At the Heart of Heart of the Church

of the Church

~⌒~

SELECTED DOCUMENTS OF
CATHOLIC EDUCATION

CATHOLIC EDUCATION STUDIES DIVISION

Alliance for Catholic Education Press
at the University of Notre Dame

AT THE
Heart
OF THE
Church

SELECTED DOCUMENTS OF
CATHOLIC EDUCATION

Edited by Ronald J. Nuzzi and Thomas C. Hunt

Alliance for Catholic Education Press

Notre Dame, Indiana

Library of Congress Cataloging-in-Publication Data

Catholic Church.
 [Works. Selections. 2012]
 At the heart of the Church : selected documents of Catholic education / Edited by Ronald J. Nuzzi, Thomas C. Hunt.
   pages cm
 Includes bibliographical references.
 Summary: "Selection of official documents of the Catholic Church that present the Catholic school as integral to the mission of the Church and at the heart of its efforts at evangelization"--Provided by publisher.
  ISBN 978-1-935788-08-9 (hardcover : alk. paper) 1. Catholic Church--Education--Papal documents. 2. Catholic schools. I. Nuzzi, Ronald James, 1958- II. Hunt, Thomas C., 1930- III. Title.
 LC473.C26 2012
 371.071'2--dc23
                    2011045512

Table of Contents

Why Documents?

RONALD J. NUZZI

Since 1983, Catholic colleges and universities in the United States have been deliberate and intentional in planning for the future of Catholic schools. This planning has taken form in what universities do best, namely educating and forming our human resources—those women and men who will serve as future Catholic school educators. With the decline in the numbers of available vowed religious personnel in the decades following Vatican II, Catholic schools were faced with serious staffing challenges. Who would recruit the next generation of Catholic school teachers and principals? Where would they be educated, certified, and prepared for ministry in the Catholic school? And more importantly, if the next generation of leaders was to come from the ranks of lay men and women, called to vocation in marriage or the single life, where would they experience the religious formation and education that we came to take for granted among the religious sisters, brothers, and priests who once staffed most Catholic schools?

One answer came in the formation of the Association of Catholic Leadership Programs (ACLP) in 1983.[1] Inspired by the vision of Sister Mary Peter Traviss, O.P., at the University of San Francisco and guided by the organizational skills of Dr. Donald Frericks at the University of Dayton, the ACLP brought together professors, researchers, and practitioners of educational leadership to share ideas, plan programs, develop resources, and otherwise professionalize the preparation and formation of Catholic school principals.

By creating a national network of Catholic educational leaders, ACLP sought to identify common standards and program goals for all who would aspire to Catholic school leadership. While a national curriculum was never the proximate goal of the ACLP, the organization was highly successful in creating a common language and vision for preparation programs, and in disseminating and incarnating that vision at dozens of Catholic colleges and universities across the country. At its zenith, the ACLP had thirty member institutions from coast to coast, all with specialized programming designed explicitly for aspiring Catholic school leaders.[2]

Recently, the ACLP has grown and expanded in a new organization, Catholic Higher Education Supporting Catholic Schools (CHESCS), a more inclusive umbrella organization bringing together even more constituent members. The new name reflects a desire for a broader focus, inclusive of all Catholic colleges and universities which support Catholic elementary and secondary schools through degree programs, certificate/licensure programs, seminars and professional development experiences for all working in Catholic education ministries.[3] The success of such efforts to galvanize support for K-12 Catholic schools at Catholic colleges and universities through explicit programming for the preparation and formation of future leaders is well documented.[4]

During this period of growth for the ACLP and CHESCS, graduate programming has become increasingly available for

1

aspiring Catholic educational leaders at several of the leading member institutions. Such programs include academic work for a graduate degree, state licensure and certification requirements, professional development opportunities, retreats and other organized efforts at spiritual formation, workshops, research conferences, and various enrichment activities. At every turn, organizers and designers have attempted to keep the unique needs of Catholic school leaders in mind. There is, however, a recurring question in all of these programs. The question centers on what we today call Catholic identity and the constitutive elements of Catholicity.

It is commonplace today to assume a certain homogeneity across schools. Schools are schools after all some say, and whether they are public, private, independent, Catholic, Christian, Jewish, or charter, they share similar characteristics, structures, and operating principles that should be obvious to all. Such thinking also further assumes that adjectives like Catholic, Jewish, Lutheran, and Muslim add little to the essential specifications of a school, but simply flavor the ethos in ways that are explicitly sectarian, with the additions of denominationally oriented religious services and perhaps even a religion class. In this way of thinking and organizing a school, one begins with the basics of a school—classrooms, teachers, students, a core curriculum and supporting texts—and once the essential elements of a school are in place, any parochial anthropology can be added to these basics to make the school a certain kind of school. Thus a Catholic school is a school to which Catholic religious services and Catholic religion classes are added.

Following this line of thinking through into the arena of professional preparation programs, it would logically follow that teaching or leading in a private or religious school is really no different than teaching or leading in any school, public or private. If schools are schools, then teaching is teaching regardless of where it occurs. From the point of view of a principal, educational administration in a building is arguably composed of the same skill set no matter the genre of school. Principals supervise teachers and staff, monitor budgets, evaluate and update curriculum, see to student safety and a safe environment, and establish and maintain good communication with parents and community stakeholders. Once you acquire the skill set to be a principal, the thinking goes, you are qualified and able to be a principal of any school, public or private. With this conceptualization, the Catholic Church respectfully disagrees.

Why? The answer can be found in the pages that follow. In this book, we have assembled an important selection of official documents on Catholic education, written and published over the years by various Catholic educational leaders. Although emanating from different sources and parts of the world, each document is official in as much as it has been promulgated by the Catholic Church as representative of its authoritative teaching responsibility. These documents express what may be called the constitutive elements of Catholic identity or the unique and essential aspects of Catholic schools, not found in other schools, public or private. These documents announce a philosophy of Catholic education, a Catholic worldview that is intended to permeate every moment of life within a Catholic school. As the astute reader will notice in these official documents, the Catholic Church has an elevated view of the Catholic school in ecclesial life and conceives of the school as integral to the mission of the Church and at the heart of its efforts at evangelization.

From the point of view of these documents, Catholic schools are not schools to which devout and pious believers have added Catholic dimensions. Rather, the Catholic school is understood to be a community of faith first, a place where the Incarnation happens in every moment of every day, where the Paschal Mystery is lived and celebrated, and the Trinity is experienced in deeply meaningful and life-giving relationships. The Catholic school community takes advantage of the educational opportunities provided in a curriculum to evangelize and sanctify, and to bring to full bloom the God-given gifts of everyone in the building. Educational advancements are the means, not the end, of the Catholic school.

Because the Catholic school has been given this primary goal of evangelization and sanctification by the Catholic Church, the school participates in the overall mission of the Church and is the privileged environment where its mission is carried out.[5] Serving as a principal in a Catholic school, therefore, requires something different than might be found in other principalships. It is not simply an additional responsibility, to be tacked on to the job of any other principal. It is not generic principalship plus Catholic seasoning. It is something different altogether from the outset. It is the formation of a community of believers in discipleship with Jesus Christ which, through the human development processes of teaching and learning, helps advance the school community toward their ultimate, common goal: salvation.

These documents repeatedly affirm the special and exalted responsibility of the Catholic school. They provide the answer to the question about what is distinctive about Catholic schools and they together constitute part of the unique knowledge base and skill set that are absolutely essential for those who would lead Catholic schools today.

Types of Documents

Four different types of documents have been selected as exemplars of this unique Catholic educational philosophy: a papal encyclical; a declaration from Vatican II; documents from the Congregation for Catholic Education, the Vatican office with oversight responsibility for Catholic schools; and pastoral messages and a statement from the United States Conference of Catholic Bishops (USCCB). The origin and authorship of these different types of documents are closely related to their differing levels of authority and intended audiences.

Papal encyclicals are typically pastoral teachings authored and disseminated by a pope for the purpose of teaching and upholding the beliefs, convictions, practices, and tradition of the Church. They are conceived as circular letters to the worldwide church, often addressed to bishops, priests, and the faithful. Our selection from papal encyclicals is *Divini Illius Magistri* by Pope Pius XI. Readers will find there not only a traditional articulation of the spiritual ends of a Catholic education, but a vision of the Church as an oasis of grace in an otherwise troubled world. And that was in 1929.

The document with the highest authority in this collection, a document for the universal Church, written and published by an ecumenical council and promulgated by the pope in union with the bishops worldwide, is *Gravissimum Educationis*, the Declaration on Christian Education. Amazingly, this highest ranking document on education in the Catholic Church affirms the right of parents to choose the best education for their children and argues that governments ought to fund parental options equally and justly.[6]

Several documents come from the Congregation for Catholic Education, once known as the Sacred Congregation for Catholic Education, and before that as the Congregation for Catholic Institutes and Seminaries. These documents are among the most articulate and poetic expressions of the purpose and mission of Catholic schools, offering a unified and universal vision for Catholic educational leaders. Largely ignored by K-12 Catholic educators, these documents announce standards for school culture, teachers, principals, vowed religious, parents, and even prod governments to fully fund parental choice. They should be required reading in any pre-service formation and preparation program for Catholic educators and included in induction programs for those educators new to Catholic schools.

Documents from the U.S. bishops are also included. Because of the changing structure of the bishops' conference, some carry the authorship of the National Conference of Catholic Bishops (NCCB), others the United States Catholic Conference (USCC), and still others the United States Conference of Catholic Bishops (USCCB). All of the bishops' documents chronicle the support of the U.S. for K-12 Catholic schools and detail some of their ongoing efforts to help sustain, strengthen, and transform K-12 Catholic schools.

While there are dozens of other documents pertaining to Catholic education more broadly,[7] and even more directed specifically at K-12 Catholic schools, the editors have made these selections with the hope that readers would find here the best and clearest official expression of the unique purpose of the Catholic school and an expanding understanding of the constitutive elements of Catholic identity. If these assembled documents accomplish that modest goal, those so motivated can pursue these other documents to advance similar goals and deepen their own understanding of and appreciation for a Catholic vision of K-12 schooling.

Towards a Theology of Educational Administration

Because Catholic schools are an essential component of the Church's overall educational and evangelical efforts, it stands to reason that such a school will be a place that operationalizes a Catholic worldview and a Catholic culture. Catholic schools are not isolated, independent entities, advancing their own self-selected goals and purposes. Rather, to be a Catholic school is to be part and parcel of the Catholic Church. Stated differently, Catholic schools do not have a mission, the mission has schools. While it is standard industry practice today for every school to have a well formulated mission statement, such statements in the Catholic sector are best understood as the community's effort to state, in a particular time and place, precisely how this school participates in the Church's overall mission. The Catholic school does not and cannot have a mission separate from the Catholic Church. The mission of the Catholic Church is the mission of the Catholic school. Thus, the school does not have a mission; the mission has schools.

Identifying distinguishing characteristics of the Catholic Church, therefore, will be a helpful prelude to understanding what is unique about Catholic schools and Catholic school leadership. The theological tradition found in Catholicism is particularly instrumental in discerning what is essential from what is peripheral. With a view to prioritizing these essential elements, four central mysteries of the Catholic faith demand our attention: the Incarnation, the Trinity, the Paschal Mystery, and greatest of all mysteries, the Eucharist. In these four core convictions, firmly based in the Catholic theological tradition, we find the unique and enduring elements of Catholic life.

The Incarnation affirms the Catholic conviction that, at a certain point in history, God took definitive action and intervened in human history by sending us His son, Jesus Christ, in the flesh.[8] Catholics do not believe that Jesus was an apparition or somehow making appearances in the flesh. No, Catholics believe that Jesus was fully human, took on human flesh, and was like us "in all things but sin" (Hebrews 2:17; 4:15). Because of the

4

Incarnation and following upon Jesus' full humanity and full divinity, Catholics have understood the Incarnation to have an abiding influence throughout all of creation. Indeed, because in Jesus the flesh was made holy, all of creation remains caught up in the mystery of God and in God's plan for the universe.

Every year on December 25, a feast liturgically known as the Nativity of the Lord, Catholics commemorate that day in history, that first Christmas, when the Incarnation occurred. But the Incarnation's abiding significance leads believers in every generation to affirm the goodness of creation, the inherent dignity of all people, and the conviction that in and through humanity, God's purposes can be realized. The Incarnation is a reminder that, as it was for Jesus, it can be for us. Humanity can be perfected as divinity. Celebrating Christmas, therefore, is as much about that first Incarnation as it is about God's enduring presence and power in the world today. We celebrate the historical Incarnation not only to commemorate the one-time event, but also to remind ourselves that the Incarnation of Jesus has lasting and eternal consequences for all humanity.

Catholic homes, families, schools, parishes, and hospitals are places where the Incarnation happens all the time. It is actually part of what makes them Catholic, namely, that believers see in these earthly institutions and relationships a spark of the divine. The Incarnation makes us believers in God's abiding presence in everything human. Saint Irenaeus captured this conviction early in Christian history by stating that "the glory of God is the human person fully alive."[9] A modern theologian said it more simply: "Whatever humanizes, divinizes."[10]

Such an incarnational worldview is critical to Catholic education. It is the Incarnation that inspires Catholic educators to claim that there are no secular subjects, for whatever humanizes, divinizes. Whatever brings the image of God in a child to a fuller articulation and expression, helps that child to grow in holiness. Whatever knowledge or skill is taught in school or in sports helps to bring the glory of God fully alive, and in so doing, advances the learner on the path to holiness. It is this incarnational worldview that affirms that parenting, teaching, coaching, and leading are truly religious in nature because by being present to others in helpful, supportive ways that help them grow and learn, God's work is done, and all processes aimed at humanization are really divinization at their core. With this understanding, Catholics operate schools as places of ongoing incarnation, where the pursuit of holiness unfolds in the human development activities of teaching and learning. It is critical, therefore, that those who serve in Catholic schools understand this incarnational principle and assist all in the school community to embrace this truth. Math, English, Social Studies, Volleyball, Theater, Art, Music, Science, and Lacrosse, because they help the image of God to grow in every child, are religious subjects and their teachers and coaches are religion teachers. The religion class itself is just icing on the cake. The incarnational aspect of Catholic education makes all of these subjects and activities holy as well.

The doctrine of the Trinity maintains that our experience of God throughout history has been threefold. God has been revealed in Scripture as triune, Father, Son, and Spirit. It is this theological conviction about the oneness of God in three persons that animates the Catholic notion of community and undergirds the theology of communion. Trinity Sunday is a liturgical feast on the calendar, and we affirm the Trinity every time we make the sign of the cross, perhaps the most often repeated of all Catholic prayers and practices. In addition to affirming the nature of God, the doctrine of the Trinity says something important about relationships and community.

Simply stated, the doctrine of the Trinity says that God is in relationship—Father, Son, and Spirit—and what it means to be God is to be in perfect relationship. God is characterized by relationship.

Because of the Trinity, we come to understand that all relationships are of God. Our human relationships participate in the union of the Trinity and when such relationships are loving and healthy, draw us more deeply into the mystery of God's love for us all. The Trinity is, therefore, the divine model for all human relationships. It is the nature of God to be in relationship and it is the nature of relationships to lead us back to God. Far from being some esoteric and effete principle of theology, the doctrine of the Trinity has practical ramifications for believers who see in every human exchange, the potential for divine significance. Relationships, all relationships, take on theological meaning for in coming to know and love others more deeply, we draw into deeper union with God.

Among the most common similes used to speak of Catholic parishes and schools is that of family. "My school is like my family" a student will say, or "the parish family" as many pastors say. It is a helpful comparison, calling attention to the bonds of community experienced in these institutions. Some leaders even speak of building community in parishes and schools, by which they mean promoting activities and gatherings that help people feel welcome and create a certain positive affect among the group. Most people of faith understand what is meant by the family simile and readily grasp the notion that fundraisers and social events can help build this sense of community.

But from a strictly understood Trinitarian perspective, we do not build community. God has in fact already done so. Jesus established this oneness in humanity, dying to save us all and rising from the dead. We are by God's design and doing, one human family, brothers and sisters all in Christ Jesus. The community is already built, won, and redeemed by God's grace. When God looks at us, that is what God sees: one human family. Our meager efforts to grow closer to one another and build community must be understood for what they truly are, namely, a simple unveiling of the truth of whom we really are. We never really build community. We simply come to see it, have it revealed to us, have our eyes opened and the veiled pulled back so we can see the goodness of our God and the oneness of the family. Community is who we are and the Trinity is our model, our goal. Thus, it is the doctrine of the Trinity that impels us into deeper and more meaningful relationships and it is the very being of God we experience in and through our human loves. The doctrine of the Trinity says relationships matter and eternally so.

This doctrine is at its core the theological foundation for our notion of community. In the Catholic school and classroom, the Trinity calls teachers and students alike to work together and collaborate, to grow and to learn, to develop and to change, all within the embrace of a loving community. It is no wonder that educational research in the secular arena also affirms that learning happens best in caring communities.[11] When a particular class or classroom truly excels, their joy is evident and tangible. Moreover, their unity and friendship is a reflection of the very love of God, found in the Trinity.

At the level of leadership, principals are also called to establish, protect, grow and if necessary, heal relationships. Relationships are what make the school function, and heathy relationships, in as much as they reflect the love of God, bless the entire learning community. Sadly, the opposite is also true. Bad relationships can poison a community, making even routine conversations troublesome. For these reasons, Catholic school educators must not only know this central doctrine of the faith, they are also called to see in all human relationships the potential for God's abiding grace. Those who appreciate the importance of this doctrine prize good relationships.

The Paschal Mystery refers to the suffering, death, and resurrection of Jesus, an event of which St. Paul writes that were it not true, our faith would be in vain (I Corinthians 15:17). Easter is the day we commemorate Jesus' victory over death and Sunday in the Christian dispensation is understood to be a "little Easter" for every Sunday memorializes the first Easter morning. In the Paschal mystery, we find meaning in suffering, courage in the face of death itself, and hope that, like Jesus, we too will be raised to glory with God in heaven.

Like the other mysteries, the Paschal Mystery is not simply about affirming some long-past historical watershed moment. It is that, of course, but the Paschal Mystery, too, has immensely important significance today, for as Scripture attests, "we who were baptized into Christ Jesus were baptized into his death" (Romans 6:3). Our faith in Jesus and in his resurrection points us to a similar resurrection in our own lives. Followers of Jesus understand that life is immersion in the Paschal Mystery and that all of the ups and downs of life, the joys and sorrows of our days, are all somehow caught up in the dying and rising of Jesus. This is the order of the universe by God's design—death and resurrection—and there is no escaping it.

Belief in the Paschal Mystery means that suffering and death have purpose, that good ultimately prevails, and that the power at the center of the universe is gracious and loving. We embrace the Paschal Mystery not only at our own death or the death of those we loved. We walk in its shadow every day, surrendering our will to the greater good, our youth to the passage of the years, our control to forces beyond ourselves. The Paschal Mystery reminds us that all of life is about letting go, about loving more freely and deeply, about dying and rising.

In terms of human development and education, there is no mystery more directly applicable to the school setting than the Paschal Mystery, for this mystery teaches the entire community that all of the successes and failures of life—the aced quizzes as well as the failed tests, the state championship trophy as well as the career-ending injury—are simply different ways to identify with Jesus Christ and to participate in the Paschal Mystery. They are ways of dying with Christ in order to rise with him. Educators of every sort depend on the Paschal Mystery as a primary way of giving witness to the Gospel, of affirming faith in Christ, and the good news that if we die with him, we shall also rise with him. An education absent such a central conviction about the order and direction of the universe might well be judged incomplete if not inadequate by people of faith.

The greatest of the mysteries of the faith, however, is the mystery of the Eucharist, what Vatican II called the source and summit of the Christian life.[12] The Eucharist constitutes Christ's abiding and real presence in the world, through the sacrament of His body and blood. Moreover, Jesus' command, repeated in all the Gospels, was specific and clear. We are to partake of the Eucharist and in so doing we eat His body and drink his blood, so deep and personal is our relationship with Him and He with us. Every Eucharistic celebration in its own way follows from Jesus' command at the Last Supper and takes us back to that important event.

As a church, the Eucharist is arguably the most important thing we do. In celebrating the Eucharist, we encounter all of the great mysteries wrapped up into one. The celebration of the Eucharist involves and engages all of the great mysteries of the faith. What happens at the Eucharist is that a community of disciples of Jesus Christ who share a common faith (a relationship rooted in the Trinity), come together and recount the story of Jesus' death and resurrection (the Paschal Mystery) and in so doing, make Jesus present anew in the community (Incarnation) through the sacrament of His body and blood. It is a beautiful, tantalizing thought, to realize that the Eucharist helps us to appreciate and understand, to taste and to see, the goodness of our God.

In her wisdom, the Catholic Church teaches that immersion in these mysteries is so crucial to Catholic life that the Eucharist will be celebrated every day. That is, it is so essential to enter into these mysteries—to understand, live, and proclaim them—that the Church provides the opportunity every day. Additionally, at a minimum, the Church directs that all Catholics partake of the Eucharist weekly, on Sundays, so vital is our attention to these great mysteries in our quest to become more Christ-like. Thus the Church has consistently taught that participation in the Sunday Eucharist is a *sine qua non* of the faith. Celebrating the Eucharist affirms the importance of relationships, the beauty of a shared faith, the dying and rising pattern present in our daily lives, and the real and abiding presence of Jesus, the Word made flesh. The Eucharist brings into sharp focus our dependence on God and one another, and leads us to reflect on the struggles of our lives, while finding strength for the journey. The Eucharist has the power to open our eyes and our hearts as it calls us to see the signs in our own lives of the Trinity, Paschal Mystery, and Incarnation.

Anyone who would teach in a Catholic school or serve as a principal of a Catholic school has a great responsibility to understand, value, and proclaim these great mysteries. They are part of the distinctive and essential attributes of the Catholic faith and as such, are crucial to the success of a Catholic school. Such a knowledge base would serve the mission well, for it would help all school stakeholders to understand more fully the nature, focus, and ultimate goal of a Catholic school education. Moreover, it is not simply a knowledge of Scripture or Christian history, or theology that is called for. Deep immersion into the great mysteries is needed, and Catholic educators need to know how the Incarnation, Trinity, and Paschal Mystery are occurring in their own lives. They must be able to name and own these mysteries on a personal level, and find a way to give voice and witness to these same mysteries in their ministry with other believers. In short, Catholic educators must be people of prayer, reflecting often on God's will for their lives and the unfolding of God's plan in and through all that happens in the life of a school.

Preparing to Be a Catholic Educational Leader

Catholic schools play an important role in the mission of the Church and in the overall educational efforts provided in the Church's name. In the United States, Catholic schools have been indispensable in serving the poor, new immigrants, racial and ethnic minorities, and even a goodly number of non-Catholics. As such, Catholic schools have made a significant and irreplaceable contribution to the republic while doing the work of evangelization and sanctification called for by the Church's mission. Contemporary church leaders are wise to value and support such schools, for they have been the most effective means of passing on the faith while preparing, educating, and forming the next generation.

As way to fully illuminate the true and sacred goal of a Catholic education, we have organized this selection of Church documents. While each document must be read and studied in its own historical context, the collection examines with great perspicacity the unique attributes of an education in a Catholic school. The documents will lead you through history and to Scripture, and will invite thoughtful and prayerful reflection on the great mysteries of the faith. They will uncover the community that is already always established among us, and will encourage an ongoing effort to discern and interpret God's ongoing revelation in our midst. They will nurture a spirit of perseverance in turmoil, and offer a sure place of safety through the storms of life. They will, at every juncture, point to life in Christ, the final destiny of us all.

While Catholic schools have been tremendously successful in the United States, the road to success was often less than straight and many challenges have been overcome along the way. Through the lens of church documents, the following essay provides an insightful background on American Catholic school history.

Notes

1. "Mission and Aims," accessed October 19, 2011, http://aclp.ncea.org/mission.html

2. Paige A. Smith and Ronald J. Nuzzi, "Beyond Religious Congregations: Responding to New Challenges in Catholic Education," in Gerald R. Grace and Joseph O'Keefe, eds., *International Handbook of Catholic Education* (London: Springer, 2007), 103-124.

3. "Chief Administrators of Catholic Education, Programs and Services," accessed October 19, 2011, http://www.ncea.org/departments/cace/EventsServices.asp#ACLP

4. Ronald J. Nuzzi, "Francis and Dominic: Toward a Spirituality of Leadership," in John L. Watzke, ed., *Beyond Alternative Teacher Education* (Notre Dame, IN: Alliance for Catholic Education Press, 2007), 209-230; Sorin E. Spohn, "Preparing for the Post-ACE Principalship," in John L. Watzke, ed., *Beyond Alternative Teacher Education* (Notre Dame, IN: Alliance for Catholic Education Press, 2007), 231-236; Michael P. Caruso, "Association of Catholic Leadership Programs (ACLP)," in Thomas C. Hunt, Ellis A. Joseph, and Ronald J. Nuzzi, eds., *Catholic Schools in the United States: An Encyclopedia* (Westport, CT: Greenwood, 2004), 51-52.

5. Congregation for Catholic Education, *The Catholic School on the Threshold of the Third Millennium*, http://www.vatican.va/roman_curia/congregations/ccatheduc/documents/rc_con_ccatheduc_doc_27041998_school2000_en.html, para. 10.

6. Vatican Council II, *Gravissimum Educationis*, http://www.vatican.va/archive/hist_councils/ii_vatican_council/documents/vat-ii_decl_19651028_gravissimum-educationis_en.html, para. 6.

7. Ronald J. Nuzzi, "Selected Church Documents: The Organization of Centralized Authority in Catholic Educational Administration," in Thomas C. Hunt, Ellis A. Joseph, and Ronald J. Nuzzi, eds., *Handbook of Research on Catholic Education* (Greenwich, CT: Information Age Publishing, 2001), 1-26; Gini Shimabukuro, "A Role Analysis Based on Church Documents, Dissertations and Recent Research," in Thomas C. Hunt, Ellis A. Joseph, and Ronald J. Nuzzi, eds., *Handbook of Research on Catholic Education* (Greenwich, CT: Information Age Publishing, 2001), 125-146.

8. Richard P. McBrien, *Catholicism* (San Francisco: HarperSan Francisco, 1994), 3-16.

9. St. Irenaeus of Lyons, *Against the Heresies*, trans. Dominic J. Unger (New York: Paulist Press, 1992).

10. Michael Himes, "Keynote Address," *Faith-Filled Future* [DVD] (Washington, DC: National Catholic Educational Association, 2004).

11. Nel Noddings, *The Challenge to Care in Schools: An Alternative Approach to Education* (New York: Teachers College Press, 2005).

12. Vatican Council II, *Sacrosanctum Concilium*, http://www.vatican.va/archive/hist_councils/ii_vatican_council/documents/vat-ii_const_19631204_sacrosanctum-concilium_en.html

Selected Episcopal and Papal Documents on Catholic Education (1792-1962)

THOMAS C. HUNT

The Eighteenth Century

John Carroll and the Formative Years

The Catholic population in what was to become the United States of America was small, scattered, and relatively impoverished prior to the Revolution. Additionally, the Catholic Church was subject to many prejudices, sometimes imposed legally, that had been brought from Europe. These included restrictions on the citizenship of Catholics, prohibitions on their practice of the faith, slogans in Massachusetts and Virginia such as "No Popery," and events such as the annual "Pope Day" (in which the Pope was burned in effigy) at Harvard College.[1] It was this environment in which John Carroll, the former Jesuit, was consecrated the country's first bishop on August 15, 1790.[2]

Beset by internal problems, such as Trusteeism, as well as external bigotry, Carroll emphasized the importance of a Christian education. In his "Pastoral" of 1792, which followed the first Synod of the United States in 1791, Carroll wrote of "The Advantages of a Christian Education." In this letter to the Catholic faithful, Carroll stated that "the principles instilled in the course of a Christian education, are generally preserved throughout life." He told parents that they should never tire of instilling the "habits of virtue and religion" in their children and thus render an "acceptable service to God." If they do this, he claimed, their children "will remember with gratitude, and repay with religious duty, your solicitude for them."[3]

The Nineteenth Century

The climate for Catholicism in the United States can scarcely be said to have improved during the nineteenth century. For instance, the incoming Irish immigrants were faced with religious and ethnic bigotry as they settled in the American cities along the east coast. The hostility enveloped the schools, as in New York City under the actions of the New York Free (Public) School Society, an allegedly nonsectarian Christian group. Religious practices, featuring the devotional reading of the King James Version of the Bible and the recitation of Protestant prayers, textbooks, which gave an inaccurate and biased portrayal of the Church's teaching and history, and slogans, such as the use of the term "Popery," abounded.[4] Irish-Americans were accosted with statements in one text, *An Irish Heart*, that if their immigration to the United States continued the nation would become the "common sewer of Ireland."[5]

The nineteenth century was to witness remarkable growth in the number of Catholics and in Catholic institutions, including schools. As the presence of the Church increased, its leaders met in council to address a multitude of issues that the infant Church in the United States faced. Schools were prominent among these concerns.

The First Provincial Council of Baltimore (1829)

Baltimore was the first metropolitan see of the Catholic Church in the United States.

Buetow estimates that the Catholic population in the United States was approximately 500,000 in 1829, out of a total American population that was about twelve million.[6] Bishop John England of Charleston, who had been calling for a Council of the American hierarchy, succeeded in his efforts and the First Provincial Council of Baltimore opened on October 1, 1829. Among the items to be considered were the "best method of counteracting the pernicious influences of the anti-Catholic groups in the country, of regulating the instruction of Catholic youth, and of encouraging and supporting religious communities, especially of women devoted to educational work."[7]

Two pastoral letters were promulgated by the Council, one to the laity and the second to the clergy. Bishop England authored the letter to the laity, which contained several references to education. Parents were instructed on the eternal consequences of seeing to a proper religious education for their children, in their own households and also from "teachers who will cultivate the seed which you have sown" and be "vigilant" regarding the "spiritual concerns" of their children.[8]

The Council Fathers also passed two decrees relevant to education. The thirty-fourth, in which they judged it "absolutely necessary that schools be established in which the young may be taught the principles of faith and morality, while being instructed in letters," and the thirty-fifth, in which they legislated for textbooks that would accurately communicate Catholic doctrine and worship and Catholic history.[9]

In reference to Bishop England's call for religious communities of women to minister in Catholic schools, Buetow notes that the first two of the forty-four non-diocesan communities of women founded in the United States between 1829 and 1884 were established in the United States in 1829.[10] These vowed religious women, often called "nuns," were to play an indispensable role in the development of Catholic education in the United States.

The Second Provincial Council of Baltimore (1833)

Guilday observes that much had happened that affected Catholicism in the United States in the few years between the first two Provincial Councils of Baltimore. The Catholic Emancipation Act of 1829 was passed in England. Some Catholic churches were burned in the country, and the American Protestant Association was founded in New York City in 1830. Nativism was on the rise with a concomitant increase in anti-Catholic sentiment.[11]

The Council Fathers again addressed the issue of Catholic education in their "Pastoral" of 1833. The education of the "rising generation," they wrote, is a "subject of the first importance." Their concern extended beyond seminaries to "colleges and schools" so that Catholic children might have "the best opportunities of literature and science, united to a strict protection of their morals and the best safeguards of their faith."[12]

The Third Provincial Council of Baltimore (1837)

The intervening years between the Second and Third Provincial Councils of Baltimore witnessed more instances of anti-Catholic bigotry in the United States. The Ursuline convent was burned in Charlestown, Massachusetts; Samuel F. B. Morse published his attack on the Leopoldine Association, located in Vienna, which, he claimed, posed a danger to the United States because of its support of Catholic immigration; and "revelatory" books, namely Rebecca Reed's *Six Months in a Convent* and Maria Monk's *Awful Disclosures* were published, along with *The Downfall of Babylon*, authored by Samuel Smith, the editor of the *Protestant*, a publication of the American

Protestant Association.[13] The institution of the common school, an allegedly nonsectarian Christian, but overwhelmingly Protestant institution, was begun in Massachusetts under the leadership of Horace Mann.

There was no explicit decree that dealt with Catholic schools in the Council but the "Pastoral" of 1837 did address the tribulations faced by the Church in the United States and had a section entitled "Education of the Young," in which they called on the faithful to join with them in making the institutions they had created "for the education of your children...as perfect as possible."[14]

The Fourth Provincial
Council of Baltimore (1840)

The Fourth Provincial Council of Baltimore opened on May 17, 1840. Guilday contends that a major concern of the Council was "safe-guarding the faith of the children who attended the public schools."[15]

The importance the bishops attached to Catholic schools is evident in the "Pastoral" that they issued, in which they called providing schools for Catholic children one of their "most pressing obligations."[16] They expressed their displeasure at some Catholic parents who, they said, were "not always so ready to aid in defraying the expenses" incurred in providing these schools.[17] Failure to provide Catholic schools resulted in the children being deprived of the "most important subject of religion," which could well lead to the "total abandonment of their religious practices."[18]

Noting the prevalent practice of the devotional reading of the King James version of the Scriptures in the recently-established common schools, the bishops warned against its "indiscriminate use," and called for "discreet and pious guides" to teach this "rich treasure." As it was, they doubted its value, and the practice would likely produce "more contempt than veneration," which

constituted another reason for attendance at Catholic schools.[19]

Textbooks in use in the common schools constituted another difficulty, the bishops averred. There was hardly one in "general use" in the public educational institutions at all levels that "covert and insidious efforts are not made to misrepresent our principles, to distort our truths, to vilify our practices and to bring contempt upon our Church and its members."[20]

The bishops set forth eleven decrees at this Council. The sixth decree called attention to the grave risks to the faith for Catholic children in the public or common schools, and directed pastors to prevent Catholic students in these schools from being forced to join in Protestant religious services.[21]

The Fifth Provincial
Council of Baltimore (1843)

Nativist (anti-Catholic) tactics changed a bit in the early 1840s. The Catholic Church was pictured as the enemy of the Bible and the opponent of the recently founded common schools. Nativists continued in their assault on institutional Catholicism, though, portraying convents as being "one vast brothel," and the Pope of being the anti-Christ. Organizations such as the "Committee on the Romish Church, Public Morals and Infidelity" at Princeton University were founded to disseminate information about "Popery" among both the students and local citizens.[22]

The Fifth Provincial Council of Baltimore was convened in this inflamed atmosphere. The Council set down eleven decrees, the tenth of which approved the creation of publishing houses in Cincinnati and Baltimore for the printing of books to be used in Catholic schools.[23] The Council Fathers were more forceful in their criticism of the public schools in their Pastoral in which they exhorted Catholic parents to vigilance and reminded them of the responsibility they had in the raising of their children, words that bear repeating:

> We have seen with serious alarm, efforts made to poison the fountains of public education, by giving it a sectarian hue, and accustoming children to the use of a version of the Bible made under sectarian bias, and placing in their hands books of various kinds replete with offensive and dangerous matter....Parents are strictly bound, like faithful Abraham, to teach their children the truths which God has revealed; and if they suffer them to be led astray, the souls of the children will be required at their hands. Let them, therefore...see that no interference with the faith of their children be used in public schools and no attempt made to induce conformity in any thing contrary to the laws of the Catholic Church.[24]

The Sixth Provincial
Council of Baltimore (1846)

The year 1844 saw Nativist rhetoric lead to action, especially in the Philadelphia Bible riots. In 1844, the Philadelphia School Board accepted Bishop Kenrick's request that Catholic children in the Philadelphia public schools be allowed to read the Douay (Catholic) Version of the Bible in the public schools. Nativists protested, with the result that Catholic Church property, including churches, were burned, along with the homes of Irish-American Catholics. Thirteen persons were killed and more than fifty wounded by mob violence before order was restored. After the conflagration, Nativist sentiment was expressed in statements such as "the Papists deserve this and much more" and "it were well if every Popish church in the world were leveled with the ground."[25]

Anti-Catholic books, such as the 1845 *History of the Papacy in the United States*, a scurrilous attack on the Church, was published, with a call to Americans to oppose the "man of sin."[26] Meanwhile the Catholic presence in the United States continued to grow. There were in 1846 twenty-one suffragan sees to Baltimore, twenty-six bishops, 675 churches, 709 priests (508 secular), twenty-two seminaries, fifteen colleges, over one million Catholics, and fourteen publications, weekly and monthly.[27]

There was no specific reference to Catholic schools in the "Pastoral" letter of this Council.

The First Plenary
Council of Baltimore (1852)

Strife and conflict over education continued as the first half of the nineteenth century came to a close. Social tensions increased with the steady flow of immigrants, many of whom were Irish and Catholic. Between 1821 and 1850 nearly 2.5 million entered the country, with over 1.7 million in the 1840s.[28] As a result, the Catholic population in the nation on the eve of the First Plenary Council of Baltimore in 1852 had reached almost two million.[29] These tensions spilled over into the schools, with sectarian, especially Catholic, schools looked upon as "un-American" and divisive, and the pan-Protestant common schools of Horace Mann steadily gaining momentum, acceptance, and support. The religious practices, textbooks, and overall orientation of the common schools contributed to the establishment of Catholic parish schools, established to teach the Catholic faith "in its entirety."[30]

The Catholic bishops encountered this situation when they congregated at the First Plenary Council of Baltimore on May 5, 1852. Guilday reports that the bishops "were exhorted to build parochial schools in all their parishes."[31] Recognizing that one of their most important needs was to "provide for the Catholic education of our youth," the Fathers emphasized the crucial importance of

Catholic education in their "Pastoral," following the example of their "Divine Master" who taught "by word and example." They pledged to regard with "more than ordinary sentiments of affection the younger members of our flock," and accepted their duty to guard "carefully those little ones of Christ."[32]

Identifying parents as "representatives of God," the bishops told them to watch over their children's faith and morals and avoid the judgment of the Almighty by giving them a "Christian education," one which was "always subordinate to religious influence." They cautioned parents not to be "led astray" by "false and delusive theories which are so prevalent, and which leave youth without religion." Do not, they advised, "listen to those who would separate religion from secular education." Rather, they said, "Listen to our voices...to bring up your children as you were brought up by your pious parents."[33]

To make this happen, parents were instructed to "encourage the establishment and support of Catholic schools; make every sacrifice which may be necessary for this object," and thus spare us the sight of "all the evils of an uncatholic education, evils too multiplied and too obvious to require that we should do more than raise our voices in solemn protest against the system from which they spring."[34]

The First Plenary Council closed with the publication of twenty-five decrees, the thirteenth of which was devoted to parochial schools. It called on all the bishops to begin the erection of parochial schools where they did not as yet exist as soon as possible due to the "grave danger" encountered by Catholic children in schools not directed by religious motives.[35]

The Provincial Councils of Cincinnati (1855), (1858), and (1861)

The Know-Nothing Party, fearful of the growing political influence of the Catholic Church, was founded to combat this perceived growth and experienced considerable political success. For instance, in 1854 it elected seventy-five men to Congress, had considerable influence in a number of states, and dominated politics in Massachusetts.[36] The growth of the Catholic Church was evident as it grew with the nation as the latter spread across the land. Several of the new dioceses were heavily German, namely Cincinnati, St. Louis, and Milwaukee, which together formed the so-called "German triangle" of the Midwest.

The Diocese of Cincinnati deserves special attention, given its commitment to Catholic schools. In the First Provincial Council of Cincinnati in 1855 the Fathers directed pastors to "strive by all the means in their power" to prevent Catholic children from attending schools that they cannot attend without "grave danger to their faith and morals." In that same Pastoral they called on Catholic parents to "aid and sustain" Catholic schools.[37] This was, the Fathers wrote, their "solemn obligation." Religion, they penned, "is an essential element—nay the very foundation—of all sound education." Accordingly, they maintained that "The erection of Catholic schools is, in many respects, as important an object as the building of new churches." The Catholic Church, they held, doesn't sever education from religion, which is its "main support and solid foundation."[38] Reflecting the German orientation of Cincinnati and the German commitment to Catholic schools, the assembled bishops called on English-speaking Catholics to emulate their German-speaking brethren:

Our excellent German congregations leave us nothing to desire on this subject. The children attend Mass every morning, they sing with one accord the power of God, they go from the church to the school. They are accustomed to cleanliness and neatness of dress, to diligent and affectionate respect for their parents, the reverend Clergy, and their teachers. We have nothing more at heart than that the pupils of our English schools should imitate their example.[39]

This commitment to Catholic schools was reiterated in the Second Provincial Council of Cincinnati that met in 1858. This time the Fathers spoke forcefully and directly in its Thirteenth Decree to the Diocese's pastors, holding them accountable, under "pain of mortal sin," to see that the parishes that they headed had parish schools, "whenever conditions warranted."[40]

Three years later, in 1861, The bishops of the Province of Cincinnati scrutinized the public school system, and termed it "plausible, but most unwise" and held it accountable for the "rising generation" being schooled without definite principles or with "false, at least, more or less, exaggerated and fanatical principles." The system itself, they said, "if carried out according to its alleged intent of abstaining from any definite religious instruction is well calculated to raise up a generation of religious indifferentists, if not of practical infidels; and if not thus carried out, its tendency is to develop false or very defective, if not dangerous principles." The only "fair and equitable" system of education would be to make it "entirely free."[41]

The "Syllabus of Errors"

Pius IX was crowned Pope in the midst of turmoil and upheaval in Europe. The revolution in Italy was threatening to take away the Papal States from the Church, described by Pius IX as the "seamless robe of Christ."[42] Pius believed that the preservation of this territory for the Church was a sacred trust bestowed on him by his predecessors that must be preserved against the secularist revolutionaries.

A few months before issuing the "Syllabus," the Pontiff had sent a letter to the Archbishop of Fribourg in which he outlined the proper role of the Church in education. He rejected the idea that the Church should withdraw her "salutary direction" of the "popular schools," saying that would be acting against the wishes of her "Divine Founder." In those countries or places where the Church's authority had been removed from the schools the Church was "bound to use all her zeal and efforts, and spare no pains at any time that the young should receive the necessary religious education, but is also bound to admonish all the faithful and declare to them that such schools, being hostile to the Catholic Church, cannot in conscience be frequented."[43]

It was in this context, and beset by the political and philosophical challenges to the Church's position in Europe, that Pius issued the "Syllabus of Errors," also known as "On Thought and Politics," on December 8, 1864. The following excerpts, taken from Cardinal Manning's translation, are significant "errors" relating to the questions of the church's role in education, which were condemned by the Pontiff:

45. The entire direction of public schools, in which the youth of Christian states are educated, except (to a certain extent) in the case of Episcopal seminaries, may and must appertain to the civil power, and belong to it so far that no other authority whatsoever shall be recognized as having any right to interfere in the discipline of the schools, the arrangement of the studies, the taking of degrees, or the choice and approval of teachers.

47. The best theory of civil society requires that popular schools open to the children of all classes, and generally, all public institutes intended for instruction in letters and philosophy, and for conducting the education of the young, should be freed from all ecclesiastical authority, government, and interference, and should be fully subject to the civil and political power,

in conformity with the will of rulers and the prevalent opinions of the age.

48. This system of instructing youth, which consists in separating it from the Catholic faith and from the power of the Church, and in teaching exclusively, or at least primarily, the knowledge of natural things and the earthly ends of social life alone, may be approved by Catholics.[44]

Cardinal Antonelli's "Introduction" makes clear how the "Syllabus" was to be received by Catholics, when he stated that the Pope ordered it to be "sent to all the Bishops of the Catholic world, in order that these Bishops may have before their eyes all the errors and pernicious doctrines which he has repudiated and condemned."[45] The Pope himself, in his encyclical "Quanta Cura," sent to all the bishops of the world on the same day the "Syllabus" was promulgated, set forth his position on how his pronouncements were to be received by the world's Catholics. Catholics could not reject them "without sinning and without departing in the least bit from the profession of the Catholic faith." Acceptance of his teaching was not limited to "dogmas of faith or morals," and this was in accord with what "Christ our Lord taught, who with his divine authority gave to the Roman Pontiff the supreme power of shepherding, ruling, and governing the Church."[46]

The Second Plenary Council of Baltimore (1866)

There were many changes that occurred between the First and Second Plenary Councils that affected life in the United States, most notably the Civil War and the issue of the freed slaves that followed it. The Church was affected by these, and had other grave matters to deal with as well. Hostility that generated at least in part from the Know-Nothing party, especially in the years prior to the Civil War, had manifested itself in the rude treatment accorded Archbishop Gaetano Bedini during his visit to the United States in 1853-54, followed by the shameful conduct toward Father John Babst in Maine in October 1854. These events preceded bloody riots in several American cities, especially in Louisville in 1855.[47] The Church had experienced phenomenal growth during the fourteen years between these two plenary Councils, with its population increasing from 1,980,000 to 3,842,000, its priests from 1,321 to 2,770, and its churches from 1,411 to 3,366.[48]

On February 16, 1866, Pope Pius IX had given his approval to a plenary council, and appointed Archbishop Martin Spalding of Baltimore as its president. The Council formally opened on October 7, 1866.[49] It addressed educational issues in its Decrees and in its "Pastoral" letter. Title IX of the fourteen Decrees had three chapters, the first of which exhorted pastors to build and maintain schools.[50]

The "Pastoral" of the Second Baltimore Plenary Council was issued on October 22, 1866. Under Section VII, "Education of Youth," it repeated the teaching of the First Plenary Council that "religious teaching and religious training should form part of every system of school education." Parents were advised not to consult their children as to their wishes for school attendance, and were told to accustom their children

from their earliest years to habits of obedience, industry, and thrift; and deeply impress on their minds the great principle, that happiness and success in life, as well as acceptance with God, do not so much depend on the station we fill, as on the fidelity with which we discharge its duties. Teach them, that the groundwork of true happiness must be placed in habitual and cheerful submission of our wills to the dispensations of Providence.[51]

The "Instruction" of the Propagation of the Faith (de Fide) (1875)

That there was a division of opinion over the necessity of Catholic schools for the benefit of the Church is evident from some of the comments made by individual bishops and some influential laymen in the years following the Council. Bishops from the Midwest, Ohio and Indiana in particular (an area of the country with a heavy German population), were prominent among the most ardent backers of Catholic schools. A brief exposition of their comments, and a consideration of the role that influential laity had in enlisting the Vatican to their cause, is appropriate prior to delving into the response of the Congregation itself.

In 1872 Bishop John Baptist Purcell of Cincinnati stated that the "Catholic school is the nursery of the Catholic congregation" and expressed doubt as to how parents who "willfully and deliberately" neglect their responsibility of sending their children to Catholic schools can "worthily approach, or be conscientiously admitted to the sacraments." How, he wondered, could parents submit their still pure offspring to the "kind of education received in Godless sectarian schools."[52] His successor in Cincinnati, Archbishop William Elder, pronounced that the Church's teaching on Catholic schools was so clear that "there is nothing for a Catholic to do but obey them or else renounce his religion."[53]

Two other Ohio bishops addressed the issue in their Lenten "Pastorals" of 1873. Bishop Gilmour of Cleveland recommended that if a parish could not build both a church and a school at the same time it should erect the school first and delay the building of the church, since there was "little danger of the old losing their faith, but there is every danger that the young will." There could be no deviation on the school question, he said: "Either we are Catholics or we are not." He authorized confessors to deny absolution to parents who sent their children to public schools as these "despise the laws of the Church and disobey the command of both priest and Bishop." Parents "sin who in their pride send their children to public schools," because one "cannot serve God and the devil."[54]

His neighbor in Columbus, Bishop Rosecrans, equated support of Catholic schools to belief in the Real Presence of Christ in the Eucharist and the Divinity of Jesus in Catholic doctrine.[55]

Ohio's bishops were not alone. In the neighboring state of Indiana, Bishop St. Palais of Vincennes voiced his opposition to public schools on a number of grounds, including the "infidel source from which they originated," and the "exclusion of the teaching of religion" in them which will "inevitably produce religious indifference if not infidelity."[56] Bishop Joseph Dwenger of Fort Wayne chose to ridicule non-Catholics with the statement that it appeared they were "so poor that they cannot support them (the public schools) without taxing the Catholics."[57]

Episcopal concern was not limited to the Midwest. In New York State, for instance, Bishop Bernard McQuaid of Rochester was an outspoken advocate of Catholic schools. He complained that the civil state had stepped in and replaced parents as children's primary educators. Catholic and Protestant parents were entitled to receive financial aid from the state to determine the education of their children, which was their God-given right. What Americans should fear, he opined, was not the union of church and state, but the "tyranny of no religion and open infidelity."[58] Catholics simply wanted justice in education, which would occur when they received their share of the tax fund for their children for their schools.

Finally, James Gibbons, while Bishop of Richmond (Virginia) in 1873 had written that the "religious and secular education" of children couldn't be "divorced" without "inflicting a fatal wound to the soul." This wound usually resulted in a "spirit of indifference in matters of faith." The "loss of Catholic faith" is a consequence of this separation. Looking to the future, Gibbons predicted that "if no provision is made for the Christian culture of the rising youth it is feared that twenty years hence, it will be much easier to find churches for a congregation, than a congregation for the churches."[59]

Dissatisfaction over the educational situation was not limited to the hierarchy. Influential lay people, perhaps James A. McMaster, the editor of the *Freeman's Journal* in New York City was foremost among them, spoke out on the issue. McMaster used his paper to "promote parochial schools and to attack public education." McMaster criticized bishops and pastors whom he thought were "lukewarm" on the parochial school issue, but focused most of his rhetoric on what he called the "godless" and "pagan" public schools.[60]

Catholic conservatives were in the lead of those who remained concerned with the large number of Catholic parents who ignored official Church teaching and sent their children to public schools. McMaster was in the lead of those who wanted to force Catholic parents to follow the Catholic leadership's urgings. When his campaign was unsuccessful in the United States, he turned to the Vatican for support.[61] The Vatican responded, asking the American archbishops questions about the "evils" of American public education, and wanted to know why Catholic parents sent their children to these schools. The archbishops doubted the wisdom of refusing absolution to parents who defied Church teaching on the school question. They pointed out that in some rural areas there were no Catholic schools and in some large cities parochial schools were inferior to their public counterparts. Denial of the sacraments would not be a solution to the problem, they felt.[62]

Walch writes that the Vatican response, the "Instruction" of the Propagation of the Faith, the agency of the Curia that had responsibility for the American Church, since the United States was officially still a "mission" country, was unpleasing to some of the American hierarchy.[63] What were the provisions of this "Instruction," and why did they arouse the ire of some American prelates?

First, it is well to note that the Vatican was responding to a request by a number of American bishops for a formal document from the Congregation, "to impress upon the faithful the seriousness of the matter and to strengthen their own authority in persuading pastors to build parish schools."[64]

The Congregation's "Instruction" on the school question in the United States was listed in eight points, which followed an Introduction that stated the Congregation had heard a number of times that "evils of the gravest kind are likely to result from the so-called public schools."[65] First, the Congregation declared that the system of public education was opposed to Catholicism since it excluded all religious instruction and thus constituted a great evil if children were exposed to it.

Second, since the schools were not under the control of the Church, teachers were selected "from every sect indiscriminately." Additionally, the document pointed to the practice of coeducation, which further endangered the children's morals.

Third, the danger of perversion of the faith or morals of children must be rendered remote for them to attend these schools, because if it were proximate then the natural, divine, and universal law would dictate that Catholic children cannot in conscience attend such schools.

Fourth, the bishops were instructed to use every means to prevent Catholics from "all contact with the public schools," to establish Catholic schools, and to improve existing parochial schools. All Catholics, especially the wealthy and influential, were reminded that they had the duty of financially supporting these schools.

Fifth, there was nothing to prevent Catholics of the United States from "averting, with God's help, the dangers with which Catholicity is threatened from the public school system," and having their own schools.

Sixth, the existence of special circumstances that would exempt parents from sending their children to the Catholic school "is to be left to the conscience and judgment of the Bishop." Examples of these circumstances would be no available Catholic school or one that is unsuitable. Even then, though, the danger of perversion of the children's faith must be made remote. If it is not, then attendance at that public school "must be shunned at whatever cost, even life itself."

Seventh, parents and pastors must make provisions for Christian training for children who attend public schools, prior to their attendance at those institutions. Pastors and parents were to insure that Catholic children were to avoid contact with their peers "whose company might be dangerous to their faith or morals."

Eighth, parents who neglect to give Christian training to their children, or who allow their children to go to schools "in which the ruin of their souls is inevitable," or those parents who send their children to public schools without sufficient reason, and without rendering the danger of perversion remote, if obstinate, "cannot be absolved," which is "evident from the moral teaching of the Church."[66]

The Third Plenary Council of Baltimore (1884)

The "Instruction" of the Propagation of the Faith did not settle the perplexing problem within the Catholic Church in the United States over the issue of parochial schools. In addition, Catholicism in general and Catholic schools in particular continued to face prejudice. Public schools developed in the years following the Civil War, especially in the North, and became increasingly equated with "Americanism." Private schools, particularly those with religious and ethnic orientations, as were a considerable number of Catholic schools, were suspect as to their patriotism and were sometimes looked on as "un-American."

Separation of church and state was advocated, as in the remarks of President Ulysses S. Grant to the veterans of the Army of the Tennessee at Des Moines, Iowa, on September 29, 1875, in which he called for the encouragement of "free schools, and resolve that not one dollar appropriated for their support" be given to any "sectarian school."[67]

Several months later Congressman James G. Blaine of Maine presented a proposed constitutional amendment to the Congress that would have prohibited "any money raised by school taxation in any State for the support of public schools," to ever be under the "control of any religious sect."[68] The "Blaine Amendment" as it became known passed the House of Representatives by a vote of 180 to 7 but failed to reach the two-thirds margin required in the Senate due to a 28 to 16 vote.[69] Congress did pass a requirement, however, that any state admitted to the union in the future have a "system of public schools which shall be open to all the children of said State and free from sectarian control."[70] These sentiments, which depicted the mood of the nation, contributed to the difficulties parochial schools faced. Walch notes that the Blaine Amendment was to have a significant effect nationally, through the actions of the several states. Between 1877 and 1917 "some twenty-nine states incorporated the amendment into their constitutions."[71]

Observing the situation years later, Catholic historian Peter Guilday remarked after considering the progress public schools made between the end of the Civil War and 1884 that "Step by step with that progress went an increasing abandonment of religious teaching and influence. There's no doubt that during these years the problem of Catholic children in these schools was the dominant anxiety of our prelates and clergy."[72]

James Gibbons, now the Archbishop of Baltimore in 1883, attested to the crucial role of Catholic schools in the life of the Church when he said "It may safely be asserted that the future status of Catholicity in the United States is to be determined by the success or failure of our day schools."[73] The necessity of Catholic schools for the good of the nation, Gibbons averred, was demonstrated by the failure of the "imperfect and vicious system of education, which undermines the religion of youth," as documented by the increase of social problems, such as crime, that were contemporary with the development of the public school system.[74]

The Catholic hierarchy, generally speaking, had committed itself to the cause of Catholic schools. The Vatican had become involved in the struggle with its "Instruction" by the Propagation of the Faith in 1875. The issue was deemed critical on both sides of the Atlantic, so it came as no surprise when three American archbishops were called to Rome where the Propagation presented them with an agenda for a plenary council. The American prelates were able to make some changes in the agenda since it had been prepared by the Propaganda and not by Pope Leo XIII.[75] Archbishop Gibbons was selected to preside over the Council.

Education was to have a prominent place in the Council. Almost one quarter of the Council's decrees were devoted to Catholic schools.[76] The "Pastoral" of the Council, dated December 7, 1884, was signed by Archbishop Gibbons. In a section, entitled "Christian Education" the Fathers wrote that "education of the laity" was secondary only to that of the clergy. Education of lay Catholics was so crucial because, as they wrote, "In the great coming combat between truth and error, between Faith and agnosticism, an important part of the fray must be borne by the laity, and woe to them, if they are not prepared." Catholics, they maintained, need to be able to "withstand the noxious influence of popularized irreligion."[77] Civilization, the bishops declared, depends on "sound popular education," which in turn requires "moral and religious training" as well as intellectual and physical. In the history of the world, "there never has been a civilization worthy of the name without religion."[78] Hence education, in order to "foster civilization, must foster religion."[79]

The Council Fathers elaborated on the role that religion could play in society. True education, they contended, required the support of three agencies, "the home, the Church, and the school." They contended that some wish to keep religion out of schools and "advocate as the best school system that which necessarily excludes religion." This is erroneous for the school is an important factor in the "forming of childhood and youth." Thus, "to shut religion out of the school, and keep it for home and the Church, is logically, to train up a generation that will consider religion good for the home and the Church but not for the practical business of real life." This action, the bishops described as "but a more false and pernicious notion could not be imagined." Religion, "in order to inspire a people, should inspire their whole life, and rule their relations with one another." Thus the school, "which principally gives the knowledge fitting for practical life, ought to be pre-eminently under the holy influence of religion."[80] Christian education is an attempt to "preserve truth and morality among the people by fostering religion in the young." It is not antagonistic to the state. On the "contrary it is an honest endeavor to give to the State better citizens, by making them better Christians," something that the State cannot do because it cannot teach religion.[81]

Turning their attention to Catholic schools the bishops wrote, "Two objects therefore, dear brethren, we have in view, to multiply our schools, and to perfect them. We must multiply them till every Catholic child in the land shall have within its reach the means of education." Much work needs to be done in this regard, they noted. "Pastors and parents should not rest until this deficit be remedied. No parish is complete till it has schools adequate to the needs of its children."[82]

Multiplication of Catholic schools was necessary, but not sufficient. The Fathers held that "But, then, we must also perfect our schools." They repudiated the idea that the Catholic school need be inferior in any way to any school. The bishops implored Catholic people to elevate their schools "to the highest educational excellence," and implored parents "not to hasten to take their children from school, but to give them all the time and all the advantages that they have the capacity to profit by, so that, in after life, their children may 'rise up and call them blessed.'"[83]

The Fathers at Baltimore III went beyond the mere urging of pastors to build schools and parents to send their children to these schools. They issued two decrees that have gone down in history in support of parochial schools. It is apparent from their texts that the binding decisions in each instance will be made by the local bishop.

> I. That near every church, a parish school, where one does not yet exist is to be built and maintained in perpetuum within two years of the promulgation of this council, unless the bishop should decide that because of serious difficulties a delay may be granted.

> IV. That all Catholic parents are bound to send their children to the parish school,

unless it is evident that a sufficient training in religion is given either in their own homes, or in other Catholic schools, or when because of a sufficient reason, approved by the bishop, with all due precautions and safeguards, it is licit to send them to other schools. What constitutes a Catholic school is left to the decision of the bishop.[84]

The result of Baltimore III was a compromise of sorts. Catholic schools were officially endorsed, but parents were not bound under pain of mortal sin to send their children to Catholic schools and pastors were warned to avoid excessive zeal in dealing with school attendance. The key was the decision of the local bishop. When he granted freedom of choice to parents, and only he could make this decision, no denial of the sacraments was allowed at the parish level.[85]

Pope Leo XIII and Catholic Schools

Education, in the eyes of the Catholic Church, was a "mixed matter," i.e., one in which several agencies had rights. In this case, those agencies were the home, the church, and the state. During his pontificate, Leo XIII addressed the thorny relationship between church and state, including their involvement in the field of education, on a number of occasions. Given the leadership position that the Pope held in the Catholic Church, and the binding force of his statements on Catholics, his teaching on the topic merits inclusion.

In 1878, Leo called the separation of public instruction from the "salutary direction of the Church" a "source of the evils present in the contemporary world." This had resulted in "unbridled freedom" in education, which was a logical consequence of the violation, and obstruction of the Church's "right to instruct and bring up youth." Liberty, in its present state, provided only delusive civilization and the Pope told the world's bishops to make all education in accord with the Catholic faith.[86] Two years later he reminded Catholic parents that they were "bound to give all care and watchful thought to the education of their offspring and their virtuous bringing up."[87]

Leo continued to write on the topic as the decade of the 1880s progressed. In 1885 he stated unambiguously that "The Church of Christ is the true and sole teacher of virtue and guardian of morality." Catholics, he insisted, were bound "to love the Church as their common mother, to obey her laws, promote her honor, defend her rights, and endeavor to make her loved and respected by those over whom they have authority."[88]

Leo's teaching had an impact on Catholic bishops and writers, as one would expect. For instance, Archbishop Gibbons of Baltimore penned in 1887 that the "vicious system of public school education" threatened the stability of our government. He went on to explain why attendance at Catholic school was necessary for Catholic children:

> The religious and secular education of our children cannot be divorced from each other without inflicting a fatal wound upon the soul. The usual consequence of such a separation is to paralyze the moral faculties and so foment a spirit of indifference in matters of faith.[89]

Catholic writers of the time joined in the critiques of public education. For instance, one accused these schools of being "heartless," because they relied on a diet of "parched rationalism in science, on which the heavenly dew of religion does not fall"; of being "headless," because they were "heartless"; and since they proposed to get along without religion they were "Godless."[90]

Bishops and other writers were joined in their advocacy of Catholic schools by the Catholic Lay Congress, which met in Baltimore in 1889. The attending delegates chose to "continue to support our own schools" since there was "no provision for teaching religion" in the state-regulated public schools, and to continue that support until the "benefits of a Christian education may be brought within the reach of every Catholic child in these United States."[91]

Archbishop Gibbons, meanwhile, persisted in repeating the theme that education had to include religion in order to deal with the whole person and that without religion; education was "defective" and inflicted a "fatal wound upon the soul."[92] Gibbons was joined by a stalwart supporter of Catholic education, Bishop Bernard McQuaid of Rochester, New York, who charged that the public school system was "liable to blunders innumerable, to inefficiency of accomplishments, and to the perpetrating of injustice." He accused the public schools of being the agent of "state paternalism," suppressing the basic rights of parents through the creeping tentacles of state control.[93]

Meanwhile Pope Leo XIII continued to address the relationship between church and state in a manner that alarmed many non-Catholic Americans. In January of 1890 he promulgated another encyclical to the world's bishops and through them to the Catholics of the world. He maintained that the duties Catholics have to the Church take priority over all others because Catholics owe the Church the "life that will live forever." They were to be submissive to the "Church and the Roman Pontiff, as to God." This submission called for "assent to all that the Church teaches." This includes the duty of the Church to oppose human laws that "encroach on the right of the Church."[94] Educational teachings came under this umbrella of submission. Parents, the repositories of God's plan for directing the education of their children, were duty-bound to imbue their children with the "principles of Christian morality, and absolutely oppose their children from frequenting schools where they are exposed to the fatal poison of impiety." Leo ended his controversial letter with praise for "Catholics of all nationalities" who "at the expense of much money and more zeal, have erected schools for the education of their children."[95]

The "Manifesto" of the Wisconsin Catholic Bishops (1890)

The decrees of Baltimore III did not settle the Catholic school attendance question within the Catholic world, as we shall subsequently see. Nor was the strife between the civil state and the Catholic Church amicably resolved in American society. Wisconsin was one state where the conflict reached crisis proportions. The immediate cause was the Bennett Law, passed by the Wisconsin legislature and signed into law by Governor William Dempster Hoard in 1889. The two most objectionable features of the law, in the eyes of the Wisconsin bishops and their Lutheran allies, were the provisions that defined a school as a place where certain subjects were taught in the English language and a provision that required the school-age children of the state to attend school in the public school division in which they resided.[96] In the wake of Pope Leo's encyclical letter, "Sapientiae Christianae," Wisconsin's three Catholic bishops, Michael Heiss, Archbishop of Milwaukee, Kilian C. Flasch, Bishop of LaCrosse, and Frederick X. Katzer, Bishop of Green Bay, issued their "Manifesto," which directly criticized the state legislation.

The bishops made it clear at the outset that their protest was not merely exhortative, when they maintained that the law "interferes with the rights of the church and of parents." They declared that the "object of the law" was to "bring our parochial and private schools under the control of the state. And in this attempt, we cannot but apprehend the ultimate intention—gradually to destroy the parochial school system."[97] Specifically, the bishops charged that the law was "unnecessary, offensive, and unjust."[98] It was "unnecessary" because with few exceptions, the state's Catholic schools used English and those exceptions would be healed by the passage of time, not by coercive legislation. It was "offensive" because the Catholics of the state had not asked for, nor received, one cent from the state to build their schools. Finally, it was "unjust" because it empowered the civil state to interfere with the "inalienable rights of parents" to educate their children. When parents of the state chose Catholic schools as the places where they want their children educated, "their schools should not be molested by any interference on the part of the state."[99]

The bishops pointed out that in Catholic Church teaching the rights of parents in education were not unlimited, but were to be exercised in accord with the teaching of the Church. Pointing to the teaching of the Church on education in Baltimore III and other sources, they declared that "no one can be a true member of the church and at the same time hold a different view or follow a different practice than this."[100]

The three prelates concluded their protest with the assertion that it had been made as a matter of duty, not pleasure, and alleged that it had been forced upon them by the action of the state. They announced: "We have never received one single cent of state help for our schools—we want no state interference with them either."[101] In their eyes, the Bennett Law represented such interference.

Internal Dissent on the School Question: Archbishop John Ireland and His Critics

John Ireland was the liberal bishop of the St. Paul, Minnesota diocese. Asked to speak at the 1890 meeting of the National Education Association (NEA) in St. Paul, Ireland infuriated some of his fellow bishops by his praise of public schools. He said:

> Free schools. Blest indeed is the nation whose vales and hillsides they adorn. And blest the generation upon whose souls are poured their treasure. No tax is more legitimate than that which is levied for the dispelling of mental darkness and the building up within a nation's bosom of intelligent manhood and womanhood.[102]

To those who condemned the public schools, Ireland called for a curse on them: "The free school of America—withered be the hand raised in sign of its destruction."[103]

Concerned that the "great mass of children in America are growing up without religion," and motivated by the financial difficulties the Catholic Church was experiencing in providing for parish schools, Ireland called for a compromise in which the state would reimburse all denominations for teaching the secular subjects in denominational schools.[104] He subsequently authored his Faribault-Stillwater plan that called for the public school board to rent the denominational school building, no religion would be taught during regular school hours, the state would certify and pay the teachers, and the pastor would control the building at times when the school was not in session, as a way to implement his idea.

Ireland's address received widespread attention across the nation. It aroused the ire of a number of his fellow bishops, especially Archbishop Michael Corrigan of New York City and Bishop Bernard McQuaid of Rochester, New York, who complained to the Vatican about Ireland's talk.[105] Ireland defended himself in a clarification to Cardinal Gibbons, in which he said that he had sought to dispel the notion that the Catholic Church was opposed to public schools "because she is opposed to the education of the children of the people."[106] Ireland identified Archbishop Katzer of Milwaukee, at the time embroiled in

a conflict with state authorities in Wisconsin over the Bennett Law, as a culprit because he claimed Katzer denied the state the right to enact school legislation, resulting in parents being free to raise their children in ignorance if they so desired.[107] He told Gibbons that he deplored the substance and frequency of the denunciations of the public schools by the Catholic clergy, particularly members of the hierarchy, and regretted the spiritual harm done to Catholic parents by episcopal anathemas for their failure to send their children to Catholic schools. The mission of the Church was not to be found in "writing and ciphering," Ireland averred. The public schools, were not, as portrayed by some Catholic prelates, "positively bad" and "hotbeds of vice."[108] Bishop McQuaid was particularly critical of Ireland, whom he accused of sacrificing the "spiritual interests" of Catholic children.[109] The criticism was so strident and strong that Cardinal Gibbons wrote to Pope Leo, requesting that he not censure Ireland for his NEA address because such an act would have a "disastrous effect" on the Catholic Church in the United States.[110]

Ireland came in for more criticism for his Faribault-Stillwater plan. Archbishop Katzer of Milwaukee termed the plan a "surrender of a Catholic school to state authorities."[111] Some non-Catholic leaders, including members of the Protestant clergy, were also opposed to the plan, believing it was a give-away to the Catholic Church. The plan lasted but a year, becoming a casualty to local non-Catholic hostility.

The internal controversy over the school question spread within the Church. Each side had a leading author take up the cudgels on behalf of its position. Dr. Thomas J. Bouquillon of the Catholic University of America represented the liberal interests. He argued that the civil government, as social authority, had the right and mission to educate, along with the family and Church. His pamphlet,

"Education: To Whom Does It Belong?" enraged conservative Catholics. A response was not long in coming. It was penned by the Rev. Rene I. Holaind, S.J., and was entitled "The Parent First." He argued that the state, especially the non-Christian one, did not have the authority that Bouquillon gave it. The authors kept up a running battle in the pages of Catholic journals. Warring members of the hierarchy attempted to enlist the Vatican on their side. Ireland warned of an American *Kulturkampf* over the school issue; the bishops of the New York Province told the pope not to be threatened by such a fear.[112] Pope Leo replied by repeating his support for Catholic schools, "in which children are instructed in religion by persons whom the bishops know to be capable of such teaching." He also held the bishops responsible for seeing that nothing offensive to the consciences of Catholic children or opposed to their religion be allowed at schools conducted "at public expense."[113]

The Vatican Gets Involved

The strife among the American hierarchy reached such proportions that a plea to them by a Vatican leader, Cardinal Ledochowski, for "peace and Christian union" to replace "promptly the deplorable agitation which saddens us all" fell on deaf ears.[114] Conflicting interpretations had been rendered to the Propagation of the Faith's "tolerari potest" ("can be allowed") response to Archbishop Ireland's Faribault-Stillwater plan ranging from Archbishop Corrigan of New York City who said it had been condemned, to Ireland himself who said it meant "fully allowed," to one Catholic writer who asserted it had received "official sanction."[115] Bishop McQuaid had further ignited the conflict when he announced that it was "time that the impudence of Archbishop Ireland should be checked."[116]

Pope Leo determined that it was time to act. Accordingly, he sent a personal legate, Archbishop Francesco Satolli to the United States to bring peace to the American Church. The Pontiff made it clear that Satolli would speak in his name:

> We command all whom it concerns to recognize in you, as Apostolic delegate, the supreme power of the delegating Pontiff; we command that they give you aid, concurrence and obedience in all things.... Whatever sentence or penalty you shall declare or inflict duly against those who oppose your authority, we will ratify.[117]

The American archbishops, who were to meet with Satolli, expected a dialogue. Satolli, though, presented fourteen propositions to the archbishops at a meeting on November 17, 1892.[118] The propositions called for the American Church to build Catholic schools and to improve those already in existence, and urged lay Catholics to send their children to them. Attendance at public schools was permitted if the "danger of perversion" of faith or morals was remote, as determined by the bishop of the diocese. No "bishop or priest" was to "exclude from the sacraments, as unworthy" parents who send their children to public schools, and this held especially for the children themselves. Satolli also stated that the clergy should not "show less love for the children that attend public schools than for those that attend the parochial schools."[119]

Those members of the American episcopacy who were ardent advocates of parochial schools were crushed. Bishop McQuaid was the most vocal of that group. His criticism went beyond Satolli to include Pope Leo himself. He wrote to Corrigan:

> We are all in a nice pickle, thanks to Leo XIII and his delegate. Just as our arduous work of the last forty years was beginning to bear ample fruit, they arbitrarily upset the whole. If an enemy had done this! It is only a question of time, when present

Roman legislation having wrought incalculable mischief, that we, school-children of the hierarchy, will again receive a lesson in our catechism from another Italian sent out to enlighten us.[120]

John Lancaster Spalding, the educator bishop of Peoria, Illinois, referred to "Faribaultism" after Satolli's presentation and offered a gloomy prediction that "without parish schools there is no hope that the Church will be able to maintain itself in America."[121] The bishops of the Province of Cincinnati, strong backers of Catholic schools, protested that Satolli's propositions had undermined their efforts on behalf of Catholic schools.[122]

Satolli's visit created confusion among the leaders of the American Church and others over just what was the official position of the Catholic Church on the school question. Recognizing this, Cardinal Gibbons wrote the Pope asking for clarification. On May 31, 1893 Leo replied, a letter that officially ended the dispute. He said that the decrees of the Third Plenary Council of Baltimore were to be followed; that Catholic schools were to be "most sedulously promoted," and that it was up to the "judgment and conscience of the ordinary to decide, according to the circumstances, when it is lawful and when it is unlawful to attend public schools." Public schools, he wrote, are "not to be entirely condemned." He ended his letter with a plea for cooperation and unity among the diverse factions of the controversy:

> Wherefore, we confidently hope that having put away every cause of error and of all anxiety you will work together with hearts united in perfect charity, for the wider and wider spread of the kingdom of God in your immense country.[123]

Leo's intervention had brought an end to the open conflict between members of the American hierarchy over the school issue. Gibbons wrote Cardinal Rampolla at the Vatican that he had "most gratefully" received the Pope's letter which "thanks to Almighty God and the most Holy Father," had ended the school controversy and "brought longed for peace to the American church."[124]

Catholic school enrollment continued to grow as the nineteenth century neared its close due to the combined efforts of some American bishops, the dedicated service of vowed religious women, leadership of pastors, and the commitment of members of the Catholic laity. Despite these efforts Catholic schools were not able to enroll much beyond fifty percent of eligible children. The Church simply did not have the resources. They had provided religious training and secular education for legions of Catholic children in the nineteenth century, many of whom were the offspring of immigrants and poor. They were to face new challenges in the next century.

The Twentieth Century

The Code of Canon Law (1918)

Bouscaren and Ellis allege that "by the beginning of the twentieth century the laws of the Church were once more in a state of considerable confusion."[125] Pope Pius X began the process of codification of all Church laws in 1904. The work went on through World War I and was completed in the pontificate of Benedict XV after the death of Pius. Pope Benedict promulgated the new Code of Canon Law on Pentecost, May 27, 1917, to become effective on Pentecost, May 19, 1918.[126]

A number of canons treat the subject of Catholic schools, either directly or indirectly. For instance, Canon 1113 states that:

> Parents are bound by a most serious obligation to provide to the best of their power for the religious and moral as well as for the physical and civil education

of their children, and also to provide for their temporal welfare.[127]

Parents, the authors write, have "by the law of nature parental authority." This law entitles them to be "free from unreasonable state control." Education that "fails to reveal to the child the only true purpose of life, that is, the attainment of his supernatural destiny, is not education."[128]

In Volume 2 of Woywod and Smith's commentary on Canon Law, Title XXII "Of Schools," schools are dealt with directly. Canon 1372 addresses the necessity of students being instructed in Catholic doctrine. Canon 1373 specifies that this instruction must be given "in every elementary school," according to the age of the students. Canon 1374 identifies the local bishop as the person who decides if attendance at a non-Catholic or "mixed" school can be tolerated. Canon 1375 postulates that the Church has the right to establish schools at all levels.[129]

Canon 1379 places the responsibility of providing Catholic schools on the shoulders of the local bishop. Catholics should contribute "according to their means" to the erection and maintenance of these schools. It is the local Ordinary's "right and duty" to see that "nothing is taught or done contrary to faith or good morals in any of the schools in their territory," according to Canon 1381. Local bishops have the "right to approve the teachers of religion and the books," and to replace teachers and books "in the interest of religion and morals."[130] They also have the authority to visit any Catholic school to "investigate all matters connected with religious and moral instruction" (Canon 1382).[131] The Code teaches that the "bishop of the diocese is appointed by the divine law the guardian of faith and morality in his territory." The Code admits "no exception," except in the case of the "internal school for professed members in exempt organizations."[132]

The Pastoral Letter of 1919

At the conclusion of World War I the American hierarchy decided that an annual meeting was in order. The first such meeting was held in Washington, D.C., in September of 1919 and its "Pastoral" was issued on September 26 of that year.[133] Section thirteen, of the fourteen sections, was entitled "Catholic Education."[134] The Fathers noted that the global conflict had consequences for education and the nation because it had "swept around all sources of thought, and has centered upon the school. There, especially, the interests of morality and religion are at stake; and there, more than anywhere else, the future of the nation is determined."[135]

The bishops' "Pastoral" praised the dedication of the men and women who "have consecrated their lives to the service of Christian education." It was through "their singleness of purpose and their sacrifice" that the Church "expressed the truth that education is indeed a holy work, not merely a service to the individual and society."[136] They lauded Catholic school teachers for giving Catholic youth their "education in its completeness from Catholic sources" and hailed the "zeal and liberality" of those who have "aided us in building up our schools." These patrons were cited not only for their "material help" but also "chiefly" for the evidence such help "affords of their spiritual sense and perception." Their assistance demonstrates their appreciation of "both the necessity of Catholic education and the unselfish devotion of our teachers."[137]

Divini Illius Magistri (The Christian Education of Youth, 1929)

Catholic elementary schools had evolved into a settled system in the United States by 1920, at which date their enrollment had increased from 405,234 in 2,246 schools in 1880 to 1,701,219 in 5,852 schools in 1920.[138] Yet, there were dangers in the near future that threatened their very existence, this time from legal action. With the aid of the Ku Klux Klan the State of Oregon, following a favorable referendum, enacted a law that required all children within its borders between the ages of eight and sixteen to attend public schools while they were in session. The source of the law came from the anti-foreign sentiment that existed in the nation after World War I, with the concomitant feeling that private schools, were divisive, even "un-American," and that attendance at public school was necessary for "good citizenship."

The Sisters of the Holy Names of Jesus and Mary, joined by the Hill Military Academy, contested the legislation in court, arguing that the intent of the law was the destruction of private and parochial schools. The case reached the Supreme Court of the United States, where the Court ruled against the State of Oregon, stating that the enforcement of the law would result in the destruction of the appellees' schools. The Court adjudged that attendance at public school was not necessary to form good citizens, and that parents have the right to send their children to private schools, which provide religious and secular education. The child, the Court ruled, "is not the mere creature of the state."[139]

Meanwhile, in Europe totalitarian systems, which claimed to have primary and even exclusive rights in education, had taken control. Communism was ensconced in the Soviet Union and Fascism was on the rise in Italy and Germany. So it was that Pope Pius XI issued his famous encyclical, *Divini Illius Magistri* (The Christian Education of Youth), on December 31, 1929. Pius highlighted the beginning of his letter to the world's bishops and through them to the Catholic faithful with the words of Christ, "Suffer the little children to come unto me" (Mark 10:14). The pontiff recognized the vital importance of Christian education, since education consists "essentially in preparing man for what he must be and what he must do here below, in order to attain the last end for which he was created." Therefore, there can be "no true education which is not wholly directed to man's last end."[140]

Education is a social activity, the Pope wrote, belonging as it does to three societies: the home, the state, and the Church. It is to the Church that it belongs "pre-eminently." The Church, in its role as supernatural mother, is "independent of any earthly power" in the conduct of schooling. It is in this capacity that the Church promotes all education, in so far as "necessary or helpful to Christian education."[141] The roles of family and state, as well as that of individuals, are to be in "complete harmony" with that of the Church. The family holds its mission to educate its offspring directly "from the creator," and this responsibility of the parents "continues up to the time when the child is in a position to provide for himself."[142]

The claim advanced by some advocates of state control, that the state has absolute control over the education of the citizen is "untenable." Existence does "not come from the State, but from the parents."[143] Nor is the parents' right to educate absolute, for it is subordinated to the "last end and to natural and divine law." It is the responsibility of parents to thwart any attempt to invade "their rights in this matter," and above all to refuse to send their children to "those schools in which there is danger of imbibing the deadly poison of impiety."[144] Two facts of supreme importance in education declare that the "mission of education regards before all, above all, primarily the Church and the family, and this by natural and divine law, and that therefore it cannot be slighted, cannot be avoided, cannot be supplanted."[145] The state has the right and duty to protect the rights of the child, and to supply deficiencies when such occur, but "always in conformity with the natural rights of the child and the supernatural rights of the Church."[146]

The creation of the school, a social institution, which followed the family and Church, is by its "very nature and institution subsidiary and complementary to the family and to the Church." The "so-called 'neutral'" school, from which religion is excluded, "cannot exist in practice; it is bound to become irreligious." Attendance at these schools is "forbidden for Catholic children" and can be "at most tolerated, on the approval of the Ordinary alone." It is not sufficient only to give religious instruction for a school to be a Catholic school, but also "every other subject taught, be permeated with Christian piety."[147] "Catholic education in Catholic schools for all the Catholic youth," Pius averred, was the goal.[148] Moreover, attendance at Catholic schools benefits society, for a Catholic student educated in schools such as these "precisely because of his Catholic principles, makes the better citizen."[149]

Perfect schools, the Pope wrote, "are the result not so much of good methods as of good teachers," teachers who are "thoroughly prepared" and who labor "unselfishly with zeal and perseverance."[150] It is in schools such as this that the "proper and immediate end of Christian education" can be realized. That end is to "cooperate with divine grace in forming the true and perfect Christian, that is, to form Christ Himself in those regenerated by baptism."[151] Thus:

> Christian education takes in the whole aggregate of human life, physical and spiritual, intellectual and moral, individual, domestic, and social, not with a view of reducing it in any way, but in order to elevate, regulate and perfect it, in accordance with the example and teaching of Christ.[152]

The product of such schooling, the "true Christian," is the "supernatural man who thinks, judges, and acts constantly and consistently in accordance with right reason illumined by the supernatural light of the example and teaching of Christ."[153]

"The Child: Citizen of Two Worlds" (1950)

McCluskey remarks that this statement by the American hierarchy, issued at the conclusion of their annual meeting in the nation's capital in the fall of 1950, is a statement on the "philosophy of Catholic education." He terms it an "impressive statement of that philosophy."[154]

Following prefatory comments, the document is divided into four sections: "Sense of God," "Sense of Direction," "Sense of Responsibility," and "Sense of Mission."[155] The bishops state at the outset that the "child must be seen whole and entire." He "belongs to this world but from his earliest years he must be taught that his chief significance comes from the fact that he is created by God and is destined for life with God in eternity."[156]

Under the caption "Sense of God," the bishops begin with the statement that the "child is not complete in himself. He will find his completion only in life with God; and that life must begin here upon earth."[157] Suggestions to parents how to initiate this process follow. The child's education during school years should continue that early beginning. Catholic schools offer the opportunity for God-centered education, and if one is not available, parents "have a grave obligation to provide for their child's religious instruction in some other way."[158]

Achieving a "Sense of Direction" will result if the child knows God, not merely knows about God. The Church, the family, and the schools "have a part to play in this process." Parents have a special responsibility to watch over their child and prevent him or her from being influenced by the many "unsalutary influences at work in modern society."[159]

The bishops opened their treatment of the "Sense of Responsibility" with the observation that a "common complaint registered against the home and the school today is that they do not sharpen the child's sense of responsibility." This section contains their advice to parents and schools as how to inculcate this sense in the child. Spiritual helps occupy a prominent place in their advice, including instilling a sense that "his time and talents belong to God."[160]

The fourth, and final, section of this document is entitled "Sense of Mission." Upon learning that he is "accountable to God for the use of his time and talents the child will acquire not only a sense of responsibility, but a sense of mission as well." Parents and teachers are instructed to help the child "choose and to follow a calling for which he is fitted and in which he can best serve God." The bishops ended their instruction with a reminder that the vocation of those who have care of the child is to "show him that he is a citizen, not only of this world, but of that other world which lies beyond with God whose kingdom is the kingdom of children."[161]

The Teaching of Pope Pius XII

Pope Pius XII gave eighty addresses concerning education during his pontificate. The titles of these are listed in Vincent A. Yzermans' edited book, *Pope Pius XII and Catholic Education*.[162] Yzermans has several headings in his "Introduction" that categorize the Pope's position on education. Under the first of these, "The Aim of Education," he writes that Pius identifies the goal of education as consisting in "collaboration with divine grace for the formation of the true and perfect Christian." He goes on to say that "In this perfection is included the ideal that the Christian as such, be in condition to face and to overcome the difficulties and correspond to the demands of the times in which it is his lot to live." Pius'

description of the "perfect Christian" is:

the Christian of today, child of his own era, knowing and cultivating all the advances made by science and technical skill. He is a citizen and not something apart from the life led in his own country today. The world will have nothing to regret if an ever increasing number of these Christians is placed in all sectors of public and private life.[163]

On Sunday, September 4, 1949, Pius addressed the participants in the Second Congress of the Italian Catholic Union of Secondary School Teachers on the topic of "Religious, Moral and Intellectual Training of Youth." Referring to the dignity of the teaching profession, he stated that "it is, perhaps, the most noble of all undertakings." The charge for teachers was to prepare the ideal of the human being. They would find that ideal "fundamentally designed in the perfect Christian."[164]

A little more than a year later, on October 14, 1950, the Pontiff spoke to some 600 delegates to the first World Catechetical Congress on the subject of the "Vocation of the Religion Teacher." Religious instruction, he said, which is "important to all ages," must "include everything that is essential to the body of the Church's teaching: dogmas of faith, moral laws and divine worship."[165]

The Italian Catholic Action movement had set aside Sunday, March 23, 1952, as "Family Day" in all the parishes of Italy. Pius XII chose that day to deliver a radio message on the subject of "The Christian Conscience as an Object of Education." During this speech he pointed out that the "substance and aim of education in the natural order is the growth of the child in order to become a complete man." The substance and aim of Christian education, he stated, "is the formation of the new human being, reborn in baptism, unto the stature of a perfect Christian."[166] To form the Christian conscience, it was necessary, "before all else," in enlightening the minds of humans regarding "the will of Christ, His Law and His Way" in order to bring the "inner self" to the "free and constant carrying out of the divine will. This is the most exalted duty of education."[167]

On January 4, 1954, Pius XII spoke to the Delegates to the National Sessions of the Italian Catholic Union of Middle School Teachers on the "Aims of an Italian Teachers Union." In a section entitled "Teachers Work with God," he noted that the "Christian educator cannot be satisfied with letting nature do its work. He must fight "against the lower inclinations" and work to "make the higher ones develop. He struggles patiently and firmly against the defects of his pupils and trains them in virtue." [168]

"The Secret of Good Schools" was the subject of the Pope's radio address on the occasion of the Fifth Inter-American Congress on Catholic Education that met in Havana, Cuba, in January of 1954. Focusing on the "Qualities of Good Teachers," he proclaimed that they "should have perfect human formation, intellectual and moral," as befits someone who holds such a "lofty position." Good teachers do more than "merely instruct," they educate, and are "capable, above all, of forming and of molding souls chiefly through contact with their own."[169]

The final sample of Pius' speeches on education is taken from "The Ideal Teacher." It was delivered on November 4, 1955, to 10,000 primary school teachers in St. Peter's Basilica to mark the climax of the convention of the Italian Association of Catholic Schoolmasters. The schoolmaster, he said, is a "person who knows how to create a close relationship between his own soul and the soul of a child." He is the person who "molds the pupil's intellect and will so as to fashion as best he can a being of human and Christian perfection." True schoolmasters "must be complete persons and integral Christians. That is, they must be imitators of the only Divine Master, Jesus Christ."[170]

Speaking directly to the teachers, he said that "As teachers, they must see to it that children acquire all the knowledge which is absolutely indispensable to life. As "Catholic teachers, you should be particularly careful that children learn religion in a clear, organic, and vivid manner....For religion is an indispensable factor in living." It is, he maintained,

> not only a solution to doubts and uncertainties, but also an aid in overcoming strife....It is a refuge against early temptations to sin and a light and guide for children's actions, duties, renunciation, and relations with the outside world.[171]

As educators, the Pontiff instructed, they "should be eager to mold your children and urge them to exercise the human virtues: loyalty, courage, and devotion to duty, family, and country."[172] As Catholic educators he said their duty was to "make every person a good Christian and to make many of them attempt a direct ascent of the holy mount of God, encouraged and sustained by you." He reminded them that "Jesus wants saints among today's children."[173]

On the Eve of the Second Vatican Council

In 1957 Archbishop Albert G. Meyer of Milwaukee, at the time President of the National Catholic Educational Association (NCEA) lauded both the quantity and quality of American Catholic elementary and secondary education.[174] There were signs of strain, however, as Timothy Walch has pointed out, especially in large cities like Chicago, New York, and Philadelphia where, despite the firm support of the ordinaries of those archdioceses, demand outstripped the supply.[175] Nationally, Catholic school enrollment had grown dramatically: in 1959, there were 4,101,792 students in elementary schools and 810,768 in secondary schools.[176] The Catholic

Church was hard-pressed to meet the demands for Catholic schools for their parishioners. Non-public school enrollment, the vast majority of which was in Catholic schools, had increased 118 percent between the years 1940 and 1959 compared with a growth rate of 36 percent in the public sector.[177]

Ideologically, McCluskey had written accurately in 1959 that the Catholic position on schooling had not changed since the days of Bishop John Hughes in New York City in 1840.[178] The Catholic world, including its educational arm, was about to be shaken in the wake of the Second Vatican Council, convened by Pope John XXIII in October of 1962.

Notes

[1] Ray Allen Billington, *The Protestant Crusade, 1800-1860*. New York: Macmillan, 1938, 9.

[2] Peter Guilday, *The Life and Times of John Carroll*. New York: The Encyclopedia Press, 1922, 369.

[3] Peter Guilday, ed., *The National Pastorals of the American Hierarchy, 1792-1919*. Westminster, MD: The Newman Press, 1954, 3-4.

[4] Vincent P. Lannie, *Public Money and Parochial Education: Bishop Hughes, Governor Seward, and the New York School Controversy*. Cleveland, OH: Case Western Reserve University, 103-110.

[5] Laurence Kehoe, ed., *The Complete Works of the Most Rev. John Hughes, D.D.*, I. New York: The American News Company, 1864, 51.

[6] Harold A. Buetow, *Of Singular Benefit: The Story of U.S. Catholic Education*. New York: Macmillan, 1970, 112.

[7] "The Pastoral Letter to the Laity (1829)," in Peter Guilday, ed., *A History of the Councils of Baltimore, 1791-1884*. New York: Macmillan, 1932, 85.

[8] "The Pastoral Letter of 1833," in Guilday, ed., *The National Pastorals of the American Hierarchy, 1792-1919*, 24-25.

[9] Guilday, ed., *A History of the Councils of Baltimore, 1791-1884*, 94-95.

[10] Buetow, *Of Singular Benefit*, 115-116.

[11] Guilday, ed., *A History of the Councils of Baltimore, 1791-1884*, 100-103.

[12] "The Pastoral Letter of 1833," in Guilday, ed., *The National Pastorals of the American Hierarchy, 1792-1919*, 74.

[13] Guilday, ed., *A History of the Councils of Baltimore, 1791-1884*, 112-113.

[14] "The Pastoral Letter of 1837," in Guilday, ed., *The National Pastorals of the American Hierarchy, 1792-1919*, 115.

[15] "The Pastoral Letter of 1840," in Guilday, ed., *The National Pastorals of the American Hierarchy, 1792-1919*, 120.

[16] Ibid., 124.

[17] Ibid.

[18] Ibid., 125.

[19] Ibid., 133.

[20] Ibid., 134.

[21] Guilday, ed., *A History of the Councils of Baltimore, 1791-1884*, 124-126.

[22] Billington, *The Protestant Crusade*, 166-168.

[23] Guilday, ed., *A History of the Councils of Baltimore, 1701-1884*, 138-139.

[24] Neil G. McCluskey, ed., *Catholic Education in America*. New York: Teachers College Press, 1964, 63.

[25] See Billington, *The Protestant Crusade*, 220-237, for a treatment of the Philadelphia riots.

[26] Guilday, ed., *A History of the Councils of Baltimore, 1791-1884*, 144.

[27] Ibid., 144-145.

[28] *Report on the Population of the United States at the Eleventh Census, 1890*, Vol. 1, Part I. Washington, DC: Government Printing Office, lxxx.

[29] Guilday, ed., *A History of the Councils of Baltimore, 1791-1884*, 171.

[30] James A. Burns, *Catholic Education: A Study of Conditions*. New York: Longmans, Green, 15.

[31] "The Pastoral Letter of 1852," in Guilday, ed., *The National Pastorals of the American Hierarchy, 1792-1919*, 182.

[32] Ibid., 187-189.

[33] Ibid., 190.

[34] Ibid., 190-191.

[35] Guilday, ed., *A History of the Councils of Baltimore, 1791-1884*, 178-179.

[36] Warren A. Nord, *Religion & American Education: Rethinking a National Dilemma*. Chapel Hill: The University of North Carolina Press, 1995, 73.

[37] "Pastoral Letter to the Clergy and Laity," First Provincial Council of Cincinnati (1855), in James A. Burns and Bernard J. Kohlbrenner, *A History*

of Catholic Education in the United States. New York: Benziger Brothers, 1937, 138.

38 Ibid. in John H. Lamott, *History of the Archdiocese of Cincinnati, 1821-1921.* New York: Frederick Pustet Company, Inc., 1921, 275.

39 Ibid. in Burns and Kohlbrenner, *A History of Catholic Education in the United States,* 138.

40 "Pastoral Letter," Second Provincial Council of Cincinnati (1858), in James A. Burns, *The Growth and Development of the Catholic School System in the United States.* New York: Benziger Brothers, 1912, 186; in Lamott, *History of the Archdiocese of Cincinnati,* 216.

41 "Pastoral Letter," Third Provincial Council of Cincinnati (1861), in Thomas J. Jenkins, *The Judges of Faith: Christian versus Godless Schools.* Baltimore: John Murphy and Co., 1866, 34; in Lamott, *History of the Archdiocese of Cincinnati,* 276-277.

42 E.E.Y. Hales, *Pio Nono.* Garden City, New York: Doubleday and Co., Inc., 1962, 206.

43 Pius IX to Herman von Vicari, Archbishop of Fribourg, in James Conway, "The Rights and Duties of the Church in Regard to Education," *The American Catholic Quarterly Review IX,* 35 (October 1884): 667.

44 Pius IX, "Syllabus of Errors," in Ernest C. Helmreich, ed., *A Free Church in a Free State?* Boston: D.C. Heath and Co., 1964, 2-5.

45 Hales, *Pio Nono,* 266-267.

46 Pius IX, "Quanta Cura," in John F. Clarkson, et al., eds., *The Church Teaches: Documents of the Church in English Translation.* St. Louis: B. Herder Book Co., 1955, 85-86.

47 Guilday, ed., *A History of the Councils of Baltimore, 1791-1884,* 187.

48 Ibid., 193-194.

49 Ibid., 195, 193.

50 Ibid., 211.

51 "The Pastoral Letter of 1866," in Guilday ed., *The National Pastorals of the American Hierarchy, 1792-1919,* 215-216.

52 Jenkins, *The Judges of Faith,* 82-83.

53 Ibid., 84.

54 Ibid., 84-86.

55 Ibid., 86.

56 Ibid. 89.

57 Ibid., 92.

58 Quoted in Frederick J. Zwierlein, *The Life and Letters of Bishop McQuaid,* II. New York: The Art Print Shop, 1926, 129.

59 Jenkins, *The Judges of Faith,* 120-122.

60 Timothy Walch, *Parish School: American Catholic Education from Colonial Times to the Present.* New York: Crossroad Herder, 1996, 55.

61 Ibid., 58.

62 Ibid., 58-59.

63 Ibid., 59.

64 McCluskey, ed., *Catholic Education in America,* 121.

65 "Instruction of the Congregation of the Propaganda de Fide" (1875), in Ibid., 122.

66 Ibid., 122-126.

67 "The President's Speech at Des Moines," *Catholic World 22* (January 1876): 17.

68 Alvin W. Johnson, *The Legal Status of Church-State Relationships in the United States.* Minneapolis, MN: The University of Minnesota Press, 1934, 21.

69 Ibid.

70 R. Freeman Butts, *The American Tradition in Religion and Education.* Boston: Beacon Press, 1950, 144.

71 Walch, *Parish School: American Catholic Education from Colonial Times to the Present,* 63.

72 Guilday, ed., *A History of the Councils of Baltimore, 1791-1884,* 217.

73 Quoted in Jenkins, *The Judges of Faith,* 122.

74 James Gibbons, "The Necessity of Religion for Society," *The American Catholic Quarterly Review 9* (October 1884): 683, 674.

75 Thomas T. McAvoy, "Leo XIII and America," in *Leo XIII and the Modern World,* ed. Edward T. Gargan, New York: Sheed and Ward, 1961, 165.

76 Guilday, ed., *A History of the Councils of Baltimore, 1791-1884,* 238.

77 Guilday, ed., *The National Pastorals of the American Hierarchy, 1792-1919,* 243-244.

78 Ibid., 244-245.

79 Ibid., 245.

80 Ibid.

81 Ibid., 246.

82 Ibid.

83 Ibid., 247.

84 McCluskey, ed., *Catholic Education in America,* 93-94.

85 Guilday, ed., *A History of the Councils of Baltimore, 1791-1884,* 238-239.

86 Leo XIII, "Inscrutabili," in Joseph Husslein, ed., *Social Wellsprings*, I. Milwaukee: Bruce Publishing Co., 1940, 3-5, 9.

87 Leo XIII, "Arcanum," in Ibid., 30-33.

88 Leo XIII, "Immortale Dei," in John F. Ryan, ed., *The State and the Church*. New York: Macmillan, 1922, 16-24.

89 *Catholic Citizen*, October 22, 1887, 3, 1.

90 Patrick F. McSweeney, "Heartless, Headless and Godless," *Catholic World* 46 (January 1888): 435-437.

91 Baltimore Catholic Congress, "For Social Reform and Americanization," in Aaron R. Abell, ed., *American Catholic Thought on Social Questions*. Indianapolis: The Bobbs-Merrill Co., Inc., 1966, 185.

92 James Cardinal Gibbons, "Is Religious Instruction in the Public Schools Expedient? If So, What Should Be Its Character and Foundations?" *Public Opinion* 7 (July 13, 1889): 297.

93 Bernard J. McQuaid, "Religious Teaching in the Schools," *Forum* 8 (December 1889): 379.

94 Leo XIII, "Sapientiae Christianae," in Husslein, ed., *Social Wellspring*, I, 144-156.

95 Ibid., 158-162.

96 *The Laws of Wisconsin, Except City Charters and Their Amendments, Passed in the Biennial Session of the Legislature of 1889*, I. Madison, WI: Democrat Printing Company, 1889, 729-733.

97 Harry H. Heming, *The Catholic Church in Wisconsin*. Milwaukee: T. J. Sullivan, 1896, 283.

98 Ibid.

99 Ibid., 284.

100 Ibid., 285.

101 Ibid., 286.

102 John Ireland, "State Schools and Parish Schools—Is Union Between Them Impossible?" *National Education Association: Journal of Proceedings and Addresses. Session of the Year 1890, held at St. Paul, Minnesota*. Topeka, KS: Kansas Publishing House, Clifford C. Baker, 1890, 179-180.

103 Ibid., 180.

104 Ibid., 182-184.

105 McCluskey, ed., *Catholic Education in America*, 141.

106 John Ireland, "Clarification to Archbishop Gibbons," (1890) in Ibid., 142-143.

107 Ibid., 144.

108 Ibid., 146-148.

109 Bernard McQuaid, quoted in Colman J. Barry, *The Catholic Church and German Americans*. Milwaukee: Bruce Publishing Co., 1953, 489.

110 "Cardinal Gibbons' Report to Pope Leo XIII, December 30, 1890," in Daniel F. Reilly, *The School Controversy, 1891-1893*. New York: Arno Press and the New York Times, 1969, 242-246.

111 Reilly, *The School Controversy*, 238

112 "Archbishop Ireland's Memorial," addressed to Cardinal Ledochowski, Prefect of the Congregation of the Propagation of the Faith, undated, likely in the Spring of 1892, in Reilly, Ibid., Appendix E, 250-266; Zwierlein, *The Life and Letters of Bishop McQuaid*, III. Rochester, NY: The Art Print Shop, 1927, 171.

113 *Catholic Citizen*, July 2, 1892, 1.

114 Reilly, *The School Controversy*, 134.

115 McCluskey, ed., *Catholic Education in America*, 151; Reilly, *The School Controversy*, 160; and John Conway, "The Catholics and the Public Schools: The Significance of Tolerari Potest," *Educational Review* 4 (October 1892): 236-240.

116 *Catholic Citizen*, July 30, 1892, 4.

117 Ibid., March 11, 1893, 1.

118 Walch, *Parish School*, 97.

119 "Archbishop Satolli's Fourteen Propositions for the Settling of the School Question," in McCluskey, ed., *Catholic Education in America*, 152-160.

120 In McCluskey, ed., 161.

121 David Francis Sweeney, *The Life of John Lancaster Spalding*. New York: Herder and Herder, 1965, 213-216.

122 Reilly, *The School Controversy*, 211-212.

123 Ibid., 228-229.

124 Ibid., 230.

125 T. Lincoln Bouscaren and Adam C. Ellis, *Canon Law: A Text and Commentary*. Milwaukee: Bruce Publishing Company, 1945, 4.

126 Ibid., 4-5.

127 Ibid., 538.

128 Ibid., 539.

129 Stanislaus Woywod, revised by Callistus Smith, *A Practical Commentary on the Code of Canon Law*, II. New York: Joseph F. Wagner, Inc., 1952, 136.

130 Ibid., 139-140.

131 Ibid., 140.

132 Ibid.

[133] "The Pastoral Letter of 1919," in Guilday, ed., *The National Pastorals of the American Hierarchy, 1792-1919*, 265.

[134] Ibid., 280-282.

[135] "Pastoral Letter of 1919," in Raphael M. Huber, ed., *Our Bishops Speak, 1919-1951*. Milwaukee: Bruce Publishing Company, 1952, 14-15.

[136] Ibid., 15.

[137] Ibid., 16.

[138] Buetow, *Of Singular Benefit*, 179.

[139] *Pierce v. Society of Sisters*, 268 U.S. 510 (1925).

[140] Pius XI, "The Christian Education of Youth," in *Five Great Encyclicals*. New York: Paulist Press, 1939, 39.

[141] Ibid., 41-42.

[142] Ibid., 44-45.

[143] Ibid., 46.

[144] Ibid.

[145] Ibid.

[146] Ibid., 49.

[147] Ibid., 60.

[148] Ibid., 61.

[149] Ibid., 62.

[150] Ibid., 63.

[151] Ibid., 64.

[152] Ibid., 65.

[153] Ibid.

[154] McCluskey, ed., *Catholic Education in America*, 93.

[155] "The Child, Citizen of Two Worlds," in Ibid., 195-205.

[156] Ibid., 194.

[157] Ibid., 195.

[158] Ibid., 197.

[159] Ibid., 200-201.

[160] Ibid., 202-204.

[161] Ibid., 204-205.

[162] Vincent A. Yzermans, ed., "Introduction," in *Pope Pius XII and Catholic Education*. St. Meinrad, IN: Grail Publications, 1957, 174-178.

[163] Yzermans, ed., Ibid., *viii*.

[164] "Religious, Moral, and Intellectual Training of Youth," in Ibid., 27-28, 32.

[165] "Vocation of the Religion Teacher," in Ibid., 38, 41.

[166] "The Christian Conscience as an Object of Education," in Ibid., 78.

[167] Ibid., 80.

[168] "Aims of an Italian Teachers Union," in Ibid., 122, 126.

[169] "The Secret of Good Schools," in Ibid., 128-130.

[170] "The Ideal Teacher," in Ibid., 165, 167.

[171] Ibid., 170.

[172] Ibid.

[173] Ibid., 171.

[174] Buetow, *Of Singular Benefit*, 276.

[175] Walch, *Parish School*, 170-173.

[176] Neil G. McCluskey, *Catholic Viewpoint on Education*, Garden City, New York, 1959, 98-100.

[177] Ibid., 107.

[178] Ibid., 167.

Divini Illius Magistri
Encyclical on Christian Education

PIUS XI
December 31, 1929

To the Patriarchs, Primates, Archbishops, Bishops, and Other Ordinaries in Peace and Communion with the Apostolic See and to All the Faithful of the Catholic World.

Venerable Brethren and Beloved Children, Health and Apostolic Benediction.

Representative on earth of that divine Master who while embracing in the immensity of His love all mankind, even unworthy sinners, showed nevertheless a special tenderness and affection for children, and expressed Himself in those singularly touching words: "Suffer the little children to come unto Me."[1] We also on every occasion have endeavored to show the predilection wholly paternal which We bear towards them, particularly by our assiduous care and timely instructions with reference to the Christian education of youth.

2. And so, in the spirit of the Divine Master, We have directed a helpful word, now of admonition, now of exhortation, now of direction, to youths and to their educators, to fathers and mothers, on various points of Christian education, with that solicitude which becomes the common Father of all the Faithful, with an insistence in season and out of season, demanded by our pastoral office and inculcated by the Apostle: "Be instant in season, out of season; reprove, entreat, rebuke in all patience and doctrine."[2] Such insistence is called for in these our times, when, alas, there is so great and deplorable an absence of clear and sound principles, even regarding problems the most fundamental.

3. Now this same general condition of the times, this ceaseless agitation in various ways of the problem of educational rights nd systems in different countries, the desire expressed to Us with filial confidence by not a few of yourselves, Venerable Brethren, and by members of your flocks, as well as Our deep affection towards youth above referred to, move Us to turn more directly to this subject, if not to treat it in all its well-nigh inexhaustible range of theory and practice, at least to summarize its main principles, throw full light on its important conclusions, and point out its practical applications.

4. Let this be the record of Our Sacerdotal Jubilee which, with altogether special affection, We wish to dedicate to our beloved youth, and to commend to all those whose office and duty is the work of education.

5. Indeed never has there been so much discussion about education as nowadays; never have exponents of new pedagogical theories been so numerous, or so many methods and means devised, proposed and debated, not merely to facilitate education, but to create a new system infallibly efficacious, and capable of preparing the present generations for that earthly happiness which they so ardently desire.

6. The reason is that men, created by God to His image and likeness and destined for Him Who is infinite perfection realize today more than ever amid the most exuberant material progress, the insufficiency of earthly goods to produce true happiness either for the individual or for the nations. And hence they feel more keenly in themselves the impulse towards a perfection that is higher, which impulse is implanted in their rational nature by the Creator Himself. This perfection they seek to acquire by means of education. But many of them with, it would seem, too great insistence on the etymological meaning of the word, pretend to draw education out of human nature itself and evolve it by its own unaided powers. Such easily fall into error, because, instead of fixing their gaze on God, first principle and last end of the whole universe, they fall back upon themselves, becoming attached exclusively to passing things of earth; and thus their restlessness will never cease till they direct their attention and their efforts to God, the goal of all perfection, according to the profound saying of Saint Augustine: "Thou didst create us, O Lord, for Thyself, and our heart is restless till it rest in Thee."[3]

7. It is therefore as important to make no mistake in education, as it is to make no mistake in the pursuit of the last end, with which the whole work of education is intimately and necessarily connected. In fact, since education consists essentially in preparing man for what he must be and for what he must do here below, in order to attain the sublime end for which he was created, it is clear that there can be no true education which is not wholly directed to man's last end, and that in the present order of Providence, since God has revealed Himself to us in the Person of His Only Begotten Son, who alone is "the way, the truth and the life," there can be no ideally perfect education which is not Christian education.

8. From this we see the supreme importance of Christian education, not merely for each individual, but for families and for the whole of human society, whose perfection comes from the perfection of the elements that compose it. From these same principles, the excellence, we may well call it the unsurpassed excellence, of the work of Christian education becomes manifest and clear; for after all it aims at securing the Supreme Good, that is, God, for the souls of those who are being educated, and the maximum of well-being possible here below for human society. And this it does as efficaciously as man is capable of doing it, namely by cooperating with God in the perfecting of individuals and of society, in as much as education makes upon the soul the first, the most powerful and lasting impression for life according to the well-known saying of the Wise Man, "A young man according to his way, even when he is old, he will not depart from it."[4] With good reason therefore did St. John Chrysostom say, "What greater work is there than training the mind and forming the habits of the young?"[5]

9. But nothing discloses to us the supernatural beauty and excellence of the work of Christian education better than the sublime expression of love of our Blessed Lord, identifying Himself with children, "Whosoever shall receive one such child as this in my name, receiveth me."[6]

10. Now in order that no mistake be made in this work of utmost importance, and in order to conduct it in the best manner possible with the help of God's grace, it is necessary to have a clear and definite idea of Christian education in its essential aspects, viz., who has the mission to educate, who are the subjects to be educated, what are the necessary accompanying circumstances, what is the end and object proper to Christian education according to God's established order in the economy of His Divine Providence.

11. Education is essentially a social and not a mere individual activity. Now there are three necessary societies, distinct from one another and yet harmoniously combined by God, into which man is born: two, namely the family and civil society, belong to the natural order; the third, the Church, to the supernatural order.

12. In the first place comes the family, instituted directly by God for its peculiar purpose, the generation and formation of offspring; for this reason it has priority of nature and therefore of rights over civil society. Nevertheless, the family is an imperfect society, since it has not in itself all the means for its own complete development; whereas civil society is a perfect society, having in itself all the means for its peculiar end, which is the temporal well-being of the community; and so, in this respect, that is, in view of the common good, it has preeminence over the family, which finds its own suitable temporal perfection precisely in civil society.

13. The third society, into which man is born when through Baptism he reaches the divine life of grace, is the Church; a society of the supernatural order and of universal extent; a perfect society, because it has in itself all the means required for its own end, which is the eternal salvation of mankind; hence it is supreme in its own domain.

14. Consequently, education which is concerned with man as a whole, individually and socially, in the order of nature and in the order of grace, necessarily belongs to all these three societies, in due proportion, corresponding, according to the disposition of Divine Providence, to the coordination of their respecting ends.

15. And first of all education belongs preeminently to the Church, by reason of a double title in the supernatural order, conferred exclusively upon her by God Himself; absolutely superior therefore to any other title in the natural order.

16. The first title is founded upon the express mission and supreme authority to teach, given her by her divine Founder: "All power is given to me in heaven and in earth. Going therefore teach ye all nations, baptizing them in the name of the Father, and of the Son, and of the Holy Ghost, teaching them to observe all things whatsoever I have commanded you, and behold I am with you all days, even to the consummation of the world."[7] Upon this magisterial office Christ conferred infallibility, together with the command to teach His doctrine. Hence the Church "was set by her divine Author as the pillar and ground of truth, in order to teach the divine Faith to men, and keep whole and inviolate the deposit confided to her; to direct and fashion men, in all their actions individually and socially, to purity of morals and integrity of life, in accordance with revealed doctrine."[8]

17. The second title is the supernatural motherhood, in virtue of which the Church, spotless spouse of Christ, generates, nurtures and educates souls in the divine life of grace, with her Sacraments and her doctrine. With good reason then does St. Augustine maintain: "He has not God for father who refuses to have the Church as mother."[9]

18. Hence it is that in this proper object of her mission, that is, "in faith and morals, God Himself has made the Church sharer in the divine magisterium and, by a special privilege, granted her immunity from error; hence she is the mistress of men, supreme and absolutely sure, and she has inherent in herself an inviolable right to freedom in teaching."[10] By necessary consequence the Church is independent of any sort of earthly power as well in the origin as in the exercise of her mission as educator, not merely in regard to her proper end and object, but also in regard to the means necessary and suitable to attain that end. Hence with regard to every other kind of human learning and instruction, which is the common patrimony of individuals and society, the Church has an independent right to make use of it, and above all to decide what may help or harm Christian education. And this must be so, because the Church as a perfect society has an independent right to the means conducive to its end, and because every form of instruction, no less than every human action, has a necessary connection with man's last end, and therefore cannot be withdrawn from the dictates of the divine law, of which the Church is guardian, interpreter and infallible mistress.

19. This truth is clearly set forth by Pius X of saintly memory: "Whatever a Christian does even in the order of things of earth, he may not overlook the supernatural; indeed he must, according to the teaching of Christian wisdom, direct all things towards the supreme good as to his last end; all his actions, besides, in so far as good or evil in the order of morality, that is, in keeping or not with natural and divine law, fall under the judgment and jurisdiction of the Church."[11]

20. It is worthy of note how a layman, an excellent writer and at the same time a profound and conscientious thinker, has been able to understand well and express exactly this fundamental Catholic doctrine: "The Church does not say that morality belongs purely, in the sense of exclusively, to her; but that it belongs wholly to her. She has never maintained that outside her fold and apart from her teaching, man cannot arrive at any moral truth; she has on the contrary more

than once condemned this opinion because it has appeared under more forms than one. She does however say, has said, and will ever say, that because of her institution by Jesus Christ, because of the Holy Ghost sent her in His name by the Father, she alone possesses what she has had immediately from God and can never lose, the whole of moral truth, *omnem veritatem*, in which all individual moral truths are included, as well those which man may learn by the help of reason, as those which form part of revelation or which may be deduced from it."[12]

21. Therefore with full right the Church promotes letters, science, art in so far as necessary or helpful to Christian education, in addition to her work for the salvation of souls: founding and maintaining schools and institutions adapted to every branch of learning and degree of culture.[13] Nor may even physical culture, as it is called, be considered outside the range of her maternal supervision, for the reason that it also is a means which may help or harm Christian education.

22. And this work of the Church in every branch of culture is of immense benefit to families and nations which without Christ are lost, as St. Hilary points out correctly: "What can be more fraught with danger for the world than the rejection of Christ?"[14] Nor does it interfere in the least with the regulations of the State, because the Church in her motherly prudence is not unwilling that her schools and institutions for the education of the laity be in keeping with the legitimate dispositions of civil authority; she is in every way ready to cooperate with this authority and to make provision for a mutual understanding, should difficulties arise.

23. Again it is the inalienable right as well as the indispensable duty of the Church, to watch over the entire education of her children, in all institutions, public or private, not merely in regard to the religious instruction there given, but in regard to every other branch of learning and every regulation in so far as religion and morality are concerned.[15]

24. Nor should the exercise of this right be considered undue interference, but rather maternal care on the part of the Church in protecting her children from the grave danger of all kinds of doctrinal and moral evil. Moreover this watchfulness of the Church not merely can create no real inconvenience, but must on the contrary confer valuable assistance in the right ordering and well-being of families and of civil society; for it keeps far away from youth the moral poison which at that inexperienced and changeable age more easily penetrates the mind and more rapidly spreads its baneful effects. For it is true, as Leo XIII has wisely pointed out, that without proper religious and moral instruction "every form of intellectual culture will be injurious; for young people not accustomed to respect God, will be unable to bear the restraint of a virtuous life, and never having learned to deny themselves anything, they will easily be incited to disturb the public order."[16]

25. The extent of the Church's mission in the field of education is such as to embrace every nation, without exception, according to the command of Christ: "Teach ye all nations;"[17] and there is no power on earth that may lawfully oppose her or stand in her way. In the first place, it extends over all the Faithful, of whom she has anxious care as a tender mother. For these she has throughout the centuries created and conducted an immense number of schools and institutions in every branch of learning. As We said on a recent occasion: "Right back in the far-off middle ages when there were so many (some have even said too many) monasteries, convents, churches, collegiate churches, cathedral chapters, etc.,

there was attached to each a home of study, of teaching, of Christian education. To these we must add all the universities, spread over every country and always by the initiative and under the protection of the Holy See and the Church. That grand spectacle, which today we see better, as it is nearer to us and more imposing because of the conditions of the age, was the spectacle of all times; and they who study and compare historical events remain astounded at what the Church has been able to do in this matter, and marvel at the manner in which she had succeeded in fulfilling her God-given mission to educate generations of men to a Christian life, producing everywhere a magnificent harvest of fruitful results. But if we wonder that the Church in all times has been able to gather about her and educate hundreds, thousands, millions of students, no less wonderful is it to bear in mind what she has done not only in the field of education, but in that also of true and genuine erudition. For, if so many treasures of culture, civilization and literature have escaped destruction, this is due to the action by which the Church, even in times long past and uncivilized, has shed so bright a light in the domain of letters, of philosophy, of art and in a special manner of architecture."[18]

26. All this the Church has been able to do because her mission to educate extends equally to those outside the Fold, seeing that all men are called to enter the kingdom of God and reach eternal salvation. Just as today when her missions scatter schools by the thousand in districts and countries not yet Christian, from the banks of the Ganges to the Yellow River and the great islands and archipelagos of the Pacific Ocean, from the Dark Continent to the Land of Fire and to frozen Alaska, so in every age the Church by her missionaries has educated to Christian life and to civilization the various peoples which now constitute the Christian nations of the civilized world.

27. Hence it is evident that both by right and in fact the mission to educate belongs preeminently to the Church, and that no one free from prejudice can have a reasonable motive for opposing or impeding the Church in this her work, of which the world today enjoys the precious advantages.

28. This is the more true because the rights of the family and of the State, even the rights of individuals regarding a just liberty in the pursuit of science, of methods of science and all sorts of profane culture, not only are not opposed to this preeminence of the Church, but are in complete harmony with it. The fundamental reason for this harmony is that the supernatural order, to which the Church owes her rights, not only does not in the least destroy the natural order, to which pertain the other rights mentioned, but elevates the natural and perfects it, each affording mutual aid to the other, and completing it in a manner proportioned to its respective nature and dignity. The reason is because both come from God, who cannot contradict Himself: "The works of God are perfect and all His ways are judgments."[19]

29. This becomes clearer when we consider more closely and in detail the mission of education proper to the family and to the State.

30. In the first place the Church's mission of education is in wonderful agreement with that of the family, for both proceed from God, and in a remarkably similar manner. God directly communicates to the family, in the natural order, fecundity, which is the principle of life, and hence also the principle of education to life, together with authority, the principle of order.

31. The Angelic Doctor with his wonted clearness of thought and precision of style, says: "The father according to the flesh has in a particular way a share in that principle which in a manner universal is found in God.... The father is the principle of generation, of education and discipline and of everything that bears upon the perfecting of human life."[20]

32. The family therefore holds directly from the Creator the mission and hence the right to educate the offspring, a right inalienable because inseparably joined to the strict obligation, a right anterior to any right whatever of civil society and of the State, and therefore inviolable on the part of any power on earth.

33. That this right is inviolable St. Thomas proves as follows: "The child is naturally something of the father...so by natural right the child, before reaching the use of reason, is under the father's care. Hence it would be contrary to natural justice if the child, before the use of reason, were removed from the care of its parents, or if any disposition were made concerning him against the will of the parents."[21] And as this duty on the part of the parents continues up to the time when the child is in a position to provide for itself, this same inviolable parental right of education also endures. "Nature intends not merely the generation of the offspring, but also its development and advance to the perfection of man considered as man, that is, to the state of virtue"[22] says the same St. Thomas.

34. The wisdom of the Church in this matter is expressed with precision and clearness in the Codex of Canon Law, can. 1113: "Parents are under a grave obligation to see to the religious and moral education of their children, as well as to their physical and civic training, as far as they can, and moreover to provide for their temporal well-being."[23]

35. On this point the common sense of mankind is in such complete accord, that they would be in open contradiction with it who dared maintain that the children belong to the State before they belong to the family, and that the State has an absolute right over their education. Untenable is the reason they adduce, namely that man is born a citizen and hence belongs primarily to the State, not bearing in mind that before being a citizen man must exist; and existence does not come from the State, but from the parents, as Leo XIII wisely declared: "The children are something of the father, and as it were an extension of the person of the father; and, to be perfectly accurate, they enter into and become part of civil society, not directly by themselves, but through the family in which they were born."[24] "And therefore," says the same Leo XIII, "the father's power is of such a nature that it cannot be destroyed or absorbed by the State; for it has the same origin as human life itself."[25] It does not however follow from this that the parents' right to educate their children is absolute and despotic; for it is necessarily subordinated to the last end and to natural and divine law, as Leo XIII declares in another memorable encyclical, where He thus sums up the rights and duties of parents: "By nature parents have a right to the training of their children, but with this added duty that the education and instruction of the child be in accord with the end for which by God's blessing it was begotten. Therefore it is the duty of parents to make every effort to prevent any invasion of their rights in this matter, and to make absolutely sure that the education of their children remain under their own control in keeping with their Christian duty, and above all to refuse to send them to those schools in which there is danger of imbibing the deadly poison of impiety."[26]

36. It must be borne in mind also that the obligation of the family to bring up children, includes not only religious and moral education, but physical and civic education as well,[27] principally in so far as it touches upon religion and morality.

37. This incontestable right of the family has at various times been recognized by nations anxious to respect the natural law in their civil enactments. Thus, to give one recent example, the Supreme Court of the United States of America, in a decision on an important controversy, declared that it is not in the competence of the State to fix any uniform standard of education by forcing children to receive instruction exclusively in public schools, and it bases its decision on the natural law: the child is not the mere creature of the State; those who nurture him and direct his destiny have the right coupled with the high duty, to educate him and prepare him for the fulfillment of his obligations.[28]

38. History bears witness how, particularly in modern times, the State has violated and does violate rights conferred by God on the family. At the same time it shows magnificently how the Church has ever protected and defended these rights, a fact proved by the special confidence which parents have in Catholic schools. As We pointed out recently in Our letter to the Cardinal Secretary of State: "The family has instinctively understood this to be so, and from the earliest days of Christianity down to our own times, fathers and mothers, even those of little or no faith, have been sending or bringing their children in millions to places of education under the direction of the Church."[29]

39. It is paternal instinct, given by God, that thus turns with confidence to the Church, certain of finding in her the protection of family rights, thereby illustrating that harmony with which God has ordered all things. The Church is indeed conscious of her divine mission to all mankind, and of the obligation which all men have to practice the one true religion; and therefore she never tires of defending her right, and of reminding parents of their duty, to have all Catholic-born children baptized and brought up as Christians. On the other hand so jealous is she of the family's inviolable natural right to educate the children, that she never consents, save under peculiar circumstances and with special cautions, to baptize the children of infidels, or provide for their education against the will of the parents, till such time as the children can choose for themselves and freely embrace the Faith.[30]

40. We have therefore two facts of supreme importance. As We said in Our discourse cited above: The Church placing at the disposal of families her office of mistress and educator, and the families eager to profit by the offer, and entrusting their children to the Church in hundreds and thousands. These two facts recall and proclaim a striking truth of the greatest significance in the moral and social order. They declare that the mission of education regards before all, above all, primarily the Church and the family, and this by natural and divine law, and that therefore it cannot be slighted, cannot be evaded, cannot be supplanted.[31]

41. From such priority of rights on the part of the Church and of the family in the field of education, most important advantages, as we have seen, accrue to the whole of society. Moreover in accordance with the divinely established order of things, no damage can follow from it to the true and just rights of the State in regard to the education of its citizens.

42. These rights have been conferred upon civil society by the Author of nature Himself, not by title of fatherhood, as in the case of the Church and of the family, but in virtue of the authority which it possesses to promote the common temporal welfare, which is precisely the purpose of its existence. Consequently education cannot pertain to civil society in the same way in which it pertains to the Church and to the family, but in a different way corresponding to its own particular end and object.

43. Now this end and object, the common welfare in the temporal order, consists in that peace and security in which families and individual citizens have the free exercise of their rights, and at the same time enjoy the greatest spiritual and temporal prosperity possible in this life, by the mutual union and coordination of the work of all. The function therefore of the civil authority residing in the State is twofold, to protect and to foster, but by no means to absorb the family and the individual, or to substitute itself for them.

44. Accordingly in the matter of education, it is the right, or to speak more correctly, it is the duty of the State to protect in its legislation, the prior rights, already described, of the family as regards the Christian education of its offspring, and consequently also to respect the supernatural rights of the Church in this same realm of Christian education.

45. It also belongs to the State to protect the rights of the child itself when the parents are found wanting either physically or morally in this respect, whether by default, incapacity or misconduct, since, as has been shown, their right to educate is not an absolute and despotic one, but dependent on the natural and divine law, and therefore subject alike to the authority and jurisdiction of the Church, and to the vigilance and administrative care of the State in view of the common good. Besides, the family is not a perfect society, that is, it has not in itself all the means necessary for its full development. In such cases, exceptional no doubt, the State does not put itself in the place of the family, but merely supplies deficiencies, and provides suitable means, always in conformity with the natural rights of the child and the supernatural rights of the Church.

46. In general then it is the right and duty of the State to protect, according to the rules of right reason and faith, the moral and religious education of youth, by removing public impediments that stand in the way. In the first place it pertains to the State, in view of the common good, to promote in various ways the education and instruction of youth. It should begin by encouraging and assisting, of its own accord, the initiative and activity of the Church and the family, whose successes in this field have been clearly demonstrated by history and experience. It should moreover supplement their work whenever this falls short of what is necessary, even by means of its own schools and institutions. For the State more than any other society is provided with the means put at its disposal for the needs of all, and it is only right that it use these means to the advantage of those who have contributed them.[32]

47. Over and above this, the State can exact and take measures to secure that all its citizens have the necessary knowledge of their civic and political duties, and a certain degree of physical, intellectual and moral culture, which, considering the conditions of our times, is really necessary for the common good.

48. However it is clear that in all these ways of promoting education and instruction, both public and private, the State should respect the inherent rights of the Church and of the family concerning Christian education, and moreover have regard for distributive justice. Accordingly, unjust and unlawful is any monopoly, educational or scholastic, which,

physically or morally, forces families to make use of government schools, contrary to the dictates of their Christian conscience, or contrary even to their legitimate preferences.

49. This does not prevent the State from making due provision for the right administration of public affairs and for the protection of its peace, within or without the realm. These are things which directly concern the public good and call for special aptitudes and special preparation. The State may therefore reserve to itself the establishment and direction of schools intended to prepare for certain civic duties and especially for military service, provided it be careful not to injure the rights of the Church or of the family in what pertains to them. It is well to repeat this warning here; for in these days there is spreading a spirit of nationalism which is false and exaggerated, as well as dangerous to true peace and prosperity. Under its influence various excesses are committed in giving a military turn to the so-called physical training of boys (sometimes even of girls, contrary to the very instincts of human nature); or again in usurping unreasonably on Sunday, the time which should be devoted to religious duties and to family life at home. It is not our intention however to condemn what is good in the spirit of discipline and legitimate bravery promoted by these methods; We condemn only what is excessive, as for example violence, which must not be confounded with courage nor with the noble sentiment of military valor in defense of country and public order; or again exaltation of athleticism which even in classic pagan times marked the decline and downfall of genuine physical training.

50. In general also it belongs to civil society and the State to provide what may be called civic education, not only for its youth, but for all ages and classes. This consists in the practice of presenting publicly to groups of individuals information having an intellectual, imaginative and emotional appeal, calculated to draw their wills to what is upright and honest, and to urge its practice by a sort of moral compulsion, positively by disseminating such knowledge, and negatively by suppressing what is opposed to it.[33] This civic education, so wide and varied in itself as to include almost every activity of the State intended for the public good, ought also to be regulated by the norms of rectitude, and therefore cannot conflict with the doctrines of the Church, which is the divinely appointed teacher of these norms.

51. All that we have said so far regarding the activity of the State in educational matters, rests on the solid and immovable foundation of the Catholic doctrine of *The Christian Constitution of States* set forth in such masterly fashion by Our Predecessor Leo XIII, notably in the Encyclicals *Immortale Dei* and *Sapientiae Christianae*. He writes as follows: "God has divided the government of the human race between two authorities, ecclesiastical and civil, establishing one over things divine, the other over things human. Both are supreme, each in its own domain; each has its own fixed boundaries which limit its activities. These boundaries are determined by the peculiar nature and the proximate end of each, and describe as it were a sphere within which, with exclusive right, each may develop its influence. As however the same subjects are under the two authorities, it may happen that the same matter, though from a different point of view, may come under the competence and jurisdiction of each of them. It follows that divine Providence, whence both authorities have their origin, must have traced with due order the proper line of action for each. The powers that are, are ordained of God."[34]

52. Now the education of youth is precisely one of those matters that belong both to

the Church and to the State, "though in different ways," as explained above. Therefore, continues Leo XIII, between the two powers there must reign a well-ordered harmony. Not without reason may this mutual agreement be compared to the union of body and soul in man. Its nature and extent can only be determined by considering, as we have said, the nature of each of the two powers, and in particular the excellence and nobility of the respective ends. To one is committed directly and specifically the charge of what is helpful in worldly matters; while the other is to concern itself with the things that pertain to heaven and eternity. Everything therefore in human affairs that is in any way sacred, or has reference to the salvation of souls and the worship of God, whether by its nature or by its end, is subject to the jurisdiction and discipline of the Church. Whatever else is comprised in the civil and political order, rightly comes under the authority of the State; for Christ commanded us to give to Caesar the things that are Caesar's, and to God the things that are God's.[35]

53. Whoever refuses to admit these principles, and hence to apply them to education, must necessarily deny that Christ has founded His Church for the eternal salvation of mankind, and maintain instead that civil society and the State are not subject to God and to His law, natural and divine. Such a doctrine is manifestly impious, contrary to right reason, and, especially in this matter of education, extremely harmful to the proper training of youth, and disastrous as well for civil society as for the well-being of all mankind. On the other hand from the application of these principles, there inevitably result immense advantages for the right formation of citizens. This is abundantly proved by the history of every age. Tertullian in his *Apologeticus* could throw down a challenge to the enemies of the Church in the early days of Christianity, just as St. Augustine did in his; and we today can repeat with him: "Let those who declare the teaching of Christ to be opposed to the welfare of the State, furnish us with an army of soldiers such as Christ says soldiers ought to be; let them give us subjects, husbands, wives, parents, children, masters, servants, kings, judges, taxpayers and tax gatherers who live up to the teachings of Christ; and then let them dare assert that Christian doctrine is harmful to the State. Rather let them not hesitate one moment to acclaim that doctrine, rightly observed, the greatest safeguard of the State."[36]

54. While treating of education, it is not out of place to show here how an ecclesiastical writer, who flourished in more recent times, during the Renaissance, the holy and learned Cardinal Silvio Antoniano, to whom the cause of Christian education is greatly indebted, has set forth most clearly this well established point of Catholic doctrine. He had been a disciple of that wonderful educator of youth, St. Philip Neri; he was teacher and Latin secretary to St. Charles Borromeo, and it was at the latter's suggestion and under his inspiration that he wrote his splendid treatise on *The Christian Education of Youth.* In it he argues as follows: "The more closely the temporal power of a nation aligns itself with the spiritual, and the more it fosters and promotes the latter, by so much the more it contributes to the conservation of the commonwealth. For it is the aim of the ecclesiastical authority by the use of spiritual means, to form good Christians in accordance with its own particular end and object; and in doing this it helps at the same time to form good citizens, and prepares them to meet their obligations as members of a civil society. This follows of necessity because in the City of God, the Holy Roman Catholic Church, a good citizen and an upright man are absolutely one and the same thing. How grave

therefore is the error of those who separate things so closely united, and who think that they can produce good citizens by ways and methods other than those which make for the formation of good Christians. For, let human prudence say what it likes and reason as it pleases, it is impossible to produce true temporal peace and tranquillity by things repugnant or opposed to the peace and happiness of eternity."[37]

55. What is true of the State, is true also of science, scientific methods and scientific research; they have nothing to fear from the full and perfect mandate which the Church holds in the field of education. Our Catholic institutions, whatever their grade in the educational and scientific world, have no need of apology. The esteem they enjoy, the praise they receive, the learned works which they promote and produce in such abundance, and above all, the men, fully and splendidly equipped, whom they provide for the magistracy, for the professions, for the teaching career, in fact for every walk of life, more than sufficiently testify in their favor.[38]

56. These facts moreover present a most striking confirmation of the Catholic doctrine defined by the Vatican Council: "Not only is it impossible for faith and reason to be at variance with each other, they are on the contrary of mutual help. For while right reason establishes the foundations of Faith, and, by the help of its light, develops a knowledge of the things of God, Faith on the other hand frees and preserves reason from error and enriches it with varied knowledge. The Church therefore, far from hindering the pursuit of the arts and sciences, fosters and promotes them in many ways. For she is neither ignorant nor unappreciative of the many advantages which flow from them to mankind. On the contrary she admits that just as they come from God, Lord of all knowledge, so too if rightly used, with the help of His grace they lead to God. Nor does she prevent the sciences, each in its own sphere, from making use of principles and methods of their own. Only while acknowledging the freedom due to them, she takes every precaution to prevent them from falling into error by opposition to divine doctrine, or from overstepping their proper limits, and thus invading and disturbing the domain of Faith."[39]

57. This norm of a just freedom in things scientific, serves also as an inviolable norm of a just freedom in things didactic, or for rightly understood liberty in teaching; it should be observed therefore in whatever instruction is imparted to others. Its obligation is all the more binding in justice when there is question of instructing youth. For in this work the teacher, whether public or private, has no absolute right of his own, but only such as has been communicated to him by others. Besides every Christian child or youth has a strict right to instruction in harmony with the teaching of the Church, the pillar and ground of truth. And whoever disturbs the pupil's Faith in any way, does him grave wrong, inasmuch as he abuses the trust which children place in their teachers, and takes unfair advantage of their inexperience and of their natural craving for unrestrained liberty, at once illusory and false.

58. In fact it must never be forgotten that the subject of Christian education is man whole and entire, soul united to body in unity of nature, with all his faculties natural and supernatural, such as right reason and revelation show him to be; man, therefore, fallen from his original estate, but redeemed by Christ and restored to the supernatural condition of adopted son of God, though without the preternatural privileges of bodily immortality or perfect control of appetite. There remain therefore, in human nature the effects of original sin, the chief of which are weakness of will and disorderly inclinations.

59. "Folly is bound up in the heart of a child and the rod of correction shall drive it away."[40] Disorderly inclinations then must be corrected, good tendencies encouraged and regulated from tender childhood, and above all the mind must be enlightened and the will strengthened by supernatural truth and by the means of grace, without which it is impossible to control evil impulses, impossible to attain to the full and complete perfection of education intended by the Church, which Christ has endowed so richly with divine doctrine and with the Sacraments, the efficacious means of grace.

60. Hence every form of pedagogic naturalism which in any way excludes or weakens supernatural Christian formation in the teaching of youth, is false. Every method of education founded, wholly or in part, on the denial or forgetfulness of original sin and of grace, and relying on the sole powers of human nature, is unsound. Such, generally speaking, are those modern systems bearing various names which appeal to a pretended self-government and unrestrained freedom on the part of the child, and which diminish or even suppress the teacher's authority and action, attributing to the child an exclusive primacy of initiative, and an activity independent of any higher law, natural or divine, in the work of his education.

61. If any of these terms are used, less properly, to denote the necessity of a gradually more active cooperation on the part of the pupil in his own education; if the intention is to banish from education despotism and violence, which, by the way, just punishment is not, this would be correct, but in no way new.

It would mean only what has been taught and reduced to practice by the Church in traditional Christian education, in imitation of the method employed by God Himself towards His creatures, of whom He demands active cooperation according to the nature of each; for His Wisdom "reacheth from end to end mightily and ordereth all things sweetly."[41]

62. But alas! it is clear from the obvious meaning of the words and from experience, that what is intended by not a few, is the withdrawal of education from every sort of dependence on the divine law. So today we see, strange sight indeed, educators and philosophers who spend their lives in searching for a universal moral code of education, as if there existed no decalogue, no gospel law, no law even of nature stamped by God on the heart of man, promulgated by right reason, and codified in positive revelation by God Himself in the ten commandments. These innovators are wont to refer contemptuously to Christian education as "heteronomous," "passive," "obsolete," because founded upon the authority of God and His holy law.

63. Such men are miserably deluded in their claim to emancipate, as they say, the child, while in reality they are making him the slave of his own blind pride and of his disorderly affections, which, as a logical consequence of this false system, come to be justified as legitimate demands of a so-called autonomous nature.

64. But what is worse is the claim, not only vain but false, irreverent and dangerous, to submit to research, experiment and conclusions of a purely natural and profane order, those matters of education which belong to the supernatural order; as for example questions of priestly or religious vocation, and in general the secret workings of grace which indeed elevate the natural powers, but are

infinitely superior to them, and may nowise be subjected to physical laws, for "the Spirit breatheth where He will."[42]

65. Another very grave danger is that naturalism which nowadays invades the field of education in that most delicate matter of purity of morals. Far too common is the error of those who with dangerous assurance and under an ugly term propagate a so-called sex-education, falsely imagining they can forearm youths against the dangers of sensuality by means purely natural, such as a foolhardy initiation and precautionary instruction for all indiscriminately, even in public; and, worse still, by exposing them at an early age to the occasions, in order to accustom them, so it is argued, and as it were to harden them against such dangers.

66. Such persons grievously err in refusing to recognize the inborn weakness of human nature, and the law of which the Apostle speaks, fighting against the law of the mind;[43] and also in ignoring the experience of facts, from which it is clear that, particularly in young people, evil practices are the effect not so much of ignorance of intellect as of weakness of a will exposed to dangerous occasions, and unsupported by the means of grace.

67. In this extremely delicate matter, if, all things considered, some private instruction is found necessary and opportune, from those who hold from God the commission to teach and who have the grace of state, every precaution must be taken. Such precautions are well known in traditional Christian education, and are adequately described by Antoniano cited above, when he says: "Such is our misery and inclination to sin, that often in the very things considered to be remedies against sin, we find occasions for and inducements to sin itself. Hence it is of the highest importance that a good father, while discussing with his son a matter so delicate, should be well on his guard and not descend to details, nor refer to the various ways in which this infernal hydra destroys with its poison so large a portion of the world; otherwise it may happen that instead of extinguishing this fire, he unwittingly stirs or kindles it in the simple and tender heart of the child. Speaking generally, during the period of childhood it suffices to employ those remedies which produce the double effect of opening the door to the virtue of purity and closing the door upon vice."[44]

68. False also and harmful to Christian education is the so-called method of "coeducation." This too, by many of its supporters, is founded upon naturalism and the denial of original sin; but by all, upon a deplorable confusion of ideas that mistakes a leveling promiscuity and equality, for the legitimate association of the sexes. The Creator has ordained and disposed perfect union of the sexes only in matrimony, and, with varying degrees of contact, in the family and in society. Besides there is not in nature itself, which fashions the two quite different in organism, in temperament, in abilities, anything to suggest that there can be or ought to be promiscuity, and much less equality, in the training of the two sexes. These, in keeping with the wonderful designs of the Creator, are destined to complement each other in the family and in society, precisely because of their differences, which therefore ought to be maintained and encouraged during their years of formation, with the necessary distinction and corresponding separation, according to age and circumstances. These principles, with due regard to time and place, must, in accordance with Christian prudence, be applied to all schools, particularly in the most delicate and decisive period of formation, that, namely, of adolescence; and in gymnastic exercises and deportment, special care must be had of Christian modesty in young women and girls, which is so gravely impaired by any kind of exhibition in public.

69. Recalling the terrible words of the Divine Master: "Woe to the world because of scandals!"[45] We most earnestly appeal to your solicitude and your watchfulness, Venerable Brethren, against these pernicious errors, which, to the immense harm of youth, are spreading far and wide among Christian peoples.

70. In order to obtain perfect education, it is of the utmost importance to see that all those conditions which surround the child during the period of his formation, in other words that the combination of circumstances which we call environment, correspond exactly to the end proposed.

71. The first natural and necessary element in this environment, as regards education, is the family, and this precisely because so ordained by the Creator Himself. Accordingly that education, as a rule, will be more effective and lasting which is received in a well-ordered and well-disciplined Christian family; and more efficacious in proportion to the clear and constant good example set, first by the parents, and then by the other members of the household.

72. It is not our intention to treat formally the question of domestic education, nor even to touch upon its principal points. The subject is too vast. Besides there are not lacking special treatises on this topic by authors, both ancient and modern, well known for their solid Catholic doctrine. One which seems deserving of special mention is the golden treatise already referred to, of Antoniano, *On the Christian Education of Youth*, which St. Charles Borromeo ordered to be read in public to parents assembled in their churches.

73. Nevertheless, Venerable Brethren and beloved children, We wish to call your attention in a special manner to the present-day lamentable decline in family education. The offices and professions of a transitory and earthly life, which are certainly of far less importance, are prepared for by long and careful study; whereas for the fundamental duty and obligation of educating their children, many parents have little or no preparation, immersed as they are in temporal cares. The declining influence of domestic environment is further weakened by another tendency, prevalent almost everywhere today, which, under one pretext or another, for economic reasons, or for reasons of industry, trade or politics, causes children to be more and more frequently sent away from home even in their tenderest years. And there is a country where the children are actually being torn from the bosom of the family, to be formed (or, to speak more accurately, to be deformed and depraved) in godless schools and associations, to irreligion and hatred, according to the theories of advanced socialism; and thus is renewed in a real and more terrible manner the slaughter of the Innocents.

74. For the love of Our Savior Jesus Christ, therefore, we implore pastors of souls, by every means in their power, by instructions and catechisms, by word of mouth and written articles widely distributed, to warn Christian parents of their grave obligations. And this should be done not in a merely theoretical and general way, but with practical and specific application to the various responsibilities of parents touching the religious, moral and civil training of their children, and with indication of the methods best adapted to make their training effective, supposing always the influence of their own exemplary lives. The Apostle of the Gentiles did not hesitate to descend to such details of practical instruction in his epistles, especially in the Epistle to the Ephesians, where among other things he gives this advice: "And you, fathers, provoke not your children to anger."[46] This fault is the result not so much of excessive severity, as of impatience and of ignorance of means best calculated to effect a desired correction; it is also due to the all too common relaxation of parental discipline which fails to check the growth of evil passions in the hearts of the younger generation. Parents therefore, and all who take their place in the work of education, should be careful to make right use of the authority given them by God, whose vicars in a true sense they are. This authority is not given for their own advantage, but for the proper up-bringing of their children in a holy and filial "fear of God, the beginning of wisdom," on which foundation alone all respect for authority can rest securely; and without which, order, tranquillity and prosperity, whether in the family or in society, will be impossible.

75. To meet the weakness of man's fallen nature, God in His Goodness has provided the abundant helps of His grace and the countless means with which He has endowed the Church, the great family of Christ. The Church therefore is the educational environment most intimately and harmoniously associated with the Christian family.

76. This educational environment of the Church embraces the Sacraments, divinely efficacious means of grace, the sacred ritual, so wonderfully instructive, and the material fabric of her churches, whose liturgy and art have an immense educational value; but it also includes the great number and variety of schools, associations and institutions of all kinds, established for the training of youth in Christian piety, together with literature and the sciences, not omitting recreation and physical culture. And in this inexhaustible fecundity of educational works, how marvelous, how incomparable is the Church's maternal providence! So admirable too is the harmony which she maintains with the Christian family, that the Church and the family may be said to constitute together one and the same temple of Christian education.

77. Since however the younger generations must be trained in the arts and sciences for the advantage and prosperity of civil society, and since the family of itself is unequal to this task, it was necessary to create that social institution, the school. But let it be borne in mind that this institution owes its existence to the initiative of the family and of the Church, long before it was undertaken by the State. Hence considered in its historical origin, the school is by its very nature an institution subsidiary and complementary to the family and to the Church. It follows logically and necessarily that it must not be in opposition to, but in positive accord with those other two elements, and form with them a perfect moral union, constituting one sanctuary of education, as it were, with the family and the Church. Otherwise it is doomed to fail of its purpose, and to become instead an agent of destruction.

78. This principle we find recognized by a layman, famous for his pedagogical writings, though these because of their liberalism cannot be unreservedly praised. "The school," he writes, "if not a temple, is a den." And again: "When literary, social, domestic and religious education do not go hand in hand, man is unhappy and helpless."[47]

79. From this it follows that the so-called "neutral" or "lay" school, from which religion is excluded, is contrary to the fundamental principles of education. Such a school moreover cannot exist in practice; it is bound to become irreligious. There is no need to repeat what Our Predecessors have declared on this point, especially Pius IX and Leo XIII, at times when laicism was beginning in a special manner to infest the public school. We renew and confirm their declarations,[48] as well as the Sacred Canons in which the frequenting of non-Catholic schools, whether neutral or mixed, those namely which are open to Catholics and non-Catholics alike, is forbidden for Catholic children, and can be at most tolerated, on the approval of the Ordinary alone, under determined circumstances of place and time, and with special precautions.[49] Neither can Catholics admit that other type of mixed school, (least of all the so-called "école unique," obligatory on all), in which the students are provided with separate religious instruction, but receive other lessons in common with non-Catholic pupils from non-Catholic teachers.

80. For the mere fact that a school gives some religious instruction (often extremely stinted), does not bring it into accord with the rights of the Church and of the Christian family, or make it a fit place for Catholic students. To be this, it is necessary that all the teaching and the whole organization of the school, and its teachers, syllabus and text-books in every branch, be regulated by the Christian spirit, under the direction and maternal supervision of the Church; so that Religion may be in very truth the foundation and crown of the youth's entire training; and this in every grade of school, not only the elementary, but the intermediate and the higher institutions of learning as well. To use the words of Leo XIII: "It is necessary not only that religious instruction be given to the young at certain fixed times, but also that every other subject taught, be permeated with Christian piety. If this is wanting, if this sacred atmosphere does not pervade and warm the hearts of masters and scholars alike, little good can be expected from any kind of learning, and considerable harm will often be the consequence."[50]

81. And let no one say that in a nation where there are different religious beliefs, it is impossible to provide for public instruction otherwise than by neutral or mixed schools. In such a case it becomes the duty of the State, indeed it is the easier and more reasonable method of procedure, to leave free scope to the initiative of the Church and the family, while giving them such assistance as justice demands. That this can be done to the full satisfaction of families, and to the advantage of education and of public peace and tranquillity, is clear from the actual experience of some countries comprising different religious denominations. There the school legislation respects the rights of the family, and Catholics are free to follow their own system of teaching in schools that are entirely Catholic. Nor is distributive justice lost sight of, as is evidenced by the financial aid granted by the State to the several schools demanded by the families.

82. In other countries of mixed creeds, things are otherwise, and a heavy burden weighs upon Catholics, who under the guidance of their Bishops and with the indefatigable cooperation of the clergy, secular and regular, support Catholic schools for their children entirely at their own expense; to this they feel obliged in conscience, and with a generosity and constancy worthy of all praise, they are firmly determined to make adequate provision for what they openly profess as their motto: "Catholic education in Catholic schools for all the Catholic youth." If such education is not aided from public funds, as distributive justice requires, certainly it may not be opposed by any civil authority ready to recognize the rights of the family, and the irreducible claims of legitimate liberty.

83. Where this fundamental liberty is thwarted or interfered with, Catholics will never feel, whatever may have been the sacrifices already made, that they have done enough, for the support and defense of their schools and for the securing of laws that will do them justice.

84. For whatever Catholics do in promoting and defending the Catholic school for their children, is a genuinely religious work and therefore an important task of "Catholic Action." For this reason the associations which in various countries are so zealously engaged in this work of prime necessity, are especially dear to Our paternal heart and are deserving of every commendation.

85. Let it be loudly proclaimed and well understood and recognized by all, that Catholics, no matter what their nationality, in agitating for Catholic schools for their children, are not mixing in party politics, but are engaged in a religious enterprise demanded by conscience. They do not intend to separate their children either from the body of the nation or its spirit, but to educate them in a perfect manner, most conducive to the prosperity of the nation. Indeed a good Catholic, precisely because of his Catholic principles, makes the better citizen, attached to his country, and loyally submissive to constituted civil authority in every legitimate form of government.

86. In such a school, in harmony with the Church and the Christian family, the various branches of secular learning will not enter into conflict with religious instruction to the manifest detriment of education. And if, when occasion arises, it be deemed necessary to have the students read authors propounding false doctrine, for the purpose of refuting it, this will be done after due preparation and with such an antidote of sound doctrine, that it will not only do no harm, but will be an aid to the Christian formation of youth.

87. In such a school moreover, the study of the vernacular and of classical literature will do no damage to moral virtue. There the Christian teacher will imitate the bee, which takes the choicest part of the flower and leaves the rest, as St. Basil teaches in his discourse to youths on the study of the classics.[51] Nor will this necessary caution, suggested also by the pagan Quintilian,[52] in any way hinder the Christian teacher from gathering and turning to profit, whatever there is of real worth in the systems and methods of our modern times, mindful of the Apostle's advice: "Prove all things: hold fast that which is good."[53] Hence in accepting the new, he will not hastily abandon the old, which the experience of centuries has found expedient and profitable. This is particularly true in the teaching of Latin, which in our days is falling more and more into disuse, because of the unreasonable rejection of methods so successfully used by that sane humanism, whose highest development was reached in the schools of the Church. These noble traditions of the past require that the youth committed to Catholic schools be fully instructed in the letters and sciences in accordance with the exigencies of the times. They also demand that the doctrine imparted be deep and solid, especially in sound philosophy, avoiding the muddled superficiality of those "who perhaps would have found the necessary, had they not gone in search of the superfluous."[54] In this connection Christian teachers should keep in mind what Leo XIII says in a pithy sentence: "Greater stress must be laid on the employment of apt and solid methods of teaching, and, what is still more important, on bringing into full conformity with the Catholic faith, what is taught in literature, in the sciences, and above all in philosophy, on which depends in great part the right orientation of the other branches of knowledge."[55]

88. Perfect schools are the result not so much of good methods as of good teachers, teachers who are thoroughly prepared and well-grounded in the matter they have to teach; who possess the intellectual and moral qualifications required by their important office; who cherish a pure and holy love for the youths confided to them, because they love Jesus Christ and His Church, of which these are the children of predilection; and who have therefore sincerely at heart the true good of family and country. Indeed it fills Our soul with consolation and gratitude towards the divine Goodness to see, side by side with religious men and women engaged in teaching, such a large number of excellent lay teachers, who, for their greater spiritual advancement, are often grouped in special sodalities and associations, which are worthy of praise and encouragement as most excellent and powerful auxiliaries of "Catholic Action." All these labor unselfishly with zeal and perseverance in what St. Gregory Nazianzen calls "the art of arts and the science of sciences,"[56] the direction and formation of youth. Of them also it may be said in the words of the divine Master: "The harvest indeed is great, but the laborers few."[57] Let us then pray the Lord of the harvest to send more such workers into the field of Christian education; and let their formation be one of the principal concerns of the pastors of souls and of the superiors of Religious Orders.

89. It is no less necessary to direct and watch the education of the adolescent, "soft as wax to be moulded into vice,"[58] in whatever other environment he may happen to be, removing occasions of evil and providing occasions for good in his recreations and social intercourse; for "evil communications corrupt good manners."[59]

90. More than ever nowadays an extended and careful vigilance is necessary, inasmuch as the dangers of moral and religious shipwreck are greater for inexperienced youth. Especially is this true of impious and immoral books, often diabolically circulated at low prices; of the cinema, which multiplies every kind of exhibition; and now also of the radio, which facilitates every kind of communications. These most powerful means of publicity, which can be of great utility for instruction and education when directed by sound principles, are only too often used as an incentive to evil passions and greed for gain. St. Augustine deplored the passion for the shows of the circus which possessed even some Christians of his time, and he dramatically narrates the infatuation for them, fortunately only temporary, of his disciple and friend Alipius.[60] How often today must parents and educators bewail the corruption of youth brought about by the modern theater and the vile book!

91. Worthy of all praise and encouragement therefore are those educational associations which have for their object to point out to parents and educators, by means of suitable books and periodicals, the dangers to morals and religion that are often cunningly disguised in books and theatrical representations. In their spirit of zeal for the souls of the young, they endeavor at the same time to circulate good literature and to promote plays that are really instructive, going so far as to put up at the cost of great sacrifices, theaters and cinemas, in which virtue will have nothing to suffer and much to gain.

92. This necessary vigilance does not demand that young people be removed from the society in which they must live and save their souls; but that today more than ever they should be forewarned and forearmed as Christians against the seductions and the errors of the world, which, as Holy Writ admonishes us, is all "concupiscence of the flesh, concupiscence of the eyes and pride of life."[61] Let them be what Tertullian wrote of the first Christians, and what Christians of all times ought to be, "sharers in the possession of the world, not of its error."[62]

93. This saying of Tertullian brings us to the topic which we propose to treat in the last place, and which is of the greatest importance, that is, the true nature of Christian education, as deduced from its proper end. Its consideration reveals with noonday clearness the preeminent educational mission of the Church.

94. The proper and immediate end of Christian education is to cooperate with divine grace in forming the true and perfect Christian, that is, to form Christ Himself in those regenerated by Baptism, according to the emphatic expression of the Apostle: "My little children, of whom I am in labor again, until Christ be formed in you."[63] For the true Christian must live a supernatural life in Christ: "Christ who is your life,"[64] and display it in all his actions: "That the life also of Jesus may be made manifest in our mortal flesh."[65]

95. For precisely this reason, Christian education takes in the whole aggregate of human life, physical and spiritual, intellectual and moral, individual, domestic and social, not with a view of reducing it in any way, but in order to elevate, regulate and perfect it, in accordance with the example and teaching of Christ.

96. Hence the true Christian, product of Christian education, is the supernatural man who thinks, judges and acts constantly and consistently in accordance with right reason illumined by the supernatural light of the example and teaching of Christ; in other words, to use the current term, the true and finished man of character. For, it is not every kind of consistency and firmness of conduct based on subjective principles that makes true character, but only constancy in following the eternal principles of justice, as is admitted even by the pagan poet when he praises as one and the same "the man who is just and firm of purpose."[66] And on the other hand, there cannot be full justice except in giving to God what is due to God, as the true Christian does.

97. The scope and aim of Christian education as here described, appears to the worldly as an abstraction, or rather as something that cannot be attained without the suppression or dwarfing of the natural faculties, and without a renunciation of the activities of the present life, and hence inimical to social life and temporal prosperity, and contrary to all progress in letters, arts and sciences, and all the other elements of civilization. To a like objection raised by the ignorance and the prejudice of even cultured pagans of a former day, and repeated with greater frequency and insistence in modern times, Tertullian has replied as follows: "We are not strangers to life. We are fully aware of the gratitude we owe to God, our Lord and Creator. We reject none of the fruits of His handiwork; we only abstain from their immoderate or unlawful use. We are living in the world with you; we do not shun your forum, your markets, your baths, your shops, your factories, your stables, your places of business and traffic. We take shop with you and we serve in your armies; we are farmers and merchants with you; we interchange skilled labor and display our works in public for your service. How we can seem unprofitable to you with whom we live and of whom we are, I know not."[67]

98. The true Christian does not renounce the activities of this life, he does not stunt his natural faculties; but he develops and perfects them, by coordinating them with the supernatural. He thus ennobles what is merely natural in life and secures for it new strength in the material and temporal order, no less then in the spiritual and eternal.

99. This fact is proved by the whole history of Christianity and its institutions, which is nothing else but the history of true civilization and progress up to the present day. It stands out conspicuously in the lives of the numerous Saints, whom the Church, and she alone, produces, in whom is perfectly realized the purpose of Christian education, and who have in every way ennobled and benefited human society. Indeed, the Saints have ever been, are, and ever will be the greatest benefactors of society, and perfect models for every class and profession, for every state and condition of life, from the simple and uncultured peasant to the master of sciences and letters, from the humble artisan to the commander of armies, from the father of a family to the ruler of peoples and nations, from simple maidens and matrons of the domestic hearth to queens and empresses. What shall we say of the immense work which has been accomplished even for the temporal well-being of men by missionaries of the Gospel, who have brought and still bring to barbarous tribes the benefits of civilization together with the light of the Faith? What of the founders of so many social and charitable institutions, of the vast numbers of saintly educators, men and women, who have perpetuated and multiplied their life work, by leaving after them prolific institutions of Christian education, in aid of families and for the inestimable advantage of nations?

100. Such are the fruits of Christian education. Their price and value is derived from the supernatural virtue and life in Christ which Christian education forms and develops in man. Of this life and virtue Christ our Lord and Master is the source and dispenser. By His example He is at the same time the universal model accessible to all, especially to the young in the period of His hidden life, a life of labor and obedience, adorned with all virtues, personal, domestic and social, before God and men.

101. Now all this array of priceless educational treasures which We have barely touched upon, is so truly a property of the Church as to form her very substance, since she is the mystical body of Christ, the immaculate spouse of Christ, and consequently a most admirable mother and an incomparable and perfect teacher. This thought inspired St. Augustine, the great genius of whose blessed death we are about to celebrate the fifteenth centenary, with accents of tenderest love for so glorious a mother: "O Catholic Church, true Mother of Christians! Not only doest thou preach to us, as is meet, how purely and chastely we are to worship God Himself, Whom to possess is life most blessed; thou does moreover so cherish neighborly love and charity, that all the infirmities to which sinful souls are subject, find their most potent remedy in thee. Childlike thou are in molding the child, strong with the young man, gentle with the aged, dealing with each according to his needs of mind of body. Thou does subject child to parent in a sort of free servitude, and settest parent over child in a jurisdiction of love. Thou bindest brethren to brethren by the bond of religion, stronger and closer then the bond of blood....Thou unitest citizen to citizen, nation to nation, yea, all men, in a union not of companionship only, but of brotherhood, reminding them of their common origin. Thou teachest kings to care for their people, and biddest people to be subject to their kings. Thou teachest assiduously to whom honor is due, to whom love, to whom reverence, to whom fear, to whom comfort, to whom rebuke, to whom punishment; showing us that whilst not all things nor the same things are due to all, charity is due to all and offense to none."[68]

102. Let us then, Venerable Brethren, raise *our* hands and our hearts in supplication to heaven, "to the Shepherd and Bishop of our Souls,"[69] to the divine King "who gives laws to rulers," that in His almighty power He may cause these splendid fruits of Christian education to be gathered in ever greater abundance "in the whole world," for the lasting benefit of individuals and of nations.

As a pledge of these heavenly favors, with paternal affection We impart to you, Venerable Brethren, to your clergy and your people, the Apostolic Benediction.

Given at Rome, at St. Peter's, the thirty-first day of December, in the year 1929, the eighth of Our Pontificate.

Pius XI

---

[1] Marc., X, 14: *Sinite parvulos venir ad me.*

[2] II Tim., IV, 2: *Insta opportune importune: argue, obsecra increpa in omni patientia et doctrina.*

[3] Confess., I, I: *Fecisti nos, Domine, ad Te. et inquietum est cor nostrum donec requiescat in Te.*

[4] Prov. XXII, 6: *Adolescens iuxta viam suam etiam cum senuerit non recedet ab ea.*

[5] Hom. 60, in c. 18 Matth.: *Ouid maius quam animis moderari, quam adolescentulorum fingere mores?*

[6] Marc., IX, 36: *Quisquis unum ex huiusmodi pueris receperit in nomine meo, me recipit.*

[7] Matth., XXVIII, 18-20: *Data est mihi omnis potestas in caelo et in terra. Euntes ergo docete omnes gentes, baptizantes eos in nomine Patris, et Filii, et Spiritus Sancti: docentes eos servare omnia quaecumque mandavi vobis. Et ecce ego vobiscum sum omnibus diebus usque ad consummationem saeculi.*

[8] Pius IX, Ep. *Quum non sine,* 14 Iul, 1864: *Columna et firmamentum viritatis a Divino suo Auctore fuit constituta, ut omnes homines divinam edoceat fidem, eiusque depositum sibi traditum integrum inviolatumque custodiat, ac homines eotumque consortia et actiones ad morum honestatem vitaeque integritatem, iuxta revelatae doctrinae normam, dirigat et fingat.*

[9] *De Symbolo* ad catech., XIII: *Non habebit Deum patrem, qui Ecclesiam noluerit habere matrem.*

[10] Ep. enc. *Libertas*, 20 Iun. 1888: *in fide atque in institutione morum, divini magisterii Ecclesiam fecit Deus ipse participem, eamdemque divino eius beneficio falli nesciam: quare magistra mortalium est maxima ac tutissima, in eaque inest non violabile ius ad magisterii libertatem.*

[11] Ep. enc. *Singulari quadam*, 24 Sept. 1912: *Quidquid homo christianus agat, etiam in ordine rerum terrenarum, non ei licet bona negligere quae sunt supra naturam, immo oportet ad summum bonum, tamquam ad ultimum finem, ex christianae sapientiae praescriptis omnia dirigat: omnes autem actiones eius, quatenus bonae aut malae sunt in genere morum, id est cum iure naturali et divino congruunt aut discrepant, indicio et iurisdictioni Ecclesiae subsunt.*

[12] A. Manzoni, *Osservazioni sulla Morale Cattolica*, c. III.

[13] Codex Iuris Canonici, c. 1375.

[14] Commentar. in Matth., cap. 18: *Quid mundo tam periculosum quam non recepisse Christum?*

[15] Cod. I.C., cc. 1381, 1382.

[16] Ep. enc. *Nobilissima Gallorum Gens*, 8 Febr. 1884: *male sana omnis futura est animarum cultura: insueti ad verecundiam Dei adolescentes nullam ferre poterunt honeste vivendi disciplinam, suisque cupiditatibus nihil unquam negare ausi, facile ad miscendas civitates pertrahentur.*

[17] Matth., XXVIII, 19: *docete omnes gentes.*

[18] Discourse to the students of Mondragone College, May 14, 1929.

[19] Deut., XXXII, 4: *Dei perfecta sunt opera, et omnes viae eius indicia.*

[20] S. Th., 2-2, Q. CII, a. I: *Carnalis pater particulariter participat rationem principii quae universaliter invenitur in De....Pater est principium et generationis et educatonis et disciplinae, et omnium quae ad perfectionem humanae vitae pertinent.*

[21] S. Th., 2-2, Q. X, a. 12: *Filius enim naturaliter est aliquid patris...; ita de iure naturali est quod filius, antequam habeat usum rationis, sit sub cura patris. Unde contra iustitiam naturalem esset, si puer, antequam habeat usum rationis, a cura parentum subtrahatur, vel de eo aliquid ordinetur invitis parentibus.*

[22] Suppl. S. Th. 3; p. Q. 41, a. 1: *Non enim intendit natura solum generationem prolis, sed etiam traductionem et promotionem usque ad perfectum statum hominis in quantum homo est, qui est virtutis status.*

[23] Cod. I. C. , c. 1113: *Parentes gravissima obligatione tenentur prolis educationem tum religiosam et moralem, tum physicam et civilem pro viribus curandi, et etiam temporali eorum bono providendi.*

[24] Ep. enc. *Rerum novarum*, 15 Maii 1891: *Filii sunt aliquid patris, et velut paternae amplificatio quaedam personae proprieque loqui si volumus, non ipsi per se, sed per communitatem domesticam, in qua generati sunt, civilem ineunt ac participant societatem.*

[25] Ep. enc. *Rerum novarum*, 15 Maii 1891: *Patria potestas est eiusmodi, ut nec extingui, neque absorberi a republica possit, quia idem et commune habet cum ipsa hominum vita principium.*

[26] Ep. enc. *Sapientiae christianae*, 10 Ian. 1890: *Natura parentes habent ius suum instituendi, quos procrearint, hoc adiuncto officio, ut cum fine, cuius gratia sobolem Dei beneficio susceperunt, ipsa educatio conveniat et doctrina puerilis. Igitur parentibus est necessarium eniti et contendere, ut omnem in hoc genere propulsent iniuriam, omninoque pervincant ut sua in potestate sit educere liberos, uti par est, more christiano, maximeque prohibere scholis iis, a quibus periculum est ne malum venenum imbibant impietatis.*

[27] Cod I. C.,c.1113.

[28] "The fundamental theory of liberty upon which all governments in this Union repose excludes any general power of the State to standardize its children by forcing them to accept instruction from public teachers only. The child is not the mere creature of the State; those who nurture him and direct his destiny have the right coupled with the high duty, to recognize, and prepare him for additional duties." U.S. Supreme Court Decision in the Oregon School Case, June 1, 1925.

[29] Letter to the Cardinal Secretary of State, May 30, 1929.

[30] Cod. I. C., c. 750, & 2. S. Th., 2, 2. Q. X., a. 12.

[31] Discourse to the students of Mondragone College, May 14, 1929.

[32] Discourse to the students of Mondragone College, May 14, 1929.

[33] P. L. Taparelli, *Saggio teor. di Diritto Naturale*, n. 922; a work never sufficiently praised and recommended to university students (Cfr. Our Discourse of Dec. 18, 1927).

[34] Ep. enc. *Immortale Dei*, 1 Nov. 1885: *Deus humani generis procurationem inter duos potestates partitus est, scilicet eccesiasticam et civilem, alteram quidem divinis, alteram humanis rebus praepositam. Utraque est in suo*

genere maxima: habet utraque certos, quibus contineatur, terminos, eosque sua cuiusque natura causaque proxime definitos; unde aliquis velut orbis circumscribitur, in quo sua cuiusque actio iure proprio versetur. Sed quia utriusque imperium est in eosdem, cum usuvenire possit, ut res una atque eadem quamquam aliter atque aliter, sed tamen eadem res, ad utriusque ius iudiciumque pertineat, debet providentissimus Deus, a quo sunt ambae constitutae, utriusque itinera recte atque ordine composiusse. Quae autem sunt, a Deo ordinatae sunt (Rom., XIII, 1).

35   Ep. enc. *Immortale Dei*, 1 Nov. 1885: *Itaque inter utramque potestatem quaedam intercedat necesse est ordinata colligatio: quae quidem coniunctioni non immerito comparatur, per quam anima et corpus in homine copulantur. Qualis autem et quanta ea sit, aliter iudicari non potest, nisi respiciendo, uti diximus, ad utriusque naturam, habendaque ratione excellentiae et nobilitatis causarum; cum alteri proxime maximeque propositum sit rerum mortalium curare commoda, alteri caelestia ac sempiterna bona comparare. Quidquid igitur est in rebus humanis quoquo modo sacrum, quidquid ad salutem animorum cultumve Dei pertinet, sive tale illud sit natura sua, sive rursus tale intelligatur propter caussam ad quam refertur, id est omne in potestate arbitrioque Ecclesiae: cetera vero, quae civile et politicum genus complectitur, rectum est civili auctoritati esse subiecta, cum Iesus Christus iusserit, quae Caesaris sint, reddi Caesari, quae Dei, Deo.*

36   Ep. 138: *Proinde qui doctrinam Christi adversam dicunt esse reipublicae, dent exercitum talem, quales doctrinas Christi esse milites iussit; dent tales provinciales, tales maritos, tales coniuges, tales parentes, tales filios, tales dominos, tales servos, tales reges, tales iudices, tales denique debitorum ipsius fisci redditores et exactores, quales esse praecipit doctrina christiana, et audeant eam dicere adversam esse reipublicae, ima vero non dubitent eam confiteri magnam, si obtemperetur, salutem esse reiublicae.*

37   *Dell 'educaz. crist.*, lib. I, c. 43.

38   Letter to the Cardinal Secretary of State, May 30, 1929.

39   Conc. Vat., Sess. 3, cap. 4. *Neque solum fides et ratio inter se dissidere nunquam possunt, sed opem quoque sibi mutuam ferunt, cum recta ratio fidei fundamenta demonstret eiusque lumine illustrata rerum divinarum scientiam excolat, fides vero rationem ab erroribus liberet ac tueatur eamque multiplici cognitione instruat. Quapropter tantum abest. ut Ecclesia humanarum artium et disciplinarium culturae obsistat, ut hanc multis modis invet atque promoveat. Non enim commoda ab iis ad hominum vitam dimanantia aut ignorat aut dispicit; fatetur immo, eas, quemadmodum a Deo scientiarum Domino profectae sunt, ita, si rite pertractentur, ad Deum iuvante eius gratia*

perducere. Nec sane ipsa vetat, ne huiusmodi disciplinae in suo quaeque ambitu propriis utantur principiis et propria methodo; sed iustam hanc libertatem agnoscens, id sedulo cavet, ne divinae doctrinae repugnando errores in se suscipiant, aut fines proprios transgressae ea, quae sunt fidei, occupent et perturbent.

40   Prov., XXII, 15: *Stultitia colligata est in corde pueri: et virga disciplinae fugabit eam.*

41   Sap., VIII, 1: *attingit a fine usque ad finem fortiter, et disponit omnia suaviter.*

42   Io., III, 8: *Spiritus ubi vult spirat.*

43   Rom., VII, 23.

44   Silvio Antonio, *Dell 'educazione cristiana dei figliuoli*, lib. II, e. 88.

45   Matth., XVIII, 7: *Vae mundo a scandalis!*

46   Eph., VI, 4: *Patres, nolite ad iracundiam provocare filios vestros.*

47   Nic. Tommaseo, *Pensieri sull 'educazione*, Parte I, 3, 6.

48   Pius IX, Ep. *Quum non sine*, 14 Jul. 1864. - Syllabus, Prop. 48. - Leo XIII, alloc. *Summi Pontificatus*, 20 Aug. 1880, Ep. enc. *Nobilissima*, 8 Febr. 1884, Ep. enc. *Quod multum*, 22 Aug. 1886, Ep. *Officio sanctissimo*, 22 Dec. 1887, Ep. enc. *Caritatis*, 19 Mart. 1894, etc. (cfr. Cod. I.C. cum. Fontium Annot., c. 1374).

49   Cod. I.C., c. 1374.

50   Ep. enc. *Militantis Ecclesiae*, 1 Aug. 1897: *Necesse est non modo certis horis doceri iuvenes religionem, sed reliquam institutionem omnem christianae pietatis sensus redolere. Id si desit, si sacer hic halitus non doctorum animos ac discentum pervadat foveatque, exiguae capientur ex qualibet doctrina utilitates; damna saepe consequentur haud exigua.*

51   P.G., t. 31, 570.

52   *Inst. Or.*, I, 8.

53   I Thess., V, 21: *omnia probate; quod bonum est tenete.*

54   Seneca, Epist. 45: *invenissent forsitan necessaria nisi et superflua quaesiissent.*

55   Leo XII, Ep. enc., *Insrutabli* 21 Apr. 1878:*...alacrius adnitendum est, ut non solum apta ac solida institutionis methodus, sed maxime institutio ipsa catholicae fidei omnino confommis in litteris et disciplinis vigeat, praesertim autem in philosophia, ex qua recta aliarum scientiarum ratio magna ex parte dependet.*

56   Oratio II, P.G., t. 35, 426: *ars artium et scientia scien-*

tiarvum.

[57] Matth., IX, 37: *Messis quidem multa, operarii autem pauci.*

[58] Horat., *Art. poet.*, v. 163: *cereus in vitium flecti.*

[59] I Cor. XV, 33: *corrumpunt mores bonos colloquia mala.*

[60] Conf., VI, 8.

[61] I Io., II, 16: *concupiscentia carnis, concupiscentia oculorum et superbia vitae.*

[62] *De Idololatria,* 14: *compossessores mundi, non erroris.*

[63] Gal., IV, 19: *Filioli mei, quos iterum parturio, donec formetur Christus in vobis.*

[64] Col., III, 4: *Christus, vita vestra.*

[65] II Cor., IV, II: *ut et vita Iesu manifestetur in carne nostra mortali.*

[66] Horat., *Od.*, 1,III, od. 3, v. 1: *Iustum et tenacem propositi virum.*

[67] Apol., 42: *Non sumus exules vitae. Meminimus gratiam nos debere Deo Domino Creatori; nullum fructum operum eius repudiamus; plane temperamus, ne ultra modum aut perperam utamur. Itaque non sine foro, non sine macello, non sine balneis, tabernis, officinis, stabulis, nundinis vestris, caeterisque commerciis cohabitamus in hoc saeculo. Navigamus et nos vobiscum et militamus et rusticamur, et mercamur, proinde miscemus artes, operas nostras publicamus usui vestro. Quomodo infructuosi videamur negotiis vestris, cum quibus et de quibus vivimus, non scio.*

[68] *De moribus Eccleslae catholicae,* lib. 1, c. 30: *Merito Ecclesia catholica Mater christianorum verissima, non solum ipsum Deum, cuius adeptio Vita est beatissima, purissime atque castissime colendum praedicas; sed etiam proximi dilectionem atque charitatem ita complecteris, ut variorum morborum, quibus pro peccatis suis animae aegrotant, omnis apud te medicina praepolleat. Tu pueriliter, pueros, fortiter iuvenes, quiete senes prout cuiusque non corporis tantum, sed et animi aetas est, exerces ac doces. Tu parentibus filios libera quadam servitute subiungis, parentes filiis pia dominatione praeponis. Tu fratribus fratres religionis vinculo firmiore atque arctiore quam sanguinis nectis....Tu cives civibus, gentes gentibus, et prorsus homines primorum parentum recordatione, non societate tantum, sed quadam etiam fraternitate coniungis. Doces Reges prospicere populis; mones populos se subdere Regibus. Quibus honor debeatur, quibus affectus, quibus reverentia, quibus timor, quibus consolatio, quibus admonitio, quibus cohortatio, quibus disciplina, quibus obiurgatio, quibus supplicium, sedulo doces; ostendens quemadmodum et non omnibus omnia, et omnibus charitas, et nulli debeatur iniuria.*

[69] Cfr. I Petr., II, 25: *ad Pastorem et Episcopum animarum vrotrarum.*

Gravissimum Educationis
Declaration on Christian Education

SECOND VATICAN COUNCIL
October 28, 1965

Introduction

The Sacred Ecumenical Council has considered with care how extremely important education is in the life of man and how its influence ever grows in the social progress of this age.[1]

Indeed, the circumstances of our time have made it easier and at once more urgent to educate young people and, what is more, to continue the education of adults. Men are more aware of their own dignity and position; more and more they want to take an active part in social and especially in economic and political life.[2] Enjoying more leisure, as they sometimes do, men find that the remarkable development of technology and scientific investigation and the new means of communication offer them an opportunity of attaining more easily their cultural and spiritual inheritance and of fulfilling one another in the closer ties between groups and even between peoples.

Consequently, attempts are being made everywhere to promote more education. The rights of men to an education, particularly the primary rights of children and parents, are being proclaimed and recognized in public documents.[3] As the number of pupils rapidly increases, schools are multiplied and expanded far and wide and other educational institutions are established. New experiments are conducted in methods of education and teaching. Mighty attempts are being made to obtain education for all, even though vast numbers of children and young people are still deprived of even rudimentary training and so many others lack a suitable education in which truth and love are developed together.

To fulfill the mandate she has received from her divine founder of proclaiming the mystery of salvation to all men and of restoring all things in Christ, Holy Mother the Church must be concerned with the whole of man's life, even the secular part of it insofar as it has a bearing on his heavenly calling.[4] Therefore she has a role in the progress and development of education. Hence this sacred synod declares certain fundamental principles of Christian education especially in schools. These principles will have to be developed at greater length by a special postconciliar commission and applied by episcopal conferences to varying local situations.

1.
The Meaning of the Universal Right to an Education

All men of every race, condition and age, since they enjoy the dignity of a human being, have an inalienable right to an education[5] that is in keeping with their ultimate goal,[6] their ability, their sex, and the culture and tradition of their country, and also in harmony with their fraternal association with other peoples in the fostering of true unity and peace on earth. For a true education aims at the formation of the human person in the pursuit of his ultimate end and of the good of the societies of which, as man, he is a member, and in whose obligations, as an adult, he will share.

Therefore children and young people must be helped, with the aid of the latest advances in psychology and the arts and science of teaching, to develop harmoniously their physical, moral and intellectual endowments so that they may gradually acquire a mature sense of responsibility in striving endlessly to form their own lives properly and in pursuing true freedom as they surmount the vicissitudes of life with courage and constancy. Let them be given also, as they advance in years, a positive and prudent sexual education. Moreover they should be so trained to take their part in social life that properly instructed in the necessary and opportune skills they can become actively involved in various community organizations, open to discourse with others and willing to do their best to promote the common good.

This sacred synod likewise declares that children and young people have a right to be motivated to appraise moral values with a right conscience, to embrace them with a personal adherence, together with a deeper knowledge and love of God. Consequently it earnestly entreats all those who hold a position of public authority or who are in charge of education to see to it that youth is never deprived of this sacred right. It further exhorts the sons of the Church to give their attention with generosity to the entire field of education, having especially in mind the need of extending very soon the benefits of a suitable education and training to everyone in all parts of the world.[7]

2.
Christian Education

Since all Christians have become by rebirth of water and the Holy Spirit a new creature[8] so that they should be called and should be children of God, they have a right to a Christian education. A Christian education does not merely strive for the maturing of a human person as just now described, but has as its principal purpose this goal: that the baptized, while they are gradually introduced the knowledge of the mystery of salvation, become ever more aware of the gift of Faith they have received, and that they learn in addition how to worship God the Father in spirit and truth (cf. John 4:23) especially in liturgical action, and be conformed in their personal lives according to the new man created in justice and holiness of truth (Eph. 4:22-24); also that they develop into perfect manhood, to the mature measure of the fullness of Christ (cf. Eph. 4:13) and strive for the growth of the Mystical Body; moreover, that aware of their calling, they learn not only how to bear witness to the hope that is in them (cf. Peter 3:15) but also how to help in the Christian formation of the world that takes place when natural powers viewed in the full consideration of man redeemed by Christ contribute to the good of the whole society.[9] Wherefore this sacred synod recalls to pastors of souls their most serious obligation to see to it that all the faithful, but especially the youth who are the hope of the Church, enjoy this Christian education.[10]

3.
The Authors of Education

Since parents have given children their life, they are bound by the most serious obligation to educate their offspring and therefore must be recognized as the primary and principal educators.[11] This role in education is so important that only with difficulty can it be supplied where it is lacking. Parents are the ones who must create a family atmosphere animated by love and respect for God and man, in which the well-rounded personal and social education of children is fostered. Hence the family is the first school of the social virtues that every society needs. It is particularly in the Christian family, enriched by the grace and office of the sacrament of matrimony, that children should be taught from their early years to have a knowledge of God according to the faith received in Baptism, to worship Him, and to love their neighbor. Here, too, they find their first experience of a wholesome human society and of the Church. Finally, it is through the family that they are gradually led to a companionship with their fellowmen and with the people of God. Let parents, then, recognize the inestimable importance a truly Christian family has for the life and progress of God's own people.[12]

The family which has the primary duty of imparting education needs help of the whole community. In addition, therefore, to the rights of parents and others to whom the parents entrust a share in the work of education, certain rights and duties belong indeed to civil society, whose role is to direct what is required for the common temporal good. Its function is to promote the education of youth in many ways, namely: to protect the duties and rights of parents and others who share in education and to give them aid; according to the principle of subsidiarity, when the endeavors of parents and other societies are lacking, to carry out the work of education in accordance with the wishes of the parents; and, moreover, as the common good demands, to build schools and institutions.[13]

Finally, in a special way, the duty of educating belongs to the Church, not merely because she must be recognized as a human society capable of educating, but especially because she has the responsibility of announcing the way of salvation to all men, of communicating the life of Christ to those who believe, and, in her unfailing solicitude, of assisting men to be able to come to the fullness of this life.[14] The Church is bound as a mother to give to these children of hers an education by which their whole life can be imbued with the spirit of Christ and at the same time do all she can to promote for all peoples the complete perfection of the human person, the good of earthly society and the building of a world that is more human.[15]

4.
Various Aids to Christian Education

In fulfilling its educational role, the Church, eager to employ all suitable aids, is concerned especially about those which are her very own. Foremost among these is catechetical instruction,[16] which enlightens and strengthens the faith, nourishes life according to the spirit of Christ, leads to intelligent and active participation in the liturgical mystery[17] and gives motivation for apostolic activity. The Church esteems highly and seeks to penetrate and ennoble with her own spirit also other aids which belong to the general heritage of man and which are of great influence in forming souls and molding men, such as the media of communication,[18] various groups for mental and physical development, youth associations, and, in particular, schools.

5.
The Importance of Schools

Among all educational instruments the school has a special importance.[19] It is designed not only to develop with special care the intellectual faculties but also to form the ability to judge rightly, to hand on the cultural legacy of previous generations, to foster a sense of values, to prepare for professional life. Between pupils of different talents and backgrounds it promotes friendly relations and fosters a spirit of mutual understanding; and it establishes as it were a center whose work and progress must be shared together by families, teachers, associations of various types that foster cultural, civic, and religious life, as well as by civil society and the entire human community.

Beautiful indeed and of great importance is the vocation of all those who aid parents in fulfilling their duties and who, as representatives of the human community, undertake the task of education in schools. This vocation demands special qualities of mind and heart, very careful preparation, and continuing readiness to renew and to adapt.

6.
The Duties and Rights of Parents

Parents who have the primary and inalienable right and duty to educate their children must enjoy true liberty in their choice of schools. Consequently, the public power, which has the obligation to protect and defend the rights of citizens, must see to it, in its concern for distributive justice, that public subsidies are paid out in such a way that parents are truly free to choose according to their conscience the schools they want for their children.[20]

In addition it is the task of the state to see to it that all citizens are able to come to a suitable share in culture and are properly prepared to exercise their civic duties and rights. Therefore the state must protect the right of children to an adequate school education, check on the ability of teachers and the excellence of their training, look after the health of the pupils and in general, promote the whole school project. But it must always keep in mind the principle of subsidiarity so that there is no kind of school monopoly, for this is opposed to the native rights of the human person, to the development and spread of culture, to the peaceful association of citizens and to the pluralism that exists today in ever so many societies.[21]

Therefore this sacred synod exhorts the faithful to assist to their utmost in finding suitable methods of education and programs of study and in forming teachers who can give youth a true education. Through the associations of parents in particular they should further with their assistance all the work of the school but especially the moral education it must impart.[22]

7.
Moral and Religious Education in All Schools

Feeling very keenly the weighty responsibility of diligently caring for the moral and religious education of all her children, the Church must be present with her own special affection and help for the great number who are being trained in schools that are not Catholic. This is possible by the witness of the lives of those who teach and direct them, by the apostolic action of their fellow-students,[23] but especially by the ministry of priests and laymen who give them the doctrine of salvation in a way suited to their age and circumstances and provide spiritual aid in every way the times and conditions allow.

The Church reminds parents of the duty that is theirs to arrange and even demand that their children be able to enjoy these aids and advance in their Christian formation to a degree that is abreast of their development in secular subjects. Therefore the Church esteems highly those civil authorities and societies which, bearing in mind the pluralism of contemporary society and respecting religious freedom, assist families so that the education of their children can be imparted in all schools according to the individual moral and religious principles of the families.[24]

8.
Catholic Schools

The influence of the Church in the field of education is shown in a special manner by the

Catholic school. No less than other schools does the Catholic school pursue cultural goals and the human formation of youth. But its proper function is to create for the school community a special atmosphere animated by the Gospel spirit of freedom and charity, to help youth grow according to the new creatures they were made through baptism as they develop their own personalities, and finally to order the whole of human culture to the news of salvation so that the knowledge the students gradually acquire of the world, life and man is illumined by faith.[25] So indeed the Catholic school, while it is open, as it must be, to the situation of the contemporary world, leads its students to promote efficaciously the good of the earthly city and also prepares them for service in the spread of the Kingdom of God, so that by leading an exemplary apostolic life they become, as it were, a saving leaven in the human community.

Since, therefore, the Catholic school can be such an aid to the fulfillment of the mission of the People of God and to the fostering of the dialogue between the Church and mankind, to the benefit of both, it retains even in our present circumstances the utmost importance. Consequently this sacred synod proclaims anew what has already been taught in several documents of the magisterium,[26] namely: the right of the Church freely to establish and to conduct schools of every type and level. And the council calls to mind that the exercise of a right of this kind contributes in the highest degree to the protection of freedom of conscience, the rights of parents, as well as to the betterment of culture itself.

But let teachers recognize that the Catholic school depends upon them almost entirely for the accomplishment of its goals and programs.[27] They should therefore be very carefully prepared so that both in secular and religious knowledge they are equipped with suitable qualifications and also with a pedagogical skill that is in keeping with the findings of the contemporary world. Intimately linked in charity to one another and to their students and endowed with an apostolic spirit, may teachers by their life as much as by their instruction bear witness to Christ, the unique Teacher. Let them work as partners with parents and together with them in every phase of education give due consideration to the difference of sex and the proper ends Divine Providence assigns to each sex in the family and in society. Let them do all they can to stimulate their students to act for themselves and even after graduation to continue to assist them with advice, friendship and by establishing special associations imbued with the true spirit of the Church. The work of these teachers, this sacred synod declares, is in the real sense of the word an apostolate most suited to and necessary for our times and at once a true service offered to society. The Council also reminds Catholic parents of the duty of entrusting their children to Catholic schools wherever and whenever it is possible and of supporting these schools to the best of their ability and of cooperating with them for the education of their children.[28]

9.
Different Types of Catholic Schools

To this concept of a Catholic school all schools that are in any way dependent on the Church must conform as far as possible, though the Catholic school is to take on different forms in keeping with local circumstances.[29] Thus the Church considers very dear to her heart those Catholic schools, found especially in the areas of the new churches, which are attended also by students who are not Catholics.

Attention should be paid to the needs of today in establishing and directing Catholic schools. Therefore, though primary and secondary schools, the foundation of education, must still be fostered, great importance is to be attached to those which are required in a particular way by contemporary conditions, such as: professional[30] and technical schools, centers for educating adults and promoting social welfare, or for the retarded in need of special care, and also schools for preparing teachers for religious instruction and other types of education.

This Sacred Council of the Church earnestly entreats pastors and all the faithful to spare no sacrifice in helping Catholic schools fulfill their function in a continually more perfect way, and especially in caring for the needs of those who are poor in the goods of this world or who are deprived of the assistance and affection of a family or who are strangers to the gift of Faith.

10.
Catholic Colleges and Universities

The Church is concerned also with schools of a higher level, especially colleges and universities. In those schools dependent on her she intends that by their very constitution individual subjects be pursued according to their own principles, method, and liberty of scientific inquiry, in such a way that an ever deeper understanding in these fields may be obtained and that, as questions that are new and current are raised and investigations carefully made according to the example of the doctors of the Church and especially of St. Thomas Aquinas,[31] there may be a deeper realization of the harmony of faith and science. Thus there is accomplished a public, enduring and pervasive influence of the Christian mind in the furtherance of culture and the students of these institutions are molded into men truly outstanding in their training, ready to undertake weighty responsibilities in society and witness to the faith in the world.[32]

In Catholic universities where there is no faculty of sacred theology there should be established an institute or chair of sacred theology in which there should be lectures suited to lay students. Since science advances by means of the investigations peculiar to higher scientific studies, special attention should be given in Catholic universities and colleges to institutes that serve primarily the development of scientific research.

The sacred synod heartily recommends that Catholic colleges and universities be conveniently located in different parts of the world, but in such a way that they are outstanding not for their numbers but for their pursuit of knowledge. Matriculation should be readily available to students of real promise, even though they be of slender means, especially to students from the newly emerging nations.

Since the destiny of society and of the Church itself is intimately linked with the progress of young people pursuing higher studies,[33] the pastors of the Church are to expend their energies not only on the spiritual life of students who attend Catholic universities, but, solicitous for the spiritual formation of all their children, they must see to it, after consultations between bishops, that even at universities that are not Catholic there should be associations and university centers under Catholic auspices in which priests, religious and laity, carefully selected and prepared, should give abiding spiritual and intellectual assistance to the youth of the university. Whether in Catholic universities or others, young people of greater ability who seem suited for teaching or research should be specially helped and encouraged to undertake a teaching career.

11.
Faculties of Sacred Sciences

The Church expects much from the zealous endeavors of the faculties of the sacred sciences.[34] For to them she entrusts the very serious responsibility of preparing her own students not only for the priestly ministry, but especially for teaching in the seats of higher ecclesiastical studies or for promoting learning on their own or for undertaking the work of a more rigorous intellectual apostolate. Likewise it is the role of these very faculties to make more penetrating inquiry into the various aspects of the sacred sciences so that an ever deepening understanding of sacred Revelation is obtained, the legacy of Christian wisdom handed down by our forefathers is more fully developed, the dialogue with our separated brethren and with non-Christians is fostered, and answers are given to questions arising from the development of doctrine.[35]

Therefore ecclesiastical faculties should reappraise their own laws so that they can better promote the sacred sciences and those linked with them and, by employing up-to-date methods and aids, lead their students to more penetrating inquiry.

12.
Coordination to be Fostered in Scholastic Matters

Cooperation is the order of the day. It increases more and more to supply the demand on a diocesan, national and international level. Since it is altogether necessary in scholastic matters, every means should be employed to foster suitable cooperation between Catholic schools, and between these and other schools that collaboration should be developed which the good of all mankind requires.[36] From greater coordination and cooperative endeavor greater fruits will be derived particularly in the area of academic institutions. Therefore in every university let the various faculties work mutually to this end, insofar as their goal will permit. In addition, let the universities also endeavor to work together by promoting international gatherings, by sharing scientific inquiries with one

another, by communicating their discoveries to one another, by having exchange of professors for a time and by promoting all else that is conducive to greater assistance.

Conclusion

The sacred synod earnestly entreats young people themselves to become aware of the importance of the work of education and to prepare themselves to take it up, especially where because of a shortage of teachers the education of youth is in jeopardy. This same sacred synod, while professing its gratitude to priests, Religious men and women, and the laity who by their evangelical self-dedication are devoted to the noble work of education and of schools of every type and level, exhorts them to persevere generously in the work they have undertaken and, imbuing their students with the spirit of Christ, to strive to excel in pedagogy and the pursuit of knowledge in such a way that they not merely advance the internal renewal of the Church but preserve and enhance its beneficent influence upon today's world, especially the intellectual world.

Notes

[1] Among many documents illustrating the importance of education confer above all apostolic letter of Benedict XV, *Communes Litteras*, April 10, 1919: *AAS* 11 (1919) p. 172. Pius XI's apostolic encyclical, *Divini Illius Magistri*, Dec. 31, 1929: *AAS* 22 (1930) pp. 49-86. Pius XII's allocution to the youths of Italian Catholic Action, April 20, 1946: *Discourses and Radio Messages*, vol. 8, pp. 53-57. Allocution to fathers of French families, Sept. 18, 1951: *Discourses and Radio Messages*, vol. 13, pp. 241-245. John XXIII's 30th anniversary message on the publication of the encyclical letter, *Divini Illius Magistri*, Dec. 30, 1959: *AAS* 52 (1960) pp. 57-S9. Paul VI's allocution to members of Federated Institutes Dependent on Ecclesiastic Authority, Dec. 30, 1963: *Encyclicals and Discourses of His Holiness Paul VI*, Rome, 1964, pp. 601-603. Above all are to be consulted the Acts and Documents of the Second Vatican Council appearing in the first series of the ante-preparatory phase, vol. 3. pp. 363-364; 370-371; 373-374.

2   Cf. John XXIII's encyclical letter *Mater et Magistra*, May 15, 1961: *AAS* 53 (1961) pp. 413-415; 417-424; Encyclical letter, *Pacem in Terris*, April 11, 1963: *AAS* 55 (1963) p. 278 ff.

3   *Declaration on the Rights of Man* of Dec. 10, 1948, adopted by the General Assembly of the United Nations, and also cf. the *Declaration of the Rights of Children* of Nov. 20, 1959; additional protocol to the Convention Safeguarding the Rights of Men and Fundamental Liberties, Paris, March 20, 1952; regarding that universal profession of the character of human laws cf. apostolic letter *Pacem in Terris*, of John XXIII of April 11, 1963: *AAS* 55 (1963) p. 295 ff.

4   Cf. John XXIII's encyclical letter, *Mater et Magistra*, May 15, 1961: *AAS* 53 (1961) p. 402. Cf. Second Vatican Council's *Dogmatic Constitution on the Church*, no. 17: *AAS* 57 (1965) p. 21, and schema on the *Pastoral Constitution on the Church in the Modern World*, 1965.

5   Pius XII's radio message of Dec. 24, 1942: *AAS* 35 (1943) pp. 12-19, and John XXIII's encyclical letter, *Pacem in Terris* April 11, 1963: *AAS* 55 (1963) p. 259 ff. Also cf. declaration cited on the rights of man in footnote 3.

6   Cf. Pius XI's encyclical letter, *Divini Illius Magistri*, Dec. 31, 1929: *AAS* 22 (1930) p. 50 ff.

7   Cf. John XXIII's encyclical letter, *Mater et Magistra*, May 15, 1961: *AAS* 53 (1961) p. 441 ff.

8   Cf. Pius XI's encyclical letter, *Divini Illius Magistri*, 1, p. 83.

9   Cf. Second Vatican Council's *Dogmatic Constitution on the Church*, no. 36: *AAS* 57 (1965) p. 41 ff.

10 Cf. Second Vatican Council's schema on the *Decree on the Lay Apostolate* (1965), no. 12.

11 Cf. Pius XI's encyclical letter *Divini Illius Magistri*, 1, p. 59 ff., encyclical letter *Mit Brennender Sorge*, March 14, 1937: *AAS* 29; Pius XII's allocution to the first national congress of the Italian Catholic Teachers' Association, Sept. 8, 1946: *Discourses and Radio Messages*, vol. 8, p. 218.

12 Cf. Second Vatican Council's *Dogmatic Constitution on the Church*, nos. 11 and 35: *AAS* 57 (1965) pp. 16, 40 ff.

13 Cf. Pius XI's encyclical letter *Divini Illius Magistri*, 1, p. 63 ff. Pius XII's radio message of June 1, 1941: *AAS* 33 (1941) p. 200; allocution to the first national congress of the Association of Italian Catholic Teachers, Sept 8, 1946: *Discourses and Radio Messages*, vol. 8, 1946: *Discourses and Radio Messages*, vol. 8, p. 218. Regarding the principle of subsidiarity, cf. John XXIII's encyclical letter, *Pacem in Terris*, April 11, 1963: *AAS* 55 (1963) p. 294.

14 Cf. Pius XI's encyclical letter, *Divini Illius Magistri*, 1 pp. 53 ff. and 56 ff.; Encyclical letter, *Non Abbiamo Bisogno* June 29, 1931: *AAS* 23 (1931) p. 311 ff. Pius XII's letter from Secretariat of State to 28th Italian Social Week, Sept. 20, 1955; *L'Osservatore Romano*, Sept. 29, 1955.

15 The Church praises those local, national and international civic authorities who, conscious of the urgent necessity in these times, expend all their energy so that all peoples may benefit from more education and human culture. Cf. Paul VI's allocution to the United Nations General Assembly, Oct. 4, 1965: *L'Osservatore Romano*, Oct. 6, 1965.

16 Cf. Pius XI's motu proprio, *Orbem Catholicum*, June 29 1923: *AAS* 15 (1923) pp. 327-329; decree, *Provide Sane*, Jan. 12, 1935: *AAS* 27 (1935) pp. 145-152. Second Vatican Council's *Decree on Bishops and Pastoral Duties*, nos. 13 and 14.

17 Cf. Second Vatican Council's *Constitution on the Sacred Liturgy*, no. 14: *AAS* 56 (1964) p. 104.

18 Cf. Second Vatican Council's *Decree on Communications Media*, nos. 13 and 14: *AAS* 56 (1964) p. 149 ff.

19 Cf. Pius XI's encyclical letter, *Divini Illius Magistri*, 1, p. 76; Pius XII's allocution to Bavarian Association of Catholic Teachers, Dec. 31, 1956: *Discourses and Radio Messages*, vol. 18, p. 746.

20 Cf. Provincial Council of Cincinnati III, a. 1861: *Collatio Lacensis*, III, col. 1240, c/d; Pius XI's encyclical letter, *Divini Illius Magistri*, 1, pp. 60, 63 ff.

21 Cf. Pius XI's encyclical letter, *Divini Illius Magistri*, 1, p. 63; encyclical letter, *Non Abbiamo Misogno*, June 29, 1931: *AAS* 23 (1931) p. 305, Pius XII's letter from the Secretary of State to the 28th Italian Social Week, Sept. 20, 1955: *L'Osservatore Romano*, Sept. 29, 1955. Paul VI's allocution to the Association of Italian Christian Workers, Oct. 6, 1963: *Encyclicals and Discourses of Paul VI*, vol. 1, Rome, 1964, p. 230.

22 Cf. John XXIII's message on the 30th anniversary of the encyclical letter, *Divini Illius Magistri*, Dec. 30, 1959: *AAS* 52 (1960) p. 57.

23 The Church considers it as apostolic action of great worth also when Catholic teachers and associates work in these schools. Cf. Second Vatican Council's schema of the *Decree on the Lay Apostolate* (1965), nos. 12 and 16.

24 Cf. Second Vatican Council's schema on the *Declaration on Religious Liberty* (1965), no. 5.

25 Cf. Provincial Council of Westminster I, a. 1852: *Collatio Lacensis* III, col. 1334, a/b; Pius XI's encyclical letter, *Divini Illius Magistri*, 1, p. 77 ff.; Pius XII's allocution to the Bavarian Association of Catholic

Teachers, Dec. 31, 1956: *Discourses and Radio Messages*, vol. 18, p. 746; Paul VI's allocution to the members of Federated Institutes Dependent on Ecclesiastic Authority, Dec. 30, 1963: *Encyclicals and Discourses of Paul VI*, 1, Rome, 1964, 602 ff.

[26] Cf. especially the document mentioned in the first note; moreover this law of the Church is proclaimed by many provincial councils and in the most recent declarations of very many of the episcopal conferences.

[27] Cf. Pius XI's encyclical letter, *Divini Illius Magistri*, 1 p. 80 ff.; Pius XII's allocution to the Catholic Association of Italian Teachers in Secondary Schools, Jan. 5, 1954: *Discourses and Radio Messages*, 15, pp. 551-55B; John XXIII's allocution to the 6th Congress of the Associations of Catholic Italian Teachers Sept. 5, 1959: *Discourses, Messages, Conversations*, 1, Rome, 1960, pp. 427-431.

[28] Cf. Pius XII's allocution to the Catholic Association of Italian Teachers in Secondary Schools, Jan. 5, 1954, 1, p. 555.

[29] Cf. Paul VI's allocution to the International Office of Catholic Education, Feb. 25, 1964: *Encyclicals and Discourses of Paul VI*, 2, Rome, 1964, p. 232.

[30] Cf. Paul VI's allocution to the Christian Association of Italian Workers, Oct. 6, 1963: *Encyclicals and Discourses of Paul VI*, 1, Rome, 1964, p. 229.

[31] Cf. Paul VI's allocution to the International Thomistic Congress, Sept. 10, 1965: *L'Osservatore Romano*, Sept. 13-14, 1965.

[32] Cf. Pius XII's allocution to teachers and students of French Institutes of Higher Catholic Education, Sept. 21, 1950: *Discourses and Radio Messages*, 12, pp. 219-221; letters to the 22nd congress of Pax Romana, Aug. 12, 1952: *Discourses and Radio Messages*, 14, pp. 567-569; John XXIII's allocution to the Federation of Catholic Universities, April 1, 1959: *Discourses, Messages and Conversations*, 1, Rome, 1960, pp. 226-229; Paul VI's allocution to the Academic Senate of the Catholic University of Milan, April 5, 1964: *Encyclicals and Discourses of Paul VI*, 2, Rome, 1964, pp. 438-443.

[33] Cf. Pius XII's allocution to the academic senate and students of the University of Rome, June 15, 1952: *Discourses and Radio Messages*, 14, p. 208: "The direction of today's society principally is placed in the mentality and hearts of the universities of today."

[34] Cf. Pius XII's apostolic constitution, *Deus Scientiarum Dominus*, May 24, 1931: *AAS* 23 (1931) pp. 245-247.

[35] Cf. Pius XII's encyclical letter, *Humani Generis* Aug. 12, 1950, *AAS* 42 (1950) pp. 568 ff. and 578; Paul VI's encyclical letter, *Ecclesiam Suam*, part III Aug. 6, 1964; *AAS* 56 (1964) pp. 637-659; Second Vatican Council's *Decree on Eccumenism*: *AAS* 57 (1965) pp. 90-107.

[36] Cf. John XXIII's encyclical letter, *Pacem in Terris*, April 11, 1963: *AAS* 55 (1963) p. 284 and elsewhere.

To Teach as Jesus Did:
A Pastoral Message on Catholic Education

NATIONAL CONFERENCE OF CATHOLIC BISHOPS
November 1972

Preface

1. This pastoral message is the product of wide consultation involving many individuals and groups. It reflects a painstaking effort to obtain the views of persons from a variety of backgrounds and interests—priests, religious men and women, lay people, professional educators at all levels of education, parents, students. Much of this consultation took place at the national level but even more occurred at the local diocesan level, where bishops sought out the views of the people regarding various drafts of the document. While, in the last analysis, the pastoral represents the views of the American bishops and only they are responsible for what it says, grateful recognition is due the indispensable contributions of all those who participated in the collaborative effort involved in its preparation, itself in many ways a model of the shared responsibility for educational ministry which the document envisions and warmly recommends.

2. The pastoral is also written against the background of the Second Vatican Council's *Declaration on Christian Education* which requested national hierarchies to issue detailed statements on the educational ministry considered in the context of the Church and society in their own countries.

3. The pastoral's scope is broad but not all-encompassing. A virtually endless catalogue of programs, institutions, and activities could be gathered together under the rubric of "education." It was therefore necessary to employ some principles of exclusion to avoid producing a treatise of excessive length and, perhaps, superficiality. This document is concerned in the main with those agencies and instruments under Church sponsorship which are commonly recognized as "educational" by professional and layman alike and through which a deliberate and systematic effort is made to achieve what are commonly recognized as "educational" objectives. This is not to discount the educational/formational role played by communications media, liturgy—indeed one of the most powerful and appropriate educative instruments at the disposal of the Church—and countless other familial, social, and pastoral efforts, but only to state that they could not be considered in depth in this particular document. In addition, some extremely important educational programs are not treated here because they have already received detailed attention by the bishops elsewhere (e.g., the education of priests, which is the subject of the National Conference of Catholic Bishops' recently published *Program of Priestly Formation*).

4. As the concluding section of this document states, the pastoral is not to be regarded as the "final word" on its subject on either the theoretical or practical level. It will serve a useful purpose if it proves a catalyst for efforts to deal realistically with problems of polarization and of confusion now confronting the educational ministry. Thus one hopes that the ideas it contains will be studied closely, criticized intelligently, and, where possible, implemented successfully. In the years ahead American Catholics should continue to articulate and implement their commitment to the educational ministry in ways suited to their times and circumstances. Within both the Christian community and the educational ministry the mission to teach as Jesus did is a dynamic mandate for Christians of all times, places, and conditions.

I.
To Teach as Jesus Did

5. *"Lord," said Thomas, "we do not know where you are going. How can we know the way?" Jesus told him: "I am the way, and the truth, and the life; no one comes to the Father but through me. If you really knew me, you would know my Father also. From this point on you know him; you have seen him." (John 14:5-7)*

6. Proclaiming the Gospel is a perennial task and joy for the Church of Jesus Christ. Rarely if ever has it been more pressing a need, more urgent a duty, and more ennobling a vocation than in these times when mankind stands poised between unprecedented fulfillment and equally unprecedented calamity.

7. Catholic education is an expression of the mission entrusted by Jesus to the Church He founded. Through education the Church seeks to prepare its members to proclaim the Good News and to translate this proclamation into action. Since the Christian vocation is a call to transform oneself and society with God's help, the educational efforts of the Church must encompass the twin purposes of personal sanctification and social reform in light of Christian values.

8. Thus one crucial measure of the success or failure of the educational ministry is how well it enables men to hear the message of hope contained in the Gospel, to base their love and service of God upon this message, to achieve a vital personal relationship with Christ, and to share the Gospel's realistic view of the human condition which recognizes the fact of evil and personal sin while affirming hope.

9. Christian hope is of special importance today when many people express a naive optimism which fails to admit the reality and effects of sin upon the individual and society, and when many others, fully aware of evil in themselves and society, are tempted to indulge in crippling despair. In face of these two attitudes the Church can make a unique contribution by preaching the Gospel of hope. The Gospel proclaims the dignity and freedom of each person and gives assurance that men are right to hope for personal salvation and for the ultimate conquest of sin, isolation, injustice, privation and death because these evils have already been conquered in the person of Jesus Christ.

10. The success of the Church's educational mission will also be judged by how well it helps the Catholic community to see the dignity of human life with the vision of Jesus and involve itself in the search for solutions to the pressing problems of society. Christians are obliged to seek justice and peace in the world. Catholics individually and collectively should join wherever possible with all persons of good will in the effort to solve social problems in ways which consistently reflect Gospel values.

11. Since special knowledge and skills are needed for the effective pursuit of justice and peace, Christian education is basic to the effort to fulfill the demands of the Gospel in many different communities: family, church, neighborhood, working world, civic arena, international scene. To discern the practical demands of justice is often difficult. Yet Christians must be prepared to perform these difficult tasks of discernment; social needs "must in the years to come take first place among (their) preoccupations" (Pope Paul VI, *A Call to Action*, 7).

12. The Church is an instrument of salvation and a sign of Christ in the world today. His mission is the Church's mission; His message is the Church's message. Jesus was sent to reveal the deepest truth about God and at the same time reveal "man to himself and make his supreme calling clear" (*The Church Today*, 22). He commissioned His Church to do the same; to teach men and women about God and themselves, to foster their love of God and one another.

13. Education is one of the most important ways by which the Church fulfills its commitment to the dignity of the person and the building of community. Community is central to educational ministry both as a necessary condition and an ardently desired goal. The educational efforts of the Church must therefore be directed to forming persons-in-community; for the education of the individual Christian is important not only to his solitary destiny but also to the destinies of the many communities in which he lives.

14. The educational mission of the Church is an integrated ministry embracing three interlocking dimensions: the message revealed by God (*didache*) which the Church proclaims; fellowship in the life of the Holy Spirit (*koinonia*); service to the Christian community and the entire human community (*diakonia*). While these three essential elements can be separated for the sake of analysis, they are joined in the one educational ministry. Each educational program or institution under Church sponsorship is obliged to contribute in its own way to the realization of the three-fold purpose within the total educational ministry. Other conceptual frameworks can also be employed to present and analyze the Church's educational mission, but this one has several advantages: it corresponds to a long tradition and also meets exceptionally well the educational needs and aspirations of men and women in our times.

Message

15. *"For I have not spoken on my own; no, the Father who sent me has commanded me what to say and how to speak. Since I know that his commandment means eternal life, whatever I say is spoken just as he instructed me."* (John 12:49-50)

16. Revelation is the act by which God unfolds to mankind the mystery of Himself and His plan for salvation. In Jesus, the Son of God, the message of the Old Law was fulfilled and the fullness of God's message was communicated. At the time of the Apostles the message of salvation was completed, and we therefore "await no further new public revelation before the glorious manifestation of our Lord Jesus Christ" (*Divine Revelation*, 4). It is this message, this doctrine, which the Church is called to proclaim authentically and fully.

17. This does not preclude development in doctrine, properly understood, or change in the forms in which it is expressed. The tradition handed on by the Apostles is a "living tradition" through which God continues His conversation with His people. God "still secretly directs, through the Holy Spirit, in sacred tradition, by the light and sense of the faith, the Church, His bride, and speaks with her, so that the People of God, under the leadership of the magisterium, may attain a fuller understanding of revelation" (*General Catechetical Directory*, 13). There is, then, a growth in understanding of the message which has been handed down (*Divine Revelation*, 8).

18. In proclaiming all things which His Father commanded Him to reveal, Jesus used images from the lives of His hearers and spoke in the idiom of His day. The Church, too, must use contemporary methods and language to proclaim the message of Christ to men and women today. The proclamation of the message is therefore "not a mere repetition of ancient doctrine" (*General Catechetical Directory*, 13). Furthermore, within the fundamental unity of the faith, there is room for a plurality of cultural differences, forms of expression, and theological views. But what is taught and how it is expressed are subject to the magisterium, the teaching authority of the Church, as guarantor of authenticity.

19. The teaching Church calls upon each of us to have an active faith in God and His revealed truth. Under the influence of the Holy Spirit, man gives total adherence to God revealing Himself. Faith involves intellectual acceptance but also much more. Through faith men have a new vision of God, the world, and themselves. They must not only accept the Christian message but act on it, witnessing as individuals and a community to all that Jesus said and did. Catechesis thus "gives clarity and vigor to faith, nourishes a life lived according to the spirit of Christ, leads to a knowing and active participation in the liturgical mystery, and inspires apostolic action" (*Christian Education*, 4).

20. In sum, doctrine is not merely a matter for the intellect, but is the basis for a way of life as envisioned by St. Paul: "Let us profess the truth in love and grow to the full maturity of Christ the head" (Ephesians 4:15).

Community

21. *"I give you a new commandment: Love one another. Such as my love has been for you, so must your love be for each other. This is how all will know you for my disciples: your love for one another." (John 13:34-35)*

22. As God's plan unfolds in the life of an individual Christian, he grows in awareness that, as a child of God, he does not live in isolation from others. From the moment of Baptism he becomes a member of a new and larger family, the Christian community. Reborn in Baptism, he is joined to others in common faith, hope, and love. This community is based not on force or accident of geographic location or even on deeper ties of ethnic origin, but on the life of the Spirit which unites its members in a unique fellowship so intimate that Paul likens it to a body of which each individual is a part and Jesus Himself is the Head. In this community one person's problem is everyone's problem and one person's victory is everyone's victory. Never before and never since the coming of Jesus Christ has anyone proposed such a community.

23. Community is at the heart of Christian education not simply as a concept to be taught but as a reality to be lived. Through education, men must be moved to build community in all areas of life; they can do this best if they have learned the meaning of community by experiencing it. Formed by this experience, they are better able to build community in their families, their places of work, their neighborhoods, their nation, their world.

24. Christian fellowship grows in personal relationships of friendship, trust and love infused with a vision of men and women as children of God redeemed by Christ. It is fostered especially by the Eucharist which is at once sign of community and cause of its growth. From a Christian perspective, integral personal growth, even growth in grace and the spiritual life, is not possible without integral social life. To understand this is a high form of learning; to foster such understanding is a crucial task of education.

25. In the family children learn to believe what their parents' words and example teach about God, and parents enrich their own faith by participating in the formal religious education of their children: for example, by preparing them to receive the Sacraments of Penance, Eucharist and Confirmation. The members of a parish grow in fellowship by coming together to worship God and by making a shared response of faith on occasions of joy and stress. Creating readiness for growth in community through worship and through the events of everyday life is an integral part of the task of Catholic education, which also seeks to build community within its own programs and institutions.

26. Our nation, blessed by God with enormous resources, has a heavy responsibility in the larger community of people on this planet. Christian educational ministry includes as a dimension of high importance the education of our own people to the imperatives of justice which should direct our national political, military, cultural and economic policies. In the absence of justice no enduring peace is possible. Thus the teaching of recent Popes, the Council and the Synod of Bishops concerning peace and justice for all nations and peoples must be communicated effectively and accepted fully. In this task we invite the collaboration of mission-sending societies whose apostolate includes educating American Catholics regarding their international responsibilities.

Service

27. *"You address me as 'Teacher' and 'Lord,' and fittingly enough, for that is what I am. But if I washed your feet—I who am Teacher and Lord—then you must wash each other's feet. What I just did was to give you an example: as I have done, so you must do."* (John 13:13-15)

28. The experience of Christian community leads naturally to service. Christ gives His people different gifts not only for themselves but for others. Each must serve the other for the good of all. The Church is a servant community in which those who hunger are to be filled; the ignorant are to be taught; the homeless to receive shelter; the sick cared for; the distressed consoled; the oppressed set free— all so that men may more fully realize their human potential and more readily enjoy life with God now and eternally.

29. But the Christian community should not be concerned only for itself. Christ did not intend it to live walled off from the world any more than He intended each person to work out his destiny in isolation from others. Fidelity to the will of Christ joins His community with the total human community. "Thus the mission of the Church will show its religious, and by that very fact, its supremely human character" (*The Church Today*, 11). No human joy, no human sorrow is a matter of indifference to the community established by Jesus. In today's world this requires that the Christian community be involved in seeking solutions to a host of complex problems, such as war, poverty, racism, and environmental pollution, which undermine community within and among nations. Christians render such service by prayer and worship and also by direct participation in the cause of social reform.

30. It is imperative that the Church render the service of educational ministry today. Many institutions in society possess much larger material resources and thus can do far more to meet the material needs of man. None, however, has the unique resources of vision and values entrusted to His community by Jesus Christ. To suppose that the Church's mission of service is somehow less urgent in today's world than in the past is to fail to recognize mankind's enduring spiritual need and the unique capacity for meeting that need possessed by the Christian community.

31. Beyond question the vision of the threefold educational ministry presented here is an ambitious one. Were it of human origin, one might well despair of its attainment. But since it represents God's plan, it must be energetically pursued.

32. Even now it is being realized in many places. All three aspects of the educational mission are present, for example, in a well organized, comprehensive parish program of education where the teaching of authentic doctrine supports and is supported by the building of community, and teaching and fellowship in turn support and are supported by Christian service through sharing spiritual and temporal goods with those in need. In such a parish Catholic education's lessons are learned in classroom and pew; yet not only there, but also in the experience of living in a Christian community of faith actively engaged in service of God, Church and neighbor.

II.
A World in Transition: Faith and Technology

33. Underlying virtually all of the changes occurring in the world today, both as instrument and cause, are technology and the technological worldview. Technology is one of the most marvelous expressions of the human spirit in history; but it is not an unmixed blessing. It can enrich life immeasurably or make a tragedy of life. The choice is man's, and education has a powerful role in shaping that choice.

34. Technological progress equips man with sophisticated means of communication, analysis and research. The speed and ease of travel, the marvel of instantaneous communication via satellite, television and telephone, the "transistor revolution" which carries new information and ideas to the most remote corners of the earth—these and many other developments foster growth in awareness that the human family is one, united though diverse.

35. Scientific tools of research and analysis like the computer have created a knowledge explosion. The past itself is more accessible to people and they are able to understand it far better than before. Thus not only does the present generation of mankind experience powerful influences toward unity but its bonds with earlier cultures also grow stronger. In this context the continuity of God's living revelation and of teaching based on the enduring deposit of faith is more apparent; the beauty of God's plan for community among all His scattered children can be more readily appreciated, and the plan itself can be more easily realized.

36. On the other hand, one must acknowledge a distressing paradox: this same technology threatens the unity and even the future of mankind. Its instruments destroy ancient patterns of life and uproot peoples from their traditions and history. Values cherished for centuries are abruptly challenged, and the stability of the social order is weakened if not destroyed. If this generation is, as some suggest, moving into a new era of global culture, it simultaneously risks losing the values of particular cultures which deserve to be preserved.

37. Although technology can create unparalleled material prosperity for all men, its abuse can be a tool of human selfishness. At present, technologically advanced nations are accumulating wealth at a rate which widens the gap between themselves and the poor nations of the world. The same phenomenon—a tragic gulf between rich and poor—is also present within many technologically developed nations, including our own. Our readiness for sharing has not kept pace with our skill at acquiring.

38. Technology poses new threats to the dignity of the person. It makes possible violence and destruction on a scale hitherto undreamed of. In our own nation's wealthy society the immense output of goods and services too often distracts its citizens from awareness of their duty to God and their fellows, without satisfying their deepest needs for stability, friendship and meaning.

39. Faith suffers in the resulting climate of uncertainty and alienation. Torn between the appeals of idealism and reform on the one hand, and the seductions of greed and self-indulgence on the other, many people drift on the surface of life, without roots, without meaning, without love.

40. Yet profound human needs endure, and the educational mission of the Church must use old ways and new to meet them. This task is more difficult today than at many times in the past, precisely because turbulence and uncertainty bring with them skepticism toward the institutions of society, including those of

the Church. In evaluating and responding to this contemporary phenomenon, it would be a serious mistake to identify mere externals with essential faith, or to confuse rejection of what is merely familiar with repudiation of our basic heritage. This underlines the need for balanced discernment in place of simplistic solutions.

41. Faithful to the past and open to the future, we must accept the burden and welcome the opportunity of proclaiming the Gospel of Christ in our times. Where this is a summons to change, we must be willing to change. Where this is a call to stand firm, we must not yield. In this spirit, our discussion turns now to the concrete forms and structures of the educational mission.

III.
Giving Form to the Vision

1.
The Educational Ministry to Adults

42. The Church's educational mission takes form in many different programs and institutions adapted to the needs of those to be educated. We shall first consider those directed to adults, including in this category both adult or continuing education and also the various forms of the ministry in higher education.

Adult Education

43. Today, perhaps more than ever before, it is important to recognize that learning is a lifelong experience. Rapid, radical changes in contemporary society demand well planned, continuing efforts to assimilate new data, new insights, new modes of thinking and acting. This is necessary for adults to function efficiently, but, more important, to achieve full realization of their potential as persons whose destiny includes but also transcends this life. Thus they will also enjoy ever deepening fellowship within the many communities to which each of them belongs. Consequently the continuing education of adults is situated not at the periphery of the Church's educational mission but at its center. Like other church-sponsored educational efforts, adult programs should reflect in their own unique way the three interrelated purposes of Christian education: the teaching of doctrine, the building and experiencing of community, and service to others.

44. It is essential that such programs recognize not only the particular needs of adults, but also their maturity and experience. Those who teach in the name of the Church do not simply instruct adults, but also learn from them; they will only be heard by adults if they listen to them. For this reason adult programs must be planned and conducted in ways that emphasize self-direction, dialogue, and mutual responsibility.

45. There are many instruments of adult education, and the Church itself sponsors many such activities and programs. Their full potential in this area should be recognized and used effectively. The liturgy is one of the most powerful educational instruments at the disposal of the Church. The fact that homilies can be effective tools of adult education lends urgency to current efforts to upgrade preaching skills and to improve the entire homiletic process. The Catholic press and other communications media should be utilized creatively for continuing education.

46. Finally, formal programs of adult education at the parish and diocesan levels deserve adequate attention and support, including professional staffing and realistic funding. Adult education should also have a recognized place in the structure of church-sponsored education at all levels, parish, diocesan and national.

Adult Religious Education

47. The gradual manner of God's self-revelation, manifested in Scripture, is a model for the catechetical efforts of the Church. The full content of revelation can be communicated best to those able by reason of maturity and prior preparation to hear and respond to it. Religious education for adults is the culmination of the entire catechetical effort because it affords an opportunity to teach the whole Christian message (*General Catechetical Directory*, 20). Catechetics for children and young people should find completion in a catechetical program for adults.

48. The content of such a program will include contemporary sociological and cultural developments considered in the light of faith, current questions concerning religious and moral issues, the relationship of the "temporal" and "ecclesial" spheres of life, and the "rational foundations" of religious belief (*General Catechetical Directory*, 97). Adult religious education should strive not only to impart instruction to adults but to enable them better to assume responsibility for the building of community and for Christian service in the world.

Education for Family Life

49. Like many institutions in society, the family is under severe pressure today. Challenges to accepted values, changing sexual mores, new ideas about marriage and especially about the sanctity of life—these and other factors can threaten family life and unity.

50. To respond creatively to such pressures and to build a healthy family life, Catholic adults who have assumed or are about to assume the responsibility of marriage must see the family as an image of the Church itself and base their marriage and family life on Christian values taught by the Church in the name of Jesus. As the Church struggles to fulfill Christ's mandate to sanctify and teach men and women in the difficult circumstances of life today, so should a man and a woman, united in marriage and imbued with the Gospel ideal, seek mutual growth in Christ and strive to form, in light of Christian values, the children whom God entrusts to their care. But as all the people of the Church are imperfect human beings who live their vocations imperfectly, so parents approach their vocation conscious of their limitations but aware also that by persevering effort to meet their responsibilities, even in the face of failure and disappointment, they help their children learn what faith, hope and love mean in practice. Finally, as the Church, in imitation of Christ, must constantly seek to be more sensitive and responsive to the needs of the poor among us, so must each Christian family see Christ in those who are less fortunate and, at cost to its own convenience and comfort, strive to be Christ to them, in the parish, the neighborhood, and the larger communities of the nation and world.

51. In seeking to instill this understanding of the Christian family's role, family life education must employ such means as premarital instruction and marriage counseling, study, prayer and action groups for couples, and other adult programs which married persons themselves may plan and conduct in collaboration with Church leadership.

Parents as Educators

52. While it was relatively easy in more stable times for parents to educate their children and transmit their values to them, the immense complexity of today's society makes this a truly awesome task. Without forgetting, then, that parents are "the first to communicate the faith to their children and to educate them" (*Apostolate of the Laity*, 11), the Christian community must make a generous effort today to help them fulfill their duty. This is particularly true in regard to two matters of great sensitivity and importance, religious education and education in human sexuality.

53. Although religious education should foster unity within the family and the Church, today at times it causes division instead. There are several reasons for this. Changes in religious education in recent years have disturbed many parents, in part at least because the training their children now receive seems to bear little resemblance to their own. To the extent that this problem relates to valid pedagogical methods, it may be resolved as parents come to understand better the techniques of contemporary religious education. However, the difficulty also touches at times on more basic issues involving the orthodoxy and authenticity of what is taught.

54. Religious truth must be communicated in a relevant manner which gives each student a vital experience of faith. But it must also be transmitted fully and accurately. There is no opposition between orthodoxy and relevance. Religious truth is itself supremely relevant, and the manner in which it is presented must make this manifest. The Catholic community today faces the challenge of combining these complementary values—orthodoxy and relevance—in viable programs of religious education for the young. The steps to achieving this cannot be spelled out in the abstract but must instead be worked out in dialogue and cooperation on the parish, diocesan and national levels. Parents, religious educators, including authors and publishers of textbooks, pastors, bishops, must seek together, in a spirit of mutual respect and shared commitment to the values of orthodoxy and relevance, to solve the problems and ease the tensions that now exist. They will find guidance in such sources as the *General Catechetical Directory* issued by the Holy See, "The Basic Teachings of Catholic Religious Education" to be issued by the American bishops, and the projected U.S. national catechetical directory.

55. Continuing education will help parents understand the approach, content and methods of contemporary religious education. At the same time, however, parents must not only be helped to understand the aims and methods of catechesis; they must also be involved in planning and evaluating the catechetical programs provided for their children (*General Catechetical Directory*, 79). And in order that this evaluation may be realistic and informed, parents and other members of the Christian community have a right to expect at least that the content of these programs will be expressed in doctrinally adequate formulae as an assurance that the programs are indeed capable of transmitting the authentic Christian message.

56. If neglecting parental involvement can only contribute to further misunderstanding and polarization in catechetics, the same is equally true of the sensitive subject of education in human sexuality. In 1968 we affirmed the "value and necessity of wisely planned education of children in human sexuality" and acknowledged our "grave obligation" to assist parents, who are "primarily responsible for imparting to their children an awareness of the sacredness of sexuality" (*Human Life in Our Day*, 61). We continue to regard this as an important priority in Christian education, met in part through diocesan-approved family life education in Catholic schools and other instructional programs.

57. These efforts presuppose parental understanding and approval and require parents' cooperation with classroom teachers. The aim is not to supplant parents but to help them fulfill their obligation. They have a right to be informed about the content of such programs and to be assured that diocesan-approved textbooks and other instructional materials meet the requirements of propriety. But when these reasonable conditions have been met, parents should not allow continuing anxiety to be translated into indiscriminate opposition to all forms of classroom education in sexuality. Such opposition would be contrary to the teaching of Vatican Council II and the pastoral policy of the American bishops. Also, to the extent that it might disrupt responsible efforts to provide formal education in sexuality for the young, it would violate the rights of other, no less conscientious, parents who ask for such instruction for their own children.

58. The child's need for and right to adequate knowledge and guidance, adapted to his age and individual maturity are the paramount considerations. In all programs proper emphasis must be given to the spiritual and moral dimensions of sexuality. The child's reverence for the God-given dignity and beauty of sex is an effective safeguard of purity; it should be cultivated from the earliest years.

59. These remarks all underline the fact that a "parent component" must be part of many different church-sponsored educational programs. Where appropriate, Catholic schools can offer courses for parents. School-related parent organizations should provide opportunities for adults to learn more about child development and pedagogical method. Similar provision for educating and involving adults should be made by parish religious education programs. All this requires teachers professionally educated for work in this area.

Adult Education and Social Problems

60. "The constant expansion of population, scientific and technical progress, and the tightening of bonds between men have not only immensely widened the field of the lay apostolate. . . .These developments have themselves raised new problems which cry out for the skillful concern and attention of the laity" (*Apostolate of the Laity*, 1). Adult education must therefore deal with the critical issues of contemporary society. "The role of the Church today is very difficult; to reconcile man's modern respect for progress with the norms of humanity and of the gospel teaching" (*Mater et Magistra*, 256). Applying the Gospel message to social problems is a delicate but crucial task for which all members of the Church are responsible but which is entrusted in a specific way to lay people.

61. In proclaiming the social doctrine of the Gospel, the aim is not to antagonize but to reconcile. But the proclamation must be forthright, even where forthrightness challenges widely accepted attitudes and practices. Even though Christians may at times err in their facts, interpretations, and conclusions about social issues, they must not fail to apply the Gospel to contemporary life. Adult programs which deal with social problems in light of Gospel values thus have an extremely important place in the Church's educational mission. And, as in other areas of adult education, participants in such programs must be encouraged to bring their insights and experiences to planning and conducting them.

Higher Education

62. While higher education has always been important in the United States, our rapid evolution as a technological society since World War II has given universities and colleges an even more prominent role in American life. Americans look to them for expert knowledge in a multitude of fields and depend on them for many functions which powerfully affect social and economic life. This is reflected in the remarkable growth of college and university enrollment. Today more than half of American young people of college age attend institutions of post-secondary education. The nation should be aware, however, that many private institutions, including Catholic ones, are not now sharing in this growth. For many, rising costs and dependence on tuition have caused a student shortage which threatens their survival.

63. Like the nation, the Church is greatly influenced by higher education and indebted to it in many ways. Cooperation between these two great institutions, Church and university, is indispensable to the health of society.

64. Everything possible must be done to preserve the critically important contribution made by Catholic institutions through their commitment to the spiritual, intellectual, and moral values of the Christian tradition. Their students have a right to explore the distinctively Catholic intellectual patrimony which affirms, among other things, the existence of God and His revelation in Jesus Christ as ontological facts and essential elements in seeking and sharing truth. The Church itself looks to its colleges and universities to serve it by deep and thorough study of Catholic beliefs in an atmosphere of intellectual freedom and according to canons of intellectual criticism which should govern all pursuit of truth. The Catholic community should therefore fully support practical efforts to assure the continued, effective presence of distinctively Catholic colleges and universities in our nation.

65. The same support and concern should be extended to all of higher education. The Church desires a commitment in every college and university to the full and free pursuit and study of truth, including the place of religion in the lives of individuals and society. Catholics are further called to give their support to all of higher education by the fact that the great majority of Catholics who enter college enroll in non-Catholic institutions. These young men and women have a strong claim on the service and affection of the entire Catholic community; among them are many future leaders of the nation and the Church.

Campus Ministry

66. The Second Vatican Council urged all "pastors of the Church" not only to seek the spiritual welfare of students in Catholic institutions of higher education, but also to ensure that "at colleges and universities which are not Catholic, there are Catholic residences and centers where priests, religious and lay men who have been judiciously chosen and trained can serve on campus as sources of spiritual and intellectual assistance to young people" (*Christian Education*, 10). While the Council's emphasis reflected conditions as they were up to that time, developments since then point to the importance of campus ministry in Catholic institutions as well. These developments include a decline in the number of priests and religious engaged in Catholic higher education, the increasing number of students who have not attended church-sponsored elementary and secondary schools, and some strong pressures to secularize Catholic institutions.

67. Wherever exercised, campus ministry has a number of distinct but related goals. These include promoting theological study and reflection on man's religious nature so that intellectual, moral and spiritual growth can proceed together; sustaining a Christian community on campus with the pastoral care and liturgical worship it requires; integration of its apostolic ministry with other ministries of the local community and the diocese; and helping the Christian community on campus to serve its members and others, including the many non-students who gravitate toward the university. Campus ministry thus involves far more than pastoral care given by chaplains to students. It is pastoral, educational and prophetic, including a complex of efforts to give witness to the Gospel message to all persons within the college or university. It is conducted not only by priests and religious, but also by lay faculty and administrators, students and members of the local community.

68. Among the challenges facing campus ministry today are the special problems posed by "commuter" colleges and universities and the rapidly growing number of two-year colleges, whose enrollment is expected to reach five million by the middle of this decade. Students in these schools differ greatly from students in four-year, largely residential institutions, since most of them live at home and have jobs and many are married.

69. The work of campus ministry requires continual evaluation of traditional methods of ministry and also of new approaches which are licitly and responsibly employed. These latter can be highly appropriate in the campus setting, where there exists an audience receptive to the kind of sound innovation which may in the future prove beneficial to the larger Catholic community.

70. Religious studies, formal or informal, should be part of every campus ministry program. Neglect of such studies would risk a growth in religious indifferentism. Today, when the importance of reason and rational discourse is questioned and frequently slighted in favor of the affective side of life, there is need for emphasis on the relationship of faith and reason.

71. At the same time campus ministry must reflect the fact that young people, while deeply concerned about personal holiness and salvation, also seek meaning and values through the life of community. A community of believers engaged in analysis and practice of their faith is a sign of the continuing vitality of the Church. Such a community is sympathetic to all who search sincerely for the meaning of life and seek a foundation for values which will guide them in the pursuit of their destiny.

72. Campus ministry must have its proper place in the educational and financial planning of every diocese. The selection, preparation and continuing education of the men and women of campus ministry should have a high priority in educational planning. Regional and national programs must be developed to promote the development of campus ministry not only for its own sake but for the sake of increased dialogue between the Church and the university.

Catholic Colleges and Universities

73. The Catholic college or university seeks to give the authentic Christian message an institutional presence in the academic world. Several things follow from this. Christian commitment will characterize this academic community. While fully maintaining the autonomy concomitant to its being a college or university, the institution will manifest fidelity to the teaching of Jesus Christ as transmitted by His Church. The advancement of Christian thought will be the object of institutional commitment. The human sciences will be examined in light of Catholic faith. The best of the Christian intellectual and spiritual

tradition will be blended with the special dynamism of contemporary higher education in a way that enriches both.

74. The Catholic college or university must of course be an institution of higher education according to sound contemporary criteria. It will therefore be strongly committed to academic excellence and the responsible academic freedom required for effective teaching and research.

75. For a Catholic institution, there is a special aspect to academic freedom. While natural truth is directly accessible to us by virtue of our innate ability to comprehend reality, the datum or raw material from which theological reflection arises is not a datum of reality fully accessible to human reason. The authentic Christian message is entrusted by Jesus Christ to His community, the Church. Theological research and speculation, which are entirely legitimate and commendable enterprises, deal with divine revelation as their source and material, and the results of such investigation are therefore subject to the judgment of the magisterium.

76. Historically, Catholic colleges and universities have had varying degrees of relationship to ecclesiastical authority. The concern of Vatican Council II with these institutions centered on their nature or function, their faculty, and their role in Christian formation (*Christian Education*, 10). At present, cordial, fruitful and continuing dialogue on the complex question of the relationship of the Catholic college or university to the Church is proceeding between representatives of such schools and others officially concerned with Catholic education. The entire Catholic community stands to benefit from this continued exploration.

Theology and the Catholic University

77. As an institution committed to examination of the full range of human existence, the university should probe the religious dimension of life. Scholars engaged in theological and religious studies should thus be part of the academic community.

78. A department of theology, conceived and functioning as an integral part of the Catholic university, can encourage scholars in other disciplines to examine more deeply their own fields of study. The theological scholar himself is enriched by participating in such discussion.

79. The department of theology also encourages students to confront religious questions and explore beyond the limits of a narrow vision of life which excludes the religious dimension. At the same time, interaction with students obliges scholars to respond to the healthy challenge of reexamining their insights and modes of expression.

80. Finally, the department of theology is a vital resource to the Catholic community outside the university and must be aware of its responsibility to that community. Its scholarship can provide support to the pastoral ministry of the Church and help deepen the Church's understanding of the Gospel message. Theologians can render special assistance to bishops, whose role, like theirs, includes both the development and the defense of Christian truth.

81. While no aspect of genuine religious experience is beyond the scope of concern of the department of theology or religious studies in a Catholic university, its characteristic strength appropriately lies in the presence of scholars whose professional competence and personal commitment are rooted in the Catholic tradition. In such an institution every scholar, Catholic or not, is also obliged to respect its spirit and purpose.

2.
The Educational Ministry To Youth

82. "The future of humanity lies in the hands of those who are strong enough to provide coming generations with reasons for living and hoping" (*The Church Today*, 31). Here as in other areas of educational ministry the threefold purpose of Christian education provides a guide for developing and evaluating programs. Educational programs for the young must strive to teach doctrine, to do so within the experience of Christian community, and to prepare individuals for effective Christian witness and service to others. In doing this they help foster the student's growth in personal holiness and his relationship with Christ.

83. This ideal of Christian education will best be realized by programs which create the widest opportunities for students to receive systematic catechesis, experience daily living in a faith community, and develop commitment and skill in serving others. All who share responsibility for educational ministry should support programs which give promise of realizing this threefold purpose which is the guide and inspiration of all the Church's educational efforts.

84. The history of American education is testimony to the deeply held conviction of American Catholics that Catholic elementary and secondary schools are the best expression of the educational ministry to youth. As we shall explain at length later, this remains our conviction today, one shared, we believe, by the great majority of American Catholics.

Yet we choose to deal here first with religious education programs for children and young people who attend public and other non-Catholic schools not because Catholic schools are any less important than in the past—their importance is in fact greater now than ever before—but because the urgency and the difficulty of the educational ministry to the students outside them warrant this emphasis. Among the pastoral issues in education which today challenge the Catholic community in our nation, none is more pressing than providing Catholic education for these young people.

Religious Education
Outside the Catholic School

85. Confraternity of Christian Doctrine and other parish programs of religious education are essential instruments of catechesis. Besides enrolling some five and a half million students, they have an even larger potential outreach among the many Catholic children and young people who attend neither Catholic schools nor out-of-school religious education programs. These students, both present and potential, are the youth of whom the Second Vatican Council spoke in urging the Catholic community to be "present" to them with its "special affection and helpfulness" (*Christian Education*, 2).

86. Obviously a part-time, out-of-school program of religious education labors under special handicaps in attempting to achieve the threefold purpose of Christian education. Yet we have a grave duty toward the students for whom such programs now represent the only means of formal religious instruction available to them. Parents, educators, and pastors must do all in their power to provide these children and young people with programs which correspond as fully as possible with the ideal of Catholic education.

Doctrine, Community and Service

87. Pastoral programs of religious education for young people outside Catholic schools must be developed and conducted within the framework of the threefold purpose of Christian education. Merely "teaching about" religion is not enough. Instead such programs must strive to teach doctrine fully, foster community, and prepare their students for Christian service. Whether it takes place in a Catholic school or not, it is essential that the Catholic community offer children and young people an experience of catechesis which indeed gives "clarity and vigor" to faith, fosters living in the spirit of Christ, encourages participation in the liturgy and sacraments, and motivates involvement in the apostolate (*Christian Education*, 4).

88. Although there are inherent limitations in out-of-school programs, there are also considerable strengths which should be recognized and built upon. A limitation, which is also a potential source of strength, is their voluntary character, which, while making it more difficult to secure participation, also offers significant opportunities for the building of Christian community. The fact that participants in leadership, teaching or student roles, are volunteers provides creative planners with opportunity to develop esprit among them, and indeed, to foster a stronger sense of community within the entire parish. This is simply to apply to the out-of-school program what has long been recognized as true of the parish school, namely that the hard work and sacrifice required for success can be powerful forces for Christian fellowship.

89. In regard to service, administrators and teachers in such programs offer personal witness to the meaning of Christian service by their dedicated effort to impart Christian truth and values to the young. This must be carried further, however, by giving the programs themselves an orientation to service of both the parish community and the community outside the parish. For service is itself an efficacious means of teaching doctrine, and thus these programs should include opportunities for service as part of the educational experience they seek to provide the young. Today, when many people have more leisure time than in the past, it is appropriate that a parish increasingly turn its attention to the task of preparing its members, young and old, for service within and beyond the Christian community.

90. In many places pastoral programs of religious education are now demonstrating vitality and effectiveness in achieving the threefold purpose of Christian education, especially in parishes which are true communities of faith. Their success deserves recognition, praise and imitation. The achievements of some innovative and imaginative programs for high school students offer a bright ray of hope in a particularly difficult area. Some parishes have made substantial progress in becoming centers for the religious education of all parishioners, young and old. In short, there now exist across the nation a variety of successful models which should be studied and translated into similar efforts elsewhere.

Problems and Policies

91. Despite their achievements and bright hopes, such programs face serious problems which should concern the entire Catholic community. These programs do not reach large numbers of Catholic young people not in Catholic schools. Many of them may simply not be accessible or receptive to any systematic, organized program of religious education now available to the Church. There are many reasons for this: parental indifference; problems of scheduling; pressures of time; demands on and appeals to their loyalty by

other communities of which they are members; the inadequacy of some religious education programs, an inadequacy often due to insufficient financing and reliance on personnel who have not had proper training and support. But practical difficulties, frustrations and disappointments accentuate the need for the Catholic community to increase its effort in this crucial area. As a matter of policy, religious education programs for Catholic students who attend public and other non-Catholic schools should receive high priority everywhere, a priority expressed in adequate budgets and increased service from professional religious educators. In this light we offer the following pastoral guidelines.

Guidelines for the Future

92. The essential unity of the educational ministry should be reflected in its programmatic expressions. The educational mission of the Church is one. It takes form in many institutions, programs and activities which, different as they are, all derive inspiration, rationale and purpose from the same source: the one educational mission of the Church which is essentially a continuation in our times of the mission of Jesus Christ. Far from competing with one another for money, personnel, students, etc., they must function together harmoniously and efficiently, complementing and supplementing one another in order to achieve jointly the fullest possible realization of the threefold aim of Christian education: teaching doctrine, building community, and serving others.

93. Since religious education programs for Catholic students who do not attend Catholic schools are an essential part of the Church's total educational ministry, their staff and students should be integrated fully into the unified educational ministry of the local Christian community. In parishes this calls for efforts to draw together these programs and the Catholic schools in closer working relationships: for example, by including "CCD" students in school and parish organizations and activities to the greatest extent possible, and, in parishes which have no schools, by doing the same for students who attend Catholic schools outside the parish. The objective—integration of all pastoral and educational programs into a unified whole whose components complement and assist one another—should be a major concern of parish leadership. In this regard, consideration should be given to common funding of all catechetical education in a parish for both the school and out-of-school programs.

94. Parishes which have Catholic schools should explore new ways of placing them more directly at the service of the entire parish community. The school should be a focal point for many educational efforts on behalf of children, young people, and adults. Where there is no parish school a parish educational center should serve the same function of drawing together programs and people.

95. Where a parish school must be closed, there should be careful advance planning to provide funds and personnel for such a center.

96. Parishes without parochial schools must not limit their programs to the bare essentials of religious instruction. Their children and young people deserve Catholic education in as full a sense as possible. This suggests that traditional programs be enriched with a variety of informal experiences to help pupils discover the meaning of Christian community life and its potential for service to others. New study and effort are needed to utilize communications media and modern technology in religious education. In areas where

parishes and missions confront the problems of isolation and limited resources, regional catechetical centers, either drawing together students from a broad geographical area or sending out teams of skilled catechists into the parishes of the region, may help meet the need for high quality, comprehensive religious education. In short, far from being an excuse for an inferior program, the absence of a parochial school simply challenges a parish, either alone or in cooperation with other parishes, to expand its efforts to give its children and young people as broad a Catholic educational experience as it possibly can.

97. The effectiveness of voluntary service in religious education programs must be strengthened. Parish leadership should give recognition and moral support to the volunteers engaged in this work, but, more than that, it should provide adequately financed opportunities for their professional preparation and in-service training. Furthermore, these programs, while retaining their distinctive voluntarism, must at the same time be reinforced by the increased use of well trained, adequately paid professionals in key positions. Organizations which serve the professional needs of personnel working in this field should receive official recognition and encouragement.

98. Careful attention should be given to providing religious education for members of minority groups and to involving them in the mainstream of the catechetical effort.

99. The right of the handicapped to receive religious education adapted to their special needs also challenges the ingenuity and commitment of the Catholic community.

100. Planning is essential to create a unified system of religious education accessible and attractive to all the People of God. We must continue to explore new ways of extending the educational ministry to every Catholic child and young person. In doing so, we must be open to the possibility of new forms and structures for all Catholic education in the years ahead. With regard to the "tasks and responsibilities" of catechesis, "it is not enough to rest content with the distribution of forces already existing; it is also necessary that effort on the part of all Christians be more and more stimulated and promoted. Care must be taken to make the Christian community every day conscious of its duty" (*General Catechetical Directory*, 107). A comprehensive vision of the Christian ministry in education, and integrated structures to embody it, seem now to offer the best hope for achieving the greatest success with the largest number of Catholic children and young people, both those who attend Catholic schools and those who do not.

Catholic Schools

101. Of the educational programs available to the Catholic community, Catholic schools afford the fullest and best opportunity to realize the threefold purpose of Christian education among children and young people. Schools naturally enjoy educational advantages which other programs either cannot offer or can offer only with great difficulty. A school has a greater claim on the time and loyalty of the student and his family. It makes more accessible to students participation in the liturgy and the sacraments, which are powerful forces for the development of personal sanctity and for the building of community. It provides a more favorable pedagogical and psychological environment for teaching Christian faith. With the Second Vatican Council we affirm our conviction that the Catholic school "retains its immense importance in the circumstances of our times" and we recall the duty of Catholic parents "to

entrust their children to Catholic schools, when and where this is possible, to support such schools to the extent of their ability, and to work along with them for the welfare of their children" (*Christian Education*, 8).

Doctrine, Community, Service

102. Christian education is intended to "make men's faith become living, conscious, and active, through the light of instruction" (*The Bishops' Office in the Church*, 14). The Catholic school is the unique setting within which this ideal can be realized in the lives of Catholic children and young people.

103. Only in such a school can they experience learning and living fully integrated in the light of faith. The Catholic school "strives to relate all human culture eventually to the news of salvation, so that the life of faith will illumine the knowledge which students gradually gain of the world, of life, and of mankind" (*Christian Education*, 8). Here, therefore, students are instructed in human knowledge and skills, valued indeed for their own worth but seen simultaneously as deriving their most profound significance from God's plan for His creation. Here, too instruction in religious truth and values is an integral part of the school program. It is not one more subject alongside the rest, but instead it is perceived and functions as the underlying reality in which the student's experiences of learning and living achieve their coherence and their deepest meaning.

104. This integration of religious truth and values with the rest of life is brought about in the Catholic school not only by its unique curriculum but, more important, by the presence of teachers who express an integrated approach to learning and living in their private and professional lives. It is further reinforced by free interaction among the students themselves within their own community of youth.

105. This integration of religious truth and values with life distinguishes the Catholic school from other schools. This is a matter of crucial importance today in view of contemporary trends and pressures to compartmentalize life and learning and to isolate the religious dimension of existence from other areas of human life. A Catholic for whom religious commitment is the central, integrative reality of his life will find in the Catholic school a perception and valuation of the role of religion which matches his own.

106. More than any other program of education sponsored by the Church, the Catholic school has the opportunity and obligation to be unique, contemporary, and oriented to Christian service: unique because it is distinguished by its commitment to the threefold purpose of Christian education and by its total design and operation which foster the integration of religion with the rest of learning and living; contemporary because it enables students to address with Christian insight the multiple problems which face individuals and society today; oriented to Christian service because it helps students acquire skills, virtues, and habits of heart and mind required for effective service to others. All those involved in a Catholic school—parents, pastors, teachers, administrators, and students—must earnestly desire to make it a community of faith which is indeed "living, conscious, and active."

107. The program of studies in a Catholic school reflects the importance which the school and sponsoring community attach to Christian formation. Basic to this task, as we have said earlier, is instruction which is authentic in doctrine and contemporary in presentation. Failure on either side renders the instruction ineffective and can in fact impede the growth of living faith in the child. Thus the proper use of new catechetical methods designed with these objectives in view is to be applauded, as are many new programs for the professional development of religion teachers. They can contribute to making Catholic schools true communities of faith in which the formational efforts of Catholic families are complemented, reinforced and extended. Within such communities teachers and pupils experience together what it means to live a life of prayer, personal responsibility and freedom reflective of Gospel values. Their fellowship helps them grow in their commitment to service of God, one another, the Church, and the general community.

108. Building and living community must be prime, explicit goals of the contemporary Catholic school. Community is an especially critical need today largely because natural communities of the past have been weakened by many influences. Pressures on the family, the basic unit of society, have already been noted. Urbanization and suburbanization have radically changed the concept of neighborhood community.

109. Racial and ethnic tensions and other conflicts reflect an absence of local and national community. War and the exploitation of poor nations by the rich dramatize the same tragic lack of community on the international level. Today's Catholic school must respond to these challenges by developing in its students a commitment to community and to the social skills and virtues needed to achieve it. Participation together in the liturgy and in paraliturgical activities and spiritual exercises can effectively foster community among students and faculty. Since the Gospel spirit is one of peace, brotherhood, love, patience and respect for others, a school rooted in these principles ought to explore ways to deepen its students' concern for and skill in peacemaking and the achievement of justice. Here young people can learn together of human needs, whether in the parish, the neighborhood, the local civic community, or the world, and begin to respond to the obligation of Christian service through joint action.

110. At the level of institutional commitment, too, service of the public interest is a notable quality of Catholic and other nonpublic schools in America. "Private education has played and is playing a significant and valuable role in raising national levels of knowledge, competence and experience" (Justice Byron White in *Board of Education v. Allen* [392 U.S. 236]). Countless men and women have been better able to contribute to the political, social and economic life of the nation as a result of their education in nonpublic schools. This service has been extended not only to those already in the mainstream of social life, but also to many suffering special disadvantages, including in a notable way the physically and mentally handicapped.

111. Other benefits flow from the private educational effort into the lifeblood of the nation. These schools supply a diversity which the American educational system would otherwise lack. They provide desirable competition for the public schools, not as antagonists, but as partners in the total American educational enterprise. In a unique way they serve the community by keeping viable the right to freedom of choice under law among educational alternatives. Most important, the commitment of Catholic schools to Christian values and the Christian moral code renders a profound service to society which depends on spiritual values and good moral conduct for its very survival.

The Crisis of Catholic Schools

112. It will perhaps be objected that much of what has been said up to now paints an ideal picture of the Catholic school and its purposes. Truly it is an ideal, but little is achieved without ideals to strive for. Furthermore, Catholic schools have realized and continue to realize this ideal more successfully than is some times acknowledged today.

113. Of the Catholic school in America we say humbly, and with gratitude for the grace of God manifested in it, that it has nurtured the faith of Jesus Christ in millions of men and women who have lived vibrantly Christian lives and have given themselves generously in service to others. Scarcely a man or woman in the Church in America today has not benefited either directly or indirectly from the sacrifices of his fellow Christians in creating the Catholic school system. A full measure of gratitude is due to the dedicated teachers who have expressed their Christian vocation through the apostolate of Catholic education. All deserve the thanks of the Catholic community, especially the religious women whose resourceful leadership has been at the heart of the Catholic school effort in the United States throughout its history.

114. Today this school system is shrinking visibly. The reasons are many and include complex sociological, demographic and psychological factors. Some believe there has been an excessive effort in formal education and too much concentration on schools at the expense of other educational programs. Some are convinced that other forms of Christian service take unequivocal priority over service rendered in the classroom. Some feel American Catholics no longer have the material resources to support so ambitious an educational enterprise.

115. Financial problems have contributed significantly to the present crisis. Burdened by the spiraling costs of both public and nonpublic education, those who support nonpublic schools have placed their cause before their fellow Americans. While legislators have responded in many instances, courts have often rejected laws favorable to nonpublic education, sometimes on grounds which many find extremely difficult to understand or accept.

116. The chief obstacle to meaningful public aid to nonpublic elementary and secondary schools continues to be the United States Supreme Court's interpretation of the First and Fourteenth Amendments. The Court, however, has decided only the cases brought before it; it has not rendered judgment on every conceivable plan. To some it appears that the Court has raised an impenetrable barrier between government and church-sponsored schools; but to others, who are knowledgeable about its jurisprudence and procedures, it appears that the Court, having acknowledged that it is walking a tightrope between the First Amendment's free exercise and establishment clauses, may eventually see a way to give realistic support to parents' freedom to choose a nonpublic school.

117. The words of Pope Pius XI, written some 40 years ago in the encyclical on Christian education, afford timely encouragement to those seeking justice for Catholic schools. "Catholics will never feel, whatever may have been the sacrifices already made, that they have done enough, for the support and defense of their schools and for the securing of laws that will do them justice" (*Christian Education of Youth*).

118. We are well aware of the problems which now face the Catholic school system in the United States. We also wish our position to be clear. For our part, as bishops, we reaffirm our conviction that Catholic schools which realize the threefold purpose of Christian education—to teach doctrine, to build community, and to serve—are the most effective means available to the Church for the education of children and young people who thus may "grow into manhood according to the mature measure of Christ" (*Christian Education*, 2; cf. Ephesians 4:13). We call upon all members of the Catholic community to do everything in their power to maintain and strengthen Catholic schools which embrace the threefold purpose of Christian education.

Action Needed Now

119. Specific steps can and should be taken now by concerned parents, educators, pastors and others to ensure the continuance and improvement of Catholic schools (Cf. for example, *Nonpublic Schools and the Public Good*, Final Report: The President's Panel on Nonpublic Education).

120. These will include such things as stating clearly and compellingly the distinctive goals of the Catholic school; increasing associations with other nonpublic and public schools; practicing fiscal, professional, academic and civic accountability; conducting vigorous programs of student recruitment; joining with other nonpublic schools in public relations efforts; exercising firm control over operating costs and practicing greater efficiency in the use of facilities and personnel; intensifying efforts to increase income from private sources, including those which have generally gone untapped up to now; entering into partnership with institutions of higher learning; undertaking school consolidations at the elementary and secondary levels where circumstances make this educationally desirable; and participating fully in the search for solutions to the racial crisis in American education.

121. The unfinished business on the agenda of Catholic schools, like many other schools, also includes the task of providing quality education for the poor and disadvantaged of our nation. Generous, sustained sacrifice is demanded of those whom God has favored in order to make available educational programs which meet the need of the poor to be self-determining, free persons in all areas of individual and social life. Recognition of past failures should not obscure the fact that the Church in many places does provide a wide variety of services for the poor, including schools of high quality, often at the cost of heroic sacrifice and with encouraging success. What is now being accomplished, however, should serve only as a spur to renewed commitment and continued effort in this area so crucial to the good of society and so central to the mission of the Church.

122. If the Catholic community is convinced of the values and advantages of Catholic schools, it must and will act now to adopt such measures and face such challenges as these. In particular all those involved in the Catholic school effort should avoid a defeatist attitude which would regard present problems as a prelude to disaster. Difficult as they may be, they are not insoluble, given the will and the intelligence to seek and adopt solutions.

Catholic Schools Called to Reorganization

123. Like other schools in our nation, Catholic schools are called to a renewal of purpose, and some to reorganization. The goals appropriate to today's Catholic educational effort, and thus to today's Catholic schools, are in some ways more challenging than in the past, including as they do the need to prepare young men and women to be witnesses to faith during an era of instability and at the same time to act as agents of creative institutional change for which adequate models hardly exist. While the Christian purpose of the Catholic school must always be clearly evident, no one form is prescribed for it.

124. The search for new forms of schooling should therefore continue. Some may bear little resemblance to schooling as we have known it: the parish education center; the family education center; the school without walls, drawing extensively on community resources; the counseling center; etc. We do not mention these new forms to canonize what some may regard as educational fads or to presume a kind of knowledge we do not possess. The point is that one must be open to the possibility that the school of the future, including the Catholic school, will in many ways be very different from the school of the past. Consideration should also be given to the relationship of parish and school where circumstances suggest that the traditional parish may no longer provide the best framework for formal schooling.

125. New forms require pilot programs along with study and evaluation. Catholic schools have the capacity and freedom to experiment. Administrators and teachers should therefore cooperate with parents in designing experimental models or pilot programs to improve educational standards and results.

126. Reorganization may also involve new models of sponsorship and collaboration. Various forms of cooperation with public schools should be explored. In supporting a school system which provides an alternative to the system sponsored by the state, the Catholic community does not wish to ignore or be isolated from public schools. On all levels of education, and particularly on a system-wide basis, Catholic educators should seek actively to cooperate with their public school counterparts and their colleagues in other nonpublic schools, sharing ideas, plans, personnel, technology, and other resources where mutually feasible and beneficial. The possibility of institutional cooperation with other Christian groups in the field of education should be explored. Approached with candor and intelligence, cooperative planning need not threaten the identity or independence of any school system and can benefit all.

Youth Ministry

127. Youth ministry today faces challenges created by the problems and needs of youth in our society. Mirroring to a great extent the alienation and uncertainty of adults, many young people in this country, as well as in other nations of the world, feel estranged both from traditional values and from an adult society whose actions often belie its own professed commitment to these values. These young people grope for the deeper meaning of life and for roles consonant with their sense of human dignity. The Christian community should be anxious to understand the causes of their uncertainty and eager to respond to what is often an unvoiced cry for help.

128. Other young people, more positively oriented toward society, exhibit encouraging energy and optimism. But even many of them feel unrest and apathy as a result of a socially imposed prolonged adolescence during which they are impeded in their growth to adulthood and frustrated in their efforts to act as responsible persons.

129. Disenchantment with organized religion is often part of the alienation of the young today. This seems in many instances not to be disenchantment with God or with the spiritual dimension of life but with some institutional forms and functions. Even as society grows more secularistic, many young people, reflecting genuine religious concern, express growing interest in Jesus Christ. Their quest for authentic values by which to live has urgency and commendable authenticity.

130. Christians should be sensitive and discerning in their approach to the young, who through their Baptism and Confirmation have been incorporated into full membership in the Christian community. This community does have solutions to many of the questions which trouble today's youth, but it cannot realistically expect young people to accept them unless it, for its part, is willing to listen to their problems. Thus it must strive not only to teach the young but to learn from them and to see its own institutions through their eyes and to make prudent changes which this insight may suggest.

131. There are thus three distinct tasks for the ministry to youth: to enable young people to take part in the Church's mission to the world in ways appropriate to their age and responsive to their interests; to give a specific dimension—education in service—to religious education; and to interpret young people, their problems and their concerns to the Christian and general communities.

132. Youth have a right and duty to be active participants in the work of the Church in the world. Obviously, however, they face certain obstacles because they are young and lack experience, organizational skills, and other necessary abilities. Adults engaged in youth ministry therefore should function mainly as guides and helpers by giving young people direction and support.

133. Those engaged in youth ministry are by that fact involved in religious education. Their efforts complement the formal religious education carried on in Catholic schools and out-of-school programs. They bring a specific focus to the work of religious education, namely, education for mission. This is done through programs which provide young people with opportunity to engage in action projects exemplifying what it means to be a Christian in the world today. Such projects should be designed and conducted in a way that helps youth see their participation as a true expression of Christian concern and not simply as a natural response to human needs.

134. The youth ministry should also provide for another educational need of the young, education in community. As maturing Christians, young people need to experience a wide variety of communities. They particularly need the experience of being in a community which brings together young people from both Catholic and public schools. Youth programs under Church sponsorship should base their concept of "community" upon the Gospel values proclaimed by Jesus Christ.

135. Among the major responsibilities of a diocesan youth director and others engaged in youth ministry is that of interpreting youth and advocating their legitimate causes to the Christian community and to other communities to which the young belong. Their informal and immediate contact with the young often gives those engaged in youth work a deep insight into the needs and concerns of youth. It is appropriate that they share these concerns with other adults and plead youth's cause with them.

136. Finally, all those involved in Catholic youth work should recognize the value of what is called peer group ministry. Young people themselves "must become the first and immediate apostles to youth exercising their apostolate among themselves and through themselves" (*Apostolate of the Laity*, 12). Young people should be welcomed as co-workers in this genuinely prophetic form of education, and programs which develop their leadership talents should have a central place in the youth ministry.

IV.
Planning the Educational Mission

137. This pastoral message has stressed the need of many different educational programs and institutions and insisted that each is an important part of the total educational ministry. This may seem of questionable value at a time when the material resources available to the Church for education are limited and, perhaps, diminishing. But only if the Catholic community of our nation is fully aware of and committed to various elements of the educational ministry is it likely to provide the resources which are needed. The cooperation of all is vital if the vision sketched here is to be a reality now or in the future.

138. While it is difficult to define and plan the Church's educational mission in this period of rapid institutional change, the effort must continue. Educational needs must be clearly identified; goals and objectives must be established which are simultaneously realistic and creative; programs consistent with these needs and objectives must be designed carefully, conducted efficiently and evaluated honestly.

139. Under the leadership of the Ordinary and his priests, planning and implementing the educational mission of the Church must involve the entire Catholic community. Representative structures and processes should be the normative means by which the community, particularly Catholic parents, addresses fundamental questions about educational needs, objectives, programs and resources. Such structures and processes, already operating in many dioceses and parishes in the United States, should become universal.

140. Vatican Council II urged the establishment of agencies by which the laity can "express their opinion of things which concern the good of the Church" (*Constitution on the Church*, 37). One such agency, long a part of the American experience and in recent years increasingly widespread in Catholic education, is the representative board of education, which, acting on behalf of the community it serves, seeks patiently and conscientiously to direct the entire range of educational institutions and programs within the educational ministry.

141. On the diocesan level, the educational mission can best be coordinated by a single board of education concerned with the needs of the entire local church. Many such boards have already been established and are now rendering important service to the Church and education. They work best when they are broadly representative of all the people of the diocese, laity, priests and religious. Membership should be open to people of many points of view, including those who may perceive needs and advocate approaches different from those expressed in this pastoral.

142. Participatory approaches to decision making are desirable not only in regard to educational policy but in the entire area of pastoral need. Although the Ordinary has ultimate responsibility for coordinating pastoral programs in the diocese, a significant role in setting priorities can be played by the diocesan pastoral council, itself a structure

strongly recommended by Vatican II (*The Bishops' Pastoral Office in the Church*, 27).

143. Much progress has already been made in educational planning by the Church in the United States. Many dioceses and institutions, for example, have sponsored valuable educational research carried out by professional agencies. Sharing the results of these studies through a national clearinghouse would make it easier to exchange data, provide guidance for new studies, help avoid duplication, and assist planning.

An Invitation to Cooperation

144. The planning and collaboration invited here will only come about through the active cooperation of all involved in the educational apostolate. We especially seek the collaboration of the teachers—priests, religious, and laity—who serve in Catholic schools and other educational programs. If the threefold purpose of Christian education is to be realized, it must be through their commitment to give instruction to their students, to build community among them, and to serve them. Furthermore, teachers bring insights and experience to planning the total educational mission of the Church. We invite and urge their creative contribution to the effort of the entire community to meet the current challenges.

145. The involvement of religious men and women in educational ministry has long provided example and support to the Christian community. They are publicly identified as persons committed to giving witness to Gospel values, notably the value of community. The stability which religious communities have brought to the apostolate has made it possible to continue many schools and programs which could hardly have survived otherwise. Their witness, always valuable, is needed more than ever today. The entire Church will be enriched by authentic renewal of religious communities. All Catholics look forward to their continued presence as a vital force in the total teaching mission of the Church.

146. The number of religious teachers, upon whom Catholic education has historically depended, is declining at present. The entire Catholic community should seek to understand the causes of this phenomenon and should adopt appropriate measures in an attempt to reverse the trend. Clarification of the ecclesial role of women could be a factor in the solution of the much deplored vocations crisis among religious communities of women.

147. A continuing shortage of religious teachers now is one of those signs of the times which Catholics must confront realistically in carrying on the educational ministry. It emphasizes the fact that reliance on lay persons in the work of Catholic education will not only continue in the years ahead but will certainly increase. This is not to suggest, however, that the presence of lay teachers and administrators in Catholic schools and other educational programs is merely a stopgap. They are full partners in the Catholic educational enterprise, and the dramatic increase of their numbers and influence in recent years is welcome and desirable in itself. As with religious, so with lay teachers and administrators, the Catholic community invites not only their continued service but also their increased participation in planning and decision making and their continued emergence in leadership roles.

148. It is also imperative that the Catholic community collaborate with all Americans committed to educational freedom. The right of parents to exercise genuine freedom of choice in education in ways consistent with the principles of justice and equality must be recognized and made operative. In this connection one must hope that our nation will arrive at a satisfactory accommodation on the role of religion in public education, one which respects the rights and legitimate interests of all parents and students.

149. While steps must be taken to ensure legitimate freedom of choice in education for all, special attention should be given to extending it to those in our country who suffer most from educational disadvantage. Efforts at educational self-determination already undertaken by some members of such groups are truly a significant manifestation of man's struggle to be free, akin to the Catholic community's historic effort to be free to direct its educational destiny. Incompatible with such freedom is a philosophy which would demand, in effect, that all educational efforts be subsumed in one educational system. In an area so intimately related to fundamental human needs and rights as is education, coercive theory or practice which results in the elimination of viable educational alternatives is intolerable, however it may be rationalized.

150. The development of Catholic education in this country up to now reflects the religious freedom which Catholics enjoy in the United States. For its part the Catholic community has a long tradition of cooperating with public authority in promoting civic interests in many fields including education. Thus it is important that persons in government and public service, who influence and regulate the educational activities of the state, understand our convictions about what church-sponsored, faith-inspired education contributes to the general good of the nation.

V.
A Ministry of Hope

151. This pastoral document is not the final word on Christian education. In a sense the final word has already been spoken by Jesus Christ whose mission the Christian community continues today in many ways, including the educational ministry. In another sense the final word will never be spoken; it is the task of each generation of Christians to assess their own times and carry on the mission of Christ by means suited to the needs and opportunities they perceive.

152. The educational mission is not exhausted by any one program or institution. By their complementary functions and cooperative activities all programs and institutions contribute to the present realization of the Church's educational mission. All should remain open to new forms, new programs, new methods which give promise of fuller realization of this mission in the future.

153. The educational mission is not directed to any single group within the Christian community or mankind. All have a role to play; all should have a voice in planning and directing.

154. Like the mission and message of Jesus Christ, the Church's educational mission is universal—for all men, at all times, in all places. In our world and in our nation, the mission of Christian education is of critical importance. The truth of Jesus Christ must be taught; the love of Jesus Christ must be extended to persons who seek and suffer.

155. The Christian community has every reason for hope in confronting the challenge of educational ministry today. To all our efforts we join prayer for God's help, and for the intercession of Mary, the Mother of Jesus. We face problems; so did those who came before us, and so will those who follow. But as Christians we are confident of ultimate success, trusting not in ourselves, but in Jesus Christ, who is at once the inspiration, the content, and the goal of Christian education: "the way, and the truth, and the life."

Teach Them:
Statement on Catholic Schools

UNITED STATES CATHOLIC CONFERENCE
May 6, 1976

I. Jesus commanded His disciples to "go and teach all nations." From a tiny upper room, by the Spirit, He sent them. With fire in their hearts He sent them. To every nation and age He sent them. From those early apostolic days the flame has been passed. In the 200 years of our own nation's history we can point with pride to St. Elizabeth Seton, Blessed John Neumann, to countless families who by their sense of educational mission answered the same call. The disciples of times past did not take Jesus' command lightly, even though they went with light hearts and willing hands into His vineyard the world. In this time and place, we believe no other answer, now or at any future moment, is acceptable for a people who bear within them that same faith. The only worthy response is a wholehearted "yes" to the Lord's command to "go and teach."

As faithful servants responding to His command, we seek to meet the needs of all who hear Jesus' message or may do so. Our 1972 pastoral, *To Teach as Jesus Did*, declared our support for Catholic education in its totality: schools, parish catechetical programs, campus ministry, young adult education, family life education, adult education. That commitment stands. In this statement we are specifically concerned with the Church's educational ministry to children and young people, especially as it is expressed in Catholic schools.

A total of 8.6 million Catholic youth in this country are now enrolled in formal religious education programs, 3.5 million in Catholic schools and 5.1 million in parish catechetical programs. But, as a report published earlier this year shows, 6.6 million (3.4 at the elementary and 3.2 at the secondary level), more than twice the number a decade ago, now are not enrolled in formal religious education programs. In our opinion this is as much a pastoral problem as an educational one. Its solution will require additional data, thorough research and analysis, responsible decisions and an appropriate program of action.

In the meantime, it is obvious that all persons with a responsibility for the Church's educational ministry—to one degree or another that means all members of the Catholic community—should reach out to these 6.6 million. This suggests some immediate steps: e.g., diocesan and parish censuses; more adult, parent and family education; vigorous recruitment for Catholic schools and parish catechetical programs; more effective use of Catholic and other communications media for evangelization and religious education; completion of the National Catechetical Directory; sensitive dialogue with persons who are critical of some methods of religious education; zealous contact with parents who have abandoned much of the active practice of their faith. Indeed, alienation and lack of interest among some parents may well be reasons why a substantial number of the 6.6 million children and youth are not receiving formal religious education. Coping adequately with this problem will require much time and effort.

Our immediate and continuing concern is to provide the best possible education for children and young people in and out of Catholic schools. With respect to parish catechetical programs, many of the innovations and improvements of recent years deserve to be recognized and put more widely into effect.

As we have said, however, our focus here is primarily upon the schools. We wish to declare our belief in their future, to offer renewed encouragement to all our collaborators in the school apostolate, to call attention to signs of progress and hope, to point to new areas for investigation and action, and to do all this in a spirit of realistic hopefulness.

The remarkably positive response which has greeted *To Teach as Jesus Did* is especially heartening. Actions taken in light of its vision have done much to strengthen the Church's educational ministry. In this response we have discerned the providential working of the Spirit. The pastoral letter continues to afford many reasons for encouragement and confidence.

II. Four years ago we reaffirmed our commitment to Catholic schools; we now do so again. For we hold that "Catholic schools which realize the threefold purpose of Christian education, to teach doctrine, to build community and to serve, are the most effective means available to the Church for the education of children and young people."[1]

The integration of religious truth and values with the rest of life, which is possible in these schools, distinguishes them from others. Here the Catholic for whom religious commitment is a matter of central importance finds an appreciation of religion which parallels his or her own. The integration is expressed above all in the lives of the teachers in Catholic schools whose daily witness to the meaning of mature faith and Christian living has a profound impact upon the education and formation of their pupils. On behalf of the entire Church we affirm our debt to these dedicated ministers of education, sisters, brothers, priests and lay people, who teach by what they are.

Our support of Catholic schools is matched by the support of millions of others, those who teach in them, who send their children to them, and who support them morally and financially. The present task seems to be less to win support for the schools than to mobilize the support which already exists.

Why do we and so many others continue to support Catholic schools in the face of many obstacles and burdens, problems not substantially different from those we outlined in our pastoral four years ago? The reasons are compelling. Generally these schools are notably successful educational institutions which offer not only high quality academic programs but also instruction and formation in the beliefs, values and traditions of Catholic Christianity. They are significantly effective in preparing students for life in today's Church and society. They instill in children and young people indispensable discipline of mind and heart. They have a highly positive impact on adult religious behavior.[2]

Another benefit of Catholic schools deserves mention. They can be a focal point for dedication, energy and generosity of many different members of the Catholic community. This concerted focus, however, must not preclude an active participation in other forms of educational and ecclesial ministry. Catholic schools therefore have a rich potential for strengthening the bonds which unite a community.

In a significant way Catholic schools bear witness to the importance of religion in our local civic communities and in our society as a whole. When a sizeable segment of the American people undertakes to build and operate a great system of schools at considerable sacrifice, serious citizens are thereby encouraged to reflect upon the importance of religion in human life. Without Catholic and other church-related schools, spiritual values would find far less support in American society.

It is gratifying and encouraging that *To Teach as Jesus Did* has helped strengthen the Catholic school apostolate. Evidence of this comes from many sources, including the National Catholic Educational Association and many religious communities, which have themselves played a laudable role in "giving form to the vision" of educational ministry embodied in the pastoral. Among the beneficial results arising, at least in part, from that effort are the following.

The identification of Catholic schools as institutions which express the threefold purpose of Catholic education, stated in the Pastoral as to teach, build community and serve, has become more clear. Concrete priorities of the schools consistent with this threefold purpose have been brought into sharper focus.[3]

Programs for the formation of teachers have been strengthened. There has been increased recognition that all share in the educational ministry, not just those specifically assigned to "teach religion."[4]

The reciprocal relationship of the Catholic school and the community it serves has been recognized and fostered. New ways have been sought and put into effect by which the school can be of even greater service to the community.

Increased attention has been given to the need for a total, integrated approach to Catholic education involving schools and other educational programs. Competition and duplication have been reduced; collaboration and coordination have been increased. Significant in these encouraging developments has been the role played by parish boards of education and parish councils which have enabled the Catholic community in an orderly fashion to identify and respond to the educational needs of the total community. More

and more, schools are being recognized and used as resource centers for total parish programs of education.

Positive changes in the instructional program have been carried forward, including greater emphasis on personalized learning which meets the unique needs and capabilities of individual students. Growing attention has been given to education for justice and for authentic human liberation.

Educational planning and the practice of accountability have been encouraged. At the same time a new thrust has emerged in educational administration, emphasizing not only technical skills but the role of the administrator as one who fosters community within both schools and school systems.

Appreciation has increased for the fact that the Catholic school is not simply an institution which offers academic instruction of high quality, but, even more important, is an effective vehicle of total Christian formation. The tendency to emphasize one aspect at the expense of the other has given way to recognition that both are necessary and possible, and indeed are being accomplished in Catholic schools.

In short, much that has happened in the past four years testifies to the fact that the schools not only remain an important part of the Catholic Church in the United States but continue to grow in effectiveness as that is determined by both educational and religious measures. This favorable judgment is strongly reinforced by a recently published report on educational research by the National Opinion Research Center showing that Catholic schools have a significant positive impact on those who attend them and that the Catholic public is highly supportive of them.[5] In view of all this, our commitment to the schools is clear and undiminished.

The Second Vatican Council asked the Church "to spare no sacrifice" for Catholic schools which care "for the poor, for those who are without the help and affection of family, and those who do not have the faith."[6] In many places in the United States the Church's response has been an extremely large human and economic investment in schools whose pupils are, in the main, economically disadvantaged children residing in the poverty areas of large cities. The funding of this large investment has come from the self-sacrifice of the children's parents, support of fellow parishioners and the generosity of contributors to diocesan funds for the subsidy of schools which lack adequate parish support for all educational expenses. This action has been notably productive in the black community where the Catholic school "has been and remains the strongest point of contact for many black people with the Catholic Church....The Catholic school is a constant witness to the talented and creative potential which black youth possess and which needs only opportunity and educational nurturing."[7] Substantially the same may be said of Catholic schools which serve the unique needs of Hispanic and native American children from low income families.

A steadily increasing number of economically poor parents are making heroic personal sacrifices to raise funds for the continuation of their Catholic schools. These parents are convinced that Catholic school education affords their children a realistic and hopeful opportunity "to break out of the hellish cycle of poverty,"[8] and to move into the mainstream of our nation's good living. These schools are therefore serving a critical human need within the context of a complete education which includes religious instruction and guidance.

The challenge confronting the total Catholic community is to approximate the self-sacrifice of poverty belt parents by increasing its contributions to interparochial and diocesan funds for the ongoing and expanded support of schools in need of annual subsidy.

III. To sustain this momentum we endorse developments and trends favorable to the continuation of strong and effective Catholic schools. In this connection we turn now to the challenges and opportunities confronting specific groups involved in educational ministry.

Parents

Parental confidence in Catholic schools, a quiet but eloquent witness reinforced by great personal sacrifice, produces in others an awareness of the importance of Catholic education's ideals and values. This confidence also encourages teachers to be available and open to parents who seek to be meaningfully involved in their children's schooling.

Parent-teacher conferences, home and school associations, lay boards and committees, and teacher-aide programs are making progress because many thoughtful parents participate faithfully in these cooperative efforts to enrich their children's education. The benefits of home and school partnership are so evident that all parents should be made aware of their duty to be full partners with the school. The school administrator who does not recognize the importance of this cooperation may be depriving pupils of one of the unique advantages of Catholic schooling. In this cooperation there is a kind of reciprocal accountability; of school to parent and parent to school. Today's Catholic school is more than a means for safeguarding faith and virtue; it is a center in which parents and teachers, guided by the Holy Spirit, collaborate in giving children a complete Catholic education.

Teachers

The new awareness that all members of the faculty, at least by their example, are an integral part of the process of religious education has brought with it a more conscientious approach to the selecting of teachers and the professional development of staff. Teachers' life style and character are as important as their professional credentials. We commend this trend and urge the development of appropriate ceremonies by which the Church can publicly express its appreciation for their role in the Church's educational ministry.

Teacher-initiated instructional programs are implementing the principles contained in the pastoral. Educational approaches emphasizing doctrine, community and service as central concepts have helped teachers implement methodologies which are responsive to the individual needs of students. Reciprocally the thrust toward personalized learning with emphasis on the total educational environment makes clear that the atmosphere and relationships in the school are as much the focus of the Catholic school as is the formal religious education class. In other wider applications numerous faculties have used the pastoral in self studies that are having profound, positive effects on the daily experiences of the school.

Administrators

In the area of school administration we note with great satisfaction the growing awareness and acceptance of the twin concepts of accountability and evaluation. This represents a recognition of the school's obligation to serve and be accountable to the Catholic community in relation to the three-fold ideal set forth in the pastoral.

We urge administrators to exercise their gifts of educational leadership by promoting structures and cooperative procedures which will render such accountability and evaluation meaningful and useful to all in the Catholic educational community—parents, teachers and the Catholic community generally. They should exercise their responsibility particularly with reference to the selection, motivation and development of teaching personnel, keeping ever in mind the apostolic goals and character of the Catholic school.

Pastors and the Community

The leadership role of pastors and their associates is a significant factor in the Catholic school apostolate. Through their words, their presence and their support in so many ways they supply a needed leadership to those who look to such commitment as a sign of the importance of their own sacrifices.

Recognition of the pastor's increased importance as a facilitator of community among the professional educational staff of the parish is a positive development. The members of such a total educational team view one another as colleagues in a common work carried on through a variety of approaches.

Pastoral leadership can likewise foster in the Catholic community the realization that Catholic schools in parishes and dioceses can be immense spiritual assets which benefit all and give witness to the faith of the entire community. Such schools, like all other aspects of the educational ministry, deserve the support of all members of the Catholic community because, directly or indirectly, they serve all. Not to support such schools merely because they do not enroll all the children of the community would, in our opinion, reflect an inaccurate and damaging view of the Church's educational mission.

Community support is manifested also by the presence of the larger community as volunteer staff for the parish educational program and by the witness to that program which these persons give in their contacts with friends and neighbors.

United States Catholic Conference

We ask the Committee on Education and the Department of Education to consider the following steps.

1. Careful study of recent research on Catholic schools, especially as it relates to their progress toward the goals set forth

in *To Teach as Jesus Did*. In a special way there is a need for careful identification of the facts, both quantitative and qualitative, concerning the Catholic school's role in educating those who have suffered economic deprivation or experienced discrimination because of racial, cultural or linguistic differences. This will help both to demonstrate the contribution now being made in this way by Catholic schools to American society generally and to foster the formulation of proposals for further steps to maintain and strengthen this commitment, including the possibility of some form of nationwide action.

Professional guidance and assistance are also needed for making realistic predictions of future enrollment and estimates of future costs, notably for teachers' salaries. We will be assisted by documented success reports describing how particular school systems or individual schools have solved problems relating to downward enrollment, soaring expenses, tensions in governance, and disputes about religious instruction. For it is entirely possible that a solution in one diocese or individual school within a diocese can be replicated elsewhere. We hope also for the discovery or development of promising models, instruments and processes to facilitate educational planning at the local level.

2. Development and promotion at all levels, local, diocesan and national, of effective programs of public relations on behalf of Catholic schools.

3. Encouragement for the development and organization of parents, teachers, and other citizens which can articulate the just demands of the nonpublic school community with respect to government aid.

4. Pursuit and publicizing of every appropriate constitutional possibility of public assistance to Catholic and other nonpublic school pupils.

IV. We urge that the entire nation realistically acknowledge the contributions which Catholic and other nonpublic schools make to the total educational enterprise in our country. Although Congress and several state legislatures, reflecting growing public appreciation of this kind, have expressed such recognition in recent years by enacting programs to assist the education of nonpublic school children, it is a deplorable fact that courts have often overturned this legislation for reasons we and others consider tenuous and at times offensive. In doing so, they have inflicted a harsh injustice on supporters of nonpublic schools, increased their burdens, and caused serious suffering to many of them. It is our hope that this situation will be corrected by more perceptive rulings which reflect the authentic American tradition, firmly rooted in our history, concerning Church and state, and which recognize both the needs and rights of nonpublic school students and parents and the best interests of American education generally. We affirm, as Pope Pius XI did some 40 years ago, that "Catholics will never feel, whatever may have been the sacrifices already made, that they have done enough for the support and defense of their schools and for the securing of laws that will do them justice."[9]

V. Last September 15, the day following the canonization of St. Elizabeth Seton, who is celebrated as the foundress of the parochial school system in the United States, Pope Paul VI spoke to some 80 of us concerning his hopes for our country. He spoke among other things of Catholic schools.

"We know the difficulties involved in preserving the Catholic schools and the uncertainties of the future," he said, "and yet we rely on the help of God and your own zealous collaboration and untiring efforts so that Catholic schools can continue, despite grave obstacles, to fulfill (their) providential role at the service of genuine Catholic education and at the service of your country."

How consistent this is with the first command of Jesus to teach. We receive these words of the Holy Father in the light of the centuries-old tradition of those who have given us so much that we take for granted. Our call now is to all who see with undimmed sight this same apostolic responsibility as their own and will join in carrying out this commitment in the years ahead: the commitment of handing on the faith to the next generation, not merely preserved, but more glorious, more efficacious, more valued by those who in their turn will take up the charge to "go and teach."

1. *To Teach as Jesus Did* (Washington, D.C.: National Conference of Catholic Bishops, November 1972), #101.

2. Andrew M. Greeley, William C. McCready, and Kathleen McCourt, *Catholic Schools in a Declining Church* (Kansas City: Sheed & Ward, Inc., 1976).

3. "*To Teach as Jesus Did*: Educational Developments since the Pastoral," *Notre Dame Journal of Education* (Vol. 6, No. 3, Fall 1975).

4. *Qualities and Competencies of Teaching Religion* (Washington, D.C.: National Catholic Educational Association, 1973).

5. Greeley, McCready and McCourt, *ibid.*

6. *Declaration on Christian Education*, Vatican Council II, the Conciliar and Post Conciliar Documents, #9.

7. "The Crisis of Catholic Education in the Black Community," *Special Statement* (National Office for Black Catholics, January 15, 1976).

8. Letter of Pope Paul VI to French Social Action Groups meeting in France, July 1st, 1970.

9. *Christian Education of Youth*, The Encyclical Letter of His Holiness Pope Pius XI, December 31, 1929, (reprinted by the United States Catholic Conference, Washington, D.C., 1968).

The Catholic School

SACRED CONGREGATION FOR CATHOLIC EDUCATION
March 19, 1977

Introduction

1. The Catholic school is receiving more and more attention in the Church since the Second Vatican Council, with particular emphasis on the Church as she appears in the Constitutions *Lumen Gentium* and *Gaudium et Spes*. In the Council's Declaration *Gravissimum Educationis* it is discussed in the wider sphere of Christian education. The present document develops the idea of this Declaration, limiting itself to a deeper reflection on the Catholic school.

2. The Sacred Congregation for Catholic Education is aware of the serious problems which are an integral part of Christian education in a pluralistic society. It regards as a prime duty, therefore, the focusing of any attention on the nature and distinctive characteristics of school which would present itself as Catholic. Yet the diverse situations and legal systems in which the Catholic school has to function in Christian and non-Christian countries demand that local problems be faced and solved by each Church within its own social-cultural context.

3. While acknowledging this duty of the local Churches, the Sacred Congregation believes that now is the opportune moment to offer its own contribution by re-emphasizing clearly the educational value of the Catholic school. It is in this value that the Catholic school's fundamental reason for existing and the basis of its genuine apostolate is to be found. This document does not pretend to be an exhaustive treatment of the subject; it merely proposes to state the premises that will lead to further fruitful study and implementation.

4. To Episcopal Conferences, pastorally concerned for all young Catholics whatever school they attend,[1] the Sacred Congregation for Catholic Education entrusts this present document in order that they may seek to achieve an effective system of education at all levels which corresponds to the total educational needs of young people today in Catholic schools. The Sacred Congregation also addresses itself to all who are responsible for education—parents, teachers, young people and school authorities—and urges them to pool all their resources and the means at their disposal to enable Catholic schools to provide a service which is truly civic and apostolic.

I.
The Catholic School and the Salvific Mission of the Church

The Salvific Mission of the Church

5. In the fullness of time, in His mysterious plan of love, God the Father sent His only Son to begin the Kingdom of God on earth and bring about the spiritual rebirth of mankind. To continue His work of salvation, Jesus Christ founded the Church as a visible organism, living by the power of the Spirit.

6. Moved by the same Spirit, the Church is constantly deepening her awareness of herself and meditating on the mystery of her being and mission.[2] Thus she is ever rediscovering her living relationship with Christ "in order to discover greater light, energy, and joy in fulfilling her mission and determining the best way to ensure that her relationship with humanity is closer and more efficacious"[3]—that humanity of which she is a part and yet so undeniably distinct. Her destiny is to serve humanity until it reaches its fullness in Christ.

7. Evangelization is, therefore, the mission of the Church; that is she must proclaim the good news of salvation to all, generate new creatures in Christ through Baptism, and train them to live knowingly as children of God.

Means Available for the Mission of the Church

8. To carry out her saving mission, the Church uses, above all, the means which Jesus Christ has given her. She also uses other means which at different times and in different cultures have proved effective in achieving and, promoting the development of the human person. The Church adapts these means to the changing conditions and emerging needs of mankind.[4] In her encounter with differing cultures and with man's progressive achievements, the Church proclaims the faith and reveals "to all ages the transcendent goal which alone gives life its full meaning."[5] She establishes her own schools because she considers them as a privileged means of promoting the formation of the whole man, since the school is a center in which a specific concept of the world, of man, and of history is developed and conveyed.

Contribution of the Catholic School Towards the Salvific Mission of the Church

9. The Catholic school forms part of the saving mission of the Church, especially for education in the faith. Remembering that "the simultaneous development of man's psychological and moral consciousness is demanded by Christ almost as a pre-condition for the reception of the befitting divine gifts of truth and grace,"[6] the Church fulfills her obligation to foster in her children a full awareness of their rebirth to a new life.[7] It is precisely in the Gospel of Christ, taking root in the minds and lives of the faithful, that the Catholic school finds its definition as it comes to terms with the cultural conditions of the times.

The Church's Educational Involvement and Cultural Pluralism

10. In the course of the centuries "while constantly holding to the fullness of divine truth"[8] the Church has progressively used the sources and the means of culture in order to deepen her understanding of revelation and promote constructive dialogue with the world. Moved by the faith through which she firmly believes herself to be led by the Spirit of the Lord, the Church seeks to discern in the events, needs and hopes of our era[9] the most insistent demands which she must answer if she is to carry out God's plan.

11. One such demand is a pressing need to ensure the presence of a Christian mentality in the society of the present day, marked, among other things, by cultural pluralism. For it is Christian thought which constitutes a sound criterion of judgment in the midst of conflicting concepts and behavior: "Reference to Jesus Christ teaches man to discern the values which ennoble from those which degrade him."[10]

12. Cultural pluralism, therefore, leads the Church to reaffirm her mission of education to insure strong character formation. Her children, then, will be capable both of resisting the debilitating influence of relativism and of living up to the demands made on them by their Baptism. It also stimulates her to foster truly Christian living and apostolic communities, equipped to make their own positive contribution, in a spirit of cooperation, to the building up of the secular society. For this reason the Church is prompted to mobilize her educational resources in the face of the materialism, pragmatism and technocracy of contemporary society.

13. The Church upholds the principle of a plurality of school systems in order to safeguard her objectives in the face of cultural pluralism. In other words, she encourages the co-existence and, if possible, the cooperation of diverse educational institutions which will allow young people to be formed by value judgments based on a specific view of the world and to be trained to take an active part in the construction of a community through which the building of society itself is promoted.

14. Thus, while policies and opportunities differ from place to place, the Catholic school has its place in any national school system. By offering such an alternative the Church wishes to respond to the obvious need for cooperation in a society characterized by cultural pluralism. Moreover, in this way she helps to promote that freedom of teaching which champions and guarantees freedom of conscience and the parental right to choose the school best suited to parents' educational purpose.[11]

15. Finally, the Church is absolutely convinced that the educational aims of the Catholic school in the world of today perform an essential and unique service for the Church herself. It is, in fact, through the school that she participates in the dialogue of culture with her own positive contribution to the cause of the total formation of man. The absence of the Catholic school would be a great loss[12] for civilization and for the natural and supernatural destiny of man.

II.
Present Difficulties
Over Catholic Schools

16. In the light of her mission of salvation, the Church considers that the Catholic school provides a privileged environment for the complete formation of her members, and that it also provides a highly important service to mankind. Nevertheless, she is aware of the many problems that exist and objections that are made against Catholic schools sometimes regarding the very validity of their existence and their functions. The issue is really part of a much wider problem which faces all institutions as such in a society as the present, characterized by rapid and profound change.

Objections Raised Against Catholic schools

17. In the debate about Catholic schools there are some easily identifiable central objections and difficulties. These need to be borne in mind if discussion is to be relevant to the actual situation and if teachers are to make a serious attempt to adapt their work to the needs of the contemporary world.

18. In the first place many people, both inside and outside the Church, motivated by a mistaken sense of the lay role in secular society, attack Catholic schools as institutions. They do not admit that, apart from the individual witness of her members, the Church also may offer witness by means of her institutions, e.g.

those dedicated to the search for truth or to works of charity.

19. Others claim that Catholic schools make use of a human institution for religious and confessional purposes. Christian education can sometimes run into the danger of a so-called proselytism, of imparting a one-sided outlook. This can happen only when Christian educators misunderstand the nature and methods of Christian education. Complete education necessarily includes a religious dimension. Religion is an effective contribution to the development of other aspects of a personality in the measure in which it is integrated into general education.

20. According to others, Catholic schools have outlived their time; as institutions they were a necessary substitute in the past but have no place at a time when civil authority assumes responsibility for education. In fact, as the State increasingly takes control of education and establishes its own so-called neutral and monolithic system, the survival of those natural communities, based on a shared concept of life, is threatened. Faced with this situation, the Catholic school offers an alternative which is in conformity with the wishes of the members of the community of the Church.

21. In some countries Catholic schools have been obliged to restrict their educational activities to wealthier social classes, thus giving an impression of social and economic discrimination in education. But this occurs only where the State has not weighed the advantages of an alternative presence in their pluralistic society. From such nearsightedness considerable difficulties have arisen for Catholic schools.

22. Allied to these points, objections are raised concerning the educational results of the Catholic school. They are sometimes accused of not knowing how to form convinced, articulate Christians ready to take their place in social and political life. Every educational enterprise, however, involves the risk of failure and one must not be too discouraged by apparent or even real failures, since there are very many formative influences on young people and results often have to be calculated on a long-term basis.

23. Before concluding these comments on the objections raised against Catholic schools, one must remember the context in which contemporary work in the field of education is undertaken, and especially in the Church. The school problem in our rapidly changing society is serious for everyone. The Second Vatican Council has encouraged a more openminded approach which has sometimes been misrepresented in theory and practice. There are difficulties in the provision of adequate staff and finance. In such a situation should the Church perhaps give up her apostolic mission in Catholic schools, as some people would like her to do, and direct her energy to a more direct work of evangelization in sectors considered to be of higher priority or more suited to her spiritual mission, or should she make State schools the sole object of her pastoral activity? Such a solution would not only be contrary to the directives of the Vatican Council, but would also be opposed to the Church's mission and to what is expected of her by Christian people. What follows emphasizes this fact.

Some Aspects of Schools Today

24. To understand the real nature of the Catholic school one cannot divorce it from wider modern problems concerning schools in general. Apart from the ideas advanced by the promoters of de-schooling—a theory which now seems of minor significance—

contemporary society tends to place greater importance than ever on the specific function of the school: its social significance (parental participation, increased democratization, equality of opportunity); its tendency to co-ordinate and eventually include the educational work of other institutions; the extension of the statutory duration of attendance at school.

III.
The School as a Center of Human Formation

25. To understand fully the specific mission of the Catholic school it is essential to keep in mind the basic concept of what a school is; that which does not reproduce the characteristic features of a school cannot be a Catholic school.

The General Purpose of a School

26. A close examination of the various definitions of school and of new educational trends at every level, leads one to formulate the concept of school as a place of integral formation by means of a systematic and critical assimilation of culture. A school is, therefore, a privileged place in which, through a living encounter with a cultural inheritance, integral formation occurs.

27. This vital approach takes place in the school in the form of personal contacts and commitments which consider absolute values in a life-context and seek to insert them into a life-framework. Indeed, culture is only educational when young people can relate their study to real-life situations with which they are familiar. The school must stimulate the pupil to exercise his intelligence through the dynamics of understanding to attain clarity and inventiveness. It must help him spell out the meaning of his experiences and their truths. Any school which neglects this duty and which offers merely pre-cast conclusions hinders the personal development of its pupils.

School and Attitudes of Life

28. From this it is clear that the school has to review its entire program of formation, both its content and the methods used, in the light of that vision of the reality from which it draws its inspiration and on which it depends.

29. Either implicit or explicit reference to a determined attitude to life (*Weltanschauung*) is unavoidable in education because it comes into every decision that is made. It is, therefore, essential, if for no other reason than for a unity in teaching, that each member of the school community, albeit with differing degrees of awareness, adopts a common vision, a common outlook on life, based on adherence to a scale of values in which he believes. This is what gives teachers and adults authority to educate. It must never be forgotten that the purpose of instruction at school is education, that is, the development of man from within, freeing him from that conditioning which would prevent him from becoming a fully integrated human being. The school must begin from the principle that its educational program is intentionally directed to the growth of the whole person.

30. It is one of the formal tasks of a school, as an institution for education, to draw out the ethical dimension for the precise purpose of arousing the individual's inner spiritual dynamism and to aid his achieving that moral freedom which complements the psychological. Behind this moral freedom, however, stand those absolute values which alone give meaning and value to human life. This has to be said because the tendency to adopt present-day values as a yardstick is not absent even in the educational world. The danger is always to react to passing, superficial ideas and to lose sight of the much deeper needs of the contemporary world.

The School in Today's Society

31. Precisely because the school endeavors to answer the needs of a society characterized by depersonalization and a mass production mentality which so easily result from scientific and technological developments, it must develop into an authentically formational school, reducing such risks to a minimum. It must develop persons who are responsible and inner-directed, capable of choosing freely in conformity with their conscience. This is simply another way of saying that the school is an institution where young people gradually learn to open themselves up to life as it is, and to create in themselves a definite attitude to life as it should be.

32. When seen in this light, a school is not only a place where one is given a choice of intellectual values, but a place where one has presented an array of values which are actively lived. The school must be a community whose values are communicated through the interpersonal and sincere relationships of its members and through both individual and corporative adherence to the outlook on life that permeates the school.

IV.
The Educational Work of the Catholic School

Specific Character of the Catholic School

33. Having stated the characteristics of the Catholic school from the point of view of "school" we can now examine its Catholic quality, namely its reference to a Christian concept of life centered on Jesus Christ.

34. Christ is the foundation of the whole educational enterprise in a Catholic school. His revelation gives new meaning to life and helps man to direct his thought, action and will according to the Gospel, making the beatitudes his norm of life. The fact that in their own individual ways all members of the school community share this Christian vision, makes the school "Catholic"; principles of the Gospel in this manner become the educational norms since the school then has them as its internal motivation and final goal.

35. The Catholic school is committed thus to the development of the whole man, since in Christ, the Perfect Man, all human values find their fulfillment and unity. Herein lies the specifically Catholic character of the school. Its duty to cultivate human values in their own legitimate right in accordance with its particular mission to serve all men has its origin in the figure of Christ. He is the One Who ennobles man, gives meaning to human life, and is the Model which the Catholic school offers to its pupils.

36. If, like every other school, the Catholic school has as its aim the critical communication of human culture and the total formation of the individual, it works towards this goal guided by its Christian vision of reality "through which our cultural heritage acquires its special place in the total vocational life of man."[13] Mindful of the fact that man has been redeemed by Christ, the Catholic school aims at forming in the Christian those particular virtues which will enable him to live a new life in Christ and help him to play faithfully his part in building up the Kingdom of God.[14]

37. These premises indicate the duties and the content of the Catholic school. Its task is fundamentally a synthesis of culture and faith, and a synthesis of faith and life: the first is reached by integrating all the different aspects of human knowledge through the subjects taught, in the light of the Gospel; the second in the growth of the virtues characteristic of the Christian.

Integration of Faith and Culture

38. In helping pupils to achieve through the medium of its teaching an integration of faith and culture, the Catholic school sets out with a deep awareness of the value of knowledge as such. Under no circumstances does it wish to divert the imparting of knowledge from its rightful objective.

39. Individual subjects must be taught according to their own particular methods. It would be wrong to consider subjects as mere adjuncts to faith or as a useful means of teaching apologetics. They enable the pupil to assimilate skills, knowledge, intellectual methods and moral and social attitudes, all of which help to develop his personality and lead him to take his place as an active member of the community of man. Their aim is not merely the attainment of knowledge but the acquisition of values and the discovery of truth.

40. Since the educative mission of the Catholic school is so wide, the teacher is in an excellent position to guide the pupil to a deepening of his faith and to enrich and enlighten his human knowledge with the data of the faith. While there are many occasions in teaching when pupils can be stimulated by insights of faith, a Christian education acknowledges the valid contribution which can be made by academic subjects towards the development of a mature Christian. The teacher can form the mind and heart of his pupils and guide them to develop a total commitment to

Christ, with their whole personality enriched by human culture.

41. The school considers human knowledge as a truth to be discovered. In the measure in which subjects rare taught by someone who knowingly and without restraint seeks the truth, they are to that extent Christian. Discovery and awareness of truth leads man to the discovery of Truth itself. A teacher who is full of Christian wisdom, well prepared in his own subject, does more than convey the sense of what he is teaching to his pupils. Over and above what he says, he guides his pupils beyond his mere words to the heart of total Truth.

42. The cultural heritage of mankind includes other values apart from the specific ambient of truth. When the Christian teacher helps a pupil to grasp, appreciate and assimilate these values, he is guiding him towards eternal realities. This movement towards the Uncreated Source of all knowledge highlights the importance of teaching for the growth of faith.

43. The achievement of this specific aim of the Catholic school depends not so much on subject matter or methodology as on the people who work there. The extent to which the Christian message is transmitted through education depends to a very great extent on the teachers. The integration of culture and faith is mediated by the other integration of faith and life in the person of the teacher. The nobility of the task to which teachers are called demands that, in imitation of Christ, the only Teacher, they reveal the Christian message not only by word but also by every gesture of their behavior. This is what makes the difference between a school whose education is permeated by the Christian spirit and one in which religion is only regarded as an academic subject like any other.

Integration of Faith and Life

44. The fundamental aim of teaching is the assimilation of objective values, and, when this is undertaken for an apostolic purpose, it does not stop at an integration of faith and culture but leads the pupil on to a personal integration of faith and life.

45. The Catholic school has as its specific duty the complete Christian formation of its pupils, and this task is of special significance today because of the inadequacy of the family and society. It knows that this integration of faith and life is part of a life-long process of conversion until the pupil becomes what God wishes him to be. Young people have to be taught to share their personal lives with God. They are to overcome their individualism and discover, in the light of faith, their specific vocation to live responsibly in a community with others. The very pattern of the Christian life draws them to commit themselves to serve God in their brethren and to make the world a better place for man to live in.

46. The Catholic school should teach its pupils to discern in the voice of the universe the Creator Whom it reveals and, in the conquests of science, to know God and man better. In the daily life of the school, the pupil should learn that he is called to be a living witness to God's love for men by the way he acts, and that he is part of that salvation history which has Christ, the Savior of the world, as its goal.

47. Being aware that Baptism by itself does not make a Christian—living and acting in conformity with the Gospel is necessary—the Catholic school tries to create within its walls a climate[15] in which the pupil's faith will gradually mature and enable him to assume the responsibility placed on him by Baptism. It will give pride of place in the education it provides through Christian Doctrine to the gradual formation of conscience in fundamental, permanent virtues—above all the theological virtues, and charity in particular, which is, so to speak, the life-giving spirit which transforms a man of virtue into a man of Christ. Christ, therefore, is the teaching-center, the Model on Whom the Christian shapes his life. In Him the Catholic school differs from all others which limit themselves to forming men. Its task is to form Christian men, and, by its teaching and witness, show non-Christians something of the mystery of Christ Who surpasses all human understanding.[16]

48. The Catholic school will work closely with other Christian bodies (the family, the parish and Christian community, youth associations, etc.). But one must not overlook many other spheres of activity in society which are sources of information and in their various ways have an educational influence. Alongside this so-called "parallel school," the school proper is an active force through the systematic formation of the pupils' critical faculties to bring them to a measure of self control[17] and the ability to choose freely and conscientiously in the face of what is offered by the organs of social communication. They must be taught to subject these things to a critical and personal analysis,[18] take what is good, and integrate it into their Christian human culture.

Religious Teaching

49. The specific mission of the school, then, is a critical, systematic transmission of culture in the light of faith and the bringing forth of the power of Christian virtue by the integration of culture with faith and of faith with living.

Consequently, the Catholic school is aware of the importance of the Gospel-teaching as transmitted through the Catholic Church. It is, indeed, the fundamental element in the educative process as it helps the pupil towards his conscious choice of living a responsible and coherent way of life.

50. Without entering into the whole problem of teaching religion in schools, it must be emphasized that, while such teaching is not merely confined to "religious classes" within the school curriculum, it must, nevertheless, also be imparted explicitly and in a systematic manner to prevent a distortion in the child's mind between general and religious culture. The fundamental difference between religious and other forms of education is that its aim is not simply intellectual assent to religious truths but also a total commitment of one's whole being to the Person of Christ.

51. It is recognized that the proper place for catechesis is the family helped by other Christian communities, especially the local parish. But the importance and need for catechetical instruction in Catholic schools cannot be sufficiently emphasized. Here young people are helped to grow towards maturity in faith.

52. The Catholic school must be alert at all times to developments in the fields of child psychology, pedagogy and particularly catechetics, and should especially keep abreast of directives from competent ecclesiastical authorities. The school must do everything in its power to aid the Church to fulfill its catechetical mission and so must have the best possible qualified teachers of religion.

The Catholic School as the Center of the Educative Christian Community

53. For all these reasons, Catholic schools must be seen as "meeting places for those who wish to express Christian values in education."[19] The Catholic school, far more than

any other, must be a community whose aim is the transmission of values for living. Its work is seen as promoting a faith-relationship with Christ in Whom all values find fulfillment. But faith is principally assimilated through contact with people whose daily life bears witness to it. Christian faith, in fact, is born and grows inside a community.

54. The community aspect of the Catholic school is necessary because of the nature of the faith and not simply because of the nature of man and the nature of the educational process which is common to every school. No Catholic school can adequately fulfill its educational role on its own. It must continually be fed and stimulated by its Source of life, the Saving Word of Christ as it is expressed in Sacred Scripture, in Tradition, especially liturgical and sacramental tradition, and in the lives of people, past and present, who bear witness to that Word.

55. The Catholic school loses its purpose without constant reference to the Gospel and a frequent encounter with Christ. It derives all the energy necessary for its educational work from Him and thus "creates in the school community an atmosphere permeated with the Gospel spirit of freedom and love."[20] In this setting the pupil experiences his dignity as a person before he knows its definition. Faithful, therefore, to the claims of man and of God, the Catholic school makes its own contribution towards man's liberation, making him, in other words, what his destiny implies, one who talks consciously with God, one who is there for God to love.

56. "This simple religious doctrine is the cornerstone of the existential, Christian metaphysic."[21] This is the basis of a Catholic school's educational work. Education is not given for the purpose of gaining power but as an aid towards a fuller understanding of, and communion with man, events and things. Knowledge is not to be considered as a means of material prosperity and success, but as a call to serve and to be responsible for others.

Other Aspects of the Educational Process in Catholic Schools

57. Whether or not the Catholic community forms its young people in the faith by means of a Catholic school, a Catholic school in itself is far from being divisive or presumptuous. It does not exacerbate differences, but rather aids cooperation and contact with others. It opens itself to others and respects their way of thinking and of living. It wants to share their anxieties and their hopes as it, indeed, shares their present and future lot in this world.

58. Since it is motivated by the Christian ideal, the Catholic school is particularly sensitive to the call from every part of the world for a more just society, and it tries to make its own contribution towards it. It does not stop at the courageous teaching of the demands of justice even in the face of local opposition, but tries to put these demands into practice in its own community in the daily life of the school. In some countries, because of local laws and economic conditions, the Catholic school runs the risk of giving counter-witness by admitting a majority of children from wealthier families. Schools may have done this because of their need to be financially self supporting. This situation is of great concern to those responsible for Catholic education, because first and foremost the Church offers its educational service to "the poor or those who are deprived of family help and affection or those who are far from the faith."[22] Since education is an important means of improving the social and economic condition of the individual and of peoples, if the Catholic school were to turn its attention exclusively or predominantly to those from the wealthier social classes, it could be contributing towards maintaining their privileged position, and could thereby continue to favor a society which is unjust.

59. It is obvious that in such a demanding educational policy all participants must be committed to it freely. It cannot be imposed, but is offered as a possibility, as good news, and as such can be refused. However, in order to bring it into being and to maintain it, the school must be able to count on the unity of purpose and conviction of all its members.

The Participation of the Christian Community in the Catholic Schools' Work

60. From the outset the Catholic school declares its program and its determination to uphold it. It is a genuine community bent on imparting, over and above an academic education, all the help it can to its members to adopt a Christian way of life. For the Catholic school mutual respect means service to the Person of Christ. Cooperation is between brothers and sisters in Christ. A policy of working for the common good is undertaken seriously as working for the building up of the Kingdom of God.

61. The cooperation required for the realization of this aim is a duty in conscience for all the members of the community teachers, parents, pupils, administrative personnel. Each has his or her own part to play. Cooperation of all, given in the spirit of the Gospel, is by its very nature a witness not only to Christ as the corner-stone of the community, but also as the light Who shines far beyond it.

The Catholic School as a Service to the Church and to Society

62. The Catholic school community, therefore, is an irreplaceable source of service, not only to the pupils and its other members, but also to society. Today especially one sees a world which clamors for solidarity and yet experiences the rise of new forms of individualism. Society can take note from the Catholic school that it is possible to create true communities out of a common effort for the common good. In the pluralistic society of today the Catholic school, moreover, by maintaining an institutional Christian presence in the academic world, proclaims by its very existence the enriching power of the faith as the answer to the enormous problems which afflict mankind. Above all, it is called to render a humble loving service to the Church by ensuring that she is present in the scholastic field for the benefit of the human family.

63. In this way the Catholic school performs "an authentic apostolate."[23] To work, therefore, in this apostolate "means apostolate performing a unique and invaluable work for the Church."[24]

V.
The Responsibility of the Catholic School Today

64. The real problem facing the Catholic school is to identify and lay down the conditions necessary for it to fulfill its mission. It is, therefore, a problem requiring clear and positive thinking, courage, perseverance and cooperation to tackle the necessary measures without being overawed by the size of the difficulties from within and without, nor "by persistent and outdated slogans,"[25] which in the last analysis aim to abolish Catholic schools.[26] To give into them would be suicidal. To favor in a more or less radical form a merely non-institutional presence of the Church in the scholastic field, is a dangerous illusion.[27]

65. At great cost and sacrifice our forebears were inspired by the teaching of the Church to establish schools which enriched mankind

and responded to the needs of time and place. While it recognizes its own inadequacies, the Catholic school is conscious of its responsibility to continue this service. Today, as in the past, some scholastic institutions which bear the name Catholic do not appear to correspond fully to the principles of education which should be their distinguishing feature and, therefore, do not fulfill the duties which the Church and the society has every right to expect of them. Without pretending to make an exhaustive enquiry into the factors which may explain the difficulties under which the Catholic school labors, here are a few points in the hope of encouraging some thought as a stimulus to courageous reform.

66. Often what is perhaps fundamentally lacking among Catholics who work in a school is a clear realization of the identity of a Catholic school and the courage to follow all the consequences of its uniqueness. One must recognize that, more than ever before, a Catholic school's job is infinitely more difficult, more complex, since this is a time when Christianity demands to be clothed in fresh garments, when all manner of changes have been introduced in the Church and in secular life, and, particularly, when a pluralist mentality dominates and the Christian Gospel is increasingly pushed to the side-lines.

67. It is because of this that loyalty to the educational aims of the Catholic school demands constant self-criticism and return to basic principles, to the motives which inspire the Church's involvement in education. They do not provide a quick answer to contemporary problems, but they give a direction which can begin to solve them. Account has to be taken of new pedagogical insights and collaboration with others, irrespective of religious allegiance, who work honestly for the true development of mankind—first and foremost with schools of other Christians—

in the interests, even in this field, of Christian unity but also with State schools. In addition to meetings of teachers and mutual research, this collaboration can be extended to the pupils themselves and their families.

68. In conclusion it is only right to repeat what has been said above[28] about the considerable difficulties arising from legal and economic systems operating in different countries which hinder the activities of the Catholic school, difficulties which prevent them from extending their service to all social and economic classes and compel them to give the false impression of providing schools simply for the rich.

VI.
Practical Directions

69. After reflecting on the difficulties which the Catholic school encounters, we turn now to the practical possibilities open to those who work in, or are responsible for, these schools. The following more serious questions have been selected for special comment: organization and planning, ensuring the distinctive Catholic character of the school, the involvement of religious in the school apostolate, the Catholic school in mission countries, pastoral care of teachers, professional associations, the economic question.

The Organization and Planning of the Catholic School

70. Catholic education is inspired by the general principles enunciated by the Second Vatican Council concerning collaboration between the hierarchy and those who work in the apostolate. In consequence of the principle of participation and co-responsibility, the various groupings which constitute the educational community are, according to their several competencies, to be associated in decision-making concerning the Catholic school and in the application of decisions once taken.[29] It is first and foremost at the stage of planning and of putting into operation an educational project that this principle of the Council is to be applied. The assigning of various responsibilities is governed by the principle of subsidiarity, and, with reference to this principle, ecclesiastical authority respects the competence of the professionals in teaching and education. Indeed, "the right and duty of exercising the apostolate is common to all the faithful, clerical and lay, and laypeople have their own proper competence in the building up of the Church."[30]

71. This principle enunciated by the Second Vatican Council is particularly applicable to the apostolate of the Catholic school which so closely unites teaching and religious education to a well-defined professional activity. It is here, above all, that the particular mission of the lay person is put into effect, a mission which has become "all the more imperative in view of the fact that many areas of human life have become very largely autonomous. This is as it should be, but it sometimes involves a certain withdrawal from ethical and religious influences and thereby creates a serious danger to Christian life."[31] Moreover, lay involvement in Catholic schools is an invitation "to cooperate more closely with the apostolate of the Bishops,"[32] both in the field of religious instruction[33] and in more general religious education which they endeavor to promote by assisting the pupils to a personal integration of culture and faith and of faith and living. The Catholic school in this sense, therefore, receives from the Bishops in some manner the "mandate" of an apostolic undertaking.[34]

72. The essential element of such a mandate is "union with those whom the Holy Spirit has assigned to rule God's Church"[35] and this link is expressed especially in overall pastoral strategy. "In the whole diocese or in given areas of it the coordination and close interconnection of all apostolic works should be fostered under the direction of the Bishop. In this way all undertakings and organization, whether catechetical, missionary, charitable, social, family, educational, or any other program serving a pastoral goal will be coordinated. Moreover, the unity of the diocese will thereby be made more evident."[36] This is something which is obviously indispensable for the Catholic school, inasmuch as it involves "apostolic cooperation on the part of both branches of the clergy, as well as of the religious and the laity."[37]

Ensuring the Distinctive Catholic Character of the School

73. This is the framework which guarantees the distinctive Catholic character of the school. While the Bishop's authority is to watch over the orthodoxy of religious instruction and the observance of Christian morals in the Catholic schools, it is the task of the whole educative community to ensure that a distinctive Christian educational environment is maintained in practice. This responsibility applies chiefly to Christian parents who confide their children to the school. Having chosen it does not relieve them of a personal duty to give their children a Christian upbringing. They are bound to cooperate actively with the school—which means supporting the educational efforts of the school and utilizing the structures offered for parental involvement, in order to make certain that the school remains faithful to Christian principles of education. An equally important role belongs to the teachers in safeguarding and developing the distinctive mission of the Catholic school, particularly with regard to the Christian atmosphere which should characterize its life and teaching. Where

difficulties and conflicts arise about the authentic Christian character of the Catholic school, hierarchical authority can and must intervene.

Involvement of Religious in the School Apostolate

74. Some problems arise from the fact that certain Religious Institutes, founded for the school apostolate, have subsequently abandoned school work because of social or political changes and have involved themselves in other activities. In some cases they have given up their schools as a result of their efforts to adapt their lives and mission to the recommendations of the Second Vatican Council and to the spirit of their original foundation.

75. It is necessary, however, to re-assess certain arguments adopted against the teaching apostolate. Some would say they have chosen a "more direct" apostolate,[38] forgetting the excellence and the apostolic value of educational work in the school.[39] Others would appeal to the greater importance of individual over community involvement, of personal over institutional work. The advantages, however, of a community apostolate in the educational field are self evident. Sometimes the abandonment of Catholic schools is justified on the grounds of an apparent failure to gain perceptible results in pursuing certain objectives. If this were true, it would surely be an invitation to undertake a fundamental revision of the whole conduct of the school, reminding everyone who ventures into education of the need for humility and hope and the conviction that his work cannot be assessed by the same rationalistic criteria which apply to other professions.[40]

76. It is the responsibility of competent local ecclesiastical authority to evaluate the advisability and necessity of any change to other forms of apostolic work whenever particular circumstances dictate the need for a re-assessment of the school apostolate, keeping in mind the observations above on overall pastoral strategy.[41]

The Catholic School in Mission Countries

77. The importance of the Catholic school apostolate is much greater when it is a question of the foreign missions. Where the young Churches still rely on the presence of foreign missionaries, the effectiveness of the Catholic school will largely depend on its ability to adapt to local needs. It must ensure that it is a true expression of the local and national Catholic community and that it contributes to the community's willingness to cooperate. In countries where the Christian community is still at its beginning and incapable of assuming responsibility for its own schools, the Bishops will have to undertake this responsibility themselves for the time being, but must endeavor little by little to fulfill the aims outlined above in connection with the organization of the Catholic schools.[42]

Pastoral Care of Teachers

78. By their witness and their behavior teachers are of the first importance to impart a distinctive character to Catholic schools. It is, therefore, indispensable to ensure their continuing formation through some form of suitable pastoral provision. This must aim to animate them as witnesses of Christ in the classroom and tackle the problems of their particular apostolate, especially regarding a Christian vision of the world and of education, problems also connected with the art of teaching in accordance with the principles of the Gospel. A huge field is thus opened up for national and international organizations which bring together Catholic teachers and educational institutions at all levels.

79. Professional organizations whose aim is to protect the interests of those who work in the educational field cannot themselves be divorced from the specific mission of the Catholic school. The rights of the people who are involved in the school must be safeguarded in strict justice. But, no matter what material interests may be at stake, or what social and moral conditions affect their professional development, the principle of the Second Vatican Council has a special application in this context: "The faithful should learn how to distinguish carefully between those rights and duties which are theirs as members of the Church, and those which they have as members of society. Let them strive to harmonize the two, remembering that in every temporal affair they must be guided by a Christian conscience."[43] Moreover, "even when preoccupied with temporal cares, the laity can and must perform valuable work for the evangelization of the world."[44] Therefore, the special organizations set up to protect the rights of teachers, parents and pupils must not forget the special mission of the Catholic school to be of service in the Christian education of youth. "The layman is at the same time a believer and a citizen and should be constantly led by Christian conscience alone."[45]

80. In the light of what has been said, these associations, while being concerned for the rights of their members, must also be alive to the responsibilities which are part and parcel of the specific apostolate of the Catholic school. Catholic teachers who freely accept posts in schools, which have a distinctive character, are obliged to respect that character and give their active support to it under the direction of those responsible.

Economic Situation of Catholic Schools

81. From the economic point of view the position of very many Catholic schools has improved and in some countries is perfectly acceptable. This is the case where governments have appreciated the advantages and the necessity of a plurality of school systems which offer alternatives to a single State system. While at first Catholic schools received various public grants, often merely conceded, they later began to enter into agreements, conventions, contracts, etc. which guarantee both the preservation of the special status of the Catholic school and its ability to perform its function adequately. Catholic schools are thereby more or less closely associated with the national system and are assured of an economic and juridical status similar to State schools.

82. Such agreements have been reached through the good offices of the respective governments, which have recognized the public service provided by Catholic schools, and through the determination of the Bishops and the Catholic community at the national level. These solutions are an encouragement to those responsible for Catholic schools in countries where the Catholic community must still shoulder a very heavy burden of cost to maintain an often highly important network of Catholic schools. These Catholics need to be assured, as they strive to regularize the frequent injustices in their school situation, that they are not only helping to provide every child with an education that respects his complete development, but they are also defending freedom of teaching and the right of parents to choose an education for their children which conforms to their legitimate requirements.[46]

VII.
Courageous and Unified Commitment

83. To commit oneself to working in accordance with the aims of a Catholic school is to make a great act of faith in the necessity and influence of this apostolate. Only one who has this conviction and accepts Christ's message, who has a love for and understands today's young people, who appreciates what people's real problems and difficulties are, will be led to contribute with courage and even audacity to the progress of this apostolate in building up a Catholic school, which puts its theory into practice, which renews itself according to its ideals and to present needs.

84. The validity of the educational results of a Catholic school, however, cannot be measured by immediate efficiency. In the field of Christian education, not only is the freedom-factor of teacher and pupil relationship with each other to be considered, but also the factor of grace. Freedom and grace come to fruition in the spiritual order which defies any merely temporal assessment. When grace infuses human liberty, it makes freedom fully free and raises it to its highest perfection in the freedom of the Spirit. It is when the Catholic school adds its weight, consciously and overtly, to the liberating power of grace, that it becomes the Christian leaven in the world.

85. In the certainty that the Spirit is at work in every person, the Catholic school offers itself to all, non-Christians included, with all its distinctive aims and means, acknowledging, preserving and promoting the spiritual and moral qualities, the social and cultural values, which characterize different civilizations.[47]

86. Such an outlook overrides any question of the disproportion between resources available and the number of children reached directly by the Catholic school; nothing can stop it from continuing to render its service. The only condition it would make, as is its right, for its continued existence would be remaining faithful to the educational aims of the Catholic school. Loyalty to these aims is, moreover, the basic motive which must inspire any needed reorganization of the Catholic school institution.

87. If all who are responsible for the Catholic school would never lose sight of their mission and the apostolic value of their teaching, the school would enjoy better conditions in which to function in the present and would faithfully hand on its mission to future generations. They themselves, moreover, would most surely be filled with a deep conviction, joy and spirit of sacrifice in the knowledge that they are offering innumerable young people the opportunity of growing in faith, of accepting and living its precious principles of truth, charity and hope.

88. The Sacred Congregation for Catholic Education, to foster the full realization of the aims of the Catholic school, extends once more its warmest and heartfelt encouragement to all who work in these schools. There can be no doubt whatever of the importance of the apostolate of teaching in the total saving mission of the Church.

89. The Church herself in particular looks with confidence and trust to Religious Institutes which have received a special charism of the Holy Spirit and have been most active in the education of the young. May they be faithful to the inspiration of their founders and give their whole-hearted support to the apostolic work of education in Catholic schools and not allow themselves to be diverted from this by attractive invitations to undertake other, often seemingly more effective, apostolates.

90. A little more than ten years after the end of the Second Vatican Council the Sacred Congregation for Catholic Education repeats the final exhortation of the Declaration on Christian Education to the priests, religious

and lay people who fulfill their mission in the Catholic school. It reads. "They are urged to persevere generously in their chosen duty, continuing to instill into their pupils the spirit of Christ; let them endeavor to excel in the art of teaching and in the advancement of knowledge. Thus they will not only foster the internal renewal of the Church, but will safeguard and intensify her beneficial presence in the modern world, and above all, in the world of the intellect."[48]

Conclusion

91. This document in no way wishes to minimize the value of the witness and work of the many Catholics who teach in State schools throughout the world. In describing the task confided to the Catholic school it is intended to encourage every effort to promote the cause of Catholic education, since in the pluralistic world in which we live, the Catholic school is in a unique position to offer, more than ever before, a most valuable and necessary service. With the principles of the Gospel as its abiding point of reference, it offers its collaboration to those who are building a new world—one which is freed from a hedonistic mentality and from the efficiency syndrome of modern consumer society.

92. We appeal to each Episcopal Conference to consider and to develop these principles which should inspire the Catholic school and to translate them into concrete programs which will meet the real needs of the educational systems operating in their countries.

93. Realizing that the problems are both delicate and highly complex, the Sacred Congregation for Catholic Education also addresses itself to the whole People of God. In the economy of salvation we poor humans must confront problems, suffer their consequences and work might and main to solve them. We are certain that in the last analysis success in any venture does not come from trust in our own solutions but from trust in Jesus Who allowed Himself to be called Teacher. May He inspire, guide, support and bring to a safe conclusion all that is undertaken in His name.

Rome, March 19th, 1977, the Feast of St. Joseph

† **Gabriel-Marie Cardinal Garrone**
Prefect

† **Antonio M. Javierre**
Secretary
Titular Archbishop of Meta

[1] Cf. Second Vatican Council, *Declaration on Christian Education* [Gravissimum Educationis], 7.

[2] Cf. Paul VI, *Encyclical Letter* [Ecclesiam suam], 7.

[3] Ibid. 13.

[4] Cf Second Vatican Council, *Pastoral Constitution on the Church in the Modern World* [Gaudium et Spes], 4.

[5] Paul VI, *Allocution to Cardinal Gabriel-Marie Garrone*, November 27th, 1972.

[6] Paul VI, *Encyclical Letter* [Ecclesiam suam], 15.

[7] Cf Second Vatican Council, *Declaration on Christian Education* [Gravissimum Educationis], 3.

[8] Second Vatican Council, *Dogmatic Constitution on Divine Revelation* [Dei Verbum], 8.

[9] Cf. Second Vatican Council, *Pastoral Constitution on the Church in the Modern World* [Gaudium et Spes], 11.

[10] Paul VI, *Allocution to the Ninth Congress of the Catholic International Education Office* (O.I.E.C.), in *L'Osservatore Romano*, June 9th, 1974.

[11] Cf. Second Vatican Council, *Declaration on Christian Education* [Gravissimum Educationis], 8.

[12] Cf. Paul VI, *Allocution to the Ninth Congress of the O.I.E.C.*, in *L'Osservatore Romano*, June 9th, 1974.

[13] Second Vatican Council, *Pastoral Constitution on the Church in the Modern World* [Gaudium et Spes], 57

[14] Cf. Second Vatican Council, *Declaration on Christian Education* [Gravissimum Educationis], 2.

[15] Cf. Second Vatican Council, *Declaration on Christian Education* [Gravissimum Educationis], 8.

[16] Cf. Eph. 3, 18-19.

[17] Cf. *Pastoral Instruction "Communio et Progressio,"* 67.

[18] Cf. Ibid.

[19] Paul VI, *Allocution to the Ninth Congress of the Catholic International Education Office* (O.I.E.C.), in *L'Osservatore Romano*, June 9th, 1974.

[20] Second Vatican Council, *Declaration on Christian Education* [Gravissimum Educationis] 8.

[21] Paul VI, *Valore dell'oblazione nella vita*, in *The Teaching of Pope Paul VI*, vol. 8 (1970), p. 97.

[22] Second Vatican Council, *Declaration on Christian Education* [Gravissimum Educationis], 9.

[23] Second Vatican Council, *Declaration on Christian Education* [Gravissimum Educationis], 8.

[24] Paul VI, to Prof. Giuseppe Lazzati, Rector of the University of the Sacred Heart (Milano), in *The Teaching of Pope Paul VI*, vol. 9, p. 1082.

[25] Paul VI, *Allocution to the Ninth Congress of the O.I.E.C.*, in *L'Osservatore Romano*, June 9th, 1974.

[26] Cf. above, nn. 18, 20, 23.

[27] Cf. Paul VI, *Allocution to the Ninth Congress of the O.I.E.C.*, in *L'Osservatore Romano*, June 9th, 1974.

[28] Cf. above, n. 58.

[29] Cf. Second Vatican Council, *Pastoral Constitution on the Church in the Modern World* [Gaudium et Spes], 43.

[30] Second Vatican Council, *Decree on the Apostolate of the Laity* [Apostolicam Actuositatem], 25.

[31] Second Vatican Council, *Decree on the Apostolate of the Laity* [Apostolicam Actuositatem], 1.

[32] Second Vatican Council, *Dogmatic Constitution on the Church* [Lumen Gentium], 33.

[33] Cf. Second Vatican Council, *Decree on the Apostolate of the Laity* [Apostolicam Actuositatem], 10.

[34] Ibid., 24.

[35] Ibid., 23.

[36] Second Vatican Council, *Decree on the Bishop's Pastoral Office in the Church* [Christus Dominus], 17.

[37] Second Vatican Council, *Decree on the Apostolate of the Laity* [Apostolicam Actuositatem], 23.

[38] Cf. above, 23.

[39] Cf. above, nn. 38-48.

[40] Cf. above, n. 22.

[41] Cf. above, nn. 70-72.

[42] Cfr. above, nn. 70-72.

[43] Second Vatican Council, *Dogmatic Constitution on the Church* [Lumen Gentium], 36.

[44] Second Vatican Council, *Dogmatic Constitution on the Church* [Lumen Gentium], 35.

45 Second Vatican Council, *Decree on the Apostolate of the Laity* [Apostolicam Actuositatem], 5.

46 Cf Second Vatican Council, *Declaration on Christian Education* [Gravissimum Educationis], 6.

47 Cf Second Vatican Council, *Declaration on the Relationship of the Church to Non-Christian Religions* [Nostra Aetate], 2.

48 Second Vatican Council, *Declaration on Christian Education* [Gravissimum Educationis], Conclusion.

Lay Catholics in Schools:
Witnesses to Faith

SACRED CONGREGATION FOR CATHOLIC EDUCATION
October 15, 1982

Introduction

1. Lay Catholics, both men and women, who devote their lives to teaching in primary and secondary schools, have become more and more vitally important in recent years.[1] Whether we look at schools in general, or Catholic schools in particular, the importance is deserved.

For it is the lay teachers, and indeed all lay persons, believers or not, who will substantially determine whether or not a school realizes its aims and accomplishes its objectives.[2] In the Second Vatican Council, and specifically in the Declaration on Christian Education, the Church recognized the role and the responsibility that this situation confers on all those lay Catholics who work in any type of elementary and secondary schools, whether as teachers, directors, administrators, or auxiliary staff. The Declaration invites us to expand on its contents and deepen them; in doing this, it is not our intention to ignore or minimize the significant accomplishments of Christians who belong to other Churches, or of non-Christians, in the field of education.

2. The most basic reason for this new role for Catholic laity, a role which the Church regards as positive and enriching, is theological. Especially in the course of the last century, the authentic image of the laity within the People of God has become increasingly clear; it has now been set down in two documents of the Second Vatican Council, which give profound expression to the richness and uniqueness of the lay vocation: The Dogmatic Constitution on the Church, and the Decree on the Apostolate of the Laity.

3. Theological development has been reinforced by the social, economic, and political developments of recent years. The cultural level has progressively risen; because this is closely tied to advances in science and technology, every profession requires a more extensive preparation. To this must be added a more general awareness of the fact that every person has a right to an integral education, an education which responds to all of the needs of the human person. These two advances in human life have required, and in part have created, an extensive development of school systems everywhere in the world, together with an extraordinary increase in the number of people who are professionally trained in education. As a result, there is a corresponding growth in the number of Catholic laity who work in the field.

This process has coincided with a notable decrease in the number of priests and Religious, both men and women, dedicated to teaching. The decrease is due to a lack of vocations, to the urgent call of other apostolic needs, and—at times—to the erroneous opinion that a school is no longer an appropriate place for the Church's pastoral activity.[3] The efficacious work that so many different Religious Congregations have traditionally accomplished through teaching activities is greatly esteemed by the Church; and so she can do no less than regret the decline in

Religious personnel which has had such a profound effect on Catholic schools, especially in some countries. The Church believes that, for an integral education of children and young people, both Religious and lay Catholics are needed in the schools.

4. This Sacred Congregation sees a genuine "sign of the times" for schools in the various facts and causes described above; it is an invitation to give special attention to the role of lay Catholics, as witnesses to the faith in what can only be described as a privileged environment for human formation. Without claiming to be exhaustive, but after serious and prolonged reflection on the importance of the theme, it desires to offer some considerations which will complete what has already been said in the document, *The Catholic School*, and which will be of help to all those interested in the problem, inspiring them to undertake further and more extended developments of the same.

I.
The Identity of the Lay Catholic in a School

5. It seems necessary to begin by trying to delineate the identity of the lay Catholics who work in a school; the way in which they bear witness to the faith will depend on this specific identity, in the Church and in this particular field of labor. In trying to contribute to the investigation, it is the intention of this Sacred Congregation to offer a service to lay Catholics who work in schools (and who should have a clear idea of the specific character of their vocation), and also to the People of God (who need to have a true picture of the laity as an active element, accomplishing an important task for the entire Church through their labor).

The Laity in the Church

6. The lay Catholic working in a school is, along with every Christian, a member of the People of God. As such, united to Christ through Baptism, he or she shares in the basic dignity that is common to all members. For, "they share a common dignity from their rebirth in Christ. They have the same filial grace and the same vocation to perfection. They possess in common one salvation, one hope, and one undivided charity."[4] Although it is true that, in the Church, "by the will of Christ, some are made teachers, dispensers of mysteries and shepherds on behalf of others, yet all share a true equality with regard to the dignity and to the activity common to all the faithful for the building up of the Body of Christ."[5]

Every Christian, and therefore also every lay person, has been made a sharer in "the priestly, prophetic, and kingly functions of Christ,"[6] and their apostolate "is a participation in the saving mission of the Church itself....All are commissioned to that apostolate by the Lord Himself."[7]

7. This call to personal holiness and to apostolic mission is common to all believers; but there are many cases in which the life of a lay person takes on specific characteristics which transform this life into a specific "wonderful" vocation within the Church. The laity "seeks the kingdom of God by engaging in temporal affairs and by ordering them according to the plan of God."[8] They live in the midst of the world's activities and professions, and in the ordinary circumstances of family and social life; and there they are called by God so that by exercising their proper function and being led by the spirit of the Gospel they can work for the sanctification of the world from within, in the manner of leaven. In this way they can make Christ known to others, especially by the testimony of a life resplendent in faith, hope, and charity."[9]

8. The renewal of the temporal order, giving it a Christian inspiration, is the special role of the laity; this should encourage them to heal "the institutions and conditions of the world"[10] when it is seen that these can be inducements to sin. In this way, human reality is raised up, and conformed to the Gospel as far as this is possible; and "the world is permeated by the Spirit of Christ, and more effectively achieves its purpose in justice, charity, and peace."[11] "Therefore, by their competence in secular fields, and by their personal activity, elevated from within by the grace of Christ, let them labor vigorously so that, by human labor, technical skill, and civic culture, created goods may be perfected for the benefit of every last person...and be more suitably distributed among them."[12]

9. The evangelization of the world involves an encounter with such a wide variety and complexity of different situations that very frequently, in concrete circumstances and for most people, only the laity can be effective witnesses of the Gospel. Therefore, "the laity are called in a special way to make the Church present and operative in those places and circumstances where only through them can she become the salt of the earth."[13] In order to achieve this presence of the whole Church, and of the Savior whom she proclaims, lay people must be ready to proclaim the message through their words, and witness to it in what they do.

10. Because of the experiences that lay people acquire in their lives, and through their presence in all of the various spheres of human activity, they will be especially capable of recognizing and clarifying the signs of the times that characterize the present historical period of the People of God. Therefore, as a proper part of their vocation, they should contribute their initiative, their creativity, and their competent, conscious, and enthusiastic labor to this task. In this way, the whole People of God will be able to distinguish more precisely those elements of the signs that are Gospel values, or values contrary to the Gospel.

Lay Catholics in the Schools

11. All those elements proper to the lay vocation in the Church are, surely, also true of those lay people who live their vocation in a school. But the fact that lay people can concretize their specific vocation in a variety of different sectors and areas of human life would seem to imply that the one common vocation will receive different specific characteristics from the different situations and states of life in which it is lived.

If, then, we are to have a better understanding of the school vocation of the lay Catholic, we must first look more precisely at the school.

The School

12. While it is true that parents are the first and foremost educators of their children[14] and that the rights and duties that they have in this regard are "original and primary with respect to the educational role of others,"[15] it is also true that among the means which will assist and complement the exercise of the educational rights and duties of the family, the school has a value and an importance that are fundamental. In virtue of its mission, then, the school must be concerned with constant and careful attention to cultivating in students the intellectual, creative, and aesthetic faculties of the human person; to develop in them the ability to make correct use of their judgment, will, and affectivity; to promote in them a sense of values; to encourage just attitudes and prudent behavior; to introduce them to the cultural patrimony handed down from previous generations; to prepare them for professional life, and to encourage the friendly interchange among students of diverse cultures and backgrounds that will lead to mutual understanding.[16] For all of these reasons, the school enters into the specific mission of the Church.

13. The function exercised by the school in society has no substitute; it is the most important institution that society has so far developed to respond to the right of each individual to an education and, therefore, to full personal development; it is one of the decisive elements in the structuring and the life of society itself. In today's world, social interchange and mass media grow in importance (and their influence is sometimes harmful or counter-productive); the cultural milieu continues to expand; preparation for professional life is becoming ever more complex, more varied, and more specialized. The family, on its own, is less and less able to confront all of these serious problems; the presence of the school, then, becomes more and more necessary.

14. If the school is such an important educational instrument, then the individual being educated has the right to choose the system of education—and therefore the type of school—that he or she prefers.[17] (When a person does not yet have the capacity to do this, then the parents, who have the primary rights in the education of their children,[18] have the right to make this choice). From this it clearly follows that, in principle, a State monopoly of education is not permissible,[19] and that only a pluralism of school systems will respect the fundamental right and the freedom of individuals—although the exercise of this right may be conditioned by a multiplicity of factors, according to the social realities of each country. The Church offers the Catholic school as a specific and enriching contribution to this variety of school possibilities. The lay Catholic, however, exercises the role of

evangelization in all the different schools, not only in the Catholic school, to the extent that this is possible in the diverse socio-political contexts of the present world.

The Lay Catholic as an Educator

15. The Second Vatican Council gives specific attention to the vocation of an educator, a vocation which is as proper to the laity[20] as to those who follow other states of life in the Church.

Every person who contributes to integral human formation is an educator; but teachers have made integral human formation their very profession. When, then, we discuss the school, teachers deserve special consideration: because of their number, but also because of the institutional purpose of the school. But everyone who has a share in this formation is also to be included in the discussion: especially those who are responsible for the direction of the school, or are counselors, tutors or coordinators; also those who complement and complete the educational activities of the teacher or help in administrative and auxiliary positions. While the present analysis of the lay Catholic as an educator will concentrate on the role of the teacher, the analysis is applicable to all of the other roles, each according to their own proper activity. The material can be a basis for deep personal reflection.

16. The teacher under discussion here is not simply a professional person who systematically transmits a body of knowledge in the context of a school; "teacher" is to be understood as "educator"—one who helps to form human persons. The task of a teacher goes well beyond transmission of knowledge, although that is not excluded. Therefore, if adequate professional preparation is required in order to transmit knowledge, then adequate professional preparation is even more necessary in order to fulfill the role of a genuine teacher. It is an indispensable human formation, and without it, it would be foolish to undertake any educational work.

One specific characteristic of the educational profession assumes its most profound significance in the Catholic educator: the communication of truth. For the Catholic educator, whatever is true is a participation in Him who is the Truth; the communication of truth, therefore, as a professional activity, is thus fundamentally transformed into a unique participation in the prophetic mission of Christ, carried on through one's teaching.

17. The integral formation of the human person, which is the purpose of education, includes the development of all the human faculties of the students, together with preparation for professional life, formation of ethical and social awareness, becoming aware of the transcendental, and religious education. Every school, and every educator in the school, ought to be striving "to form strong and responsible individuals, who are capable of making free and correct choices," thus preparing young people "to open themselves more and more to reality, and to form in themselves a clear idea of the meaning of life."[21]

18. Each type of education, moreover, is influenced by a particular concept of what it means to be a human person. In today's pluralistic world, the Catholic educator must consciously inspire his or her activity with the Christian concept of the person, in communion with the Magisterium of the Church. It is a concept which includes a defense of human rights, but also attributes to the human person the dignity of a child of God; it attributes the fullest liberty, freed from sin itself by Christ, the most exalted destiny, which is the definitive and total possession of God Himself, through love. It establishes the strictest possible relationship of solidarity among all persons; through mutual love and

an ecclesial community. It calls for the fullest development of all that is human, because we have been made masters of the world by its Creator. Finally, it proposes Christ, Incarnate Son of God and perfect Man, as both model and means; to imitate Him, is, for all men and women, the inexhaustible source of personal and communal perfection. Thus, Catholic educators can be certain that they make human beings more human.[22] Moreover, the special task of those educators who are lay persons is to offer to their students a concrete example of the fact that people deeply immersed in the world, living fully the same secular life as the vast majority of the human family, possess this same exalted dignity.

19. The vocation of every Catholic educator includes the work of ongoing social development: to form men and women who will be ready to take their place in society, preparing them in such a way that they will make the kind of social commitment which will enable them to work for the improvement of social structures, making these structures more conformed to the principles of the Gospel. Thus, they will form human beings who will make human society more peaceful, fraternal, and communitarian. Today's world has tremendous problems: hunger, illiteracy and human exploitation; sharp contrasts in the standard of living of individuals and of countries; aggression and violence, a growing drug problem, legalization of abortion, along with many other examples of the degradation of human life. All of this demands that Catholic educators develop in themselves, and cultivate in their students, a keen social awareness and a profound sense of civic and political responsibility. The Catholic educator, in other words, must be committed to the task of forming men and women who will make the "civilization of love"[23] a reality.

But lay educators must bring the experience of their own lives to this social development and social awareness, so that students can be prepared to take their place in society with an appreciation of the specific role of the lay person—for this is the life that nearly all of the students will be called to live.

20. A school uses its own specific means for the integral formation of the human person: the communication of culture. It is extremely important, then, that the Catholic educator reflect on the profound relationship that exists between culture and the Church. For the Church not only influences culture and is, in turn, conditioned by culture; the Church embraces everything in human culture which is compatible with Revelation and which it needs in order to proclaim the message of Christ and express it more adequately according to the cultural characteristics of each people and each age. The close relationship between culture and the life of the Church is an especially clear manifestation of the unity that exists between creation and redemption.

For this reason, if the communication of culture is to be a genuine educational activity, it must not only be organic, but also critical and evaluative, historical and dynamic. Faith will provide Catholic educators with some essential principles for critique and evaluation; faith will help them to see all of human history as a history of salvation which culminates in the fulness of the Kingdom. This puts culture into a creative context, constantly being perfected.

Here too, in the communication of culture, lay educators have a special role to play. They are the authors of, and the sharers in, the more lay aspects of culture; their mission, then, is to help the students come to understand, from a lay point of view, the global character that is proper to culture, the synthesis which will join together the lay and the religious aspects of culture, and the personal

contribution which those in the lay state can be expected to make to culture.

21. The communication of culture in an educational context involves a methodology, whose principles and techniques are collected together into a consistent pedagogy. A variety of pedagogical theories exist; the choice of the Catholic educator, based on a Christian concept of the human person, should be the practice of a pedagogy which gives special emphasis to direct and personal contact with the students. If the teacher undertakes this contact with the conviction that students are already in possession of fundamentally positive values, the relationship will allow for an openness and a dialogue which will facilitate an understanding of the witness to faith that is revealed through the behavior of the teacher.

22. Everything that the Catholic educator does in a school takes place within the structure of an educational community, made up of the contacts and the collaboration among all of the various groups—students, parents, teachers, directors, non-teaching staff—that together are responsible for making the school an instrument for integral formation. Although it is not exhaustive, this concept of the scholary institution as an educational community, together with a more widespread awareness of this concept, is one of the most enriching developments for the contemporary school. The Catholic educator exercises his or her profession as a member of one of the constitutive elements of this community. The professional structure itself offers an excellent opportunity to live—and bring to life in the students the communitarian dimension of the human person. Every human being is called to live in a community, as a social being, and as a member of the People of God.

Therefore, the educational community of a school is itself a "school." It teaches one how to be a member of the wider social communities; and when the educational community is at the same time a Christian community—and this is what the educational community of a Catholic school must always be striving toward—then it offers a great opportunity for the teachers to provide the students with a living example of what it means to be a member of that great community which is the Church.

23. The communitarian structure of the school brings the Catholic educator into contact with a wide and rich assortment of people; not only the students, who are the reason why the school and the teaching profession exist, but also with one's colleagues in the work of education, with parents, with other personnel in the school, with the school directors. The Catholic educator must be a source of spiritual inspiration for each of these groups, as well as for each of the scholastic and cultural organizations that the school comes in contact with, for the local Church and the parishes, for the entire human ambience in which he or she is inserted and, in a variety of ways, should have an effect on. In this way, the Catholic educator is called to display that kind of spiritual inspiration which will manifest different forms of evangelization.

24. To summarize: The lay Catholic educator is a person who exercises a specific mission within the Church by living, in faith, a secular vocation in the communitarian structure of the school: with the best possible professional qualifications, with an apostolic intention inspired by faith, for the integral formation of the human person, in a communication of culture, in an exercise of that pedagogy which will give emphasis to direct and personal contact with students, giving spiritual inspiration to the educational community of which he or she is a member, as well as to all the different persons related to the educational community. To this lay person, as a member of this community, the family and the Church entrust the school's educational endeavor. Lay teachers must be profoundly convinced that they share in the sanctifying, and therefore educational mission of the Church; they cannot regard themselves as cut off from the ecclesial complex.

II.
How to Live One's Personal Identity

25. The human person is called to be a worker; work is one of the characteristics which distinguish human beings from the rest of creatures.[24] From this it is evident that it is not enough to possess a vocational identity, an identity which involves the whole person; it must be lived. More concretely, if, through their work, human beings must contribute "above all to elevating unceasingly the cultural and moral level of society,"[25] then the educator who does not educate can no longer truly be called an educator. And if there is no trace of Catholic identity in the education, the educator can hardly be called a Catholic educator. Some of the aspects of this living out of one's identity are common and essential; they must be present no matter what the school is in which the lay educator exercises his or her vocation. Others will differ according to the diverse nature of various types of schools.

Common Elements of an Identity That Is Being Lived

Realism Combined With Hope

26. The identity of the lay Catholic educator is, of necessity, an ideal; innumerable obstacles stand in the way of its accomplishment. Some are the result of one's own personal situation; others are due to deficiencies in the school and in society; all of them have their strongest effect on children and young people. Identity crisis, loss of trust in social structures, the resulting insecurity and loss of any personal convictions, the contagion of a progressive secularization of society, loss of the proper concept of authority and lack of a proper use of freedom—these are only a few of the multitude of difficulties which, in varying degrees, according to the diverse cultures and the different countries, the adolescents and young people of today bring to the Catholic educator. Moreover, the lay state in which the teacher lives is itself seriously threatened by crises in the family and in the world of labor.

These present difficulties should be realistically recognized. But they should, at the same time, be viewed and confronted with a healthy optimism, and with the forceful courage that Christian hope and a sharing in the mystery of the Cross demand of all believers. Therefore, the first indispensable necessity in one who is going to live the identity of a lay Catholic educator is to sincerely share in, and make one's own, the statements that the Church, illuminated by Divine Revelation, has made about the identity of an educator. The strength needed to do this should be found through a personal identification with Christ.

Professionalism:
A Christian Concept of Humanity and of Life

27. Professionalism is one of the most important characteristics in the identity of every lay Catholic. The first requirement, then, for a lay educator who wishes to live out his or her ecclesial vocation, is the acquisition of a solid professional formation. In the case of an educator, this includes competency in a wide range of cultural, psychological, and pedagogical areas.[26] However, it is not enough that the initial training be at a good level; this must be maintained and deepened, always bringing it up to date. This can be very difficult for a lay teacher, and to ignore this fact is to ignore reality: salaries are often inadequate,

and supplementary employment is often a necessity. Such a situation is incompatible with professional development, either because of the time required for other work, or because of the fatigue that results. In many countries, especially in those less developed, the problem is insoluble at the present time.

Even so, educators must realize that poor teaching, resulting from insufficient preparation of classes or outdated pedagogical methods, is going to hinder them severely in their call to contribute to an integral formation of the students; it will also obscure the life witness that they must present.

28. The entire effort of the Catholic teacher is oriented toward an integral formation of each student. New horizons will be opened to students through the responses that Christian revelation brings to questions about the ultimate meaning of the human person, of human life, of history, and of the world. These must be offered to the students as responses which flow out of the profound faith of the educator, but at the same time with the greatest sensitive respect for the conscience of each student. Students will surely have many different levels of faith response; the Christian vision of existence must be presented in such a way that it meets all of these levels, ranging from the most elementary evangelization all the way to communion in the same faith. And whatever the situation, the presentation must always be in the nature of a gift: though offered insistently and urgently, it cannot be imposed.

On the other hand, the gift cannot be offered coldly and abstractly. It must be seen as a vital reality, one which deserves the commitment of the entire person, something which is to become a part of one's own life.

Synthesis of Faith, Culture and Life

29. For the accomplishment of this vast undertaking, many different educational elements must converge; in each of them, the lay Catholic must appear as a witness to faith. An organic, critical, and value-oriented communication of culture[27] clearly includes the communication of truth and knowledge; while doing this, a Catholic teacher should always be alert for opportunities to initiate the appropriate dialogue between culture and faith—two things which are intimately related—in order to bring the interior synthesis of the student to this deeper level. It is, of course, a synthesis which should already exist in the teacher.

30. Critical transmission also involves the presentation of a set of values and counter-values. These must be judged within the context of an appropriate concept of life and of the human person. The Catholic teacher, therefore, cannot be content simply to present Christian values as a set of abstract objectives to be admired, even if this be done positively and with imagination; they must be presented as values which generate human attitudes, and these attitudes must be encouraged in the students. Examples of such attitudes would be these: a freedom which includes respect for others; conscientious responsibility; a sincere and constant search for truth; a calm and peaceful critical spirit; a spirit of solidarity with and service toward all other persons; a sensitivity for justice; a special awareness of being called to be positive agents of change in a society that is undergoing continuous transformation.

Since Catholic teachers frequently have to exercise their mission within a general atmosphere of secularization and unbelief, it is important that they not be limited to a mentality that is merely experimental and critical; thus, they will be able to bring the students to an awareness of the transcendental, and dispose them to welcome revealed truth.

31. In the process of developing attitudes such as these, the teacher can more easily show the positive nature of the behavior that flows from such attitudes. Ideally, attitudes and behavior will gradually be motivated by, and flow out of, the interior faith of the individual student. In this way, the fulness of faith will be achieved; it will then extend to such things as filial prayer, sacramental life, love for one another, and a following of Jesus Christ—all of the elements that form a part of the specific heritage of the faithful. Knowledge, values, attitudes, and behavior fully integrated with faith will result in the student's personal synthesis of life and faith. Very few Catholics, then, have the opportunity that the educator has to accomplish the very purpose of evangelization: the incarnation of the Christian message in the lives of men and women.

Personal Life Witness:
Direct and Personal Contact with Students

32. Conduct is always much more important than speech; this fact becomes especially important in the formation period of students. The more completely an educator can give concrete witness to the model of the ideal person that is being presented to the students, the more this ideal will be believed and imitated. For it will then be seen as something reasonable and worthy of being lived, something concrete and realizable. It is in this context that the faith witness of the lay teacher becomes especially important. Students should see in their teachers the Christian attitude and behavior that is often so conspicuously absent from the secular atmosphere in which they live. Without this witness, living in such an atmosphere, they may begin to regard Christian behavior as an impossible ideal. It must never be forgotten that, in the crises "which have their greatest effect on the younger generations," the most important element in the educational endeavor is "always the individual person: the person, and the moral dignity of that person which is the result of his or her principles, and the conformity of actions with those principles."[28]

33. In this context, what was said above about direct and personal contact between teachers and students[29] becomes especially significant: it is a privileged opportunity for giving witness. A personal relationship is always a dialogue rather than a monologue, and the teacher must be convinced that the enrichment in the relationship is mutual. But the mission must never be lost sight of: the educator can never forget that students need a companion and guide during their period of growth; they need help from others in order to overcome doubts and disorientation. Also, rapport with the students ought to be a prudent combination of familiarity and distance; and this must be adapted to the need of each individual student. Familiarity will make a personal relationship easier, but a certain distance is also needed: students need to learn how to express their own personality without being pre-conditioned; they need to be freed from inhibitions in the responsible exercise of their freedom.

It is good to remember here that a responsible use of freedom also involves the choice of one's own state of life. In contacts with those students who are believers, Catholic teachers should not be hesitant to discuss the question of one's personal vocation in the Church. They should try to discover and cultivate vocations to the priesthood or to Religious life, or the call to live a private commitment in a Secular Institute or Catholic apostolic organization; these latter possibilities are areas which are often neglected. And they should also help students to discern a vocation to marriage or to celibacy, including consecrated celibacy, within the lay state.

This direct and personal contact is not just a methodology by which the teacher can help in the formation of the students; it is also the means by which teachers learn what they need to know about the students in order to guide them adequately. The difference in generation is deeper, and the time between generations is shorter, today more than ever before; direct contact, then, is more necessary than ever.

Communitarian Aspects

34. Along with a proper development of their individual personalities, and as an integral part of this process, students should be guided by their Catholic teachers toward the development of an attitude of sociability: toward others in the educational community, in the other communities that they may belong to, and with the entire human community. Lay Catholic educators are also members of the educational community; they influence, and are influenced by, the social ambience of the school. Therefore, close relationship should be established with one's colleagues; they should work together as a team. And teachers should establish close relationships with the other groups that make up the educational community, and be willing to contribute their share to all of the diverse activities that make up the common educational endeavor of a scholastic institution.

The family is "the first and fundamental school of social living"[30] therefore, there is a special duty to accept willingly and even to encourage opportunities for contact with the parents of students. These contacts are very necessary, because the educational task of the family and that of the school complement one another in many concrete areas; and they will facilitate the "serious duty" that parents have "to commit themselves totally to a cordial and active relationship with the teachers and the school authorities."[31] Finally, such contacts will offer to many families the assistance they need in order to educate their own children properly; and thus fulfill the "irreplaceable and inalienable"[32] function that is theirs.

35. A teacher must also be constantly attentive to the socio-cultural, economic, and political environment of the school: in the immediate area that the school is located in, and also in the region and the nation. Given today's means of communication, the national scene exerts a great influence on the local situation. Only close attention to the global reality—local, national, and international—will provide the data needed to give the kind of formation that students need now, and to prepare them for the future that can now be predicted.

36. While it is only natural to expect lay Catholic educators to give preference to Catholic professional associations, it is not foreign to their educational role to participate in and collaborate with all educational groups and associations, along with other groups that are connected with education. They should also lend support to the struggle for an adequate national educational policy, in whatever ways such support is possible. Their involvement may also include Trade Union activity, though always mindful of human rights and Christian educational principles.[33] Lay teachers should be reminded that professional life can sometimes be very remote from the activities of associations; they should realize that if they are never involved in or even aware of these activities, this absence could be seriously harmful to important educational issues.

It is true that there is often no reward for such activities; success or failure depends on the generosity of those who participate. But when there are issues at stake so vital that the Catholic teacher cannot ignore them, then generosity is urgently needed.

A Vocation, Rather than a Profession

37. The work of a lay educator has an undeniably professional aspect; but it cannot be reduced to professionalism alone. Professionalism is marked by, and raised to, a super-natural Christian vocation. The life of the Catholic teacher must be marked by the exercise of a personal vocation in the Church, and not simply by the exercise of a profession. In a lay vocation, detachment and generosity are joined to legitimate defense of personal rights; but it is still a vocation, with the fulness of life and the personal commitment that the word implies. It offers ample opportunity for a life filled with enthusiasm.

It is, therefore, very desirable that every lay Catholic educator become fully aware of the importance, the richness, and the responsibility of this vocation. They should fully respond to all of its demands, secure in the knowledge that their response is vital for the construction and ongoing renewal of the earthly city, and for the evangelization of the world.

Elements of the Catholic Educational Vocation Which Are Specific to Different Types of Schools

In the Catholic School

38. The distinctive feature of the Catholic school is "to create for the school community an atmosphere enlivened by the gospel spirit of freedom and charity. It aims to help the adolescent in such a way that the development of his or her own personality will be matched by the growth of that new creation which he or she becomes by baptism. It strives to relate all human culture eventually to the news of salvation, so that the light of faith will illumine the knowledge which students gradually gain of the world, of life and of the human race."[34] From all this, it is obvious that the Catholic school "fully enters into the salvific mission of the Church, especially in the need for education in the faith,"[35] and involves a sincere adherence to the Magisterium of the Church, a presentation of Christ as the supreme model of the human person, and a special care for the quality of the religious education in the school.

The lay Catholic who works in a Catholic school should be aware of the ideals and specific objectives which constitute the general educational philosophy of the institution, and realize that it is because of this educational philosophy that the Catholic school is the school in which the vocation of a lay Catholic teacher can be lived most freely and most completely. It is the model for the apostolic activity of lay Catholics in all other schools, according to the possibilities that each one of them offers. This realization will inspire lay Catholics in Catholic schools to commit themselves sincerely and personally to share in the responsibility for the attainment of these ideals and objectives. This is not to deny that difficulties exist; among them we mention, because of the great consequences that it has, the great heterogeneity of both students and teachers within the Catholic schools of many countries today.

39. Certain elements will be characteristic of all Catholic schools. But these can be expressed in a variety of ways; often enough, the concrete expression will correspond to the specific charism of the Religious Institute that founded the school and continues to direct it. Whatever be its origin—diocesan, Religious, or lay—each Catholic school can preserve its own specific character, spelled out in an educational philosophy, rationale, or in its own pedagogy. Lay Catholics should try to understand the special characteristics of the school they are working in, and the reasons that have inspired them. They should try to so identify themselves with these characteristics that their own work will help toward realizing the specific nature of the school.

40. As a visible manifestation of the faith they profess and the life witness they are supposed to manifest,[36] it is important that lay Catholics who work in a Catholic school participate simply and actively in the liturgical and sacramental life of the school. Students will share in this life more readily when they have concrete examples: when they see the importance that this life has for believers. In today's secularized world, students will see many lay people who call themselves Catholics, but who never take part in liturgy or sacraments. It is very important that they also have the example of lay adults who take such things seriously, who find in them a source and nourishment for Christian living.

41. The educational community of a Catholic school should be trying to become a Christian community: a genuine community of faith. This will not take place, it will not even begin to happen, unless there is a sharing of the Christian commitment among at least a portion of each of the principal groups that make up the educational community: parents, teachers, and students. It is highly desirable that every lay Catholic, especially the educator, be ready to participate actively in groups of pastoral inspiration, or in other groups capable of nourishing a life lived according to the Gospel.

42. At times there are students in Catholic schools who do not profess the Catholic faith, or perhaps are without any religious faith at all. Faith does not admit of violence; it is a free response of the human person to God as He reveals Himself. Therefore, while Catholic educators will teach doctrine in conformity with their own religious convictions and in accord with the identity of the school, they must at the same time have the greatest respect for those students who are not Catholics. They should be open at all times to authentic dialogue, convinced that in these circumstances the best testimony that they can give of their own faith is a warm and sincere appreciation for anyone who is honestly seeking God according to his or her own conscience.[37]

43. Education in the faith is a part of the finality of a Catholic school. The more fully the educational community represents the richness of the ecclesial community, the more capable it will be of fulfilling this mission. When priests, men and women Religious, and lay people are all present together in a school, they will present students with a living image of this richness, which can lead to a better understanding of the reality of the Church. Lay Catholics should reflect on the importance of their presence, from this point of view, alongside the priests and Religious. For each of these types of ecclesial vocation presents to the students its own distinct incarnational model: lay Catholics, the intimate dependence of earthly realities on God in Christ, the lay professional as one who disposes the world toward God; the priest, the multiple sources of grace offered by Christ to all believers through the sacraments, the revealing light of the Word, and the character of service which clothes the hierarchical structure of the Church; Religious, the radical spirit of Beatitudes, the continuous call of the Kingdom as the single definitive reality, the love of Christ, and the love of all men and women in Christ.

44. If each vocation has its own distinct characteristics, then all should be aware of the fact that a mutual and complementary presence will be a great help in ensuring the character of the Catholic school. This means that each one should be dedicated to the search for unity and coordination. Furthermore, the attitude of the lay people should be one which will help to insert the Catholic school into pastoral activities, in union with the local Church—a perspective which must never be forgotten—in ways that are complementary to the activities of parish ministry. The initiatives and experiences of lay people should also help to bring about more effective relationships and closer collaboration among Catholic schools, as well as between Catholic schools and other schools—especially those which share a Christian orientation—and with society as a whole.

45. Lay Catholic educators must be very aware of the real impoverishment which will result if priests and Religious disappear from the Catholic schools, or noticeably decline in number. This is to be avoided as far as is possible; and yet, the laity must prepare themselves in such a way that they will be able to maintain Catholic schools on their own whenever this becomes necessary or at least more desirable, in the present or in the future. Historical forces at work in the schools of today lead to the conclusion that, at least for the immediate future, continued existence of Catholic schools in many traditionally Catholic countries is going to depend largely on the laity, just as that existence has depended and does depend, with great fruit, on lay people in so many of the young Churches. This responsibility cannot be assumed with passive attitudes of fear and regret; it is a responsibility that offers a challenge to firm and effective action. And this action should even now look to and plan for the future with the help of the Religious Institutes who see their possibilities diminishing in the days immediately ahead.

46. There are times in which the Bishops will take advantage of the availability of competent lay persons who wish to give clear Christian witness in the field of education, and will entrust them with complete direction of Catholic schools, thus incorporating them more closely into the apostolic mission of the Church.[38]

Given the ever greater expansion of the field of education, the Church needs to take advantage of every available resource for the Christian education of youth. To increase the participation of lay Catholic educators is not meant to diminish the importance of those schools directed by Religious Congregations in any way. The unique kind of witness that men and women Religious give in their own teaching centers, whether as individuals or as a community, surely implies that these schools are more necessary than ever in a secularized world.

Few situations are as apt as their own schools for the members of a Religious community to give this kind of witness. For in the schools, Religious men and women establish an immediate and lasting contact with young people, in a context in which the truths of faith frequently come up spontaneously as a means to illuminate the varied dimensions of existence. This contact has a special importance at a time of life in which ideas and experiences leave such a lasting impression on the personality of the students.

However, the call of the Church to lay Catholic educators, to commit themselves to an active apostolate in education, is not a call limited to the Church's own schools. It is a call that extends to the entire vast teaching field, to the extent in which it may be possible to give Christian witness in teaching.

In Schools That Have Different Educational Philosophies

47. We now consider all those schools, public or private, whose educational philosophy is different from that of the Catholic school, but is not essentially incompatible with the Christian concept of the human person and of life. Schools of this type form the vast majority of the schools that exist in the world. Their educational philosophy may be developed by means of a well-defined concept of the human person and of life; more simply and narrowly, they may have a determined ideology;[39] or the school may admit the coexistence of a variety of philosophies and ideologies among the teachers, within the framework of some general principles. "Coexistence" should be understood here as a manifestation of pluralism: in such schools, each of the educators gives lessons, explains principles, and promotes values according to his or her own concept of the human person, and specific ideology. We do not speak here about the so-called neutral school because, in practice, such a school does not exist.

48. In today's pluralistic and secularized world, it will frequently happen that the presence of lay Catholics in these schools is the only way in which the Church is present. This is a concrete example of what was said above: that the Church can only reach out to certain situations or institutions through the laity.[40] A clear awareness of this fact will be a great help to encourage lay Cathoics to assume the responsibility that is theirs.

49. Lay Catholic teachers should be influenced by a Christian faith vision in the way they teach their course, to the extent that this is consistent with the subject matter, and the circumstances of the student body and the school. In doing this, they will help students to discover true human values; and even though they must work within the limitations proper to a school that makes no attempt to educate in the faith, in which many factors will actually work directly against faith education, they will still be able to contribute to the beginnings of a dialogue between faith and culture. It is a dialogue which may, one day, lead to the students' genuine synthesis of the two. This effort can be especially fruitful for those students who are Catholics; it can be a form of evangelization for those who are not.

50. In a pluralistic school, living according to one's faith must be joined to careful respect for the ideological convictions and the work of the other educators, assuming always that they do not violate the human rights of the students. Mutual respect should lead to constructive dialogue, especially with other Christians, but with all men and women of good will. In this way it can become clearly evident that religious and human freedom, the logical fruit of a pluralistic society, is not only defended in theory by Christian faith, but also concretely practiced.

51. Active participation in the activities of colleagues, in relationships with other members of the educational community; and especially in relationships with parents of the students, is extremely important. In this way the objectives, programs, and teaching methods of the school in which the lay Catholic is working can be gradually impregnated with the spirit of the Gospel.

52. Professional commitment; support of truth, justice and freedom; openness to the point of view of others, combined with an habitual attitude of service; personal commitment to the students, and fraternal solidarity with everyone; a life that is integrally moral in all its aspects. The lay Catholic who brings all of this to his or her work in a pluralist school becomes a living mirror, in whom every individual in the educational community will see reflected an image of one inspired by the Gospel.

In Other Schools

53. Here we consider more specifically the situation in schools of what are called mission countries, or countries where the practice of Christianity has almost totally disappeared. The lay Catholic may be the only presence of the Church, not only in the school, but also in the place in which he or she is living. The call of faith makes this situation especially compelling: the lay Catholic teacher may be the only voice that proclaims the message of the Gospel: to students, to other members of the educational community, to everyone that he or she comes in contact with, as an educator or simply as a person.[41] Everything that has been said above about awareness of responsibility, a Christian perspective in teaching (and in education more generally), respect for the convictions of others, constructive dialogue with other Christians as well as with those who do not believe in Christianity, active participation in various school groups, and, most important of all, personal life witness all of these things become crucially important in this type of school situation.

54. Finally, we cannot forget those lay Catholics who work in schools in countries where the Church is persecuted, where one who is known to be a Christian is forbidden to function as an educator. The orientation of the school is atheist; laity who work in them must conceal the fact that they are believers. In this difficult situation simple presence, if it is the silent but vital presence of a person inspired by the Gospel, is already an efficacious proclamation of the message of Christ. It is a counterbalance to the pernicious intentions of those who promote an atheistic education in the school. And this witness, when joined to personal contact with the students, can, in spite of the difficulties, lead to opportunities for more explicit evangelization. Although forced to live his or her Catholicism anonymously, the lay educator can still be (because of regrettable human and religious motives) the only way that many of the young people in these countries can come to some genuine knowledge of the Gospel and of the Church, which are distorted and attacked in the school.

55. In every kind of school, the Catholic educator will not infrequently come in contact with non-Catholic students, especially in some countries. The attitude should not only be one of respect, but also welcoming, and open to dialogue motivated by a universal Christian love. Furthermore, they should always remember that true education is not limited to the imparting of knowledge; it promotes human dignity and genuine human relationships, and prepares the way for opening oneself to the Truth that is Christ.

The Lay Catholic Educator as a Teacher of Religion

56. Religious instruction is appropriate in every school, for the purpose of the school is human formation in all of its fundamental dimensions, and the religious dimension is an integral part of this formation. Religious education is actually a right—with the corresponding duties—of the student and of the parents. It is also, at least in the case of the Catholic religion, an extremely important instrument for attaining the adequate synthesis of faith and culture that has been insisted on so often.

Therefore, the teaching of the Catholic religion, distinct from and at the same time complementary to catechesis properly so-called,[42] ought to form a part of the curriculum of every school.

57. The teaching of religion is, along with catechesis, "an eminent form of the lay apostolate."[43] Because of this, and because of the number of religion teachers needed for today's vast school systems, lay people will have the responsibility for religious education in the majority of cases, especially at the level of basic education.

58. Lay Catholics, therefore, in different places and according to different circumstances, should become aware of the great role that is offered to them in this field of religious education. Without their generous collaboration, the number of religious teachers will not be adequate to meet the need that exists; this is already the situation in some countries. In this respect, as in so many others, the Church depends on lay collaboration. The need can be especially urgent in young Churches.

59. The role of the religion teacher is of first importance; for "what is asked for is not that one impart one's own doctrine, or that of some other teacher, but the teaching of Jesus Christ Himself."[44] In their teaching, therefore, taking into account the nature of the group being taught, teachers of religion (and also catechists) "should take advantage of every opportunity to profit from the fruits of theological research, which can shed light on their own reflections and also on their teaching, always taking care...to be faithful to the genuine sources, and to the light of the Magisterium," on which they depend for the proper fulfillment of their role; and "they should refrain from upsetting the minds of children and young people...with outlandish theories."[45] The norms of the local bishop should be faithfully followed in everything that has to do with their own theological and pedagogical formation, and also in the course syllabi; and they should remember that, in this area above all, life witness and an intensely lived spirituality have an especially great importance.

III.
The Formation That Is Needed if Lay Catholics Are to Give Witness to the Faith in a School

60. The concrete living out of a vocation as rich and profound as that of the lay Catholic in a school requires an appropriate formation, both on the professional plane and on the religious plane. Most especially, it requires the educator to have a mature spiritual personality, expressed in a profound Christian life. "This calling," says the Second Vatican Council, speaking about educators, requires "extremely careful preparation."[46] "(Teachers) should therefore be trained with particular care, so that they may be enriched with both secular and religious knowledge, appropriately certified, and may be equipped with an educational skill which reflects modern day findings."[47] The need for an adequate formation is often felt most acutely in religious and spiritual areas; all too frequently, lay Catholics have not had a religious formation that is equal to their general, cultural, and, most especially, professional formation.

Awareness and Stimulation

61. Generally speaking, lay Catholics preparing themselves for work in a school have a genuine human vocation; they are very aware of the good professional formation that they need in order to become educators. But an awareness that is limited only to the professional level is not what ought to characterize a lay Catholic, whose educational work is the basic instrument for personal sanctification and the exercise of an apostolic mission. What is being asked of lay Catholics who work in schools is precisely an awareness that what they are doing is exercising a vocation. To what extent they actually do have such an awareness is something that these lay people should be asking themselves.

62. The need for religious formation is related to this specific awareness that is being asked of lay Catholics; religious formation must be broadened and be kept up to date, on the same level as, and in harmony with, human formation as a whole. Lay Catholics need to be keenly aware of the need for this kind of religious formation; it is not only the

exercise of an apostolate that depends on it, but even an appropriate professional competence, especially when the competence is in the field of education.

63. The purpose of these reflections is to help awaken such a consciousness, and to help each individual to consider his or her own personal situation in an area which is so fundamental for the full exercise of the lay vocation of a Catholic educator. What is at stake is so essential that simply to become aware of it should be a major stimulus toward putting forth the effort needed: to acquire whatever may have been lacking in formation, and to maintain at an adequate level all that has been already acquired. Lay Catholic educators also have a right to expect that, within the ecclesial community, bishops, priests, and Religious, especially those dedicated to the apostolate of education, and also various groups and associations of lay Catholic educators, will help to awaken them to their personal needs in the area of formation, and will find the means to stimulate them so that they can give themselves more totally to the social commitment that such a formation requires.

Professional and Religious Formation

64. It may be worth noting that centers of teacher formation will differ in their ability to provide the kind of professional training that will best help Catholic educators to fulfill their educational mission. The reason for this is the close relationship that exists between the way a discipline (especially in the humanities) is taught, and the teacher's basic concept of the human person, of life, and of the world. If the ideological orientation of a center for teacher formation is pluralist, it can easily happen that the future Catholic educator will have to do supplementary work in order to make a personal synthesis of faith and culture in the different disciplines that are being studied. It must never be forgotten, during the days of formation, that the role of a teacher is to present the class materials in such a way that students can easily discover a dialogue between faith and culture, and gradually be led to a personal synthesis of these. If we take all of this into account, it follows that it would be better to attend a center for teacher formation under the direction of the Church where one exists, and to create such centers, if possible, where they do not yet exist.

65. For the Catholic educator, religious formation does not come to an end with the completion of basic education; it must be a part of and a complement to one's professional formation, and so be proportionate to adult faith, human culture, and the specific lay vocation. This means that religious formation must be oriented toward both personal sanctification and apostolic mission, for these are two inseparable elements in a Christian vocation. "Formation for apostolic mission means a certain human and well-rounded formation, adapted to the natural abilities and circumstances of each person" and requires "in addition to spiritual formation,... solid doctrinal instruction...in theology, ethics and philosophy."[48] Nor can we forget, in the case of an educator, adequate formation in the social teachings of the Church, which are "an integral part of the Christian concept of life,"[49] and help to keep intensely alive the kind of social sensitivity that is needed.[50]

With regard to the doctrinal plane, and speaking more specifically of teachers, it may be worth recalling that the Second Vatican Council speaks of the need for religious knowledge guaranteed by appropriate certification.[51] It is highly recommended, therefore, that all Catholics who work in schools, and most especially those who are educators, obtain the necessary qualifications by pursuing programs of religious formation in

Ecclesiastical Faculties or in Institutes of Religious Science that are suitable for this purpose, wherever this is possible.

66. With appropriate degrees, and with an adequate preparation in religious pedagogy, they will have the basic training needed for the teaching of religion. Bishops will promote and provide for the necessary training, both for teachers of religion and for catechists; at the same time, they will not neglect the kind of dialogue with the corps of teachers being formed that can be mutually enlightening.

Updating Permanent Formation

67. Recent years have witnessed an extraordinary growth in science and technology; every object, situation, or value is subjected to a constant critical analysis. One effect is that our age is characterized by change; change that is constant and accelerated, that affects every last aspect of the human person and the society that he or she lives in. Because of change, knowledge that has been acquired, and structures that have been established, are quickly outdated; the need for new attitudes and new methods is constant.

68. Faced with this reality, which lay people are the first to experience, the Catholic educator has an obvious and constant need for updating: in personal attitudes, in the content of the subjects, that are taught, in the pedagogical methods that are used. Recall that the vocation of an educator requires "a constant readiness to begin anew and to adapt."[52] If the need for updating is constant, then the formation must be permanent. This need is not limited to professional formation; it includes religious formation and, in general, the enrichment of the whole person. In this way, the Church will constantly adapt its pastoral mission to the circumstances of the men and women of each age, so that the message of

Jesus Christ can be brought to them in a way that is understandable and adapted to their condition.

69. Permanent formation involves a wide variety of different elements; a constant search for ways to bring it about is therefore required of both individuals and the community. Among the variety of means for permanent formation, some have become ordinary and virtually indispensable instruments: reading periodicals and pertinent books, attending conferences and seminars, participating in workshops, assemblies and congresses, making appropriate use of periods of free time for formation. All lay Catholics who work in schools should make these a habitual part of their own human, professional, and religious life.

70. No one can deny that permanent formation, as the name itself suggests, is a difficult task; not everyone succeeds in doing it. This becomes especially true in the face of the growing complexity of contemporary life and the difficult nature of the educational mission, combined with the economic insecurity that so often accompanies it. But in spite of all these factors, no lay Catholic who works in a school can ignore this present-day need. To do so would be to remain locked up in outdated knowledge, criteria, and attitudes. To reject a formation that is permanent and that involves the whole person—human, professional, and religious—is to isolate oneself from that very world that has to be brought closer to the Gospel.

IV.
The Support That the Church Offers to Lay Catholics Working in Schools

71. The different circumstances in which lay Catholics have to carry out their work in schools can often create feelings of isolation or misunderstanding, and as a result lead to depression, or even to the giving up of teaching responsibilities. In order to find help in overcoming such difficulties; in order, more generally, to be helped to fulfill the vocation to which they are called, lay Catholics who work in schools should always be able to count on the support and aid of the entire Church.

Support in the Faith, in the Word, and in Sacramental Life

72. Above all else, lay Catholics will find support in their own faith. Faith is the unfailing source of the humility, the hope, and the charity needed for perseverence in their vocation.[53] For every educator is in need of humility in order to recognize one's own limitations, one's mistakes, along with the need for constant growth, and the realization that the ideal being pursued is always beyond one's grasp. Every educator needs a firm hope, because the teacher is never the one who truly reaps the fruits of the labor expended on the students. And, finally, every educator is in need of a permanent and growing charity, in order to love each of the students as an individual created in the image and likeness of God, raised to the status of a child of God by the redemption of Jesus Christ.

This humble faith, this hope, and this charity are supported by the Church through the Word, the life of the Sacraments, and the prayer of the entire People of God.

For the Word will speak to educators, and remind them of the tremendous greatness of their identity and of their task; Sacramental life will give them the strength they need to live this career, and bring support when they fail; the prayer of the whole Church will present to God, with them and for them, with the assured response that Jesus Christ has promised, all that the human heart desires and pleads for, and even the things that it does not dare to desire or plead for.

Community Support

73. The work of education is arduous, and very important; for that reason, its realization is delicate and complex. It requires calm, interior peace, freedom from an excessive amount of work, continuous cultural and religious enrichment. In today's society, it is seldom that conditions can all be met simultaneously. The nature of the educational vocation of lay Catholics should be publicized more frequently and more profoundly among the People of God by those in the Church most capable of doing it. The theme of education, with all that is implied in this term, should be developed more insistently; for education is one of the great opportunities for the salvific mission of the Church.

74. From this knowledge will logically flow understanding and proper esteem. All of the faithful should be conscious of the fact that, without lay Catholics as educators, the Church's education in the faith would lack one of its important basic elements. As far as they can, therefore, all believers should actively collaborate in the work of helping educators to reach the social status and the economic level that is their due, together with the stability and the security that they must have if they are to accomplish their task. No members of the Church can be considered exempt from the struggle to ensure that, in each of their countries, both the legislation of educational policy and the practical carrying out of this legislation reflect, as far as possible, Christian educational principles.

75. Contemporary world conditions should be an inducement for the hierarchy, along with those Religious Institutes that have a commitment to education, to give their support to existing groups, movements, and Catholic Associations of lay believers engaged in education; and also to create other, new groups, always searching for the type of association that will best respond to the needs of the times and the different situations in different countries. The vocation of the lay Catholic educator requires the fulfillment of many educational objectives, along with the social and religious objectives that flow from them. These will be virtually impossible to bring into reality without the united strength of strong associations.

The Support of the Educational Institutions Themselves: The Catholic School and the Laity

76. The importance of the Catholic school suggests that we reflect specifically on this case; it can serve as a concrete example of how other Catholic institutions should support the lay people who work in them. In speaking about lay people, this Sacred Congregation has declared without hesitation that "by their witness and behavior, teachers are of the first importance to impart a distinctive character to Catholic schools."[54]

77. Before all else, lay people should find in a Catholic school an atmosphere of sincere respect and cordiality; it should be a place in which authentic human relationships can be formed among all of the educators. Priests, men and women Religious, and lay persons, each preserving their specific vocational identity,[55] should be integrated fully into one educational community; and each one should be treated as a fully equal member of that community.

78. If the directors of the school and the lay people who work in the school are to live according to the same ideals, two things are essential. First, lay people must receive an adequate salary, guaranteed by a well defined contract, for the work they do in the school: a salary that will permit them to live in dignity, without excessive work or a need for additional employment that will interfere with the duties of an educator. This may not be immediately possible without putting an enormous financial burden on the families, or making the school so expensive that it becomes a school for a small elite group; but so long as a truly adequate salary is not being paid, the laity should see in the school directors a genuine preoccupation to find the resources necessary to achieve this end. Secondly, laity should participate authentically in the responsibility for the school; this assumes that they have the ability that is needed in all areas, and are sincerely committed to the educational objectives which characterize a Catholic school. And the school should use every means possible to encourage this kind of commitment; without it, the objectives of the school can never be fully realized. It must never be forgotten that the school itself is always in the process of being created, due to the labor brought to fruition by all those who have a role to play in it, and most especially by those who are teachers.[56] To achieve the kind of participation that is desirable, several conditions are indispensable: genuine esteem of the lay vocation, sharing the information that is necessary, deep confidence, and, finally, when it should become necessary, turning over the distinct responsibilities for teaching, administration, and government of the school, to the laity.

79. As a part of its mission, an element proper to the school is solicitous care for the permanent professional and religious formation of its lay members. Lay people should be able to look to the school for the orientation and the assistance that they need, including the willingness to make time available when this is needed. Formation is indispensable; without it, the school will wander further and further away from its objectives. Often enough, if it will join forces with other educational centers and with Catholic professional organizations, a Catholic school will not find it too difficult to organize conferences, seminars, and other meetings which will provide the needed formation. According to circumstances, these could be expanded to include other lay Catholic educators who do not work in Catholic schools; these people would thus be offered an opportunity they are frequently in need of, and do not easily find elsewhere.

80. The ongoing improvement of the Catholic school, and the assistance which the school, joined to other educational institutions of the Church, can offer to lay Catholic educators, depend heavily on the support that Catholic families offer to the school—families in general, and most especially those that send their children to these schools. Families should recognize the level of their responsibility for a support that extends to all aspects of the school: interest, esteem, collaboration, and economic assistance. Not everyone can collaborate to the same degree or in the same way; nonetheless, each one should be ready to be as generous as possible, according to the resources that are available. Collaboration of the families should extend to a share in accomplishing the objectives of the school, and also sharing in responsibility for the school. And the school should keep the families informed about the ways in which the educational philosophy is being applied or improved on, about formation, about administration, and, in certain cases, about the management.

Conclusion

81. Lay Catholic educators in schools, whether teachers, directors, administrators, or auxiliary staff, must never have any doubts about the fact that they constitute an element of great hope for the Church. The Church puts its trust in them entrusting them with the task of gradually bringing about an integration of temporal reality with the Gospel, so that the Gospel can thus reach into the lives of all men and women. More particularly, it has entrusted them with the integral human formation and the faith education of young people. These young people are the ones who will determine whether the world of tomorrow is more closely or more loosely bound to Christ.

82. This Sacred Congregation for Catholic Education echoes the same hope. When it considers the tremendous evangelical resource embodied in the millions of lay Catholics who devote their lives to schools, it recalls the words with which the Second Vatican Council ended its Decree on the Apostolate of the Laity, and "earnestly entreats in the Lord that all lay persons give a glad, generous, and prompt response to the voice of Christ, who is giving them an especially urgent invitation at this moment;...they should respond to it eagerly and magnanimously...and, recognizing that what is His is also their own (Phil 2, 5), to associate themselves with Him in His saving mission....Thus they can show that they are His co-workers in the various forms and methods of the Church's one apostolate, which must be constantly adapted to the new needs of the times. May they always abound in the works of God, knowing that they will not labor in vain when their labor is for Him (Cf. I Cor 15, 58)."[57]

Rome, October 15, 1982, Feast of St. Teresa of Jesus, in the Fourth Centenary of her death

† **William Cardinal Baum**
Prefect

† **Antonio M. Javierre**
Titular Archbishop of Meta
Secretary

[1] Second Vatican Council: Const. *Lumen Gentium*, n. 31: "The term laity is here understood to mean all the faithful except those in holy orders and those in a religious state sanctioned by the Church."

[2] Cf. Second Vatican Council: Decl. *Gravissimum educationis*, n. 8.

[3] Cf. Sacred Congregation for Catholic Education: *The Catholic School*, March 19, 1979, nn. 18-22.

[4] Second Vatican Council: Const. *Lumen Gentium*, n. 32.

[5] Ibid.

[6] Ibid., n. 31.

[7] Ibid., n. 33.

[8] Ibid., n. 31.

[9] Ibid.

[10] Second Vatican Council: Const. *Lumen Gentium*, n. 36; Cf. Decl. *Apostolicam actuositatem*, n. 7.

[11] Second Vatican Council: Const. *Lumen Gentium*, n. 36.

[12] Ibid.

[13] Ibid., n. 33.

[14] Cf. Second Vatican Council: Decl. *Gravissimum educationis*, n. 3.

[15] John Paul II, Apostolic Exhortation *Familiaris consortio*, Nov. 22, 1981, *AAS*, 74 (1982) n. 36. Pag. 126.

[16] Cf. Second Vatican Council: Decl. *Gravissimum educationis*, n. 5.

[17] Ibid., n. 3.

[18] Ibid., n. 6; *Universal Declaration on Human Rights*, art. 26, 3.

[19] Cf. Second Vatican Council: Decl. *Gravissimum educationis*, n. 6.

[20] Ibid., n. 5; Cf. Paul VI, Apostolic Exhortation *Evangelii nuntiandi*, December 8, 1975, *AAS* 68 (1976) n. 70, pp. 59-60.

[21] Sacred Congregation for Catholic Education: *The Catholic School*, n. 31.

[22] Cf. Paul VI, Encyclical Letter *Populorum progressio*; March 26, 1967, *AAS* 59 (1967), n. 19, pp. 267-268; cf. John Paul II, *Discourse to UNESCO*, June 2, 1980, *AAS* 72 (1980) n. 11, p. 742.

[23] Paul VI, *Discourse on Christmas Night*, December 25, 1976, *AAS* 68 (1976) p. 145.

[24] Cf. John Paul II, Encyclical Letter *Laborem exercens*, 14. Sept. 1981, *AAS* 73 (1981), Foreword, p. 578.

25 John Paul II, Encyclical Letter *Laborem exercens*, ibid. p. 577.

26 Cf. above, n. 16.

27 Cf. above, n. 20.

28 John Paul II, *Discourse to UNESCO*, June 2, 1980, *AAS* 72 (1980) n. 11, p. 742.

29 Cf. above, n. 21.

30 John Paul II, Apostolic Exhortation *Familiaris consortio*, *AAS*, 74 (1982) n. 37, p. 127.

31 Ibid., n. 40.

32 Ibid., n. 36.

33 Cf. John Paul II, Encyclical Letter *Laborem exercens*, September 14, 1981, *AAS* 73 (1981) n. 20, pp. 629-632.

34 Second Vatican Council, Decl. *Gravissimum educationis*, n. 8; cf. Sacred Congregation for Catholic Education: *The Catholic School*, n. 34.

35 Sacred Congregation for Catholic Education: *The Catholic School*, n. 9.

36 Cf. above, n. 29 and n. 32.

37 Cf. Second Vatican Council, Decl. *Dignitatis humanae*, n. 3.

38 Cf. *Apostolicam actuositatem*, n. 2.

39 The concept here is a more ample one: a system of ideas joined to social, economic, and/or political structures.

40 Cf. above n. 9.

41 Cf. Second Vatican Council, Decl. *Ad Gentes*, n. 21.

42 Cf. John Paul II, *Discourse to the Clerics of Rome Concerning the Teaching of Religion and Catechesis*, March 5, 1981, *Insegnamenti di Giovanni Paolo II*, 1981, IV, I, n. 3, p. 630.

43 John Paul II, Apostolic Exhortation *Catechesi tradendae*, October 16, 1979, *AAS* 71 n. 66, p. 1331.

44 Ibid., n. 6.

45 Ibid., n. 61.

46 Second Vatican Council: Decl. *Gravissimum educationis*, n. 5.

47 Ibid., n. 8.

48 Second Vatican Council: Decree *Apostolicam actuositatem*, n. 29.

49 John Paul II, *Discourse on the Occasion of the 90th Anniversary of Rerum Novarum*, May 13, 1981 (not delivered), *L'Osservatore Romano*, May 15, 1981.

50 Cf. Ibid.

51 Cf. Second Vatican Council, Decl. *Gravissimum educationis*, n. 8.

52 Second Vatican Council, Decl. *Gravissimum educationis*, n. 5.

53 Cf. Sacred Congregation for Catholic Education, *The Catholic School*, n. 75.

54 Sacred Congregation for Catholic Education, *The Catholic School*, n. 78.

55 Cf above, n. 43

56 Cf. John Paul II, Encyclical Letter *Laborem Exercens*, *AAS*, 73, (1981) n. 14, p. 614.

57 Second Vatican Council, Decree *Apostolicam actuositatem*, n. 33.

The Religious Dimension of Education in a Catholic School: Guidelines for Reflection and Renewal

CONGREGATION FOR CATHOLIC EDUCATION
April 7, 1988

Introduction

1. On October 28, 1965, the Second Vatican Council promulgated the Declaration on Christian Education *Gravissimum educationis*. The document describes the distinguishing characteristic of a Catholic school in this way; "The Catholic school pursues cultural goals and the natural development of youth to the same degree as any other school. What makes the Catholic school distinctive is its attempt to generate a community climate in the school that is permeated by the Gospel spirit of freedom and love. It tries to guide the adolescents in such a way that personality development goes hand in hand with the development of the 'new creature' that each one has become through baptism. It tries to relate all of human culture to the good news of salvation so that the light of faith will illumine everything that the students will gradually come to learn about the world, about life, and about the human person."[1]

The Council, therefore, declared that what makes the Catholic school distinctive is its religious dimension, and that this is to be found in (*a*) the educational climate, (*b*) the personal development of each student, (*c*) the relationship established between culture and the Gospel, (*d*) the illumination of all knowledge with the light of faith.

2. More than twenty years have passed since this declaration of the Council. In response to suggestions received from many parts of the world, the Congregation for Catholic Education warmly invites local ordinaries and the superiors of Religious Congregations dedicated to the education of young people to examine whether or not the words of the Council have become a reality. The Second Extraordinary General Assembly of the Synod of Bishops of 1985 said that this opportunity should not be missed! The reflection should lead to concrete decisions about what can and should be done to make Catholic schools more effective in meeting the expectations of the Church, expectations shared by many families and students.

3. In order to be of assistance in implementing the Council's declaration, the Congregation for Catholic Education has already published several papers dealing with questions of concern to Catholic schools. *The Catholic School*[2] develops a basic outline of the specific identity and mission of the school in today's world. *Lay Catholics in Schools: Witnesses to the Faith*[3] emphasizes the contributions of lay people, who complement the valuable service offered in the past and still offered today by so many Religious Congregations of men and women. This present document is closely linked to the preceding ones; it is based on the same sources, appropriately applied to the world of today.[4]

4. The present document restricts its attention to Catholic schools: that is, educational institutions of whatever type, devoted to the formation of young people at all pre-university levels, dependent on ecclesiastical authority, and therefore falling within the competence of this Dicastery. This clearly leaves many other questions untouched, but it is better to concentrate our attention on one area rather than try to deal with several different issues at once. We are confident that attention will be given to the other questions at some appropriate time.[5]

5. The pages which follow contain guidelines which are rather general. Different regions, different schools, and even different classes within the same school will have their own distinct history, ambience, and personal characteristics. The Congregation asks bishops, Religious superiors and those in charge of the schools to study these general guidelines and adapt them to their own local situations.

6. Not all students in Catholic schools are members of the Catholic Church; not all are Christians. There are, in fact, countries in which the vast majority of the students are not Catholics—a reality which the Council called attention to.[6] The religious freedom and the personal conscience of individual students and their families must be respected, and this freedom is explicitly recognized by the Church.[7] On the other hand, a Catholic school cannot relinquish its own freedom to proclaim the Gospel and to offer a formation based on the values to be found in a Christian education; this is its right and its duty. To proclaim or to offer is not to impose, however; the latter suggests a moral violence which is strictly forbidden, both by the Gospel and by Church law.[8]

I.
The Religious Dimension in the Lives of Today's Youth

Youth in a Changing World

7. The Council provided a realistic analysis of the religious condition in the world today,[9] and paid explicit attention to the special situation of young people;[10] educators must do the same. Whatever methods they employ to do this, they should be attentive to the results of research with youth done at the local level, and they should be mindful of the fact that the young today are, in some respects, different from those that the Council had in mind.

8. Many Catholic schools are located in countries which are undergoing radical changes in outlook and in lifestyle: these countries are becoming urbanized and industrialized, and are moving into the so-called "tertiary" economy, characterized by a high standard of living, a wide choice of educational opportunities, and complex communication systems. Young people in these countries are familiar with the media from their infancy; they have been exposed to a wide variety of opinions on every possible topic, and are surprisingly well-informed even when they are still very young.

9. These young people absorb a wide and varied assortment of knowledge from all kinds of sources, including the school. But they are not yet capable of ordering or prioritizing what they have learned. Often enough, they do not yet have the critical ability needed to distinguish the true and good from their opposites; they have not acquired the necessary religious and moral criteria that will enable them to remain objective and independent when faced with the prevailing attitudes and habits of society. Concepts such as truth, beauty and goodness have become so vague today that young people do not know where to turn to find help; even when they are able to hold on to certain values, they do not yet have the capacity to develop these values into a way of life; all too often they are more inclined simply to go their own way, accepting whatever is popular at the moment.

Changes occur in different ways and at different rates. Each school will have to look carefully at the religious behavior of the young people "in loco" in order to discover their thought processes, their lifestyle, their reaction to change. Depending on the situation, the change may be profound, it may be only beginning, or the local culture may be resistant to change. Even a culture resistant to change is being influenced by the all-pervasive mass media!

Some Common Characteristics of the Young

10. Although local situations create great diversity, there are characteristics that today's young people have in common, and educators need to be aware of them.

Many young people find themselves in a condition of radical instability. On the one hand they live in a one dimensional universe in which the only criterion is practical utility and the only value is economic and technological progress. On the other hand, these same young people seem to be progressing to a stage beyond this narrow universe; nearly everywhere, evidence can be found of a desire to be released from it.

11. Others live in an environment devoid of truly human relationships; as a result, they suffer from loneliness and a lack of affection. This is a widespread phenomenon that seems to be independent of lifestyle: it is found in oppressive regimes, among the homeless, and in the cold and impersonal dwellings of the rich. Young people today are notably more depressed than in the past; this is surely a sign of the poverty of human relationships in families and in society today.

12. Large numbers of today's youth are very worried about an uncertain future. They have been influenced by a world in which human values are in chaos because these values are no longer rooted in God; the result is that these young people are very much afraid when they think about the appalling problems in the world: the threat of nuclear annihilation, vast unemployment, the high number of marriages that end in separation or divorce, widespread poverty, etc. Their worry and insecurity become an almost irresistible urge to focus in on themselves, and this can lead to violence when young people are together—a violence that is not always limited to words.

13. Not a few young people, unable to find any meaning in life or trying to find an escape from loneliness, turn to alcohol, drugs, the erotic, the exotic, etc. Christian education is faced with the huge challenge of helping these young people discover something of value in their lives.

14. The normal instability of youth is accentuated by the times they are living in. Their decisions are not solidly based: today's "yes" easily becomes tomorrow's "no."

Finally, a vague sort of generosity is characteristic of many young people. Filled with enthusiasm, they are eager to join in popular causes. Too often, however, these movements are without any specific orientation or inner coherence. It is important to channel this potential for good and, when possible, give it the orientation that comes from the light of faith.

15. In some parts of the world it might be profitable to pay particular attention to the reasons why young people abandon their faith. Often enough, this begins by giving up religious practices. As time goes on, it can develop into a hostility toward Church structures and a crisis of conscience regarding the truths of faith and their accompanying moral values. This can be especially true in those countries where education in general is secular or even imbued with atheism. The crisis seems to occur more frequently in places where there is high economic development and rapid social and cultural change. Sometimes the phenomenon is not recent; it is something that the parents went through, and they are now passing their own attitudes along to the new generation. When this is the case, it is no longer a personal crisis, but one that has become religious and social. It has been called a "split between the Gospel and culture."[11]

16. A break with the faith often takes the form of total religious indifference. Experts suggest that certain patterns of behavior found among young people are actually attempts to fill the religious void with some sort of a substitute: the pagan cult of the body, drug escape, or even those massive "youth events" which sometimes deteriorate into fanaticism and total alienation from reality.

17. Educators cannot be content with merely observing these behavior patterns; they have to search for the causes. It may be some lack at the start, some problem in the family background. Or it may be that parish and Church organizations are deficient. Christian formation given in childhood and early adolescence is not always proof against the influence of the environment. Perhaps there are cases in which the fault lies with the Catholic school itself.

18. There are also a number of positive signs, which give grounds for encouragement. In a Catholic school, as in any school, one can find young people who are outstanding in every way—in religious attitude, moral behavior, and academic achievement. When we look for the cause, we often discover an excellent family background reinforced by both Church and school. There is always a combination of factors, open to the interior workings of grace.

Some young people are searching for a deeper understanding of their religion; as they reflect on the real meaning of life they begin to find answers to their questions in the Gospel. Others have already passed through the crisis of indifference and doubt, and are now ready to commit themselves—or recommit themselves—to a Christian way of life. These positive signs give us reason to hope that a sense of religion can develop in more of today's young people, and that it can be more deeply rooted in them.

19. For some of today's youth, the years spent in a Catholic school seem to have scarcely any effect. They seem to have a negative attitude toward all the various ways in which a Christian life is expressed—prayer, participation in the Mass, or frequenting of the Sacraments. Some even reject these expressions outright, especially those associated with an institutional Church. If a school is excellent as an academic institution, but does not witness to authentic values, then both good pedagogy and a concern for pastoral care make it obvious that renewal is called for—not only in the content and methodology of religious instruction, but in the overall school planning which governs the whole process of formation of the students.

20. The religious questioning of young people today needs to be better understood. Many of them are asking about the value of science and technology when everything could end in a nuclear holocaust; they look at how modern civilization floods the world with material goods, beautiful and useful as these may be, and they wonder whether the purpose of life is really to possess many "things" or whether there may not be something far more valuable; they are deeply disturbed by the injustice which divides the free and the rich from the poor and the oppressed.

21. For many young people, a critical look at the world they are living in leads to crucial questions on the religious plane. They ask whether religion can provide any answers to the pressing problems afflicting humanity. Large numbers of them sincerely want to know how to deepen their faith and live a meaningful life. Then there is the further practical question of how to translate responsible commitment into effective action. Future historians will have to evaluate the "youth group" phenomenon, along with the movements founded for spiritual growth, apostolic work, or service of others. But these are signs that words are not enough for the young people of today. They want to be active—to do something worthwhile for themselves and for others.

22. Catholic schools are spread throughout the world and enroll literally millions of students.[12] These students are children of their own race, nationality, traditions, and family. They are also the children of our age. Each student has a distinct origin and is a unique individual. A Catholic school is not simply a place where lessons are taught; it is a center that has an operative educational philosophy, attentive to the needs of today's youth and illumined by the Gospel message. A thorough and exact knowledge of the real situation will suggest the best educational methods.

23. We must be ready to repeat the basic essentials over and over again, so long as the need is present. We need to integrate what has already been learned, and respond to the questions which come from the restless and critical minds of the young. We need to break through the wall of indifference, and at the same time be ready to help those who are doing well to discover a "better way," offering them a knowledge that also embraces Christian wisdom.[13] The specific methods and the steps used to accomplish the educational

philosophy of the school will, therefore, be conditioned and guided by an intimate knowledge of each student's unique situation.[14]

II.
The Religious Dimension of the School Climate

What is a Christian School Climate?

24. In pedagogical circles, today as in the past, great stress is put on the climate of a school: the sum total of the different components at work in the school which interact with one another in such a way as to create favorable conditions for a formation process. Education always takes place within certain specific conditions of space and time, through the activities of a group of individuals who are active and also interactive among themselves. They follow a program of studies which is logically ordered and freely accepted. Therefore, the elements to be considered in developing an organic vision of a school climate are: persons, space, time, relationships, teaching, study, and various other activities.

25. From the first moment that a student sets foot in a Catholic school, he or she ought to have the impression of entering a new environment, one illumined by the light of faith, and having its own unique characteristics. The Council summed this up by speaking of an environment permeated with the Gospel spirit of love and freedom.[15] In a Catholic school, everyone should be aware of the living presence of Jesus the "Master" who, today as always, is with us in our journey through life as the one genuine "Teacher," the perfect Man in whom all human values find their fullest perfection. The inspiration of Jesus must be translated from the ideal into the real. The Gospel spirit should be evident in a Christian way of thought and life which permeates all facets of the educational climate. Having crucifixes in the school will remind everyone, teachers and students alike, of this familiar and moving presence of Jesus, the "Master" who gave his most complete and sublime teaching from the cross.

26. Prime responsibility for creating this unique Christian school climate rests with the teachers, as individuals and as a community. The religious dimension of the school climate is expressed through the celebration of Christian values in Word and Sacrament, in individual behavior, in friendly and harmonious interpersonal relationships, and in a ready availability. Through this daily witness, the students will come to appreciate the uniqueness of the environment to which their youth has been entrusted. If it is not present, then there is little left which can make the school Catholic.

The Physical Environment of a Catholic School

27. Many of the students will attend a Catholic school—often the same school—from the time they are very young children until they are nearly adults. It is only natural that they should come to think of the school as an extension of their own homes, and therefore a "school-home" ought to have some of the amenities which can create a pleasant and happy family atmosphere. When this is missing from the home, the school can often do a great deal to make up for it.

28. The first thing that will help to create a pleasant environment is an adequate physical facility: one that includes sufficient space for classrooms, sports and recreation, and also such things as a staff room and rooms for parent-teacher meetings, group work, etc. The possibilities for this vary from place to place; we have to be honest enough to admit that some school buildings are unsuitable and

unpleasant. But students can be made to feel "at home" even when the surroundings are modest, if the climate is humanly and spiritually rich.

29. A Catholic school should be an example of simplicity and evangelical poverty, but this is not inconsistent with having the materials needed to educate properly. Because of rapid technological progress, a school today must have access to equipment that, at times, is complex and expensive. This is not a luxury; it is simply what a school needs to carry out its role as an educational institution. Catholic schools, therefore, have a right to expect the help from others that will make the purchase of modern educational materials possible.[16] Both individuals and public bodies have a duty to provide this support.

Students should feel a responsibility for their "school-home"; they should take care of it and help to keep it as clean and neat as possible. Concern for the environment is part of a formation in ecological awareness, the need for which is becoming increasingly apparent.

An awareness of Mary's presence can be a great help toward making the school into a "home." Mary, Mother and Teacher of the Church, accompanied her Son as he grew in wisdom and grace; from its earliest days, she has accompanied the Church in its mission of salvation.

30. The physical proximity of the school to a church can contribute a great deal toward achieving the educational aims. A church should not be seen as something extraneous, but as a familiar and intimate place where those young people who are believers can find the presence of the Lord: "Behold, I am with you all days."[17] Liturgy planning should be especially careful to bring the school community and the local Church together.

The Ecclesial and Educational Climate of the School

31. The declaration *Gravissimum educationis*[18] notes an important advance in the way a Catholic school is thought of: the transition from the school as an institution to the school as a community. This community dimension is, perhaps, one result of the new awareness of the Church's nature as developed by the Council. In the Council texts, the community dimension is primarily a theological concept rather than a sociological category; this is the sense in which it is used in the second chapter of *Lumen gentium*, where the Church is described as the People of God.

As it reflects on the mission entrusted to it by the Lord, the Church gradually develops its pastoral instruments so that they may become ever more effective in proclaiming the Gospel and promoting total human formation. The Catholic school is one of these pastoral instruments; its specific pastoral service consists in mediating between faith and culture: being faithful to the newness of the Gospel while at the same time respecting the autonomy and the methods proper to human knowledge.

32. Everyone directly involved in the school is a part of the school community: teachers, directors, administrative and auxiliary staff. Parents are central figures, since they are the natural and irreplaceable agents in the education of their children. And the community also includes the students, since they must be active agents in their own education.[19]

33. At least since the time of the Council, therefore, the Catholic school has had a clear identity, not only as a presence of the Church in society, but also as a genuine and proper instrument of the Church. It is a place of evangelization, of authentic apostolate and of pastoral action—not through complementary or parallel or extracurricular activity, but of its very nature: its work of educating the Christian person. The words of the present Holy Father make this abundantly clear: "the Catholic school is not a marginal or secondary element in the pastoral mission of the bishop. Its function is not merely to be an instrument with which to combat the education given in a State school."[20]

34. The Catholic school finds its true justification in the mission of the Church; it is based on an educational philosophy in which faith, culture and life are brought into harmony. Through it, the local Church evangelizes, educates, and contributes to the formation of a healthy and morally sound lifestyle among its members. The Holy Father affirms that "the need for the Catholic school becomes evidently clear when we consider what it contributes to the development of the mission of the People of God, to the dialogue between Church and the human community, to the safeguarding of freedom of conscience...." Above all, according to the Holy Father, the Catholic school helps in achieving a double objective: "of its nature it guides men and women to human and Christian perfection, and at the same time helps them to become mature in their faith. For those who believe in Christ, these are two facets of a single reality."[21]

35. Most Catholic schools are under the direction of Religious Congregations, whose consecrated members enrich the educational climate by bringing to it the values of their own Religious communities. These men and women have dedicated themselves to the service of the students without thought of personal gain, because they are convinced that it is really the Lord whom they are serving.[22]

Through the prayer, work and love that make up their life in community, they express in a visible way the life of the Church. Each

Congregation brings the richness of its own educational tradition to the school, found in its original charism; its members each bring the careful professional preparation that is required by the call to be an educator. The strength and gentleness of their total dedication to God enlightens their work, and students gradually come to appreciate the value of this witness. They come to love these educators who seem to have the gift of eternal spiritual youth, and it is an affection which endures long after students leave the school.

36. The Church offers encouragement to these men and women who have dedicated their lives to the fulfillment of an educational charism.[23] It urges those in education not to give up this work, even in situations where it involves suffering and persecution. In fact, the Church hopes that many others will be called to this special vocation. When afflicted by doubts and uncertainty, when difficulties are multiplied, these Religious men and women should recall the nature of their consecration, which is a type of holocaust[24]—a holocaust which is offered "in the perfection of love, which is the scope of the consecrated life."[25] Their merit is the greater because their offering is made on behalf of young people, who are the hope of the Church.

37. At the side of the priests and Religious, lay teachers contribute their competence and their faith witness to the Catholic school. Ideally, this lay witness is a concrete example of the lay vocation that most of the students will be called to. The Congregation has devoted a specific document to lay teachers,[26] meant to remind lay people of their apostolic responsibility in the field of education and to summon them to participate in a common mission, whose point of convergence is found in the unity of the Church. For all are active members of one Church and cooperate in its one mission, even though the fields of labor and the states of life are different because of the personal call each one receives from God.

38. The Church, therefore, is willing to give lay people charge of the schools that it has established, and the laity themselves establish schools. The recognition of the school as a Catholic school is, however, always reserved to the competent ecclesiastical authority.[27] When lay people do establish schools, they should be especially concerned with the creation of a community climate permeated by the Gospel spirit of freedom and love, and they should witness to this in their own lives.

39. The more the members of the educational community develop a real willingness to collaborate among themselves, the more fruitful their work will be. Achieving the educational aims of the school should be an equal priority for teachers, students and families alike, each one according to his or her own role, always in the Gospel spirit of freedom and love. Therefore channels of communication should be open among all those concerned with the school. Frequent meetings will help to make this possible, and a willingness to discuss common problems candidly will enrich this communication.

The daily problems of school life are sometimes aggravated by misunderstandings and various tensions. A determination to collaborate in achieving common educational goals can help to overcome these difficulties and reconcile different points of view. A willingness to collaborate helps to facilitate decisions that need to be made about the ways to achieve these goals and, while preserving proper respect for school authorities, even makes it possible to conduct a critical evaluation of the school—a process in which teachers, students and families can all take part because of their common concern to work for the good of all.

40. Considering the special age group they are working with, primary schools should try to create a community school climate that reproduces, as far as possible, the warm and intimate atmosphere of family life. Those responsible for these schools will, therefore, do everything they can to promote a common spirit of trust and spontaneity. In addition, they will take great care to promote close and constant collaboration with the parents of these pupils. An integration of school and home is an essential condition for the birth and development of all of the potential which these children manifest in one or the other of these two situations—including their openness to religion with all that this implies.

41. The Congregation wishes to express its appreciation to all those dioceses which have worked to establish primary schools in their parishes; these deserve the strong support of all Catholics. It also wishes to thank the Religious Congregations helping to sustain these primary schools, often at great sacrifice. Moreover, the Congregation offers enthusiastic encouragement to those dioceses and Religious Congregations who wish to establish new schools. Such things as film clubs and sports groups are not enough; not even classes in catechism instruction are sufficient. What is needed is a school. This is a goal which, in some countries, was the starting point. There are countries in which the Church began with schools and only later was able to construct Churches and to establish a new Christian community.[28]

The Catholic School as an Open Community

42. Partnership between a Catholic school and the families of the students must continue and be strengthened: not simply to be able to deal with academic problems that may arise, but rather so that the educational goals of the school can be achieved. Close cooperation with the family is especially important when treating sensitive issues such as religious, moral, or sexual education, orientation toward a profession, or a choice of one's vocation in life. It is not a question of convenience, but a partnership based on faith. Catholic tradition teaches that God has bestowed on the family its own specific and unique educational mission.

43. The first and primary educators of children are their parents.[29] The school is aware of this fact but, unfortunately, the same is not always true of the families themselves; it is the school's responsibility to give them this awareness. Every school should initiate meetings and other programs which will make the parents more conscious of their role, and help to establish a partnership; it is impossible to do too much along these lines. It often happens that a meeting called to talk about the children becomes an opportunity to raise the consciousness of the parents. In addition, the school should try to involve the family as much as possible in the educational aims of the school—both in helping to plan these goals and in helping to achieve them. Experience shows that parents who were once totally unaware of their role can be transformed into excellent partners.

44. "The involvement of the Church in the field of education is demonstrated especially by the Catholic school."[30] This affirmation of the Council has both historical and practical importance. Church schools first appeared centuries ago, growing up alongside monasteries, cathedrals and parish churches. The Church has always had a love for its schools, because this is where its children receive their formation. These schools have continued to flourish with the help of bishops, countless Religious Congregations, and laity; the Church has never ceased to support the schools in their difficulties and to defend them against governments seeking to close or confiscate them.

Just as the Church is present in the school, so the school is present in the Church; this is a logical consequence of their reciprocal commitment. The Church, through which the Redemption of Christ is revealed and made operative, is where the Catholic school receives its spirit. It recognizes the Holy Father as the center and the measure of unity in the entire Christian community. Love for and fidelity to the Church is the organizing principle and the source of strength of a Catholic school.

Teachers find the light and the courage for authentic Religious education in their unity among themselves and their generous and humble communion with the Holy Father. Concretely, the educational goals of the school include a concern for the life and the problems of the Church, both local and universal. These goals are attentive to the Magisterium, and include cooperation with Church authorities. Catholic students are helped to become active members of the parish and diocesan communities. They have opportunities to join Church associations and Church youth groups, and they are taught to collaborate in local Church projects.

Mutual esteem and reciprocal collaboration will be established between the Catholic school and the bishop and other Church authorities through direct contacts. We are pleased to note that a concern for Catholic schools is becoming more of a priority of local Churches in many parts of the world.[31]

45. A Christian education must promote respect for the State and its representatives, the observance of just laws, and a search for the common good. Therefore, traditional civic values such as freedom, justice, the nobility of work and the need to pursue social progress are all included among the school goals, and the life of the school gives witness to them. The national anniversaries and other important civic events are commemorated and celebrated in appropriate ways in the schools of each country.

The school life should also reflect an awareness of international society. Christian education sees all of humanity as one large family, divided perhaps by historical and political events, but always one in God who is Father of all. Therefore a Catholic school should be sensitive to and help to promulgate Church appeals for peace, justice, freedom, progress for all peoples and assistance for countries in need. And it should not ignore similar appeals coming from recognized international organizations such as UNESCO and the United Nations.

46. That Catholic schools help to form good citizens is a fact apparent to everyone. Both government policy and public opinion should, therefore, recognize the work these schools do as a real service to society. It is unjust to accept the service and ignore or fight against its source. Fortunately, a good number of countries seem to have a growing understanding of and sympathy for the Catholic school.[32] A recent survey conducted by the Congregation demonstrates that a new age may be dawning.

III.
The Religious Dimension of School Life and Work

The Religious Dimension of School Life

47. Students spend a large share of each day and the greater part of their youth either at school or doing activities that are related to school. "School" is often identified with "teaching"; actually, classes and lessons are only a small part of school life. Along with the lessons that a teacher gives, there is the active participation of the students individually or as a group: study, research, exercises, para-curricular activities, examinations, relationships with teachers and with one another, group activities, class meetings, school assemblies. While the Catholic school is like any other school in this complex variety of events that make up the life of the school, there is one essential difference: it draws its inspiration and its strength from the Gospel in which it is rooted. The principle that no human act is morally indifferent to one's conscience or before God has clear applications to school life: examples of it are school work accepted as a duty and done with good will; courage and perseverance when difficulties come; respect for teachers; loyalty toward and love for fellow students; sincerity, tolerance, and goodness in all relationships.

48. The educational process is not simply a human activity; it is a genuine Christian journey toward perfection. Students who are sensitive to the religious dimension of life realize that the will of God is found in the work and the human relationships of each day. They learn to follow the example of the Master, who spent his youth working and who did good to all.[33] Those students who are unaware of this religious dimension are deprived of its benefits and they run the risk of living the best years of their lives at a shallow level.

49. Within the overall process of education, special mention must be made of the intellectual work done by students. Although Christian life consists in loving God and doing his will, intellectual work is intimately involved. The light of Christian faith stimulates a desire to know the universe as God's creation. It enkindles a love for the truth that will not be satisfied with superficiality in knowledge or judgment. It awakens a critical sense which examines statements rather than accepting them blindly. It impels the mind to learn with careful order and precise methods, and to work with a sense of responsibility. It

provides the strength needed to accept the sacrifices and the perseverance required by intellectual labor. When fatigued, the Christian student remembers the command of Genesis[34] and the invitation of the Lord.[35]

50. The religious dimension enhances intellectual efforts in a variety of ways: interest in academic work is stimulated by the presence of new perspectives; Christian formation is strengthened; supernatural grace is given. How sad it would be if the young people in Catholic schools were to have no knowledge of this reality in the midst of all the difficult and tiring work they have to do!

The Religious Dimension of the School Culture

51. Intellectual development and growth as a Christian go forward hand in hand. As students move up from one class into the next it becomes increasingly imperative that a Catholic school help them become aware that a relationship exists between faith and human culture.[36] Human culture remains human, and must be taught with scientific objectivity. But the lessons of the teacher and the reception of those students who are believers will not divorce faith from this culture;[37] this would be a major spiritual loss. The world of human culture and the world of religion are not like two parallel lines that never meet; points of contact are established within the human person. For a believer is both human and a person of faith, the protagonist of culture and the subject of religion. Anyone who searches for the contact points will be able to find them.[38] Helping in the search is not solely the task of religion teachers; their time is quite limited, while other teachers have many hours at their disposal every day. Everyone should work together, each one developing his or her own subject area with professional competence, but sensitive to those opportunities in which they can help students to see beyond the limited horizon of human reality. In a Catholic school, and analogously in every school, God cannot be the Great Absent One or the unwelcome intruder. The Creator does not put obstacles in the path of someone trying to learn more about the universe he created, a universe which is given new significance when seen with the eyes of faith.

52. A Catholic secondary school will give special attention to the "challenges" that human culture poses for faith. Students will be helped to attain that synthesis of faith and culture which is necessary for faith to be mature. But a mature faith is also able to recognize and reject cultural counter-values which threaten human dignity and are therefore contrary to the Gospel.[39] No one should think that all of the problems of religion and of faith will be completely solved by academic studies; nevertheless, we are convinced that a school is a privileged place for finding adequate ways to deal with these problems. The declaration *Gravissimum educationis*,[40] echoing *Gaudium et spes*,[41] indicates that one of the characteristics of a Catholic school is that it interpret and give order to human culture in the light of faith.

53. As the Council points out, giving order to human culture in the light of the message of salvation cannot mean a lack of respect for the autonomy of the different academic disciplines and the methodology proper to them; nor can it mean that these disciplines are to be seen merely as subservient to faith. On the other hand, it is necessary to point out that a proper autonomy of culture has to be distinguished from a vision of the human person or of the world as totally autonomous, implying that one can negate spiritual values or prescind from them. We must always remember that, while faith is not to be identified with any one culture and is independent of all cultures, it must inspire every culture: "Faith

which does not become culture is faith which is not received fully, not assimilated entirely, not lived faithfully."[42]

54. In a number of countries, renewal in school programming has given increased attention to science and technology. Those teaching these subject areas must not ignore the religious dimension. They should help their students to understand that positive science, and the technology allied to it, is a part of the universe created by God. Understanding this can help encourage an interest in research: the whole of creation, from the distant celestial bodies and the immeasurable cosmic forces down to the infinitesimal particles and waves of matter and energy, all bear the imprint of the Creator's wisdom and power. The wonder that past ages felt when contemplating this universe, recorded by the Biblical authors,[43] is still valid for the students of today; the only difference is that we have a knowledge that is much more vast and profound. There can be no conflict between faith and true scientific knowledge; both find their source in God.

The student who is able to discover the harmony between faith and science will, in future professional life, be better able to put science and technology to the service of men and women, and to the service of God. It is a way of giving back to God what he has first given to us.[44]

55. A Catholic school must be committed to the development of a program which will overcome the problems of a fragmented and insufficient curriculum. Teachers dealing with areas such as anthropology, biology, psychology, sociology and philosophy all have the opportunity to present a complete picture of the human person, including the religious dimension. Students should be helped to see the human person as a living creature having both a physical and a spiritual nature; each of us has an immortal soul, and we are in need of redemption. The older students can gradually come to a more mature understanding of all that is implied in the concept of "person": intelligence and will, freedom and feelings, the capacity to be an active and creative agent; a being endowed with both rights and duties, capable of interpersonal relationships, called to a specific mission in the world.

56. The religious dimension makes a true understanding of the human person possible. A human being has a dignity and a greatness exceeding that of all other creatures: a work of God that has been elevated to the supernatural order as a child of God, and therefore having both a divine origin and an eternal destiny which transcend this physical universe.[45] Religion teachers will find the way already prepared for an organic presentation of Christian anthropology.

57. Every society has its own heritage of accumulated wisdom. Many people find inspiration in these philosophical and religious concepts which have endured for millennia. The systematic genius of classical Greek and European thought has, over the centuries, generated countless different doctrinal systems, but it has also given us a set of truths which we can recognize as a part of our permanent philosophical heritage. A Catholic school conforms to the generally accepted school programming of today, but implements these programs within an overall religious perspective. This perspective includes criteria such as the following: Respect for those who seek the truth, who raise fundamental questions about human existence.[46] Confidence in our ability to attain truth, at least in a limited way—a confidence based not on feeling but on faith. God created us "in his own image and likeness" and will not deprive us of the truth necessary to orient our lives.[47] The ability to make judgments about what is true

and what is false; and to make choices based on these judgments.[48] Making use of a systematic framework, such as that offered by our philosophical heritage, with which to find the best possible human responses to questions regarding the human person, the world, and God.[49] Lively dialogue between culture and the Gospel message.[50] The fullness of truth contained in the Gospel message itself, which embraces and integrates the wisdom of all cultures, and enriches them with the divine mysteries known only to God but which, out of love, he has chosen to reveal to us.[51] With such criteria as a basis, the student's careful and reflective study of philosophy will bring human wisdom into an encounter with divine wisdom.

58. Teachers should guide the students' work in such a way that they will be able to discover a religious dimension in the world of human history. As a preliminary, they should be encouraged to develop a taste for historical truth, and therefore to realize the need to look critically at texts and curricula which, at times, are imposed by a government or distorted by the ideology of the author. The next step is to help students see history as something real: the drama of human grandeur and human misery.[52] The protagonist of history is the human person, who projects onto the world, on a larger scale, the good and the evil that is within each individual. History is, then, a monumental struggle between these two fundamental realities,[53] and is subject to moral judgments. But such judgments must always be made with understanding.

59. To this end, the teacher should help students to see history as a whole. Looking at the grand picture, they will see the development of civilizations, and learn about progress in such things as economic development, human freedom, and international cooperation. Realizing this can help to offset the disgust that comes from learning about the darker side of human history. But even this is not the whole story. When they are ready to appreciate it, students can be invited to reflect on the fact that this human struggle takes place within the divine history of universal salvation. At this moment, the religious dimension of history begins to shine forth in all its luminous grandeur.[54]

60. The increased attention given to science and technology must not lead to a neglect of the humanities: philosophy, history, literature and art. Since earliest times, each society has developed and handed on its artistic and literary heritage, and our human patrimony is nothing more than the sum total of this cultural wealth. Thus, while teachers are helping students to develop an aesthetic sense, they can bring them to a deeper awareness of all peoples as one great human family. The simplest way to uncover the religious dimension of the artistic and literary world is to start with its concrete expressions: in every human culture, art and literature have been closely linked to religious beliefs. The artistic and literary patrimony of Christianity is vast and gives visible testimony to a faith that has been handed down through centuries.

61. Literary and artistic works depict the struggles of societies, of families, and of individuals. They spring from the depths of the human heart, revealing its lights and its shadows, its hope and its despair. The Christian perspective goes beyond the merely human, and offers more penetrating criteria for understanding the human struggle and the mysteries of the human spirit.[55] Furthermore, an adequate religious formation has been the starting point for the vocation of a number of Christian artists and art critics. In the upper grades, a teacher can bring students to an even more profound appreciation of artistic works: as a reflection of the divine

beauty in tangible form. Both the Fathers of the Church and the masters of Christian philosophy teach this in their writings on aesthetics—St. Augustine invites us to go beyond the intention of the artists in order to find the eternal order of God in the work of art; St. Thomas sees the presence of the Divine Word in art.[56]

62. A Catholic school is often attentive to issues having to do with educational methods, and this can be of great service both to civil society and to the Church. Government requirements for teacher preparation usually require historical and systematic courses in pedagogy, psychology and teaching methods. In more recent times, educational science has been subdivided into a number of areas of specialization and has been subjected to a variety of different philosophies and political ideologies; those preparing to become teachers may feel that the whole field is confused and fragmented. Teachers of pedagogical science can help these students in their bewilderment, and guide them in the formulation of a carefully thought out synthesis, whose elaboration begins with the premise that every pedagogical current of thought contains things which are true and useful. But then one must begin to reflect, judge, and choose.

63. Future teachers should be helped to realize that any genuine educational philosophy has to be based on the nature of the human person, and therefore must take into account all of the physical and spiritual powers of each individual, along with the call of each one to be an active and creative agent in service to society. And this philosophy must be open to a religious dimension. Human beings are fundamentally free; they are not the property of the state or of any human organization. The entire process of education, therefore, is a service to the individual students, helping each one to achieve the most complete formation possible.

The Christian model, based on the person of Christ, is then linked to this human concept of the person—that is, the model begins with an educational framework based on the person as human, and then enriches it with supernatural gifts, virtues, and values—and a supernatural call. It is indeed possible to speak about Christian education; the Conciliar declaration provides us with a clear synthesis of it.[57] Proper pedagogical formation, finally, will guide these students to a self-formation that is both human and Christian, because this is the best possible preparation for one who is preparing to educate others.

64. Interdisciplinary work has been introduced into Catholic schools with positive results, for there are questions and topics that are not easily treated within the limitations of a single subject area. Religious themes should be included; they arise naturally when dealing with topics such as the human person, the family, society, or history. Teachers should be adequately prepared to deal with such questions and be ready to give them the attention they deserve.

65. Religion teachers are not excluded. While their primary mission must be the systematic presentation of religion, they can also be invited—within the limitations of what is concretely possible—to assist in clarifying religious questions that come up in other classes. Conversely, they may wish to invite one of their colleagues to attend a religion class, in order to have the help of an expert when dealing with some specific issue. Whenever this happens, students will be favorably impressed by the cooperative spirit among the teachers: the one purpose all of them have in mind is to help these students grow in knowledge and in commitment.

IV.
Religious Instruction in the Classroom and the Religious Dimension of Formation

The Nature of Religious Instruction

66. The mission of the Church is to evangelize, for the interior transformation and the renewal of humanity.[58] For young people, the school is one of the ways for this evangelization to take place.[59] It may be profitable to recall what the Magisterium has said: "Together with and in collaboration with the family, schools provide possibilities for catechesis that must not be neglected....This refers especially to the Catholic school, of course: it would no longer deserve the title if, no matter how good its reputation for teaching in other areas there were just grounds for a reproach of negligence or deviation in religious education properly so-called. It is not true that such education is always given implicitly or indirectly. The special character of the Catholic school and the underlying reason for its existence, the reason why Catholic parents should prefer it, is precisely the quality of the religious instruction integrated into the overall education of the students."[60]

67. Sometimes there is an uncertainty, a difference of opinion, or an uneasiness about the underlying principles governing religious formation in a Catholic school, and therefore about the concrete approach to be taken in religious instruction. On the one hand, a Catholic school is a "civic institution"; its aim, methods and characteristics are the same as those of every other school. On the other hand, it is a "Christian community," whose educational goals are rooted in Christ and his Gospel. It is not always easy to bring these two aspects into harmony; the task requires constant attention, so that the tension between a serious effort to transmit culture and a forceful witness to the Gospel does not turn into a conflict harmful to both.

68. There is a close connection, and at the same time a clear distinction, between religious instruction and catechesis, or the handing on of the Gospel message.[61] The close connection makes it possible for a school to remain a school and still integrate culture with the message of Christianity. The distinction comes from the fact that, unlike religious instruction, catechesis presupposes that the hearer is receiving the Christian message as a salvific reality. Moreover, catechesis takes place within a community living out its faith at a level of space and time not available to a school: a whole lifetime.

69. The aim of catechesis, or handing on the Gospel message, is maturity: spiritual, liturgical, sacramental and apostolic; this happens most especially in a local Church community. The aim of the school however, is knowledge. While it uses the same elements of the Gospel message, it tries to convey a sense of the nature of Christianity, and of how Christians are trying to live their lives. It is evident, of course, that religious instruction cannot help but strengthen the faith of a believing student, just as catechesis cannot help but increase one's knowledge of the Christian message.

The distinction between religious instruction and catechesis does not change the fact that a school can and must play its specific role in the work of catechesis. Since its educational goals are rooted in Christian principles, the school as a whole is inserted into the evangelical function of the Church. It assists in and promotes faith education.

70. Recent Church teaching has added an essential note: "The basic principle which must guide us in our commitment to this sensitive area of pastoral activity is that religious instruction and catechesis are at the same time distinct and complementary. A school has as its purpose the students' integral formation. Religious instruction, therefore, should be integrated into the objectives and criteria which characterize a modern school."[62] School directors should keep this directive of the Magisterium in mind, and they should respect the distinctive characteristics of religious instruction. It should have a place in the weekly order alongside the other classes, for example; it should have its own syllabus, approved by those in authority; it should seek appropriate interdisciplinary links with other course material so that there is a coordination between human learning and religious awareness. Like other course work, it should promote culture, and it should make use of the best educational methods available to schools today. In some countries, the results of examinations in religious knowledge are included within the overall measure of student progress.

Finally, religious instruction in the school needs to be coordinated with the catechesis offered in parishes, in the family, and in youth associations.

Some Basic Presuppositions About Religious Instruction

71. It should be no surprise that young people bring with them into the classroom what they see and hear in the world around them, along with the impressions gained from the "world" of mass media. Perhaps some have become indifferent or insensitive. The school curriculum as such does not take these attitudes into account, but teachers must be very aware of them. With kindness and understanding, they will accept the students as they are, helping them to see that doubt and indifference are common phenomena, and that the reasons for this are readily understandable. But they will invite students in a friendly manner to seek and discover together the message of the Gospel, the source of joy and peace.

The teachers' attitudes and behavior should be those of one preparing the soil.[63] They then add their own spiritual lives, and the prayers they offer for the students entrusted to them.[64]

72. An excellent way to establish rapport with students is simply to talk to them—and to let them talk. Once a warm and trusting atmosphere has been established, various questions will come up naturally. These obviously depend on age and living situation, but many of the questions seem to be common among all of today's youth; and they tend to raise them at a younger age.[65] These questions are serious ones for young people, and they make a calm study of the Christian faith very difficult. Teachers should respond with patience and humility, and should avoid the type of peremptory statements that can be so easily contradicted.

Experts in history and science could be invited to class. One's own experiences and study should be used to help the students. Inspiration can be found in the numerous and carefully worked out responses which Vatican II gives to these kinds of questions. In theory at least, this patient work of clarification should take place at the beginning of each year, since it is almost certain that new questions and new difficulties will have come up during the vacation period. And experience suggests that every other opportune occasion should be taken advantage of.

73. It is not easy to develop a course syllabus for religious instruction classes which will present the Christian faith systematically and in a way suited to the young people of today.

The Second Extraordinary General Assembly of the Synod of Bishops in 1985 suggested that a new catechism be developed for the universal Church, and the Holy Father immediately created a commission to begin the preparatory work on this project. When the catechism becomes available, adaptations will be necessary in order to develop course outlines that conform to the requirements of education authorities and respond to the concrete situations that depend on local circumstances of time and place.

While we await the new synthesis of Christian doctrine—the completion of the work mandated by the Synod—we present by way of example an outline which is the fruit of experience. It is complete in content, faithful to the Gospel message, organic in form, and is developed according to a methodology based on the words and deeds of the Lord.

An Outline for an Organic Presentation of the Christian Event and the Christian Message

74. As expressed by Vatican II, the task of the teacher is to summarize Christology and present it in everyday language. Depending on the level of the class, this should be preceded by a presentation of some basic ideas about Sacred Scripture, especially those having to do with the Gospels, Divine Revelation, and the Tradition that is alive in the Church.[66] With this as a base, the class begins to learn about the Lord Jesus. His person, his message, his deeds, and the historical fact of his resurrection lead to the mystery of his divinity: "You are the Christ, the Son of the living God."[67] For more mature students, this study can be expanded to include Jesus as Savior, Priest, Teacher, and Lord of the universe. At his side is Mary his Mother, who cooperates in his mission.[68]

The discovery process is an important pedagogical method. The person of Jesus will come alive for the students. They will see again the example of his life, listen to his words, hear his invitation as addressed to them: "Come to me, all of you...."[69] Faith is thus based on knowing Jesus and following him; its growth depends on each one's good will and cooperation with grace.

75. The teacher has a reliable way to bring young people closer to the mystery of the revealed God, to the extent that this can ever be humanly possible.[70] It is the way indicated by the Savior: "Whoever has seen me, has seen the Father."[71] Through his person and his message we learn about God: we examine what he has said about the Father, and what he has done in the name of the Father. Through the Lord Jesus, therefore, we come to the mystery of God the Father, who created the universe and who sent his Son into the world so that all men and women might be saved.[72] Through Christ we come to the mystery of the Holy Spirit, sent into the world to bring the mission of the Son to fulfillment.[73] And thus we approach the supreme mystery of the Holy Trinity, in itself and as operative in the world. It is this mystery that the Church venerates and proclaims whenever it recites the Creed, repeating the words of the first Christian communities.

The process has great educational value. Its successful completion will help to strengthen the virtues of faith and of Christian religion, both of which have God as their object: Father, Son and Holy Spirit; known, loved and served in this life as we await an eternal life in union with them.

76. Students learn many things about the human person by studying science; but science has nothing to say about mystery. Teachers should help students begin to discover the mystery within the human person, just as Paul tried to help the people of Athens discover the "Unknown God." The text of John already cited[74] demonstrates that, in and through Christ, a close relationship has been established between God and each human being. The relationship has its beginning in the love of the Father; it is expressed in the

love of Jesus, which led to the ultimate sacrifice of himself: "No one has greater love than this: to lay down one's life for one's friends."[75] A crowd of people constantly surrounded Jesus; they were of all types, as if representing all of humanity. As the students see this, they will begin to ask themselves why Jesus loves everyone, why he offers an invitation to all, why he gives his life for us all. And they will be forced to conclude that each person must be a very privileged creature of God, to be the object of so much love. This is the point at which students will begin to discover another mystery—that human history unfolds within a divine history of salvation: from creation, through the first sin, the covenant with the ancient people of God, the long period of waiting until finally Jesus our Savior came, so that now we are the new People of God, pilgrims on earth journeying toward our eternal home.[76]

The educational value of Christian anthropology is obvious. Here is where students discover the true value of the human person: loved by God, with a mission on earth and a destiny that is immortal. As a result, they learn the virtues of self-respect and self-love, and of love for others—a love that is universal. In addition, each student will develop a willingness to embrace life, and also his or her own unique vocation, as a fulfillment of God's will.

77. The history of salvation continues in the Church, an historical reality that is visible to the students. They should be encouraged to discover its origins in the Gospels, in Acts, and in the Apostolic Letters; as they study these works they will see the Church at its birth, and then as it begins to grow and take its place in the world. From the way it comes into being, from its miraculous growth, and from its fidelity to the Gospel message the transition is made to the Church as a mystery. The teacher will help students to discover the

Church as the People of God, composed of women and men just like ourselves, bringing salvation to all of humanity. The Church is guided by Jesus the Eternal Shepherd; guided by his Spirit, which sustains it and is forever renewing it; guided visibly by the pastors he has ordained: the Holy Father and the bishops, assisted by priests and the deacons who are their collaborators in priesthood and in ministry. The Church, called by God to be holy in all its members, continues to be at work in the world. This is the mystery of the One, Holy, Catholic, and Apostolic Church that we celebrate in the Creed.[77]

Ecclesiology has an extremely important educational value: the ideal of a universal human family is realized in the Church. As young people come to a better knowledge of the Church they belong to, they will learn to love it with a filial affection; this has obvious consequences for life, for apostolate, and for a Christian vision of the world.

78. As they get older, many young people stop receiving the Sacraments; this may be a sign that their meaning has not been grasped. Perhaps they are seen as devotional practices for children, or a popular devotion joined to a secular feast. Teachers are familiar with this phenomenon and its dangers. They will, therefore, help students to discover the real value of the Sacraments: they accompany the believer on his or her journey through life. This journey takes place within the Church, and therefore becomes more comprehensible as students grow in an understanding of what it means to be a member of the Church. The essential point for students to understand is that Jesus Christ is always truly present in the Sacraments which he has instituted,[78] and his presence makes them efficacious means of grace. The moment of closest encounter with the Lord Jesus occurs in the Eucharist, which is both Sacrifice and Sacrament. In the Eucharist, two supreme acts of love are united: Our Lord renews his sacrifice of salvation for us, and he truly gives himself to us.

79. An understanding of the sacramental journey has profound educational implications. Students become aware that being a member of the Church is something dynamic, responding to every person's need to continue growing all through life. When we meet the Lord in the Sacraments, we are never left unchanged. Through the Spirit, he causes us to grow in the Church, offering us "grace upon grace"[79]; the only thing he asks is our cooperation. The educational consequences of this touch on our relationship with God, our witness as a Christian, and our choice of a personal vocation.[80]

80. Young people today are assaulted by distractions; the circumstances are not ideal for reflecting on the last things. An effective way to approach this mystery of faith is, however, available to the teacher: the Lord proposes it in his own unique way. In the story of Lazarus, he calls himself "the resurrection and the life."[81] In the parable of the rich man he helps us to understand that a personal judgment awaits each one of us.[82] In the impressive drama of the last judgment he points to an eternal destiny which each of us merits through our own works.[83] The good or evil done to each human being is as if done to him.[84]

81. Then, using the Creed as a pattern, the teacher can help students to learn about the Kingdom of Heaven: that it consists of those who have believed in him and spent their lives in his service. The Church calls them "saints" even if not all are formally venerated under that title. First among them is Mary, the Mother of Jesus, living a glorified life at the side of her Son. Those who have died are not separated from us. They, with us, form the one Church, the People of God, united in the "communion of saints." Those dear to us who have left us are alive and are in communion with us.[85]

These truths of faith contribute to human and Christian maturity in several important areas. They provide a sense of the dignity of the person, as destined to immortality. Christian hope offers comfort in life's difficulties. We are personally responsible in everything we do, because we must render an account to God.

An Outline for a Systematic Presentation of the Christian Life

82. As we have seen, each truth of faith has educational and ethical implications, and students should be helped to learn about these from the time when they first begin the study of religion. But a systematic presentation of Christian ethics is also needed; to assist in this task, we present here a sample outline.

As an introduction to a study of the relationship between faith and life through religious ethics it can be helpful to reflect on the first Christian communities, where the Gospel message was accompanied by prayer and the celebration of the Sacraments.[86] This has permanent value. Students will begin to understand the meaning of the virtue of faith: helped by grace, to give complete, free, personal and affective loyalty to the God who reveals himself through his Son.

This commitment is not automatic; it is itself a gift of God. We must ask for it and wait for it patiently. And students must be given time to grow and to mature.

83. The life of faith is expressed in acts of religion. The teacher will assist students to open their hearts in confidence to Father, Son, and Holy Spirit through personal and liturgical prayer. The latter is not just another way of praying; it is the official prayer of the Church, which makes the mystery of Christ present in our lives—especially through the Eucharist, Sacrifice and Sacrament, and through the Sacrament of Reconciliation. Religious experiences are then seen, not as something externally imposed, but as a free and loving response to the God who first loved us.[87] The virtues of faith and religion, thus rooted and cultivated, are enabled to develop during childhood, youth, and in all the years that follow.

84. The human person is present in all the truths of faith: created in "the image and likeness" of God; elevated by God to the dignity of a child of God; unfaithful to God in original sin, but redeemed by Christ; a temple of the Holy Spirit; a member of the Church; destined to eternal life.

Students may well object that we are a long way from this ideal. The teacher must listen to these pessimistic responses, but point out that they are also found in the Gospel.[88] Students may need to be convinced that it is better to know the positive picture of personal Christian ethics rather than to get lost in an analysis of human misery. In practice, this means respect for oneself and for others. We must cultivate intelligence and the other spiritual gifts, especially through scholastic work. We must learn to care for our body and its health, and this includes physical activity and sports. And we must be careful of our sexual integrity through the virtue of chastity, because sexual energies are also a gift of God, contributing to the perfection of the person and having a providential function for the life of society and of the Church.[89] Thus, gradually, the teacher will guide students to the idea, and then to the realization, of a process of total formation.

85. Christian love is neither sentimentalism nor humanitarianism; it is a new reality, born of faith. Teachers must remember that the love of God governs the divine plan of universal salvation. The Lord Jesus came to live among us in order to show us the Father's love. His ultimate sacrifice testifies to his love for his friends. And the Lord's new commandment is at the center of our faith: "This is my commandment: that you love one another as I have loved you."[90] The "as" is the model and the measure of Christian love.

86. Students will raise the standard objections: violence in the world, racial hatred, daily crime, both young and old concerned only with themselves and what they can get for themselves. Teachers cannot avoid discussing these issues, but they should insist that the commandment of Christ is new and revolutionary, and that it stands in opposition to all that is evil and to every form of egoism. The new Christian ethic needs to be understood and put into practice.

87. It begins at the level of family and school: affection, respect, obedience, gratitude, gentleness, goodness, helpfulness, service and good example. All manifestations of egoism, rebellion, antipathy, jealousy, hatred or revenge must be rooted out. At the broader level of Church: a love for all that excludes no one because of religion, nationality or race; prayer for all, so that all may know the Lord; laboring together in apostolic works and in efforts to relieve human suffering; a preferential option for the less fortunate, the sick, the poor, the handicapped, the lonely. As love grows in the Church, more young people may choose a life of service in it, responding to a call to the priesthood or to Religious life.

As they begin to prepare for marriage: rejecting anything that would hint at a desecration of love; discovering the newness and the depth of Christian love between man and woman, including the mutuality and reserve with which it is expressed and the sincere tenderness by which it is preserved. Young people should experience love in this way from their first friendships, gradually leading to the possibility of a commitment, until finally love is consecrated for the whole of life in the Sacrament of Matrimony.

88. Christian social ethics must always be founded on faith. From this starting point it can shed light on related disciplines such as law, economics and political science, all of which study the human situation,[91] and this is an obvious area for fruitful interdisciplinary study. But it is important to remind ourselves that God has put the world at the service of the human family.[92] As our Lord pointed out,[93] violence and injustice in society come from men and women, and they are contrary to the will of God. But in saving us, God also saves our works: a renewed world flows from a renewed heart. The works of the new Christian order of humanity are love, justice, freedom and grace.[94]

89. These, then, are the basic elements of a Christian social ethic: the human person, the central focus of the social order; justice, the recognition of the rights of each individual; honesty, the basic condition for all human relationships; freedom, the basic right of each individual and of society. World peace must then be founded on good order and the justice to which all men and women have a right as children of God; national and international well-being depend on the fact that the goods of the earth are gifts of God, and are not the privilege of some individuals or groups while others are deprived of them. Misery and hunger weigh on the conscience of humanity and cry out to God for justice.

90. This is an area which can open up broad possibilities. Students will be enriched by the principles and values they learn, and their service of society will be more effective. The Church supports and enlightens them with a social doctrine which is waiting to be put into practice by courageous and generous men and women of faith.[95]

91. The guidelines developed up to this point seem excessively optimistic. While the presentation of the Christian message as "good news" is pedagogically sound,[96] the realism of revelation, history and daily experience all require that students have a clear awareness of the evil that is at work in the world and in the human person. The Lord spoke about the "power of darkness."[97] Men and women wander far away from God, and rebel against the Gospel message; they continue to poison the world with war, violence, injustice and crime.

92. A teacher can invite the students to examine their own consciences. Which one of us can honestly claim to be without sin?[98] Thus they will acquire a sense of sin: the great sin of humanity as a whole and the personal sin which all of us discover within ourselves. Sin drives us away from God, rejects the message of Christ, and transgresses the law of love; sin betrays conscience, abuses the gift of freedom, offends the other children of God, and harms the Church of which we are all members.

93. But we are not in a hopeless situation. The teacher should help students to see, in the light of faith, that this reality has another side to it. On the world scale, the Gospel message continues to "die" as the "seed" in the soil of the earth only to blossom and bear fruit in due season.[99] At the personal level, the Lord waits for us in the Sacrament of Reconciliation. It is not just a devotional practice, but rather a personal encounter with him, through the mediation of his minister. After this celebration we can resume our journey with renewed strength and joy.

94. These truths can lead to a new and more mature understanding of Christianity. The

Lord calls us to an endless struggle: to resist the forces of evil and, with his help, to have the courage to overpower it. This is a Christianity which is alive and healthy, at work in history and within the life of each individual.[100]

The call to be a Christian involves a call to help liberate the human family from its radical slavery to sin and, therefore, from the effects of sin in the cultural, economic, social and political orders. Ultimately, these effects all result from sin; they are obstacles which prevent men and women from living according to the dignity which is theirs.[101]

95. Perfection is a theme which must be part of this systematic presentation of the Christian message. To pass over it would be disloyal: to the Lord, who calls us to limitless perfection;[102] to the Church, which invites us all to perfection;[103] and to the young people themselves, who have the right to know what the Lord and the Church expect of them. The teacher will begin by reminding believing students that, through their baptism, they have become members of the Church. The Christian perfection to which we are all called is a gift of Jesus through the mediation of the Spirit; but the gift requires our cooperation. Our apostolic witness must make this perfection visible in the world, today and in the future.

Once they get beyond feeling that too much is being asked of them, students will realize that perfection is actually within their grasp. The only thing they have to do is live their lives as students as well as they can:[104] do their best in study and work; put into practice the virtues they already know in theory—especially love, which must be lived in the classroom, at home, and among friends; accept difficulties with courage; help those in need; give good example. In addition, they must find the inspiration for their daily lives in the words and the example of Jesus. They must converse with him in prayer and receive him in the Eucharist. No student can say that these are impossible demands.

The ideal would be for each student to have an opportunity for spiritual guidance, to help in interior formation. It is the best way of giving orientation and completion to the religious instruction given in the classroom and, at the same time, of integrating this instruction into the personal experiences of each individual.

The Religion Teacher

96. The fruits of an organic presentation of the faith and of Christian ethics depend in great part on the religion teachers: who they are and what they do.

The religion teacher is the key, the vital component, if the educational goals of the school are to be achieved. But the effectiveness of religious instruction is closely tied to the personal witness given by the teacher; this witness is what brings the content of the lessons to life. Teachers of religion, therefore, must be men and women endowed with many gifts, both natural and supernatural, who are also capable of giving witness to these gifts; they must have a thorough cultural, professional, and pedagogical training, and they must be capable of genuine dialogue.

Most of all, students should be able to recognize authentic human qualities in their teachers. They are teachers of the faith; however, like Christ, they must also be teachers of what it means to be human. This includes culture, but it also includes such things as affection, tact, understanding, serenity of spirit, a balanced judgment, patience in listening to others and prudence in the way they respond, and, finally, availability for personal meetings and conversations with the students. A teacher who has a clear vision of the Christian milieu and lives in accord with it will be able to help young people develop a similar vision,

and will give them the inspiration they need to put it into practice.

97. In this area, especially, an unprepared teacher can do a great deal of harm. Everything possible must be done to ensure that Catholic schools have adequately trained religion teachers; it is a vital necessity and a legitimate expectation. In Catholic schools today, these teachers tend more and more to be lay people, and they should have the opportunity of receiving the specific experiential knowledge of the mystery of Christ and of the Church that priests and Religious automatically acquire in the course of their formation. We need to look to the future and promote the establishment of formation centers for these teachers; ecclesiastical universities and faculties should do what they can to develop appropriate programs so that the teachers of tomorrow will be able to carry out their task with the competence and efficacy that is expected of them.[105]

V.
A General Summary:
The Religious Dimension of the Formation Process as a Whole

What is a Christian Formation Process?

98. The declaration of the Council insists on the dynamic nature of integral human formation,[106] but it adds immediately that, from a Christian point of view, human development by itself is not sufficient. Education "does not merely strive to foster in the human person the maturity already described. Rather, its principal aims are these: that as the baptized person is gradually introduced into a knowledge of the mystery of salvation, he or she may daily grow more conscious of the gift of faith which has been received...."[107] What characterizes a Catholic school, therefore, is that it guide students in such a way "that the development of each one's own personality will be matched by the growth of that new creation which he or she became by baptism."[108] We need to think of Christian education as a movement or a growth process, directed toward an ideal goal which goes beyond the limitations of anything human.[109] At the same time the process must be harmonious, so that Christian formation takes place within and in the course of human formation. The two are not separate and parallel paths; they are complementary forms of education which become one in the goals of the teacher and the willing reception of the students. The Gospel notes this harmonious growth in the child Jesus.[110]

99. A Christian formation process might therefore be described as an organic set of elements with a single purpose: the gradual development of every capability of every student, enabling each one to attain an integral formation within a context that includes the Christian religious dimension and recognizes the help of grace. But what really matters is not the terminology but the reality, and this reality will be assured only if all the teachers unite their educational efforts in the pursuit of a common goal. Sporadic, partial, or uncoordinated efforts, or a situation in which there is a conflict of opinion among the teachers, will interfere with rather than assist in the students' personal development.

Educational Goals

100. The responsibility of a Catholic school is enormous and complex. It must respect and obey the laws that define methods, programs, structure, etc., and at the same time it must fulfill its own educational goals by blending human culture with the message of salvation into a coordinated program; it must help each of the students to actually become the "new creature" that each one is

potentially, and at the same time prepare them for the responsibilities of an adult member of society. This means that a Catholic school needs to have a set of educational goals which are "distinctive" in the sense that the school has a specific objective in mind, and all of the goals are related to this objective. Concretely, the educational goals provide a frame of reference which:

† defines the school's identity: in particular, the Gospel values which are its inspiration must be explicitly mentioned;

† gives a precise description of the pedagogical, educational and cultural aims of the school;

† presents the course content, along with the values that are to be transmitted through these courses;

† describes the organization and the management of the school;

† determines which policy decisions are to be reserved to professional staff (governors and teachers), which policies are to be developed with the help of parents and students, and which activities are to be left to the free initiative of teachers, parents, or students;

† indicates the ways in which student progress is to be tested and evaluated.

101. In addition, careful attention must be given to the development of general criteria which will enable each aspect of school activity to assist in the attainment of the educational objective, so that the cultural, pedagogical, social, civil and political aspects of school life are all integrated:

a. Fidelity to the Gospel as proclaimed by the Church. The activity of a Catholic school is, above all else, an activity that shares in the evangelizing mission of the

Church; it is a part of the particular local Church of the country in which it is situated, and shares in the life and work of the local Christian community.

b. Careful rigor in the study of culture and the development of a critical sense, maintaining a respect for the autonomy of human knowledge and for the rules and methods proper to each of the disciplines, and at the same time orienting the whole process toward the integral formation of the person.

c. Adapting the educational process in a way that respects the particular circumstances of individual students and their families.

d. Sharing responsibility with the Church. While school authorities are the ones primarily responsible for the educational and cultural activities of the school, the local Church should also be involved in appropriate ways; the educational goals should be the result of dialogue with this ecclesial community.

It is clear, then, that the set of educational goals is something quite distinct from internal school regulations or teaching methods; and it is not just a description of vague intentions.

102. The educational goals should be revised each year on the basis of experience and need. They will be achieved through a formation process which takes place in stages; it has a starting point, various intermediate points, and a conclusion. At each stage, teachers, students and families should determine the degree of success in achieving these goals; where there is insufficient progress they should look for the reasons and find suitable remedies. It is essential that this evaluation be seen as a common responsibility, and that it be carried out faithfully.

The end of each school year is one appropriate time for such an evaluation. From a Christian perspective, it is not enough to say that this is the time for examinations. The academic program is only one part of the process, and the end of the school year is also the time for a serious and intelligent examination of which educational goals have been achieved and which have not. A much more decisive time comes at the completion of a student's years in the school, because this is the moment when students should have reached the maximum level of an education that integrates the human and the Christian.[111]

103. The religious dimension of the school climate strengthens the quality of the formation process, so long as certain conditions are verified—conditions that depend both on teachers and students. It is worth noting, once again, that the students are not spectators; they help to determine the quality of this climate.

Some of the conditions for creating a positive and supportive climate are the following: that everyone agree with the educational goals and cooperate in achieving them; that interpersonal relationships be based on love and Christian freedom; that each individual, in daily life, be a witness to Gospel values; that every student be challenged to strive for the highest possible level of formation, both human and Christian. In addition, the climate must be one in which families are welcomed, the local Church is an active participant, and civil society—local, national, and international—is included. If all share a common faith, this can be an added advantage.

104. Strong determination is needed to do everything possible to eliminate conditions which threaten the health of the school climate. Some examples of potential problems are these: the educational goals are either not defined or are defined badly; those responsible for the school are not sufficiently trained; concern for academic achievement is excessive; relations between teachers and students are cold and impersonal; teachers are antagonistic toward one another; discipline is imposed from on high without any participation or cooperation from the students; relationships with families are formal or even strained, and families are not involved in helping to determine the educational goals; some within the school community are giving a negative witness; individuals are unwilling to work together for the common good; the school is isolated from the local Church; there is no interest in or concern for the problems of society; religious instruction is "routine." Whenever some combination of these symptoms is present, the religious dimension of the school is seriously threatened. Religious instruction can become empty words falling on deaf ears, because the authentically Christian witness that reinforces it is absent from the school climate. All symptoms of ill health have to be faced honestly and directly, remembering that the Gospel calls us to a continuous process of conversion.

105. A school exerts a great deal of effort in trying to obtain the students' active cooperation. Since they are active agents in their own formation process, this cooperation is essential. To be human is to be endowed with intelligence and freedom; it is impossible for education to be genuine without the active involvement of the one being educated. Students must act and react; with their intelligence, freedom, will, and the whole complex range of human emotions. The formation process comes to a halt when students are uninvolved and unmoved. Experienced teachers are familiar with the causes of such "blocks" in young people; the roots are both psychological and theological, and original sin is not excluded.

106. There are many ways to encourage students to become active participants in their own formation. Those with sufficient knowledge and maturity can be asked to help in the development of educational goals. While they are clearly not yet able to determine the final objective, they can help in determining the concrete means which will help to attain this objective. When students are trusted and given responsibility, when they are invited to contribute their own ideas and efforts for the common good, their gratitude rules out indifference and inertia. The more that students can be helped to realize that a school and all its activities have only one purpose—to help them in their growth toward maturity—the more those students will be willing to become actively involved.

Even students who are very young can sense whether the atmosphere in the school is pleasant or not. They are more willing to cooperate when they feel respected, trusted and loved. And their willingness to cooperate will be reinforced by a school climate which is warm and friendly, when teachers are ready to help, and when they find it easy to get along with the other students.

107. One important result of religious instruction is the development of religious values and religious motivation; these can be a great help in obtaining the willing participation of the students. But we must remember that religious values and motivation are cultivated in all subject areas and, indeed, in all of the various activities going on in the school. One way that teachers can encourage an under standing of and commitment to religious values is by frequent references to God. Teachers learn through experience how to help the students understand and appreciate the religious truths they are being taught, and this appreciation can easily develop into love, A truth which is loved by the teacher, and communicated in such a way that it is seen to be something valuable in itself, then becomes valuable to the student. One advantage of the Christological approach to religious instruction is that it can develop this love more easily in young people. The approach we have suggested concentrates on the person of Jesus. It is possible to love a person; it is rather difficult to love a formula. This love for Christ is then transferred to his message which, because it is loved, has value.

But every true educator knows that a further step is necessary: values must lead to action; they are the motivation for action. Finally, truth becomes fully alive through the supernatural dynamism of grace, which enlightens and leads to faith, to love, to action that is in accord with the will of God, through the Lord Jesus, in the Holy Spirit. The Christian process of formation is, therefore, the result of a constant interaction involving the expert labor of the teachers, the free cooperation of the students, and the help of grace.

108. We have already referred to the fact that, in many parts of the world, the student body in a Catholic school includes increasing numbers of young people from different faiths and different ideological backgrounds. In these situations it is essential to clarify the relationship between religious development and cultural growth. It is a question which must not be ignored, and dealing with it is the responsibility of each Christian member of the educational community.

In these situations, however, evangelization is not easy—it may not even be possible. We should look to pre-evangelization: to the development of a religious sense of life. In order to do this, the process of formation must constantly raise questions about the "how" and the "why" and the "what" and then point out and deepen the positive results of this investigation.

The transmission of a culture ought to be especially attentive to the practical effects of that culture, and strengthen those aspects of it which will make a person more human. In particular, it ought to pay attention to the religious dimension of the culture and the emerging ethical requirements to be found in it.

There can be unity in the midst of pluralism, and we need to exercise a wise discernment in order to distinguish between what is essential and what is accidental. Prudent use of the "why" and the "what" and the "how" will lead to integral human development in the formation process, and this is what we mean by a genuine pre-evangelization. It is fertile ground which may, at some future time, be able to bear fruit.

109. In order to describe the formation process, we have had to proceed by an analysis of its various elements; this, of course, is not the way things happen in the real world. The Catholic school is a center of life, and life is synthetic, In this vital center, the formation process is a constant interplay of action and reaction. The interplay has both a horizontal and a vertical dimension, and it is this qualification that makes the Catholic school distinctive from those other schools whose educational objectives are not inspired by Christianity.

110. The teachers love their students, and they show this love in the way they interact with them. They take advantage of every opportunity to encourage and strengthen them in those areas which will help to achieve the goals of the educational process. Their words, their witness, their encouragement and help, their advice and friendly correction are all important in achieving these goals, which must always be understood to include academic achievement, moral behavior, and a religious dimension.

When students feel loved, they will love in return. Their questioning, their trust, their critical observations and suggestions for improvement in the classroom and the school milieu will enrich the teachers and also help to facilitate a shared commitment to the formation process.

111. In a Catholic school, even this is not enough. There is also a continuous vertical interaction, through prayer; this is the fullest and most complete expression of the religious dimension.

Each of the students has his or her own life, family and social background, and these are not always happy situations. They feel the unrest of the child or adolescent, which grows more intense as they face the problems and worries of a young person approaching maturity. Teachers will pray for each of them, that the grace present in the Catholic school's milieu may permeate their whole person, enlightening them and helping them to respond adequately to all that is demanded of them in order to live Christian lives.

And the students will learn that they must pray for their teachers. As they get older, they will come to appreciate the pain and the difficulties that teaching involves. They will pray that the educational gifts of their teachers may be more effective, that they may be comforted by success in their work, that grace may sustain their dedication and bring them peace in their work.

112. Thus a relationship is built up which is both human and divine; there is a flow of love, and also of grace. And this will make the Catholic school truly authentic. As the years go by, students will have the joy of seeing themselves nearing maturity; not only physically, but also intellectually and spiritually. When they look back, they will realize that, with their cooperation, the educational objectives of the school have become a reality. And as they look forward, they will feel free and secure, because they will be able to face the new, and now proximate, life commitments.

Conclusion

113. The Congregation for Catholic Education asks local ordinaries and superiors of Religious Congregations dedicated to the education of youth to bring these reflections to the attention of all teachers and directors of Catholic schools. At the same time, the Congregation wishes to affirm once again that it is fully conscious of the important service they offer—to youth and to the Church.

114. Therefore the Congregation extends warm thanks to all those engaged in this work: for all they have done, and for all that they continue to do in spite of political, economic, and practical difficulties. For many, to continue in this mission involves great sacrifice. The Church is deeply grateful to everyone dedicated to the educational mission in a Catholic school; it is confident that, with the help of God, many others will be called to join in this mission and will respond generously.

115. The Congregation would like to suggest that further study, research, and experimentation be done in all areas that affect the religious dimension of education in Catholic schools. Much has been done, but many people are asking for even more. This is surely possible in every school whose freedom is sufficiently protected by civil law. It may be difficult in those countries which allow the Catholic school as an academic institution, but where the religious dimension leads to constant conflict. Local experience must be the determining factor in such situations; however, to the extent that it is possible, a religious dimension should always be present—either in the school or outside its walls. There has never been a shortage of families and students, of different faiths and religions, who choose a Catholic school because they appreciate the value of an education where instruction is enhanced by a religious dimension.

Educators will know the best way to respond to their expectations, knowing that, in a world of cultural pluralism, dialogue always gives grounds for hope.

Rome, April 7, 1988, Feast of Saint John Baptist de La Salle, Principal Patron of Teachers

† **William Cardinal Baum**
Prefect

† **Antonio M. Javierre Ortas**
Titular Archbishop of Meta
Secretary

---

[1] *Gravissimum educationis*, 8.

[2] March 19, 1977.

[3] October 15, 1982.

[4] From Vatican Council II: Declaration on Christian Education *Gravissimum educationis*; Dogmatic Constitution on the Church *Lumen gentium*; Pastoral Constitution on the Church in the Modern World *Gaudium et spes*; Dogmatic Constitution on Divine Revelation *Dei verbum*; Constitution on the Liturgy *Sacrosanctum Concilium*; Decree on the Apostolate of the Laity *Apostolicam actuositatem*; Decree on Missionary Activity *Ad gentes divinitus*; Declaration on Non-Christian Religions *Nostra aetate*; Decree on Ecumenism *Unitatis redintegratio*; Declaration on Religious Liberty *Dignitatis humanae*. From Paul VI, the Apostolic Exhortation *Evangelii nuntiandi* of December 8, 1975. From John Paul II, the Apostolic Exhortation *Catechesi tradendae* of October 16, 1979; in addition, a number of his talks given to educators and to young people will be cited below. From the Congregation for Clergy, the *Directorium catechisticum generale* of April 11, 1971. All of these documents will be cited by their Latin titles in the notes which follow. In a few places, pastoral letters of bishops will be quoted.

[5] Note that the Congregation has also published *Educational Guidance in Human Love: Outlines for Sex Education*, November 1, 1983. This theme, therefore, will receive only brief and passing mention in the present document.

[6] *Gravissimum educationis*, 9: "It is clear that the Church has a deep respect for those Catholic schools, especially in countries where the Church is young, which have large numbers of students who are not Catholics."

[7] Cf. *Dignitatis humanae*, 2; 9; 10; 12 *et passim*.

[8] C.I.C., canon 748 § 2: "Homines ad amplectendam fidem catholicam contra ipsorum conscientiam per coactionem adducere nemini umquam fas est."

[9] Cf *Gaudium et spes*, 4-10.

[10] Ibid., 7: "The change of mentality and of structures often call into question traditional values, especially among the young."

[11] Cf *Evangelii nuntiandi*, 20.

[12] Cf the *Annuario Statistico della Chiesa* published by the Central Statistical Office of the Church, an office within the Secretariate of State for Vatican City. By way of example, on December 31, 1985, there were 154,126 Catholic schools with 38,243,304 students.

[13] Cf 1 Cor 12:31.

[14] Various aspects of the religious attitudes of young people developed in this section have been the object of recent statements of the Holy Father. A handy compilation of these numerous talks can be found in a book edited by the Pontifical Council for the Laity, *The Holy Father Speaks to Youth: 1980-1985*. The book is published in several languages.

[15] Cf *Gravissimum educationis*, 8. For the Gospel spirit of love and freedom, cf *Gaudium et spes*, 38: "[The Lord Jesus] reveals to us that God is love (1 Jn 4:8), and at the same time teaches us that the fundamental rule for human perfection, and therefore also for the transformation of the world, is the new commandment of love." See also 2 Cor 3:17: "Where the Spirit of the Lord is present, there is freedom."

[16] This question was treated in *The Catholic School*, 81-82.

[17] Mt 28:20.

[18] 6.

[19] Cf the address of John Paul II to the parents, teachers and students from the Catholic schools of the Italian Province of Lazio, March 9, 1985, *Insegnamenti*, VIII/1, p. 620.

[20] Address of John Paul II to the bishops of Lombardy, Italy, on the occasion of their "Ad limina" visit, January 15, 1982, *Insegnamenti*, V/1, 1982, p. 105.

21 *Insegnamenti*, VIII/1, pp. 618f.

22 Mt 25:40: "For indeed I tell you, as often as you have done these things to one of these least of my brothers, you have done it to me."

23 Cf *Perfectae caritatis*, 8: "There are in the Church a great number of institutes, clerical or lay, dedicated to various aspects of the apostolate, which have different gifts according to the grace that has been given to each: 'some exercise a ministry of service; some teach' (cf Rom 12:5-8)." Also see *Ad gentes divinitus*, 40.

24 *Summa Theol.* II-II, q. 186, a. 1: "By antonomasis those are called 'religious' who dedicate themselves to the service of God as if they were offering themselves as a holocaust to the Lord."

25 Ibid., a. 2.

26 *Lay Catholics in Schools: Witnesses to the Faith.*

27 The norms of the Church in this respect are to be found in canons 800-803 of the Code of Canon Law.

28 Cf the address of Pope Paul VI to the National Congress of Diocesan Directors of the Teachers' Organizations of Catholic Action, *Insegnamenti*, I, 1963, p. 594.

29 Cf *Gravissimum educationis*, 3

30 *Gravissimum educationis*, 8

31 A number of recent documents from national Episcopal Conferences and from individual local ordinaries have had the Catholic school as their theme. These documents should be known and put into practice.

32 See, for example, the Resolution of the European Parliament on freedom of education in the European Community, approved by a large majority on March 14, 1984.

33 Cf Mk 6: 3; Acts 10: 35. Useful applications of the ethics of work to the work done in school can be found in the September 14, 1981 Encyclical *Laborem exercens* of John Paul II, especially in Part Five.

34 Gen 3: 19: "By the sweat on your face shall you get bread to eat."

35 Lk 9: 23: "...let him take up his cross each day."

36 *Gravissimum educationis*, 8: among the elements characteristic of the Catholic school, there is that of "developing the relationship between human culture and the message of salvation, so that the knowledge of the world, of life and of the human person which the students are gradually acquiring is illuminated by faith."

37 For a description of culture and of the relationship between culture and faith, see *Gaudium et spes*, 54 ff.

38 Cf Denz: Schön. 3016-3017 for the traditional doctrine on the rapport between reason and faith, as defined by Vatican Council I.

39 Cf the address of Pope John Paul II to the teachers and students of Catholic schools in Melbourne, Australia, on the occasion of his pastoral journey to East Asia and Oceania: *Insegnamenti* November 28, 1986; IX/2, 1986, pp. 1710 ff.

40 Cf 8.

41 Cf 53-62.

42 Pope John Paul II, speaking at the National Congress of Catholic Cultural Organizations: *Insegnamenti*, V/1, 1982, p. 131. See also John Paul II, *Epistula qua Pontificium Consilium pro hominum Cultura instituitur: AAS* 74 (1982), p. 685.

43 Wis 13: 5: "Through the grandeur and beauty of the creatures we may, by analogy, contemplate their Author." Ps 18(19): 2ff.: "The heavens tell of the glory of God."

44 Cf Mt 25: 14-30.

45 Cf *Gaudium et spes*, 12; 14; 17; 22.

46 Cf *Gaudium et spes*, 10.

47 Cf Denz.-Schön. 3004 for the ability to know God through human reason, and 3005 for the ability to know other truths.

48 1 Thes 5: 21: "Examine all things, hold on to what is good". Phil 4: 8: "Everything that is true, noble, or just...let all this be the object of your thoughts."

49 Cf *Gaudium et spes*, 61, on the need to hold on to certain fundamental concepts.

50 Ibid., 44: "At the same time there should be a vital exchange between the Church and the diverse cultures of peoples."

51 Cf *Dei verbum* 2.

52 Cf Blaise Pascal, *Pensées*, fr. 397.

53 *Gaudium et spes*, 37: "The whole of human history is permeated with the gigantic struggle against the powers of darkness."

54 Invaluable material for presenting the divine history of salvation can be found in *Lumen gentium* and *Dei verbum*.

55 Cf *Gaudium et spes*, 62.

56 Cf St. Augustine, *De libero arbitrio*, II, 16, 42. PL 32, 1264. St. Thomas, *Contra gentiles*, IV, 42.

57 Cf *Gravissimum educationis*, 1-2.

58 *Evangelii nuntiandi*, 18: "For the Church to evange-

lize is to bring the Good News to all aspects of humanity and, through its influence, to transform it from within, making humanity itself into something new."

59 Ibid., 44: "The effort to evangelize will bring great profit, through catechetical instruction given at Church, in schools wherever this is possible, and always within the Christian family."

60 *Catechesi tradendae*, 69.

61 Cf The address of Paul VI at the Wednesday audience of May 31, 1967, *Insegnamenti*, V, 1967, p. 788.

62 Address of John Paul II to the priests of the diocese of Rome, March 5, 1981, *Insegnamenti*, IV/1, pp. 629 f.

63 Cf Mt 3: 1-3 on the mission of the Precursor.

64 Cf Jn 17: 9, the prayer of the Lord for those entrusted to him.

65 Apart from strictly local concerns, these questions are generally the ones treated in university "apologetics" manuals, and are about the "preambles to the faith." But the questions acquire a specific nuance for today's students, because of the material they are studying and the world they are living in. Typical questions have to do with atheism, non-Christian religions, divisions among Christians, events in the life of the Church; the violence and injustice of supposedly Christian nations, etc.

66 Revelation, Scripture, Tradition and Christology are themes developed in *Dei verbum*, *Lumen gentium*, and *Gaudium et spes*. Study of the Gospels should be extended to include a study of these documents.

67 Mt 16: 16.

68 Concerning the Blessed Virgin Mary in the life of the Pilgrim Church, cf the encyclical *Redemptoris Mater* of Pope John Paul II, number 39.

69 Mt 11:28.

70 Cf Denz.-Schön. 2854: one cannot speak about God in the same way that one speaks about the objects of human knowledge.

71 Jn 14: 9.

72 Cf Lk 12: 24-28; Jn 3: 16 f.

73 Cf Jn 16: 13.

74 Cf Jn 3: 16 f.

75 Jn 15: 13.

76 From the point of view of Christian anthropology, it is essential that the history of salvation presented in *Lumen gentium* and *Gaudium et spes* be a part of what is studied in class.

77 Important and valuable material for teaching about the Church can be found in *Lumen gentium*.

78 *Sacrosanctum Concilium*, 7: "Christ is present in the Sacraments with his own authority, so that when one baptizes it is Christ himself who baptizes."

79 Jn 1: 16.

80 The content and the methods for teaching about the Sacraments can be enriched through studying parts of *Lumen gentium* and *Sacrosanctum Concilium*.

81 Jn 11: 25-27.

82 Cf Lk 16: 19-31.

83 Cf Mt 25: 31-46.

84 Cf Ibid. 25: 40.

85 Cf *Lumen gentium*, Chapter VII on the eschatological nature of the pilgrim Church and its union with the heavenly Church.

86 Cf Eph 1: 1-14 and Col 1: 13-20 for doxologies which witness to the faith of the early communities. Acts 10 speaks of evangelization, conversion, faith, and the gift of the Spirit in the house of the Roman official Cornelius. Acts 20: 7-12 describes evangelization and the Eucharist in a house at Troas.

87 1 Jn 4:10: "It is not we who have loved God, but God who first loved us."

88 Cf Mt 15: 19 f.

89 Cf the document of the Congregation for Catholic Education already referred to: *Educational Guidance in Human Love: Outlines for Sex Education*.

90 Jn 15:12.

91 Cf *Gaudium et spes*, 63-66 and related applications.

92 Cf Gen 1: 27 f.

93 Again cf Mt 15: 19 f.

94 Cf *Gaudium et spes*, 93.

95 Students should become aware of at least some of the Church's major social documents.

96 Lk 2: 10: "I bring you news of great joy."

97 Lk 22: 53: "But this is your hour; this is the reign of darkness." Evidence of this is easily found in various abuses, acts of injustice, attacks on freedom, the overwhelming weight of misery that leads to sickness, decline and death, the scandalous inequality between rich and poor, the lack of any equity or sense of solidarity in international relations. (Cf *Some Aspects of the "Theology of Liberation,"* published by the Congregation for the Doctrine of the Faith, Introduction and Part I).

98 Jn 8: 7: "Let the one who is without sin cast the first stone."

99 Cf Lk 8: 4.15.

100 Cf Eph 6: 10-17, a characteristically vigorous Pauline description.

101 Cf the *Introduction to Some Aspects of the "Theology of Liberation"* published by the Congregation for the Doctrine of the Faith, August 6, 1984.

102 Mt 5: 48: "You must be perfect as your heavenly Father is perfect."

103 *Lumen gentium*, 42: "All the faithful are invited and called to holiness and to perfection within their own state of live."

104 Ibid., 39: "This holiness of the Church... is expressed in various forms according to each individual, who in their lives and their activities join perfection to love."

105 Some aspects of this are treated in the documents already referred to: *The Catholic School*, 78-80; *Lay Catholics in Schools: Witnesses to the Faith*, especially 56-59. What is said there does not apply only to the lay teachers.

106 *Gravissimum educationis*, 1; "Children and young people should be assisted in the harmonious development of their physical, moral and intellectual gifts....They should be helped to acquire gradually a more mature sense of responsibility."

107 Ibid., 2.

108 Ibid., 8.

109 Cf Mt 5: 48.

110 Lk 2:40: "The child grew and became strong, filled with wisdom; and the favor of God was upon him." Lk 2:52: "And Jesus grew in wisdom and in stature, and in favour with God and with men."

111 Cf once again *Gravissimum educationis*, 1-2.

In Support of Catholic Elementary and Secondary Schools

UNITED STATES CATHOLIC CONFERENCE
November 1990

Our Conviction

The year 1997 will mark the twenty-fifth anniversary of our pastoral letter, *To Teach As Jesus Did*. Now, in 1990, seven years before that anniversary, we wish to commit ourselves to certain seven year goals as a sign of our affirmation of the principles laid down in that pastoral. It is our deep conviction that Catholic schools must exist for the good of the Church. Our concern for the importance of Catholic schools is set in the context of the responsibility we have by our episcopal office to ensure total Catholic education in all its phases for all ages.

In 1972 we stated: "Of the educational programs available to the Catholic community, Catholic schools afford the fullest and best opportunity to realize the three-fold purpose [message, community, and service] of Christian education among children and young people" (*To Teach As Jesus Did* [= TT], 101). In our National Catechetical Directory, *Sharing the Light of Faith*, we included worship among the purposes of Christian education, and now speak about the fourfold purpose of Catholic schools (215).

We are encouraged that our statements are reflective of the teachings of our Holy Father, Pope John Paul II, and of the official documents from the Holy See. Speaking to Catholic educators in New Orleans in 1987, the Holy Father said:

> The presence of the Church in the field of education is wonderfully manifested in the vast and dynamic network of schools and educational programs extending from the preschool through the adult years. *The entire ecclesial community*—bishops, priests, religious, the laity—the Church in all her parts, *is called to value ever more deeply the importance of this task and mission, and to continue to give it full and enthusiastic support* (emphasis in the original) (*Catholic Education: Gift to the Church, Gift to the Nation* [= CE] p. 12).

Further in the same address, the Holy Father said:

> As an institution the Catholic school has to be judged extremely favorably if we apply the sound criterion: "You will know them by their deeds" (Mt 7:16)....The heroic sacrifices of generations of Catholic parents in building up and supporting parochial and diocesan schools must never be forgotten. Rising costs may call for new approaches, new forms of partnership and sharing, new uses of financial resources. But I am sure that all concerned will face the challenge of Catholic schools with courage and dedication, and not doubt the value of the sacrifices to be made (CE, p. 15).

In 1977, the Sacred Congregation for Catholic Education wrote that "the Church is absolutely convinced that the educational aims of the Catholic school in the world of today perform an essential and unique service for the Church herself" (*The Catholic School*, 15).

A decade later, the same congregation issued *The Religious Dimension of Education in a Catholic School*. If anything, the congregation in 1988 was more insistent on the role of the school in the Church: "[T]he Congregation offers enthusiastic encouragement to those dioceses and Religious Congregations who wish to establish new schools. Such things as film clubs and sports groups are not enough; not even classes in catechism instruction are sufficient. What is needed is a school" (41).

In 1983, the bishops of the United States recognized the importance and the role of Catholic education in the formation of Hispanic youth:

> Catholic educators in the United States have a long record of excellence and dedication to the instruction and formation of millions of Catholic faithful. Now they must turn their skills to responding to the educational needs of Hispanics (*The Hispanic Presence: Challenge and Commitment*, p. 18).

In 1984, ten of our brother bishops of African American ancestry also wrote about the need for Catholic schools in *What We Have Seen and Heard: A Pastoral Letter on Evangelization from the Black Bishops of the United States*. They reaffirmed that:

> Today the Catholic school still represents for many in the Black community, especially in the urban areas, an opportunity for quality education and character development.... The Catholic school has been and remains one of the chief vehicles of evangelization within the Black community. We cannot overemphasize the tremendous importance of parochial schools for the Black community. We even dare to suggest that the efforts made to support them and to insure their continuation are a touchstone of the local Church's sincerity in the evangelization of the Black community (p. 28, St. Anthony Messenger Press).

In *To Teach As Jesus Did*, we called upon parents, educators, and pastors "to ensure the continuance and improvement of Catholic schools" (119). And we pointed to specific areas of concern: greater fiscal responsibility, quality education for the disadvantaged, and the need to look at alternative models. Much progress has been made. More needs to be done. We encourage our parents and pastors who presently are shouldering the onerous task of educating our youth in Catholic schools. In our day, it is more important than ever that they give their active support to Catholic schools.

We reaffirm our commitment to Catholic schools. We invite the whole Catholic community to address with us these and other issues of concern.

Our Successes and Challenges

In this new decade, there is good news about Catholic schools and there are challenges.

Research has shown that Catholic schools directly impact the future lives of their students. Graduates of Catholic schools are more closely bonded to the Church, more deeply committed to adult religious practices, happier, and more supportive of religious perspectives on women and have more confidence in other people, more benign images of God, and a greater awareness of the responsibility for moral decision making. They give in a committed fashion more contributions to the Catholic Church (National Opinion Research Center [NORC] 1988 General Social Survey).

Research by the United States Department of Education over the last decade has found that Catholic school students consistently outscore students in the public schools in reading, mathematics, and science. They are especially effective in educating minority and low-income students, much more so than the public schools or other private schools (National Assessment of Educational Progress Studies).

There are also some serious challenges facing Catholic schools. Costs have increased 500 percent in the last twenty years, over twice the Consumer Price Index. Fewer than 200 Catholic schools have opened since 1966 and only thirty of those were in the ten largest (arch)dioceses. In the last ten years, the percentage of potential Catholic students attending Catholic schools has dropped from 33 percent for elementary schools to 27 percent and from 22 percent for secondary schools to 19 percent. Much of this decline is due to shifting demographics and would be reversed if parishes and clusters of parishes opened schools where Catholic families now live. In many wealthy suburban areas, some parents perceive that the free public schools are better than Catholic schools, in spite of the research to the contrary. Other parents perceive that the public schools offer their children a broader cultural experience and, as a result, they opt for the public school education.

There are some dioceses that do not have education boards or commissions connected to their schools but, rather, operate with the traditional parish governance structure. There is, therefore, a lack of consistency in the relationship of the Catholic laity to the schools. Dioceses should be encouraged to study patterns of school governance and financial development with the goal of enhancing the role of parents and other interested laity, e.g., alumni, grandparents, and parishioners.

In 1972, we declared that we were well aware of the problems which face Catholic schools in the United States. We also said that we wished "to make our position clear. For our part, as bishops, we reaffirm our conviction that Catholic schools ...are the most effective means available to the Church for the education of children and young people." (TT, 118).

Therefore, we called "upon all members of the Catholic community to do everything in their power to maintain and strengthen Catholic schools" which embrace the fourfold purposes of Catholic education (TT, 118).

We will not waver from that conviction.

Our Future Goals for 1997

By the twenty-fifth anniversary of *To Teach As Jesus Did* in 1997, we commit ourselves unequivocally to the following goals:

1. That Catholic schools will continue to provide high quality education for all their students in a context infused with gospel values.

2. That serious efforts will be made to ensure that Catholic schools are available for Catholic parents who wish to send their children to them.

3. That new initiatives will be launched to secure sufficient financial assistance from both private and public sectors for Catholic parents to exercise this right.

4. That the salaries and benefits of Catholic school teachers and administrators will reflect our teaching as expressed in *Economic Justice for All*.

In order to accomplish these interrelated goals, we commit ourselves to the following initial actions.

Stewardship

We will teach clearly, consistently, and continuously that we are all stewards of the mysteries of God and disciples of Jesus Christ. This will include an understanding that God has given us gifts which are to be shared with others in the practical application of discipleship and stewardship to which all are called. We will invite all Catholics to share in the apostolate of Catholic education, realizing that financial support is a means of responding to God's call to stewardship.

Development

We commit ourselves to the establishment of diocesan educational development offices or similar initiatives that will be concerned with soliciting funds from other sources and wisely investing the money. These development efforts should include some form of endowment for Catholic schools established in accordance with diocesan guidelines. We would hope that these efforts would be in place by the fall of 1995.

Recognizing that some dioceses may need assistance in establishing and fostering their development efforts, we will open a national development office by January 1992. In addition to its educational efforts, this office will be charged with the responsibility to ensure ethical practices in the Church's development efforts. Furthermore, we challenge our successful business and community leaders to join us in supporting Catholic schools. Recognizing that there are a number of corporations which limit their charitable contributions to national projects, it is our intention to convene a group of diocesan bishops and chief executive officers from the business community to consider funding national efforts on behalf of Catholic schools.

Ensuring Parental Rights

In union with the Holy Father, we have consistently taught that parents are the first and foremost educators of their children. Almost seventy years ago, we assisted the Sisters of the Holy Names of Jesus and Mary to bring suit against one state that sought to encroach on these rights of parents. In *Pierce v. Society of Sisters*, the Supreme Court of the United States recognized that choosing the education most appropriate for the child was both the right and responsibility of parents. In 1983, in *Mueller v. Allen*, the Court held that states could constitutionally assist parents in defraying the costs associated with those educational choices. The time has come for all citizens of the United States, especially those who govern in their name, to fortify this right and promote this responsibility.

Recognizing that Catholic schools are a significant part of education in the United States, we call on all citizens to join with us in supporting federal and state legislative efforts to provide financial assistance to all parents which will ensure that they can afford to choose the type of schooling they desire for their children. For our part, we are so convinced that the Catholic community needs to enter seriously into both national and state educational discussions that we are taking immediate steps to educate all citizens of the United States about the importance of assuring that all parents have a meaningful choice of schools.

Recognizing the long-term nature of convincing the nation that parents should have not only a choice in selecting educational opportunities for their children, but also financial support to exercise that choice, we are taking immediate steps to accomplish this end.

We support and encourage the formation of diocesan, state, and national organizations of Catholic school parents. To assist in this effort, we will provide, through outside funding obtained by the General Secretary, two million dollars in seed money for a national office, which will provide assistance to diocesan and state groups and found a national parent organization.

Furthermore, from this seed money, we will fund one additional staff position in the Department of Education; the sole responsibility of this person will be to work with diocesan superintendents of schools and parent representatives to establish a national communications network. We will also fund one additional staff position in the Office of Government Liaison; this person's sole responsibility will be to work on educational issues.

Strategic Plan

Because of our long-term commitment to Catholic schools, we are instructing our Committee on Education to develop a strategic plan for Catholic schools to be presented for our consideration no later than 1995.

Conclusion

We want to acknowledge that today's children and youth are our future. Catholic schools have provided and will continue to provide an excellent total education. In doing so, they have also fostered the improvement of all of education in the United States. Many of the reforms being suggested for public education (school-based management, greater parental involvement, values education, increased homework, more rigorous courses, and even school uniforms) have long been associated with the success of Catholic schools. Our inner city Catholic schools have been especially prominent in providing quality education for the most disadvantaged to improve their future status in society. Our Church and our nation have been enriched because of the quality of education provided in Catholic schools over the last 300 years. We express our deep and prayerful thanks to the religious, priests, and laity who formed this ministry. Now we are called to sustain and expand this vitally important ministry of the Church.

In December 1989, the Administrative Board of the United States Catholic Conference authorized the General Secretary to convene a special "blue ribbon committee on financing Catholic elementary and secondary schools." Aware of the crisis existing in many parts of the United States in financing Catholic schools, the committee was charged with recommending a new effort to assist bishops as they confront the realities of financing schools. The committee made its report to the USCC Committee on Education, which unanimously approved this statement in June 1990. This present document, *In Support of Catholic Elementary and Secondary Schools*, was approved by the general membership of the United States Catholic Conference on November 21, 1990, and is authorized for publication as a document of the United States Catholic Conference by the undersigned.

Monsignor Robert N. Lynch
General Secretary
NCCB/USCC

The Catholic School on the Threshold
of the Third Millennium

CONGREGATION FOR CATHOLIC EDUCATION
December 28, 1997

Introduction

1. On the threshold of the third millennium education faces new challenges which are the result of a new socio-political and cultural context. First and foremost, we have a crisis of values which, in highly developed societies in particular, assumes the form, often exalted by the media, of subjectivism, moral relativism and nihilism. The extreme pluralism pervading contemporary society leads to behavior patterns which are at times so opposed to one another as to undermine any idea of community identity. Rapid structural changes, profound technical innovations and the globalization of the economy affect human life more and more throughout the world. Rather than prospects of development for all, we witness the widening of the gap between rich and poor, as well as massive migration from under-developed to highly-developed countries. The phenomena of multiculturalism and an increasingly multi-ethnic and multi-religious society is at the same time an enrichment and a source of further problems. To this we must add, in countries of long-standing evangelization, a growing marginalization of the Christian faith as a reference point and a source of light for an effective and convincing interpretation of existence.

2. In the specifically educational field, the scope of educational functions has broadened, becoming more complex, more specialized. The sciences of education, which concentrated in the past on the study of the child and teacher-training, have been widened to include the various stages of life, and the different spheres and situations beyond the school. New requirements have given force to the demand for new contents, new capabilities and new educational models besides those followed traditionally. Thus education and schooling become particularly difficult today.

3. Such an outlook calls for courageous renewal on the part of the Catholic school. The precious heritage of the experience gained over the centuries reveals its vitality precisely in the capacity for prudent innovation. And so, now as in the past, the Catholic school must be able to speak for itself effectively and convincingly. It is not merely a question of adaptation, but of missionary thrust, the fundamental duty to evangelize, to go towards men and women wherever they are, so that they may receive the gift of salvation.

4. Accordingly, the Congregation for Catholic Education, during this time of immediate preparation for the great jubilee of the year 2000, and as it celebrates the thirtieth anniversary of the creation of the Schools Office[1] and the twentieth anniversary of *The Catholic School*, published on 19th March 1977, proposes to "focus attention on the nature and distinctive characteristics of a school which would present itself as Catholic."[2] It therefore addresses this circular letter to all those who are engaged in Catholic schooling, in order to convey to them a word of encouragement and hope. In particular, by means of the present letter, the Congregation shares their joy for the positive fruits yielded by the Catholic school and their anxiety about the difficulties which it encounters. Furthermore, the teachings of the Second Vatican Council, innumerable interventions of the Holy Father, ordinary and extraordinary Assemblies of the Synod of Bishops, Episcopal Conferences and the pastoral solicitude of diocesan Ordinaries, as well as international Catholic organizations involved in education and schooling, all support our conviction that it is opportune to devote careful attention to certain fundamental characteristics of the Catholic school, which are of great importance if its educational activity is to be effectual in the Church and in society. Such are: *the Catholic school as a place of integral education of the human person through a clear educational project of which Christ is the foundation;*[3] *its ecclesial and cultural identity; its mission of education as a work of love; its service to society; the traits which should characterize the educating community.*

Joys and Difficulties

5. We retrace with satisfaction the positive course of the Catholic school over the past decades. First and foremost, we must recognize the contribution it makes to the evangelizing mission of the Church throughout the world, including those areas in which no other form of pastoral work is possible. Moreover, in spite of numerous obstacles, the Catholic school has continued to share responsibility for the social and cultural development of the different communities and peoples to which it belongs, participating in their joys and hopes, their sufferings and difficulties, their efforts to achieve genuine human and communitarian progress. In this respect, mention must be made of the invaluable services of the Catholic school to the spiritual and

material development of less fortunate peoples. It is our duty to express appreciation for the Catholic school's contribution to innovation in the fields of pedagogy and didactics, and the strenuous commitment of so many men and women, especially of all those religious and laity who see their teaching as a mission and true apostolate.[4] Finally, we cannot forget the part played by Catholic schools in organic pastoral work and in pastoral care for the family in particular, emphasizing in this respect their discreet insertion in the educational dynamics between parents and their children and, very especially the unpretentious yet caring and sensitive help offered in those cases, more and more numerous above all in wealthy nations, of families which are "fragile" or have broken up.

6. The school is undoubtedly a sensitive meeting-point for the problems which beseige this restless end of the millennium. The Catholic school is thus confronted with children and young people who experience the difficulties of the present time. Pupils who shun effort, are incapable of self-sacrifice and perseverance and who lack authentic models to guide them, often even in their own families. In an increasing number of instances they are not only indifferent and non-practicing, but also totally lacking in religious or moral formation. To this we must add—on the part of numerous pupils and families—a profound apathy where ethical and religious formation is concerned, to the extent that what is in fact required of the Catholic school is a certificate of studies or, at the most, quality instruction and training for employment. The atmosphere we have described produces a certain degree of pedagogical tiredness, which intensifies the ever increasing difficulty of conciliating the role of the teacher with that of the educator in today's context.

7. Among existing difficulties, there are also situations in the political, social and cultural sphere which make it harder or even impossible to attend a Catholic school. The drama of large-scale poverty and hunger in many parts of the world, internal conflicts and civil wars, urban deterioration, the spread of crime in large cities, impede the implementation of projects for formation and education. In other parts of the world, governments themselves put obstacles in the way, when they do not actually prevent the Catholic school from operating, in spite of the progress which has been made as far as attitude, democratic practice and sensitivity to human rights are concerned. Finance is a source of further difficulties, which are felt more acutely in those states in which no government aid is provided for non state schools. This places an almost unbearable financial burden on families choosing not to send their children to state schools and constitutes a serious threat to the survival of the schools themselves. Moreover, such financial strain not only affects the recruiting and stability of teachers, but can also result in the exclusion from Catholic schools of those who cannot afford to pay, leading to a selection according to means which deprives the Catholic school of one of its distinguishing features, which is to be a school for all.

Looking Ahead

8. This overview of the joys and difficulties of the Catholic school, although not pretending to exhaust its entire breadth and depth, does prompt us to reflect on the contribution it can make to the formation of the younger generation on the threshold of the third millennium, recognizing, as John Paul II has written, that "the future of the world and of the Church belongs to the *younger generation*, to those who, born in this century, will reach maturity in the next, the first century of the new millennium."[5] Thus the Catholic school

should be able to offer young people the means to acquire the knowledge they need in order to find a place in a society which is strongly characterized by technical and scientific skill. But at the same time, it should be able, above all, to impart a solid Christian formation. And for the Catholic school to be a means of education in the modern world, we are convinced that certain fundamental characteristics need to be strengthened.

The Human Person and His or Her Education

9. The Catholic school sets out to be a school for the human person and of human persons. "The person of each individual human being, in his or her material and spiritual needs, is at the heart of Christ's teaching: this is why the promotion of the human person is the goal of the Catholic school."[6] This affirmation, stressing man's vital relationship with Christ, reminds us that it is in His person that the fullness of the truth concerning man is to be found. For this reason the Catholic school, in committing itself to the development of the whole man, does so in obedience to the solicitude of the Church, in the awareness that all human values find their fulfillment and unity in Christ.[7] This awareness expresses the centrality of the human person in the educational project of the Catholic school, strengthens its educational endeavor and renders it fit to form strong personalities.

10. The social and cultural context of our time is in danger of obscuring "the educational value of the Catholic school, in which its fundamental reason for existing and the basis of its genuine apostolate is to be found."[8] Indeed, although it is true to say that in recent years there has been an increased interest and a greater sensitivity on the part of public opinion, international organizations and governments with regard to schooling and education, there has also been a noticeable tendency to reduce education to its purely technical and practical aspects. Pedagogy and the sciences of education themselves have appeared to devote greater attention to the study of phenomenology and didactics than to the essence of education as such, centered on deeply meaningful values and vision. The fragmentation of education, the generic character of the values frequently invoked and which obtain ample and easy consensus at the price of a dangerous obscuring of their content, tend to make the school step back into a supposed neutrality, which enervates its educating potential and reflects negatively on the formation of the pupils. There is a tendency to forget that education always presupposes and involves a definite concept of man and life. To claim neutrality for schools signifies in practice, more times than not, banning all reference to religion from the cultural and educational field, whereas a correct pedagogical approach ought to be open to the more decisive sphere of ultimate objectives, attending not only to "how," but also to "why," overcoming any misunderstanding as regards the claim to neutrality in education, restoring to the educational process the unity which saves it from dispersion amid the meandering of knowledge and acquired facts, and focuses on the human person in his or her integral, transcendent, historical identity. With its educational project inspired by the Gospel, the Catholic school is called to take up this challenge and respond to it in the conviction that "it is only in the mystery of the Word made flesh that the mystery of man truly becomes clear."[9]

The Catholic School at the Heart of the Church

11. The complexity of the modern world makes it all the more necessary to increase awareness of the ecclesial identity of the Catholic school. It is from its Catholic identity that the school derives its original characteristics and its "structure" as a genuine instrument of the Church, a place of real and specific pastoral ministry. The Catholic school participates in the evangelizing mission of the Church and is the privileged environment in which Christian education is carried out. In this way "Catholic schools are at once places of evangelization, of complete formation, of inculturation, of apprenticeship in a lively dialogue between young people of different religions and social backgrounds."[10] The ecclesial nature of the Catholic school, therefore, is written in the very heart of its identity as a teaching institution. It is a true and proper ecclesial entity by reason of its educational activity, "in which faith, culture and life are brought into harmony."[11] Thus it must be strongly emphasized that this ecclesial dimension is not a mere adjunct, but is a proper and specific attribute, a distinctive characteristic which penetrates and informs every moment of its educational activity, a fundamental part of its very identity and the focus of its mission.[12] The fostering of this dimension should be the aim of all those who make up the educating community.

12. By reason of its identity, therefore, the Catholic school is a place of ecclesial experience, which is molded in the Christian community. However, it should not be forgotten that the school fulfills its vocation to be a genuine experience of Church only if it takes its stand within the organic pastoral work of the Christian community. In a very special way the Catholic school affords the opportunity to meet young people in an environment which favors their Christian formation. Unfortunately, there are instances in which the Catholic school is not perceived as an integral part of organic pastoral work, at times it is considered alien, or very nearly so, to the community. It is urgent, therefore, to sensitize parochial and diocesan communities to the necessity of their devoting special care to education and schools.

13. In the life of the Church, the Catholic school is recognized above all as an expression of those Religious Institutes which, according to their proper charism or specific apostolate, have dedicated themselves generously to education. The present time is not without its difficulties, not only on account of the alarming decrease in numbers, but also of a serious misunderstanding which induces some Religious to abandon the teaching apostolate. In other words, on the one hand the commitment to schooling is separated from pastoral activity, while on the other it is not easy to reconcile concrete activities with the specific demands of religious life. The fertile intuitions of saintly founders and foundresses demonstrate, more radically than any other argumentation, the groundless and precarious nature of such attitudes. We should also remember that the presence of consecrated religious within the educating community is indispensable, since "consecrated persons are able to be especially effective in educational activities"[13]; they are an example of the unreserved and gratuitous "gift" of self to the service of others in the spirit of their religious consecration. The presence of men and women religious, side by side with priests and lay teachers, affords pupils "a vivid image of the Church and makes recognition of its riches easier."[14]

Cultural Identity of the Catholic School

14. From the nature of the Catholic school also stems one of the most significant elements of its educational project: the synthesis between culture and faith. Indeed, knowledge set in the context of faith becomes wisdom and life vision. The endeavor to interweave reason and faith, which has become the heart of individual subjects, makes for unity, articulation and coordination, bringing forth within what is learnt in school a Christian vision of the world, of life, of culture and of history. In the Catholic school's educational project there is no separation between time for learning and time for formation, between acquiring notions and growing in wisdom. The various school subjects do not present only knowledge to be attained, but also values to be acquired and truths to be discovered.[15] All of which demands an atmosphere characterized by the search for truth, in which competent, convinced and coherent educators, teachers of learning and of life, may be a reflection, albeit imperfect but still vivid, of the one Teacher. In this perspective, in the Christian educational project all subjects collaborate, each with its own specific content, to the formation of mature personalities.

"Care for learning means loving" (Sap 6, 17)

15. In its ecclesial dimension another characteristic of the Catholic school has its root: it is a school for all, with special attention to those who are weakest. In the past, the establishment of the majority of Catholic educational institutions has responded to the needs of the socially and economically disadvantaged. It is no novelty to affirm that Catholic schools have their origin in a deep concern for the education of children and young people left to their own devices and deprived of any form of schooling. In many parts of the world even today material poverty prevents many youths and children from having access to formal education and adequate human and Christian formation. In other areas new forms of poverty challenge the Catholic school. As in the past, it can come up against situations of incomprehension, mistrust and lack of material resources. The girls from poor families that were taught by the Ursuline nuns in the 15th Century, the boys that Saint Joseph of Calasanz saw running and shouting through the streets of Rome, those that De la Salle came across in the villages of France, or those that were offered shelter by Don Bosco, can be found again among those who have lost all sense of meaning in life and lack any type of inspiring ideal, those to whom no values are proposed and who do not know the beauty of faith, who come from families which are broken and incapable of love, often living in situations of material and spiritual poverty, slaves to the new idols of a society, which, not infrequently, promises them only a future of unemployment and marginalization. To these new poor the Catholic school turns in a spirit of love. Spurred on by the aim of offering to all, and especially to the poor and marginalized, the opportunity of an education, of training for a job, of human and Christian formation, it can and must find in the context of the old and new forms of poverty that original synthesis of ardor and fervent dedication which is a manifestation of Christ's love for the poor, the humble, the masses seeking for truth.

The Catholic School at the Service of Society

16. The school cannot be considered separately from other educational institutions and administered as an entity apart, but must be related to the world of politics, economy, culture and society as a whole. For her part the Catholic school must be firmly resolved to take the new cultural situation in her stride and, by her refusal to accept unquestioningly educational projects which are merely partial, be an example and stimulus for other educational institutions, in the forefront of ecclesial community's concern for education. In this way the Catholic school's public role is clearly perceived. It has not come into being as a private initiative, but as an expression of the reality of the Church, having by its very nature a public character. It fulfills a service of public usefulness and, although clearly and decidedly configured in the perspective of the Catholic faith, is not reserved to Catholics only, but is open to all those who appreciate and share its qualified educational project. This dimension of openness becomes particularly evident in countries in which Christians are not in the majority or developing countries, where Catholic schools have always promoted civil progress and human development without discrimination of any kind.[16] Catholic schools, moreover, like state schools, fulfill a public role, for their presence guarantees cultural and educational pluralism and, above all, the freedom and right of families to see that their children receive the sort of education they wish for them.[17]

17. The Catholic school, therefore, undertakes a cordial and constructive dialogue with states and civil authorities. Such dialogue and collaboration must be based on mutual respect, on the reciprocal recognition of each other's role and on a common service to mankind. To achieve this end, the Catholic school willingly occupies its place within the school system of the different countries and in the legislation of the individual states, when the latter respect the fundamental rights of the human person, starting with respect for life and religious freedom. A correct relationship between state and school, not only a Catholic school, is based not so much on institutional relations as on the right of each person to receive a suitable education of their free choice. This right is acknowledged according to the principle of subsidiarity.[18] For "The public authority, therefore, whose duty it is to protect and defend the liberty of the citizens, is bound according to the principle of distributive justice to ensure that public subsidies are so allocated that parents are truly free to select schools for their children in accordance with their conscience."[19] In the framework not only of the formal proclamation, but also in the effective exercise of this fundamental human right, in some countries there exists the crucial problem of the juridical and financial recognition of non-state schools. We share John Paul II's earnest hope, expressed yet again recently, that in all democratic countries "concrete steps finally be taken to implement true equality for non-state schools and that it be at the same time respectful of their educational project."[20]

Climate of the Educating Community

18. Before concluding, we should like to dwell briefly on the climate and role of the educating community, which is constituted by the interaction and collaboration of its various components: students, parents, teachers, directors and non-teaching staff.[21] Attention is rightly given to the importance of the relations existing between all those who make up the educating community. During childhood and adolescence a student needs to experience personal relations with outstanding educators, and what is taught has greater influence on the student's formation when placed in a context of personal involvement, genuine reciprocity, coherence of attitudes, life-styles and day to day behavior. While respecting individual roles, the community dimension should be fostered, since it is one of the most enriching developments for the contemporary school.[22] It is also helpful to bear in mind, in harmony with the Second Vatican Council,[23] that this community dimension in the Catholic school is not a merely sociological category; it has a theological foundation as well. The educating community, taken as a whole, is thus called to further the objective of a school as a place of complete formation through interpersonal relations.

19. In the Catholic school, "prime responsibility for creating this unique Christian school climate rests with the teachers, as individuals and as a community."[24] Teaching has an extraordinary moral depth and is one of man's most excellent and creative activities, for the teacher does not write on inanimate material, but on the very spirits of human beings. The personal relations between the teacher and the students, therefore, assume an enormous importance and are not limited simply to giving and taking. Moreover, we must remember that teachers and educators fulfill a specific Christian vocation and share an equally specific participation in the mission of the Church, to the extent that "it depends chiefly on them whether the Catholic school achieves its purpose."[25]

20. Parents have a particularly important part to play in the educating community, since it is to them that primary and natural responsibility for their children's education belongs. Unfortunately in our day there is a widespread tendency to delegate this unique role. Therefore it is necessary to foster initiatives which encourage commitment, but which provide at the same time the right sort of concrete support which the family needs and which involve it in the Catholic school's educational project.[26] The constant aim of the school therefore, should be contact and dialogue with the pupils' families, which should also be encouraged through the promotion of parents' associations, in order to clarify with their indispensable collaboration that personalized approach which is needed for an educational project to be efficacious.

Conclusion

21. The Holy Father has pointed out in a meaningful expression how "man is the primary and fundamental way for the Church, the way traced out by Christ himself."[27] This way cannot, then, be foreign to those who evangelize. Traveling along it, they will experience the challenge of education in all its urgency. Thus it follows that the work of the school is irreplaceable and the investment of human and material resources in the school becomes a prophetic choice. On the threshold of the third millennium we perceive the full strength of the mandate which the Church handed down to the Catholic school in that "Pentecost" which was the Second Vatican Council: "Since the Catholic school can be of such service in developing the mission of the People of God and in promoting dialogue between the Church and the community at large to the advantage of both, it is still of vital importance even in our times."[28]

Prot. N. 29096.
Rome, 28th December 1997,
Solemnity of the Holy Family

† Pio Cardinal Laghi
Prefect

† José Saraiva Martins
Tit. Archbishop of Tuburnica
Secretary

---

[1] The Sacred Congregation for Catholic Education was the new name given to the Sacred Congregation for Seminaries and Universities by the Apostolic Constitution *Regimini ecclesiae universae*, which was published on 15 August 1967 and in force as from 1 March 1968 (AAS, LIX [1967] pp. 885-928). The Congregation now comprised a third section, the Schools Office, intended "to develop further" the fundamental principles of education, especially in schools (cfr. II Vatican Council, Declaration on Christian Education *Gravissimum educationis*, Preface).

[2] S. Congregation for Catholic Education, The Catholic School, n. 2.

[3] Cfr. S. Congregation for Catholic Education, *The Catholic School*, n. 34.

[4] Cfr. II Vatican Council, Declaration on Christian Education *Gravissimum educationis*, n. 8.

[5] John Paul II, Apostolic Letter *Tertio Millennio Adveniente*, n. 58.

[6] Cfr. John Paul II, *Address to the I National Meeting of the Catholic School in Italy*, in L'Osservatore Romano, 24 November 1991, p. 4.

[7] Cfr. S. Congregation for Catholic Education, *The Catholic School*, n. 35.

[8] S. Congregation for Catholic Education, *The Catholic School*, n. 3.

[9] II Vatican Council, Pastoral Constitution on the Church in the Modern World *Gaudium et Spes*, n. 22.

[10] John Paul II, Apostolic Exhortation *Ecclesia in Africa*, n. 102.

[11] Congregation for Catholic Education, *Religious Dimension of Education in a Catholic School*, n. 34.

[12] Cfr. Congregation for Catholic Education, *Religious Dimension of Education in a Catholic school*, n. 33.

[13] John Paul II, Apostolic Exhortation *Vita Consecrata*, n. 96.

[14] John Paul II, Apostolic Exhortation *Christifideles Laici*, n. 62.

[15] Cfr. S. Congregation for Catholic Education, *The Catholic School*, n. 39.

[16] Cfr. II Vatican Council, Declaration on Christian Education *Gravissimum educationis*, n. 9.

[17] Cfr. Holy See, *Charter of Rights of the Family*, art. 5.

[18] Cfr. John Paul II, Apostolic Exhortation Familiaris consortio, n. 40; cfr. Congregation for the Doctrine of the Faith, Instruction *Libertatis conscientia*, n. 94.

[19] II Vatican Council, Declaration on Christian Education *Gravissimum educationis*, n. 6.

[20] John Paul II, Letter to the Superior General of the Piarists, in *L'Osservatore Romano*, 28 June 1997, p. 5.

[21] Cfr. S. Congregation for Catholic Education, *Lay Catholics in Schools: Witnesses to Faith*, n. 22.

[22] Cfr. Ibid.

[23] Cfr. II Vatican Council, Declaration on Christian Education *Gravissimum educationis*, n. 8.

[24] Congregation for Catholic Education, *Religious Dimension of Education in a Catholic School*, n. 26.

[25] Cfr. II Vatican Council, Declaration on Christian Education *Gravissimum educationis*, n. 8.

[26] Cfr. John Paul II, Apostolic Exhortation *Familiaris consortio*, n. 40.

[27] Cfr. John Paul II, Encyclical Letter *Redemptor hominis*, n. 14.

[28] II Vatican Council, Declaration on Christian Education *Gravissimum educationis*, n. 8.

Consecrated Persons and Their Mission in Schools: Reflections and Guidelines

CONGREGATION FOR CATHOLIC EDUCATION
October 28, 2002

Introduction

At the Beginning of the Third Millennium

1. The celebration of the two thousandth anniversary of the incarnation of the Word was for many believers a time of conversion and of opening to God's plan for the human person created in his image. The grace of the Jubilee incited in the People of God an urgency to proclaim the mystery of Jesus Christ "yesterday, today and forever" with the testimony of their lives and, in Him, the truth about the human person. Young people, moreover, expressed a surprising interest with regard to the explicit announcement of Jesus. Consecrated persons, for their part, grasped the strong call to live in a state of conversion for accomplishing their specific mission in the Church: to be witnesses of Christ, *epiphany of the love of God in the world*, recognizable signs of reconciled humanity.[1]

A Prophetic Task

2. The complex cultural situations of the beginning of the 21st century are a further appeal to a responsibility to live the present as *kairós*, a favorable time, so that the Gospel may effectively reach the men and women of today. Consecrated persons feel the importance of the prophetic task entrusted to them by the Church in these momentous but fascinating times,[2] *"recalling and serving the divine plan for humanity*, as it is announced in Scripture and as also emerges from the attentive reading of the signs of God's providential action

in history."[3] This task requires the courage of testimony and the patience of dialogue; it is a duty before the cultural tendencies that threaten the dignity of human life, especially in the crucial moments of its beginning and its ending, the harmony of creation, and the existence of peoples and peace.

The Reason for These Reflections

3. Within the context of the profound changes that assail the world of education and schools, the Congregation for Catholic Education wishes to share some reflections, offer some guidelines and incite some further investigations of the educational mission and the presence of consecrated persons in schools in general, not only Catholic schools. This document is mainly addressed to members of institutes of consecrated life and of societies of apostolic life, as well as to those who, involved in the educational mission of the Church, have assumed the evangelical counsels in other forms.

As a Continuation of Previous Ecclesial Guidelines

4. These considerations are within the lines of the Second Vatican Council, the Magisterium of the universal Church and the documents of the continental Synods regarding evangelization, the consecrated life and education, especially scholastic education. In recent years, this Congregation has offered guidelines on Catholic schools[4] and on lay people who bear witness to faith in schools.[5] As a continuation of the document on lay people, it now intends reflecting on the specific contribution of consecrated persons to the educational mission in schools in the light of the Apostolic Exhortation *Vita consecrata* and of the more recent developments of pastoral care for culture.[6] This is a result of its conviction that: "a faith that does not become culture is a faith that has not been fully received, not entirely thought through, not loyally lived."[7]

The Cultural Mediation of the Faith Today

5. The necessity for a cultural mediation of the faith is an invitation for consecrated persons to consider the meaning of their presence in schools. The altered circumstances in which they operate, in environments that are often laicized and in reduced numbers in educational communities, make it necessary to clearly express their specific contribution in cooperation with the other vocations present in schools. A time emerges in which to process answers to the fundamental questions of the young generations and to present a clear cultural proposal that clarifies the type of person and society to which it is desired to educate, and the reference to the anthropological vision inspired by the values of the gospel, in a respectful and constructive dialogue with the other concepts of life.

A Renewed Commitment in the Educational Sphere

6. The challenges of modern life give new motivations to the mission of consecrated persons, called to live the evangelic councils and bring the humanism of the beatitudes to the field of education and schools. This is not at all foreign to the mandate of the Church to announce salvation to all.[8] "At the same time, however, we are painfully aware of certain difficulties which induce your Communities to abandon the school sector. The dearth of religious vocations, estrangement from the teaching apostolate, the attraction of alternative forms of apostolate seemingly more gratifying."[9] Far from discouraging, these difficulties can be a source of purification and characterize a time *of grace and salvation* (cf. 2 Cor 6:2). They invite discernment and an attitude of constant *renewal*. The Holy Spirit, moreover, guides us to rediscover the charism, the roots and the modalities for our presence in schools, concentrating on the essential: the importance of the testimony of Christ, the poor, humble and chaste one; the priority of the person and of relationships based on love; the search for truth; the synthesis between faith, life and culture and the valid proposal of a view of man that respects God's plan.

Evangelize by Educating

It thus becomes clear that consecrated persons in schools, in communion with the Bishops, carry out an ecclesial mission that is vitally important inasmuch as while they educate they are also evangelizing. This mission requires a commitment of holiness, generosity and skilled educational professionalism so that the truth about the person as revealed by Jesus may enlighten the growth of the young generations and of the entire community. This Dicastery feels therefore that it is opportune to call attention to the profile of consecrated persons and to reflect on some well-known aspects of their educational mission in schools today.

I.
Profile of Consecrated Persons

At the School of Christ the Teacher
Ecclesial Gift for Revealing the Word

7. "The consecrated life, deeply rooted in the example and teaching of Christ the Lord, is a gift of God the Father to his Church through the Holy Spirit. By the profession of the evangelical counsels the *characteristic features of Jesus*—the chaste, poor and obedient one—*are made constantly 'visible' in the midst of the world* and the eyes of the faithful are directed towards the mystery of the Kingdom of God already at work in history, even as it awaits its full realization in heaven."[10] The aim of the consecrated life is "conformity to the Lord Jesus in *his total self-giving*,"[11] so that every consecrated person is called to assume "his mind and his way of life,"[12] his way of thinking and of acting, of being and of loving.

Identity of Consecrated Life

8. *The direct reference to Christ* and the *intimate nature of a gift* for the Church and the world,[13] are elements that define the identity and scope of the consecrated life. In them the consecrated life finds itself, its point of departure, God and his love, and its point of arrival, the human community and its requirements. It is through these elements that every religious family traces its own physiognomy, from its spirituality to its apostolate, from its style of community life to its ascetic plan, to the sharing and participation in the richness of its own charisms.

At Christ's School to Have His Mind

9. The consecrated life can be compared in some ways to a *school*, that every consecrated person is called to attend for his whole life. In fact, having the mind of the Son means to attend his school daily, to learn from him to have a heart that is meek and humble, courageous and passionate. It means allowing oneself to be *educated* by Christ, the eternal Word of the Father and, to be drawn to him, the heart and center of the world, choosing his same *form* of life.

Allowing Oneself to Be Educated and Formed by Christ, to Be Similar to Him

10. The life of a consecrated person is therefore an *educational-formative* rise and fall that educates to the truth of life and forms it to the freedom of the gift of oneself, according to the model of the Easter of the Lord. Every moment of consecrated life forms part of this rise

and fall, in its double educational and formative aspect. A consecrated person does in fact gradually learn to have the mind of the Son in him and to reveal it in *a life that is increasingly similar to his*, both at individual and community level, in initial and permanent formation. Thus the vows are an expression of the lifestyle chosen by Jesus on this earth that was essential, chaste and completely dedicated to the Father. Prayer becomes a continuation on earth of the praise of the Son to the Father for the salvation of all mankind. Community life is the demonstration that, in the name of the Lord, stronger bonds than those that come from flesh and blood can be tied. These are bonds that are able to overcome what can divide. The apostolate is the impassioned announcement of he by whom we have been conquered.

Gift for Everyone

11. The school of the mind of the Son gradually opens the consecrated life to the urgency for testimony, so that *the gift may reach everyone*. In fact, Christ "did not count equality with God a thing to be grasped" (Phil 2:6), he kept nothing for himself, but shared his wealth of being Son with all men. That is why, even when the testimony contests some elements of the local culture, consecrated persons try to enter into a dialogue in order to share the wealth which they bring. This means that the testimony must be distinct and unequivocal, clear and comprehensible for everyone, in order to demonstrate that religious consecration has much to say to every culture inasmuch as it helps to reveal the truth about human beings.

Radical Response
Anthropological Value of the Consecrated Life

12. Among the challenges that the consecrated life faces today is that of trying to demonstrate the *anthropological value* of consecration. It is a question of demonstrating that a poor, chaste and obedient life enhances intimate human dignity; that *everyone* is called, in a different way, according to his or her vocation, to be poor, obedient and chaste. The evangelical counsels do, in fact, transfigure authentically human values and desires, but they also relativize the human "by pointing to God as the absolute good."[14] The consecrated life, moreover, must be able to show that the evangelical message possesses considerable importance for living in today's world and is also comprehensible for those who live in a competitive society such as ours. Lastly, the consecrated life must try to testify that holiness is the highest humanizing proposal of man and of history; it is a project that everyone on earth can make his or her own.[15]

Charismatic Circularity

13. Consecrated persons communicate the richness of their specific vocation to the extent that they live their consecration commitments to the full. On the other hand, such a communication also arouses in the receiver a capacity for an enriching response through the participation of his personal gift and his specific vocation. This "confrontation-sharing" with the Church and with the world is of great importance for the vitality of the various religious charisms and for their interpretation in line with the modern context and their respective spiritual roots. It is the principle of *charismatic circularity*, as a result of which the charism *returns* in a sort of way to where it was born, but without simply repeating itself. In this way, the consecrated life itself is renewed, in the listening and interpretation of the signs of the times and in the creative and active fidelity of its origins.

Constructive Dialogue in the Past and in the Present

14. The validity of this principle is confirmed by history; the consecrated life has always woven a constructive dialogue with local culture, sometimes questioning and provoking it, at others defending and preserving it, but in any case allowing it to stimulate and interrogate, in a confrontation that was in some cases dialectic, but always fruitful. It is important that such a confrontation continues even in these times of renewal for the consecrated life and of cultural disorientation that risks frustrating the human heart's insuppressible need for truth.

In the Church Communion
The Church Mystery of Communion

15. The study of the ecclesial situation as a mystery of communion has led the Church, under the action of the Spirit, to increasingly understand itself as the pilgrim people of God and, at the same time as the body of Christ the members of which are in a mutual relationship with each other and with the head.

At a pastoral level, "to make the Church *the home and the school of communion*"[16] is the great challenge that we must know how to face, at the beginning of the new millennium, in order to be faithful to God's plan and to the world's deep expectations. It is first and foremost necessary to promote a *spirituality of communion* capable of becoming the educational principle in the various environments in which the human person is formed. This *spirituality* is learned by making our hearts ponder on the mystery of the Trinity, whose light is reflected in the face of every person, and welcomed and appreciated as a gift.

Consecrated Persons in the Church-Communion

16. Demands for communion have offered consecrated persons the chance to rediscover the mutual relationship with the other vocations in the people of God. In the Church they are called, in a special way, to reveal that participation in the Trinitarian communion can change human relations creating a new kind of solidarity. By professing to live *for God and of God*, consecrated persons do, in fact, undertake to preach the power of the peacemaking action of grace that overcomes the disruptive dynamisms present in the human heart.

With the Dynamism of the Specific Charism

17. Whatever the specific charism that characterizes them, consecrated persons are called, through their vocations, to be *experts of communion*, to promote human and spiritual bonds that promote the mutual exchange of gifts between all the members of the people of God. The acknowledgement of the *many forms* of vocations in the Church gives a new meaning to the presence of consecrated persons in the field of scholastic education. For them a school is a place of mission, where the prophetic role conferred by baptism and lived according to the requirements of the radicalism typical of the evangelical counsels is fulfilled. The gift of special consecration that they have received will lead them to recognizing in schools and in the educational commitment the fruitful furrow in which the Kingdom of God can grow and bear fruit.

A Consecrated Person Educates....

18. This commitment responds perfectly to the nature and to the scope of the consecrated life itself and is carried out according to that double *educational and formative* model that accompanies the growth of the individual consecrated person. Through schools, men and women religious educate, help young people to grasp their own identity and to reveal those authentic needs and desires that inhabit everyone's heart, but which often remain unknown and underestimated: thirst for authenticity and honesty, for love and fidelity, for truth and consistency, for happiness and fullness of life. Desires which in the final analysis converge in the supreme human desire: *to see the face of God.*

.... Forms

19. The second modality is that regarding formation. A school *forms* when it offers a precise proposal for fulfilling those desires, preventing them from being deformed, or only partially or weakly achieved. With the testimony of their lives consecrated persons, who are at the school of the Lord, propose that form of existence which is inspired by Christ, so that even a young person may live the freedom of being a child of God and may experiment the true joy and authentic fulfillment that spring from the project of the Father. Consecrated persons have a providential mission in schools, in the modern context, where the educational proposals seem to be increasingly poorer and man's aspirations seem to be increasingly unanswered!

In Schools, Educational Communities

20. There is no need for consecrated persons to reserve exclusive tasks for themselves in educational communities. The specificity of the consecrated life lies in its being a sign, a memory and prophecy of the values of the Gospel. Its characteristic is "to bring to bear on the world of education their radical witness to the values of the Kingdom,"[17] in cooperation with the laity called to express, in the sign of secularity, the realism of the Incarnation of God in our midst, "the intimate dependency of earthly situations on God in Christ."[18]

By Developing the Specificity of All the Vocations Present in the Educational Community

21. The different vocations operate for the growth of the body of Christ and of his mission in the world. The commitment to evangelical testimony according to the typical form of every vocation gives rise to a dynamism of mutual help to fully live membership of the mystery of Christ and of the Church in its many dimensions; a stimulus for each one to discover the evangelical richness of his or her own vocation in a gratitude-filled comparison with others.

By avoiding both confrontation and homologation, the reciprocity of vocations seems to be a particularly fertile prospect for enriching the ecclesial value of educational communities. In them the various vocations carry out a service for achieving a culture of communion. They are correlative, different and mutual paths that converge to bring to fulfillment the charism of charisms: love.

Before the World
Accounting for Hope

22. The awareness that they are living in a time that is full of challenges and new possibilities urges consecrated persons, involved in the educational mission in schools, to make good use of the gift received by accounting for the hope that animates them. Fruit of the faith in the God of history, hope is based on the word and on the life of Jesus, who lived *in the world*, without being *of the world*. He asks the same attitude from those who follow him: to live and work in history, without however allowing oneself to be imprisoned by it. Hope demands insertion in the world, but also separation; it requires prophecy and sometimes involves following or withdrawing in order to educate the children of God to freedom in a context of influences that lead to new forms of slavery.

Discernment and Contemplative Gaze

23. This way of being in history requires a deep capacity for discernment. Born from daily listening to the Word of God, this facilitates the interpreting events and prepares for becoming, as if to say, a *critical conscience*. The deeper and more authentic this commitment, the more likely it will be to grasp the action of the Spirit in the life of people and in the events of history. Such a capacity finds its foundation in contemplation and in prayer, which teach us to see persons and things from God's viewpoint. This is the contrary of a superficial glance and of an activism that is incapable of reflecting on the important and the essential. When there is no contemplation and prayer—and consecrated persons are not exempt from this risk—passion for the announcement of the Gospel is also lacking as is the capacity to fight for the life and salvation of mankind.

In Schools for Educating to Silence and to Meeting God

24. By living their vocations with generosity and eagerness, consecrated persons bring to schools their experience of a relationship with God, based on prayer, the Eucharist, the sacrament of Reconciliation and the spirituality of communion that characterizes the life of religious communities. The evangelical position that results facilitates discernment and the formation of a critical sense, a fundamental and necessary aspect of the educational process. Whatever their specific task, the presence of consecrated persons in schools *infects* the contemplative glance by educating to a silence that leads to listening to God, to paying attention to others, to the situation that surrounds us, to creation. Furthermore, by aiming at the essential, consecrated persons provoke the need for authentic encounters, they renew the capacity to be amazed and to take care of the other, rediscovered like a brother.

For Living the Gospel to the Full

25. Because of their role, consecrated persons are "*a living memorial of Jesus' way of living and acting* as the Incarnate Word in relation to the Father and in relation to the brethren."[19] The first and fundamental contribution to the educational mission in schools by

200

consecrated persons is the evangelical completeness of their lives. This way of shaping their lives, based on their generous response to God's call, becomes an invitation to all the members of the educational community to make their lives a response to God, according to their various states of life.

And Testifying a Chaste, Poor and Obedient Life

26. In this perspective, consecrated persons testify that the *chastity* of their hearts, bodies, lives is the full and strong expression of a total love for God that renders a person free, full of deep joy and ready for their mission. Thus consecrated persons contribute to guiding young men and women towards the full development of their capacity to love and a complete maturation of their personalities. This is a very important testimony in a culture that increasingly tends to trivialize human love and close itself to life. In a society where everything tends to be free, consecrated persons, through their freely chosen *poverty*, take on a simple and essential lifestyle, promoting a correct relationship with things and trusting in Divine Providence. Freedom from things makes them unreservedly ready for an educational service to the young that becomes a sign of the availability of God's love in a world where materialism and having seem to prevail over being. Finally, by living *obedience*, they remind everyone of the lordship of the only God and, against the temptation of dominion, they indicate a choice of faith that counters forms of individualism and self-sufficiency.

And Expressing Their Donation

27. Just as Jesus did for his disciples, so consecrated persons live their donation for the benefit of the receivers of their mission: students, in the first place, but also their parents and other educators. This encourages them to live prayer and their daily response to their following Christ to become an increasingly more suitable instrument for the work that God achieves through them.

The call to give themselves fully to schools, in deep and true freedom, means that consecrated men and women become a living testimony to the Lord who offers himself for everyone. This excess of gratuitousness and love makes their donation assessable over and above any type of usefulness.[20]

Looking at Mary

28. Consecrated persons find in Mary the model to inspire them in their relations with God and in living human history. Mary is the icon of prophetic hope because of her capacity to welcome and meditate at length on the Word in her heart, of interpreting history according to God's plan, of contemplating God present and working in time. In her eyes we see the wisdom that unites in harmony the ecstasy of her meeting with God and the greatest critical realism with regard to the world. The *Magnificat* is the prophecy *par excellence* of the Virgin. It always sounds new in the spirit of a consecrated person, as a constant praise to the Lord who bends down to the least and to the poor to give them life and mercy.

II.
The Educational Mission
of Consecrated Persons Today

29. A profile of consecrated persons clearly shows how their educational commitment in schools is suited to the nature of the consecrated life. In fact "thanks to their experience of the particular gifts of the Spirit, their careful listening to the Word, their constant practice of discernment and their rich heritage of pedagogical traditions amassed since the establishment of their Institutes...consecrated persons give life to educational undertakings"[21] in the educational field. On the one hand, this requires the promotion within the consecrated life of a "renewed cultural commitment which seeks to raise the level of personal preparation,"[22] and on the other of a constant conversion to follow Jesus, *the way, the truth and the life* (cf. Jn 14:6). It is an uncomfortable and tiring road that does however make it possible to take up the challenges of the present time and undertake the educational mission entrusted to the Church. While aware that it cannot be exhaustive, the Congregation for Catholic Education, intends pausing to consider just some elements of this mission. In particular it wishes to reflect on three specific contributions of the presence of consecrated persons to scholastic education: first of all the link of education to evangelization; then formation to "vertical" relationism, that is to the opening to God and lastly formation to "horizontal" relationism, that is to say to welcoming the other and to living together.

Educators Called to Evangelize

Go ... preach the Gospel to the whole creation (Mk 16:15)

The Educational Experience of Consecrated Persons

30. "To fulfill the mandate she has received from her divine founder of proclaiming the mystery of salvation to all men and of restoring all things in Christ, Holy Mother the Church must be concerned with the whole of men's life, even the secular part of it insofar as it has a bearing on his heavenly calling."[23] Both in Catholic and in other types of schools, the educational commitment for consecrated persons is a vocation and choice of life, a path to holiness, a demand for justice and solidarity especially towards the poorest young people, threatened by various forms of deviancy and risk. By devoting themselves to the educational mission in schools, consecrated persons contribute to making the bread of culture reach those in most need of it. They see in culture a fundamental condition for people to

completely fulfill themselves, achieve a level of life that conforms to their dignity and open themselves to encounter with Christ and the Gospel. Such a commitment is founded on a patrimony of pedagogical wisdom that makes it possible to confirm the value of education as a force that is able to help the maturing of a person, to draw him to the faith and to respond to the challenges of such a complex society as that which we have today.

Faced with Modern Challenges
The Globalization Process

31. The process of globalization characterizes the horizon of the new century. This is a complex phenomenon in its dynamics. It has positive effects, such as the possibility for peoples and cultures to meet, but also negative aspects, which risk producing further disparities, injustices and marginalization. The rapidity and complexity of the changes produced by globalization are also reflected in schools, which risk being exploited by the demands of the productive-economic structures, or by ideological prejudices and political calculations that obscure their educational function. This situation incites schools to strongly reassert their specific role of stimulus to reflection and critical aspiration. Because of their vocation consecrated persons undertake to promote the dignity of the human person, cooperating with schools so that they may become places of overall education, evangelization and learning of a vital dialogue between persons of different cultures, religions and social backgrounds.[24]

New Technologies

32. The growing development and diffusion of new technologies provide means and instruments that were inconceivable up to just a few years ago. However, they also give rise to questions concerning the future of human development. The vastness and depth of technological innovations influence the processes of access to knowledge, socialization, relations with nature and they foreshadow radical, not always positive, changes in huge sectors of the life of mankind. Consecrated persons cannot shirk wondering about the impact that these technologies will have on people, on means of communication, on the future of society.

Schools' Task

33. Within the context of these changes, schools have a meaningful role to play in the formation of the personalities of the new generations. The responsible use of the new technologies, especially of internet, demands an appropriate ethical formation.[25] Together with those working in schools, consecrated persons feel the need to understand the processes, languages, opportunities and challenges of the new technologies, but above all to become *communication educators*, so that these technologies may be used with discernment and wisdom.[26]

...For the Future of Man

34. Among the challenges of modern society that schools have to face are threats to life and to families, genetic manipulations, growing pollution, plundering of natural resources, the unsolved drama of the underdevelopment and poverty that crush entire populations of the south of the world. These are vital questions for everyone, which need to be faced with extensive and responsible vision, promoting a concept of life that respects the dignity of man and of creation. This means forming persons who are able to dominate and transform processes and instruments in a sense that is humanizing and filled with solidarity. This concern is shared by the whole international community, that is active in assuring that national educational programs contribute to developing training initiatives in this regard.[27]

An Explicit Anthropological View
Necessity for an Anthropological Foundation

35. The clarification of the anthropological foundation of the formative proposal of schools is an increasingly more unavoidable urgency in our complex societies.

The human person is defined by his *rationality*, that is by his intelligent and free nature, and by his *relational nature*, that is by his relationship with other persons. Living with others involves both the level of the being of the human person—man/woman—and the ethical level of his acting. The foundation of human *ethos* is in being the image and likeness of God, the Trinity of persons in communion. The existence of a person appears therefore as a call to the duty to exist for one another.

36. The commitment of a spirituality of communion for the 21st century is the expression of a concept of the human person, created in the image of God. This view enlightens the mystery of man and woman. The human person experiences his humanity to the extent that he is able to participate in the humanity of the other, the bearer of a unique and unrepeatable plan. This is a plan that can only be carried out within the context of the relation and dialogue with the *you* in a dimension of reciprocity and opening to God. This kind of reciprocity is at the basis of the gift of self and of *closeness* as an opening in solidarity with every other person. This closeness has its truest root in the mystery of Christ, the Word Incarnate, who wished to become close to man.

Within the Dimension of a Plenary Humanism

37. Faced with ideological pluralism and the proliferation of "knowledge," consecrated men and women therefore offer the contribution of a vision of *a plenary humanism*,[28] open to God, who loves everyone and invites them to become increasingly more "conformed to the image of his Son" (cf. Rm 8:29). This divine plan is the heart of Christian humanism: "Christ...fully reveals man to man himself and makes his supreme calling clear."[29] To confirm the greatness of the human creature does not mean to ignore his fragility: the image of God reflected in persons is in fact deformed by sin. The illusion of freeing oneself from all dependency, even from God, always ends up in new forms of slavery, violence and suppression. This is confirmed by the experience of each human being, by the history of blood shed in the name of ideologies and regimes that wished to construct a *new humanity* without God.[30] On the contrary, in order to be authentic, freedom must measure itself according to the truth of the person, the fullness of which is revealed in Christ, and lead to a liberation from all that denies his dignity preventing him from achieving his own good and that of others.

Witnesses of the Truth About the Human Person

38. Consecrated persons undertake to be witnesses in schools to the truth about persons and to the transforming power of the Holy Spirit. With their lives they confirm that faith enlightens the whole field of education by raising and strengthening human values. Catholic schools especially have a priority: that of "bringing forth within what is learnt in school a Christian vision of the world, of life, of culture and of history."[31]

With Cultural Mediation

39. Hence the importance of reasserting, in a pedagogical context that tends to put it in the background, the humanistic and spiritual dimension of knowledge and of the various school subjects. Through study and research a person contributes to perfecting himself and his humanity. Study becomes the path for a personal encounter with the truth, a "place" of encounter with God himself. Taken this way, knowledge can help to motivate existence, to

begin the search for God, it can be a great experience of freedom for truth, placing itself in the service of the maturation and promotion of humanity.[32] Such a commitment demands of consecrated persons an accurate analysis of the quality of their educational proposal, and also constant attention to their cultural and *professional* formation.

And Commitment in the Field of Non-Formal Education

40. Another, equally important, field of evangelization and humanization is nonformal education, that is of those who have been unable to have access to normal schooling. Consecrated persons feel that they should be present and promote innovative projects in such contexts. In these situations poorer young people should be given the chance of a suitable formation that considers their moral, spiritual and religious development and is able to promote socialization and overcome discrimination. This is no novelty, inasmuch as working classes have always been within the sphere of various religious families. It is a case of confirming today with suitable means and plans an attention that has never been lacking.

Educators Called to Accompany Towards the Other
We wish to see Jesus (Jn 12:21)

The Dynamism of Reciprocity In the Educational Community

41. The educational mission is carried out in a spirit of cooperation between various subjects—students, parents, teachers, nonteaching personnel and the school management—who form the educational community. It can create an environment for living in which the values are mediated by authentic interpersonal relations between the various members of which it is composed. Its highest aim is the complete and comprehensive education of the person. In this respect, consecrated persons can offer a decisive contribution, in the light of their experience of communion that characterizes their community lives. In fact, by committing themselves to live and communicate the spirituality of communion in the school community, through a dialogue that is constructive and able to harmonize differences, they build an environment that is rooted in the evangelical values of truth and love. Consecrated persons are thus leaven that is able to create relations of increasingly deep communion, that are in themselves educational. They promote solidarity, mutual enhancement and joint responsibility in the educational plan, and, above all, they give an explicit Christian testimony, through communication of the experience of God and of the evangelical message, even sharing the awareness of being instruments of God and bearers of a charism in the service of all men.

Within the Sphere of the Church Communion

42. The task of communicating the spirituality of communion within the school community derives from being part of the Church communion. This means that consecrated persons involved in the educational mission must be integrated, starting from their charism, in the pastoral activity of the local Church. They, in fact, carry out an ecclesial ministry in the service of a concrete community and in communion with the Diocesan Ordinary. The common educational mission entrusted to them by the Church does, however, require cooperation and greater synergy between the various religious families. Apart from offering a more skilled educational service, this synergy offers the chance for sharing charisms from which the entire Church will gain. For this reason the communion that consecrated persons are called to experiment goes well beyond their own religious family or institute. Indeed, by opening themselves to communion with other forms of consecration, consecrated persons can "rediscover their common Gospel roots and together grasp the beauty of their own identity in the variety of charisms with greater clarity."[33]

The Relational Dimension
Promoting Authentic Relations

43. The educational community expresses the variety and beauty of the various vocations and the fruitfulness at educational and pedagogical level that this contributes to the life of scholastic institutions. The commitment to promote the relational dimension of the person and the care taken in establishing authentic educational relationships with young people are undoubtedly aspects that the presence of consecrated persons can facilitate in schools, considered as microcosms in which oases are created where the bases are laid for living responsibly in the macrocosm of society. It is not, however, strange to observe, even in schools, the progressive deterioration of interpersonal relations, due to the functionalization of roles, haste, fatigue and other factors that create conflicting situations. To organize schools like gymnasiums where one exercises to establish positive relationships between the various members and to search for peaceful solutions to the conflicts is a fundamental objective not just for the life of the educational community, but also for the construction of a society of peace and harmony.

Educating to Reciprocity

44. Usually in schools there are boys and girls, as well as men and women with tasks of teaching or administration. Consideration of the single-dual dimension of the human person implies the need to educate to mutual acknowledgement, in respect and acceptance of differences. The experience of man/woman reciprocity may appear paradigmatic in the positive management of other differences,

205

including ethnic and religious ones. It does, in fact, develop and encourage positive attitudes, such as an awareness that every person can give and receive, a willingness to welcome the other, a capacity for a serene dialogue and a chance to purify and clarify one's own experience while seeking to communicate it and compare it with the other.

Through Enhancing Relations

45. In a relationship of reciprocity, interaction can be asymmetric from the point of view of roles, as it is necessarily in the educational relationship, but not from that of the dignity and uniqueness of every human person. Learning is facilitated when, without undue straining with regard to roles, educational interaction is at a level that fully recognizes the equality of the dignity of every human person. In this way it is possible to form personalities capable of having their own view of life and to agree with their choice. The involvement of families and teaching staff creates a climate of trust and respect that promotes the development of the capacity for dialogue and peaceful coexistence in the search for whatever favors the common good.

The Educational Community
Creating An Educational Environment

46. Due to their experience of community life, consecrated persons are in a most favorable position for cooperating to make the educational plan of the school promote the creation of a true community. In particular they propose an alternative model of coexistence to that of a standardized or individualistic society. In actual fact consecrated persons undertake, together with their lay colleagues, to assure that schools are structured as places of encounter, listening, communication, where students experience values in an essential way. They help, in a directed way, to guide pedagogical choices to promote overcoming

individualistic self-promotion, solidarity instead of competition, assisting the weak instead of marginalization, responsible participation instead of indifference.

Aware of the Family's Task

47. The family comes first in being responsible for the education of its children. Consecrated persons appreciate the presence of parents in the educational community and try to establish a true relation of reciprocity with them. Participating bodies, personal meetings and other initiatives are aimed at rendering increasingly more active the insertion of parents in the life of institutions and for making them aware of the educational task. Acknowledgement of this task is more necessary today than it was in the past, due to the many difficulties that families now experience. When God's original plan for families is overshadowed in peoples' minds, society receives incalculable damage and the right of children to live in an environment of fully human love is infringed. On the contrary, when a family reflects God's plan, it becomes a workshop where love and true solidarity are experienced.[34]

Consecrated persons announce this truth, which does not regard just believers, but is the patrimony of all mankind, inscribed in the heart of man. The chance of contact with the families of the children and young people is a favorable occasion for examining with them meaningful questions regarding life, human love and the nature of families and for agreeing to the proposed vision instead of other often dominating visions.

And of the Importance of Brotherhood as a Prophetic Sign

48. By testifying to Christ and living their typical life of communion, consecrated men and women offer the whole educational community the prophetic sign of brotherhood.

Community life, when woven with deep relationships "is itself *prophetic* in a society which, sometimes without realizing it, has a profound yearning for a brotherhood which knows no borders."[35] This conviction becomes visible in the commitment to make the life of the community a place of growth of persons and of mutual aid in the search and fulfillment of the common mission. In this regard it is important that the sign of brotherhood can be perceived with transparency in every moment of the life of the scholastic community.

In Network With Other Educational Agencies

49. The educational community achieves its scopes in synergy with other educational institutions present in the country.

By coordinating with other educational agencies and in the more extensive communications network a school stimulates the process of personal, professional and social growth of its students, by offering a number of proposals in integrated form. Above all, it forms a most important aid for escaping various conditionings, especially of the *media*, so helping young people to pass from simple and passive consumers to critical interlocutors, capable of positively influencing public opinion and even the quality of information.

Going Towards the Other
A Lifestyle That Questions

50. When involved in the serious search for truth through the contribution of the different subjects, the life of the educational community is constantly urged to mature in reflection, to go beyond the acquisitions achieved and to question at the existential level.

With their presence, consecrated persons offer in this context the specific contribution of their identity and vocation. Even if not always consciously, young people wish to find in them the testimony of a life lived as the answer to a call, as a journey towards God,

as the search for the signs through which He makes himself present. They expect to see persons who invite them to seriously question themselves, and to discover the deepest meaning of human existence and of history.

Guide in a Search for Meaning
Develop the Gift for Searching

51. An encounter with God is always a personal event, an answer that is by its nature, a person's free act in response to the gift of faith. Schools, even Catholic schools, do not demand adherence to the faith, however, they can prepare for it. Through the educational plan it is possible to create the conditions for a person to develop a gift for searching and to be guided in discovering the mystery of his being and of the reality that surrounds him, until he reaches the threshold of the faith.

To those who then decide to cross this threshold the necessary means are offered for continuing to deepen their experience of faith through prayer, the sacraments, the encounter with Christ in the Word, in the Eucharist, in events and persons.[36]

Educating to Freedom

52. An essential dimension of the path of searching is education to freedom, typical of every school loyal to its task. Education to freedom is a humanizing action, because it aims at the full development of personality. In fact, education itself must be seen as the acquisition, growth and possession of freedom. It is a matter of educating each student to free him/herself from the conditionings that prevent him/her from fully living as a person, to form him/herself into a strong and responsible personality, capable of making free and consistent choices.[37]

Preparing the Ground for the Choice of Faith
Educating truly free people is in itself already guiding them to the faith. The search for meaning favors the development of the

religious dimension of a person as ground in which the Christian choice can mature and the gift of faith can develop. It is ever more frequently observed that in schools, especially in western societies, the religious dimension of a person has become a *lost link*, not only in the typically educational sphere of schools, but also in the more extensive formative process that began in the family.

Yet, without it the formative process, as a whole, is strongly affected, making any search for God difficult. The immediate, the superficial, the accessory, prefabricated solutions, deviations towards magic and surrogates of mystery thus tend to grasp the interest of young people and leave no room for opening to the transcendent.

Even teachers, who call themselves non-believers, today feel the urgency to recover the religious dimension of education, necessary for forming personalities able to manage the powerful conditionings under way in society and to ethically guide the new discoveries of science and technology.

With a Style of Interpellant Education

53. By living the evangelical counsels, consecrated persons form an effective invitation to question themselves about God and the mystery of life. Such a question that requires a style of education that is able to stimulate fundamental questions on the origin and meaning of life passes through the search for the *whys* more than for the *hows*. For this reason, it is necessary to check how the contents of the various subjects are proposed in order that students may develop such questions and search for suitable replies. Moreover, children and young people should be encouraged to flee from the obvious and from the trivial, especially within the sphere of choices of life, of the family, of human love. This style is translated into a methodology of study and research that trains for reflection and

discernment. It takes the form of a strategy that cultivates in the person, from his earliest years, an inner life as the place to listen to the voice of God, cultivate the meaning of the sacred, decide to follow values, mature the recognition of one's limits and of sin, feel the growth of the responsibility for every human being.

Teaching Religion
Specialized Religious Education Itineraries

54. The teaching of religion assumes a specific role in this context. Consecrated persons, together with other educators, but with a greater responsibility, are often called to ensure specialized paths of religious education, depending on the different school situations: in some schools the majority of the pupils are Christians, in others different religious followings predominate, or there are agnostic or atheist choices.

Cultural Proposal Offered to Everyone
Their's is the duty to emphasize the value of the teaching of religion within the timetable of the institution and within the cultural program. Even while acknowledging that the teaching of religion in a Catholic school has a different function from that which it has in other schools, its scope is still that of opening to the understanding of the historical experience of Christianity, of guiding to knowledge of Jesus Christ and the study of his Gospel. In this sense, it can be described as a cultural proposal that can be offered to everyone over and above their personal choices of faith. In many contexts, Christianity already forms the spiritual *horizon* of the native culture.

Teaching of Religion in Catholic Schools
In Catholic schools, teaching of religion must help students to arrive at a personal position in religious matters that is consistent and respectful of the positions of

others, so contributing to their growth and to a more complete understanding of reality. It is important that the whole educational community, especially in Catholic schools, recognizes the value and role of the teaching of religion and contributes to its enhancement by the students. By using words that are suited to mediating the religious message, the religion teacher is called to stimulate the pupils to study the great questions concerning the meaning of life, the significance of reality and a responsible commitment to transform it in the light of the evangelical values and modern culture.

Other Formative Opportunities

The community of a Catholic school offers not only teaching of religion but also other opportunities, other moments and ways for educating to a harmony between faith and culture, faith and life.[38]

Life as a Vocation
Life as a Gift and as a Task

55. Together with other Christian educators, consecrated persons know how to grasp and enhance the vocational dimension that is intrinsic to the educational process. Life is, in fact, a gift that is accomplished in the free response to a special call, to be discovered in the concrete circumstances of each day. Care for the vocational dimension guides the person to interpret his existence in the light of God's plan.

The absence or scarce attention to the vocational dimension not only deprives young people of the assistance to which they have a right in the important discernment on the fundamental choices of their lives, but it also impoverishes society and the Church, both of which are in need of the presence of people able to devote themselves on a stable basis to the service of God, their brothers and the common good.

Culture of Vocations
Reawakening a Taste for the Big Questions

56. The promotion of a *new* vocational culture is a fundamental component of the new evangelization. Through it, one must "find courage and zest for the big questions, those related to one's future."[39] These are questions that should be reawakened even through personalized educational processes by means of which one is gradually led to discover life as a gift of God and as a task. These processes can form a real itinerary of vocational maturation, that leads to a specific vocation.

Consecrated persons especially are called to promote the *culture of vocations* in schools. They are a sign for all Christian people not only of a specific vocation, but also of vocational dynamism as a form of life, thus eloquently representing the decision of those who wish to live with attention to God's call.

Sharing Their Educational Charism

57. In the modern situation, the educational mission in schools is increasingly shared with the laity. "Whereas at times in the recent past, collaboration came about as a means of supplementing the decline of consecrated persons necessary to carry out activities, now it is growing out of the need to share responsibility not only in the carrying out of the Institute's works but especially in the hope of sharing specific aspects and moments of the spirituality and mission of the Institute."[40] Consecrated persons must therefore transmit the educational charism that animates them and promote the formation of those who feel that they are called to the same mission. To discharge this responsibility they must be careful not to get involved exclusively in academic-administrative tasks and to not be taken over by activism. What they must do is favor attention to the richness of their charism and try to develop it in response to the new social-cultural situations.

Becoming Privileged Interlocutors in the Search for God

58. In educational communities consecrated persons can promote the achievement of a mentality that is inspired by the evangelical values in a style that is typical of their charism. This in itself is already an educational service in a vocational key. Young people, in fact, and often also the other members of the educational community, more or less consciously expect to find in consecrated persons privileged interlocutors in the search for God. For this type of service, the most specific of the identity of consecrated persons, there are no age limits that would justify considering oneself retired. Even when they have to retire from professional activity, they can always continue to be available for young people and adults, as experts of life according to the Spirit, men and women educators in the sphere of faith.

The presence of consecrated men and women in schools is thus a proposal of evangelical spirituality, a reference point for the members of the educational community in their itinerary of faith and of Christian maturation.

The Vocational Dimension of the Teaching Profession

59. The quality of the teachers is fundamental in creating an educational environment that is purposeful and fertile. It is for this reason that the institutions of consecrated life and religious communities, especially when in charge of Catholic schools, propose formation itineraries for teachers. It is opportune in these to emphasize the vocational dimension of the teaching profession in order to make the teachers aware that they are participating in the educational and sanctifying mission of the Church.[41] Consecrated persons can reveal, to those who so desire, the richness of the spirituality that characterizes them and of the charism of their Institute,

encouraging them to live them in the educational ministry according to the lay identity and in forms that are suitable and accessible to young people.

Educators Called to Teach Coexistence
....all men will know that you are my disciples, if you have love for one another (Jn 13:35)

On a Human Scale
Priority Attention to the Person

60. A school's community dimension is inseparable from priority attention to the person, the focus of the scholastic educational program. *"Culture must correspond to the human person,* and overcome the temptation to a knowledge which yields to pragmatism or which loses itself in the endless meanderings of erudition. Such knowledge is incapable of giving meaning to life...knowledge enlightened by faith, far from abandoning areas of daily life, invests them with all the strength of hope and prophecy. The humanism which we desire advocates a vision of society centered on the human person and his inalienable rights, on the values of justice and peace, on a correct relationship between individuals, society and the State, on the logic of solidarity and subsidiarity. It is a humanism capable of giving a soul to economic progress itself, so that it may be directed to the *promotion of each individual and of the whole person."[42]*

Characterizing Concrete Choices in That Sense

61. Consecrated persons must be careful to safeguard the priority of the person in their educational program. For this they must cooperate in the concrete choices that are made regarding the general school program and its formative proposal. Each pupil must be considered as an individual, bearing in mind his family environment, his personal history, his skills and his interests. In a climate of mutual trust, consecrated men and women discover and cultivate each person's talents and help young people to become responsible for their own formation and to cooperate in that of their companions. This requires the total dedication and unselfishness of those who live the educational service as a mission. This dedication and unselfishness contribute to characterizing the school environment as a vital environment in which intellectual growth is harmonized with spiritual, religious, emotional and social growth.

Personalized Accompanying
Giving Precedence to Dialogue
and Attentive Listening

62. With the typical sensitivity of their formation, consecrated persons offer personalized accompanying through attentive listening and dialogue. They are, in fact, convinced that "education is a thing of the heart"[43] and that, consequently, an authentic formative process can only be initiated through a personal relationship.

Reawakening the Desire for Internal Liberation

63. Every human being feels that he is internally oppressed by tendencies to evil, even when he flaunts limitless freedom. Consecrated men and women strive to reawaken in young people the desire for an internal liberation. This is a condition for undertaking the Christian journey that is directed towards the new life of the evangelical beatitudes. The evangelical view will allow young people to take a critical attitude towards consumerism and hedonism that have wormed their way, like the tare in the wheat, into the culture and way of life of vast areas of humanity.

That is Conversion of the Heart
Fully aware that all human values find their full accomplishment and their unity in Christ, consecrated persons explicitly represent the maternal care of the Church for the complete growth of the young people of our time, communicating the conviction that there can be no true liberation if there is no conversion of the heart.[44]

The Dignity of Woman and Her Vocation
The Presence and Action of Women

64. The sensitivity of consecrated persons, so attentive to the need to develop the single-dual dimension of the human person in obedience to God's original plan (cf. Gen 2:18), can contribute to integrating differences in the educational endeavor to make maximum use of them and overcoming homologations and stereotypes. History testifies to the commitment of consecrated men and women in favor of women. Even today consecrated persons feel they have a duty to appreciate women in the field of education. In various parts of the world Catholic schools and numerous religious families are active in assuring that women are guaranteed access to education without any discrimination and that they can give their specific contribution to the good of the entire community. Everyone is aware of the contribution of women in favor of life and of the humanization of culture,[45] their readiness to care for people and to rebuild the social tissue that has often been broken and torn by tension and hate. Many initiatives of solidarity, even among peoples at war, are born from that *female genius* that promotes sensitivity for all human beings in all circumstances.[46] In this context consecrated women are called in a very special way to be, through their dedication lived in fullness and joy, *a sign of God's tender love towards the human race.*[47] The presence and appreciation of women is therefore essential for preparing a culture that really does place at its center people, the search for the peaceful settlement of conflicts, unity in diversity, assistance and solidarity.

Intercultural Outlook
Contribution of Consecrated Persons to
Intercultural Dialogue

65. In today's complex society, schools are called to provide young generations with the elements necessary for developing an intercultural vision. Consecrated persons involved in education, who often belong to institutes that are spread throughout the world, are an expression of "multi-cultural and International communities, called to 'witness to the sense of communion among peoples, races and cultures'...where mutual knowledge, respect, esteem and enrichment are being experienced."[48] For this reason they can easily consider cultural differences as a richness and propose accessible paths of encounter and dialogue. This attitude is a precious contribution for true intercultural education, something that is made increasingly urgent by the considerable phenomenon of migration. The itinerary to be followed in educational communities involves passing from tolerance of the multicultural situation to welcome and a search for reasons for mutual understanding to intercultural dialogue, which leads to acknowledging the values and limits of every culture.

Intercultural Education
Education Application Necessary

66. From a Christian viewpoint, intercultural education is essentially based on the relational model that is open to reciprocity. In the same way as happens with people, cultures also develop through the typical dynamisms of dialogue and communion. "Dialogue between cultures emerges as an intrinsic demand of human nature itself, as well as of culture. It is dialogue which protects the distinctiveness of cultures as historical and creative expressions of the underlying unity of the human family, and which sustains understanding and communion between them. The

notion of communion, which has its source in Christian revelation and finds its sublime prototype in the Triune God (cf. Jn 17:11, 21), never implies a dull uniformity or enforced homogenization or assimilation; rather it expresses the convergence of a multiform variety, and is therefore a sign of richness and a promise of growth."[49]

Coexistence of Differences

67. The intercultural prospective involves a change of paradigm at the pedagogical level. From the integration of differences one passes to a search for their coexistence. This is a model that is neither simple nor easily implemented. In the past, diversity between cultures was often a source of misunderstandings and conflicts; even today, in various parts of the world, we see the arrogant establishment of some cultures over others. No less dangerous is the tendency to homologation of cultures to models of the western world inspired by forms of radical individualism and a practically atheist concept of life.

Commitment to Seek the Ethical Foundations of the Various Cultures

68. Schools must question themselves about the fundamental ethical trends that characterize the cultural experiences of a particular community. "Cultures, like the people who give rise to them, are marked by the 'mystery of evil' at work in human history (cf. 1 Th 2:7), and they too are in need of purification and salvation. The authenticity of each human culture, the soundness of its underlying *ethos*, and hence the validity of its moral bearings, can be measured to an extent by its commitment to the human cause and by its capacity to promote human dignity at every level and in every circumstance."[50]

In his speech to the members of the 50th General Assembly of the United Nations Organization, the Pope underlined the fundamental communion between peoples, observing that the various cultures are in actual fact just different ways of dealing with the question of the meaning of personal existence. In fact, every culture is an attempt to reflect on the mystery of the world and of man, a way of expressing the transcendent dimension of human life. Seen this way, difference, rather than being a threat, can become, through respectful dialogue, a source of deep understanding of the mystery of human existence.[51]

Sharing with the Poor in Solidarity
Preferential Option for the Poor

69. The presence of consecrated persons in an educational community concurs in perfecting the sensitivity of everyone to the poverty that still torments young people, families and entire peoples. This sensitivity can become a source of profound changes in an evangelical sense, inducing a transformation of the logics of excellence and superiority into those of service, of *caring for others* and forming a heart that is open to solidarity.

The preferential option for the poor leads to avoiding all forms of exclusion. Within the school there is often an educational plan that serves the more or less well-to-do social groups, while attention for the most needy definitively takes second place. In many cases social, economic or political circumstances leave no better alternative. This, however, must not mean the exclusion of a clear idea of the evangelical criteria or of trying to apply it at a personal and community level and within the scholastic institutions themselves.

Planning Starting From the Least
Poor Young People at the Center of the Education Program

70. When the preferential option for the poorest is at the center of the educational program, the best resources and most qualified persons are initially placed at the service of the least, without in this way excluding those who have less difficulties and shortages. This is the meaning of evangelical inclusion, so distant from the logic of the world. The Church does, in fact, mean to offer its educational service *in the first place* to "those who are poor in the goods of this world or who are deprived of the assistance and affection of a family or who are strangers to the gift of Faith."[52] Unjust situations often make it difficult to implement this choice. Sometimes, however, it is Catholic educational institutions themselves that have strayed from such a preferential option, which characterized the beginnings of the majority of institutes of consecrated life devoted to teaching.

This choice, typical of the consecrated life, should therefore be cultivated from the time of initial formation, so that it is not considered as reserved only for the most generous and courageous.

Identify Situations of Poverty

71. Following in the footsteps of the Good Shepherd, consecrated persons should identify among their pupils the various poverty situations that prevent the overall maturation of the person and marginalize him or her from social life, by investigating their causes. Among these, destitution occupies an undisputable place. It often brings with it the lack of a family and of health, social maladjustment, loss of human dignity, impossibility of access to culture and consequently a deep spiritual poverty. *Becoming the voice of the poor of the world* is a challenge assumed by the Church, and all Christians should do the same.[53] Due to their choices and their publicly professed commitment of a poor personal and community lifestyle, consecrated persons are more strongly sensitive to their duty to promote justice and solidarity in the environment in which they are active.

Giving Voice to the Poor
Considering the Least

72. Access to education especially for the poor[54] is a commitment assumed at different levels by Catholic educational institutions. This requires arranging educational activity to suit the least, no matter what the social status of the pupils present in the scholastic institution. This involves, among other things, proposing the contents of the social doctrine of the Church through educational projects and requires checking the profile that the school foresees for its students. If a school listens to the poorest people and arranges itself to suit them, it will be able to interpret the subjects at the service of life, and avail of their contents in relation to the global growth of people.

Commitment in Formal and Non-Formal Education

73. By listening to the poor, consecrated persons know *where* to commit themselves even within the sphere of non-formal education and how to bring the most underprivileged to have access to instruction. Acquaintance with countries where schools are reserved for the few or encounter serious difficulties in accomplishing their task could give rise in the educational communities of the more developed countries to initiatives of solidarity, among which twinning between classes or schools. The formative advantages would be great for everyone, especially for the pupils of the more developed countries. They would learn what is essential in life and they would be assisted in not following the cultural fashions induced by consumerism.

And in the Defense of Children's Rights

74. The defense of children's rights is another particularly important challenge. The exploitation of children, in different, often aberrant, forms, is among the most disturbing aspects of our time. Consecrated persons involved in the educational mission have the inescapable duty to devote themselves to the protection and promotion of children's rights. The concrete contributions that they can make both as individuals and as an educational institution will probably be insufficient with respect to the needs, but not useless, inasmuch as aimed at making known the roots from which the abuses derive. Consecrated persons willingly unite their efforts to those of other civil and ecclesial organizations and persons of good will, to uphold the respect of human rights in for the good of everyone, starting from the most weak and helpless.

Willing Even to Give Their Lives

75. The preferential option for the poor requires living a personal and community attitude of readiness to *give one's life* where necessary. It might therefore be necessary to leave perhaps even works of prestige which are no longer able to implement suitable formative processes and consequently leave no room for the characteristics of the consecrated life. In fact, "if a school is excellent as an academic institution, but does not bear witness to authentic values, then both good pedagogy and a concern for pastoral care make it obvious that renewal is called for."[55]

Consecrated persons are therefore called to check to see if, in their educational activity, they are mainly pursuing academic prestige rather than the human and Christian maturation of the young people; if they are favoring competition rather than solidarity; if they are involved in educating, together with the other members of the school community, persons who are free, responsible and *just* according to evangelical justice.

To the Ends of the Earth

76. Precisely because of their religious consecration, consecrated persons are preeminently free to leave everything to go to preach the gospel even to the ends of the earth.[56] For them, even in the educational field, the announcement *"ad gentes"* of the Good News remains a priority. They are therefore aware of the fundamental role of Catholic schools in mission countries. In many cases, in fact, schools are the only possibility for the Church's presence, in others they are a privileged place of evangelizing and humanizing action, responsible both for the human and cultural development of the poorest people. It is important in this regard to consider the necessity of the participation of the educational charism between the religious families of the countries of ancient evangelization and those born in mission territories, which inspire them. In fact, "the older Institutes, many of which have been tested by the severest of hardships, which they have accepted courageously down the centuries can be enriched through dialogue and an exchange of gifts with the foundations appearing in our own days."[57] Such sharing is also transferred into the field of formation of consecrated persons, in sustaining new religious families and in cooperation between various institutes.

Culture of Peace
Peace Through Justice

77. The path to peace passes through justice. "Only in this way can we ensure a peaceful future for our world and remove the root causes of conflicts and wars: peace is the fruit of justice...a justice which is not content to apportion to each his own, but one which aims at creating conditions of *equal opportunity* among citizens, and therefore favoring those who, for reasons of social status or education or health, risk being left behind or being relegated to the lowest places in society, without possibility of deliverance."[58]

Educating for Peace
Starting From the Heart
Peacemakers in Their Own Environment

78. Awareness that education is the main road to peace is a fact shared by the international community. The various projects launched by international organizations for sensitizing public opinion and governments are a clear sign of this.[59] Consecrated persons, witnesses of Christ, the Prince of Peace, grasp the urgency of placing education for peace among the primary objectives of their formative action offering their specific contribution to encourage in the hearts of the pupils the desire to become peacemakers. Wars in fact are born in the hearts of men and the defenses of peace must be built in the hearts of men. By enhancing the educational process, consecrated persons undertake to excite attitudes of peace in the souls of the men of the third millennium. This "is not only the absence of conflict but requires a positive, dynamic, participatory process where dialogue is encouraged and conflicts are solved in a spirit of mutual understanding and cooperation."[60]

Consecrated persons cooperate in this undertaking with all men and women of goodwill sharing with them the effort and urgency to always seek new ways that are suited for an effective education that "has widened possibilities for strengthening a culture of peace."[61]

Through the Education to Values

79. An effective education for peace involves preparing various levels of programs and strategies. Among other things, it is a matter of proposing to the pupils an education to suitable values and attitudes for peacefully settling disputes in the respect of human dignity; of organizing activities, even extracurricular ones such as sports and theatre that favor assimilating the values of loyalty and respect of rules; of assuring equality of access to education for women; of encouraging, when necessary, a review of curricula, including textbooks.[62]

Education is also called to transmit to students an awareness of their cultural roots and respect for other cultures. When this is achieved with solid ethical reference points, education leads to a realization of the inherent limits in one's own culture and in that of others. At the same time, however, it emphasizes a common inheritance of values to the entire human race. In this way *education has a particular role to play in building a more united and peaceful world. It can help to affirm that integral humanism, open to life's ethical and religious dimension, which appreciates the importance of understanding and showing esteem for other cultures and the spiritual values present in them.*[63]

Educating for Coexistence
Educating for Active and Responsible Citizens

80. As a result of the negative effects of uncontrolled economic and cultural globalization, responsible participation in the life of the community at local, national and world levels acquires increasing importance at the beginning of the third millennium. This participation presupposes the realization of the causes of the phenomena that threaten the coexistence of people and of human life itself. As with every realization, this too finds in education, and in particular in schools, fertile ground for its development. Thus a new and difficult task takes shape: educate to have active and responsible citizens. The words of the Pope are enlightening in this regard: "promoting the right to peace ensures respect for all other rights, since it encourages the building of a society in which structures of power give way to structures of cooperation, with a view to the common good."[64] In this respect,

consecrated persons can offer the sign of a responsible brotherhood, living in communities in which "each member has a sense of co-responsibility for the faithfulness of the others; each one contributes to a serene climate of sharing life, of understanding, and of mutual help."[65]

Conclusion

81. The reflections proposed clearly indicate that the presence of consecrated persons in the world of education is a prophetic choice.[66]

The Synod on the consecrated life exhorts to assume with renewed dedication the educational mission in all levels of schools, universities and institutions of higher learning.[67] The invitation to continue the itinerary begun by those who have already offered a significant contribution to the educational mission of the Church lies within the bounds of the fidelity to their original charism: "because of their special consecration, their particular experience of the gifts of the Spirit, their constant listening to the Word of God, their practice of discernment, their rich heritage of pedagogical traditions built up since the establishment of their Institute, and their profound grasp of spiritual truth (cf. Ef 1:17), consecrated persons are able to be especially effective in educational activities and to offer a specific contribution to the work of other educators."[68]

82. In the dimension of ecclesial communion, there is a growing awareness in every consecrated person of the great cultural and pedagogical wealth that derives from sharing a common educational mission, even in the specificity of the various ministries and charisms. It is a matter of discovering and renewing an awareness of one's own identity, finding again the inspiring nucleus of a skilled educational professionalism to be rediscovered as a way of being that represents an authentic vocation.

Starting Afresh from Christ

The root of this renewed awareness is Christ. Consecrated persons working in schools must start from him to find again the motivating source of their mission. Starting afresh from Christ means contemplating his face, pausing at length with him in prayer to then be able to show him to others. It is what the Church is called to accomplish at the beginning of the new millennium, conscious that only faith can enter the mystery of that face.[69] Starting again from Christ is, therefore, also for consecrated men and women, starting afresh from faith nourished by the sacraments and supported by a hope that does not fail: "I am with you always" (Mt 28:20).

In a Renewed Commitment

Encouraged by this hope, consecrated persons are called to revive their educational passion living it in school communities as a testimony of encounter between different vocations and between generations.

The task of teaching to live, discovering the deepest meaning of life and of transcendence, to mutually interact with others, to love creation, to think freely and critically, to find fulfillment in work, to plan the future, in one word to *be*, demands a new love of consecrated persons for educational and cultural commitment in schools.

And Living in a State of Permanent Formation

83. By allowing themselves to be transformed by the Spirit and living in a state of permanent formation, consecrated men and women become able to extend their horizons and understand the profound causes of events.[70] Permanent formation also becomes the key to understanding the educational mission in schools and for carrying it out in a

way that is close to a reality that is so changeable and at the same time in need of responsible, timely and prophetic intervention. The cultural study that consecrated persons are called to cultivate for improving their professionalism in the subjects for which they are responsible, or in the administrative or management service, is a duty of justice, which cannot be shirked.

Participation in the life of the universal and particular Church involves demonstrating the bonds of communion and appreciating the directions of the Magisterium, especially with regard to such matters as life, the family, the issue of women, social justice, peace, ecumenism, inter-religious dialogue. In the climate of modern pluralism, the Magisterium of the Church is the voice of authority that interprets phenomena in the light of the Gospel.

Thanksgiving for the Important and Noble Task

84. The Congregation for Catholic Education wishes to conclude these reflections with sincere gratitude to all the consecrated persons who work in the field of school education. While aware of the complexity and often of the difficulties of their task, it wishes to underline the value of the *noble* educational service aimed at giving reasons for life and hope to the new generations, through critically processed knowledge and culture, on the basis of a concept of the person and of life inspired by the evangelical values.

Every school and every place of non formal education can become a center of a greater network which, from the smallest village to the most complex metropolis, wraps the world in hope. It is in education, in fact, that the promise of a more human future and a more harmonious society lies.

No difficulty should remove consecrated men and women from schools and from education in general, when the conviction of being called to bring the Good News of the Kingdom of God to the poor and small is so deep and vital. Modern difficulties and confusion, together with the new prospects that are appearing at the dawn of the third millennium, are a strong reminder to pass one's life in educating the new generations to become bearers of a culture of communion that may reach every people and every person. The main motive and, at the same time, the goal of the commitment of every consecrated person, is to light and trim the lamp of faith of the new generations, the "morning watchmen (cf. Is 21:11-12) at the dawn of the new millennium."[71]

The Holy Father, during the Audience granted to the undersigned Prefect, approved this document and authorized its publication.

Rome, 28th October 2002, thirty-seventh anniversary of the promulgation of the statement Gravissimum educationis of the Second Vatican Council.

† **Zenon Cardinal Grocholewski**
Prefect

† **Joseph Pittau, S.J.**
Secretary

Notes

[1] Cf. John Paul II, Apostolic exhortation *Vita consecrata*, 25th March 1996, nn. 72-73, *AAS* 88 (1996), 447-449.

[2] Cf. John Paul II, Encyclical letter *Redemptoris missio*, 7th December 1990, n. 38, *AAS* 83 (1991), 286.

[3] John Paul II, Apostolic exhortation *Vita consecrata*, n. 73, *AAS* 88 (1996), 448.

[4] Cf. Sacred Congregation for Catholic Education, *The Catholic School*, 19th March 1977; cf. Congregation for Catholic Education, *The Catholic School on the Threshold of the Third Millennium*, 28th December 1997.

[5] Cf. Sacred Congregation for Catholic Education, *Lay Catholics in Schools: Witnesses to Faith*, 15th October 1982.

[6] Cf. Pontifical Council for Culture, *Toward a Pastoral Approach to Culture*, 23rd May 1999, *L'Osservatore Romano* (English), N. 23, 9 June 1999.

[7] John Paul II, *Letter Instituting the Pontifical Council for Culture*, 20th May 1982, *AAS* 74 (1982), 685.

[8] Cf. John Paul II, Apostolic exhortation *Vita consecrata*, n. 96, *AAS* 88 (1996), 471.

[9] Congregation for Catholic Education, *Circular letter to the Reverend General Superiors and Presidents of Societies of Apostolic Life responsible for Catholic Schools*, 15th October 1996, in *Enchiridion Vaticanum*, vol. 15, 837.

[10] John Paul II, Apostolic exhortation *Vita consecrata*, n. 1, *AAS* 88 (1996), 377.

[11] Ibid., n. 65, 441.

[12] Ibid., n. 18, 391.

[13] Cf. Second Vatican Ecumenical Council, Dogmatic Constitution on the Church *Lumen gentium*, nn. 43-44.

[14] John Paul II, Apostolic exhortation *Vita consecrata*, n. 87, *AAS* 88 (1996), 463.

[15] Cf. John Paul II, Apostolic letter *Novo millennio ineunte*, 6th January 2001, n.30, *AAS* 93 (2001), 287.

[16] Ibid., n. 43, 296.

[17] John Paul II, Apostolic exhortation *Vita consecrata*, n. 96, *AAS* 88 (1996), 472.

[18] Sacred Congregation for Catholic Education, *Lay Catholics in Schools: Witnesses to Faith*, n. 43.

[19] John Paul II, Apostolic exhortation *Vita consecrata*, n. 22, *AAS* 88 (1996), 396.

[20] Cf. Ibid., n. 105, 481.

[21] Congregation for Institutes of Consecrated Life and Societies of Apostolic Life, *Starting Afresh from Christ*, 19th May 2002, n. 39.

[22] Ibid., n. 39.

[23] Second Vatican Ecumenical Council, Declaration on Christian Education *Gravissimum educationis*, Introd.

[24] Cf. Congregation for Catholic Education, *The Catholic School on the Threshold of the Third Millennium*, n. 11.

[25] Cf. Pontifical Council for Social Communications, *Ethics in Internet*, 22nd February 2002, n. 15.

[26] Cf. Pontifical Council for Social Communications *The Church and Internet*, 22nd February 2002, n. 7.

[27] Cf. UNESCO, Conférence générale, *Résolution adoptée sur le rapport de la Commission V. Séance plénière*, 12 novembre 1997.

[28] Cf. Paul VI, Encyclical letter *Populorum progressio*, 26th March 1967, n. 42, *AAS* 59 (1967), 278.

[29] Second Vatican Ecumenical Council, Pastoral Constitution on the Church in the Modern World *Gaudium et spes*, n. 22.

[30] Cf.John Paul II, Encyclical letter *Redemptoris missio*, n. 8, *AAS* 83 (1991), 256.

[31] Congregation for Catholic Education, *The Catholic School on the Threshold of the Third Millennium*, n. 14.

[32] Cf. John Paul II, *Speech to the Plenary Session of the Pontifical Academy of Sciences*, 13th November 2000, *AAS* 93 (2001), 202-206.

[33] Congregation for Institutes of Consecrated Life and Societies of Apostolic Life, *Starting Afresh from Christ*, n. 30.

[34] Cf. John Paul II, *Homily for the Jubilee of Families*, Rome, 15th October 2000, nn. 4-5, *AAS* 93 (2001), 90.

[35] John Paul II, Apostolic exhortation *Vita consecrata*, n. 85, *AAS* 88 (1996), 462.

[36] Cf. Congregation for Catholic Education, *The Religious Dimension of Education in a Catholic School*, 7th April 1988, nn. 98-112.

[37] Cf. Sacred Congregation for Catholic Education, *The Catholic School*, n. 31.

[38] Cf. Ibid., nn. 37-48.

[39] Pontifical Work for Ecclesiastical Vocations, *New Vocations for a New Europe*. Final document of the Congress of Vocations to the Priesthood and to Consecrated life, Rome, 5th -10th May 1997, n. 13 b.

[40] Congregation for Institutes of Consecrated Life and Societies of Apostolic Life, *Starting Afresh from Christ*, n. 31.

[41] Cf. Sacred Congregation for Catholic Education, *Lay Catholics in Schools: Witnesses to Faith*, n. 24.

[42] John Paul II, *Jubilee of University Professors*, Rome, 9th September 2000, nn. 3, 6, *AAS* 92 (2000), 863-865.

[43] St. John BOSCO, *Circolare del 24 gennaio 1883*, in CE-RIA E. (*a cura di*), *Epistolario di S. Giovanni Bosco*, SEI, Torino 1959, vol.IV, 209.

[44] Cf.Paul VI, Apostolic exhortation *Evangelii nuntiandi*, 8th December 1975, n. 36, *AAS* 68 (1976), 29

[45] Cf. John Paul II, Apostolic exhortation *Christifideles laici*, 30th December 1988, n. 51, *AAS* 81 (1989), 492-496..

[46] Cf. John Paul II, Apostolic letter *Mulieris dignitatem*, 15th August 1988, n. 30, *AAS* 80 (1988), 1724-1727.

[47] Cf. John Paul II, Apostolic exhortation *Vita conse-crata*, n. 57, *AAS* 88 (1996), 429.

[48] Congregation for Institutes of Consecrated Life and Societies of Apostolic Life, *Starting Afresh from Christ*, n. 29.

[49] John Paul II, *Dialogue between Cultures for a Civilisation of Love and Peace*, Message for the Celebration of the World Day of Peace, 1st January 2001, n. 10, *AAS* 93 (2001), 239.

[50] Ibid., n. 8, 238.

[51] Cf. John Paul II, *Insegnamenti*, XVIII/ 2, 1995, 730-744.

[52] Second Vatican Ecumenical Council, Declaration on Catholic Education *Gravissimum educationis*, n. 9.

[53] Cf. John Paul II, Apostolic letter *Tertio millennio adveniente*, 10th November 1994, n. 51, *AAS* 87 (1995), 36.

[54] See, for example, Office International Pour L'enseignement Catholique (OIEC), *Déclaration de la XIVème Assemblée Générale*, Rome, 5th March 1994.

[55] Congregation for Catholic Education, *The Religious Dimension of Education in a Catholic School*, n. 19.

[56] Cf. Paul VI, Apostolic exhortation *Evangelii nuntiandi*, n. 69, *AAS* 68 (1976), 58.

[57] John Paul II, Apostolic exhortation *Vita consecrata*, n. 62, *AAS* 88 (1996), 437.

[58] John Paul II, *Jubilee of Government Leaders, Members of Parliament and Politicians*, Rome, 4th November 2000, n. 2, *AAS* 93 (2001), 167.

[59] For example, the United Nations has promoted the *International Decade for a Culture of Peace and Non-violence*, (2000-2010).

[60] The United Nations, *Résolution 53/243: Déclaration et Programme d'action sur une culture de la paix*, 6 octobre 1999.

[61] Ibid., A, art. 1a; art. 4.

[62] Cf. Ibid., B, art. 9.

[63] John Paul II, *Dialogue between Cultures for a Civilisation of Love and Peace*, Message for the Celebration of the World Day of Peace, 1st January 2001, n. 20, *AAS* 93 (2001), 245.

[64] John Paul II, *Respect for Human Rights: the Secret of True Peace*, Message for the Celebration of the World Day of Peace, 1st January 1999, n. 11, *AAS* 91 (1999), 385.

[65] Congregation for Institutes of Consecrated Life and Societies of Apostolic Life, *Fraternal Life in Community*, 2nd February 1994, n. 57, in *Enchiridion Vaticanum*, vol. 14, 265.

66 Cf. Congregation for Catholic Education, *The Catholic School on the Threshold of the Third Millennium*, n. 21.

67 Cf. John Paul II, Apostolic exhortation *Vita consecrata*, n. 97, *AAS* 88 (1996), 473.

68 Ibid., n. 96, 472.

69 Cf. John Paul II, Apostolic letter *Novo millennio ineunte*, n. 19, *AAS* 93 (2001), 278-279.

70 Cf. John Paul II, Apostolic exhortation *Vita consecrata*, n. 98, *AAS* 88 (1996), 474.

71 John Paul II, Apostolic letter *Novo millennio ineunte*, n. 9, *AAS* 93 (2001), 272.

Renewing Our Commitment to Catholic Elementary and Secondary Schools in the Third Millennium

UNITED STATES CONFERENCE OF CATHOLIC BISHOPS
June 2005

Introduction

Young people are a valued treasure and the future leaders of our Church. It is the responsibility of the entire Catholic community—bishops, priests, deacons, religious, and laity—to continue to strive towards the goal of making our Catholic elementary and secondary schools available, accessible, and affordable to all Catholic parents and their children, including those who are poor and middle class. All Catholics must join together in efforts to ensure that Catholic schools have administrators and teachers who are prepared to provide an exceptional educational experience for young people—one that is both truly Catholic and of the highest academic quality.

In 1990, the Catholic bishops of the United States issued the statement *In Support of Catholic Elementary and Secondary Schools*. In it we affirmed our strong conviction that Catholic elementary and secondary schools are of great value to our Church and our nation; and that, in our role as chief teachers, we are each responsible for the total educational ministry of the local Church. We affirmed that "the entire ecclesial community ... is called to value ever more deeply the importance of this task and mission, and to continue to give it full and enthusiastic support." These Catholic schools afford the fullest and best opportunity to realize the fourfold purpose of Christian education, namely to provide an atmosphere in which the Gospel message is proclaimed, community in Christ is experienced, service to our sisters and brothers is the norm, and thanksgiving and worship of our God is cultivated (2).

In that statement we pointed to the great value and the many successes of Catholic schools and the numerous challenges that they face. We unequivocally committed ourselves and the whole Catholic community to the following set of goals:

† Catholic schools will continue to provide a Gospel-based education of the highest quality.

† Catholic schools will be available, accessible, and affordable.

† The bishops will launch initiatives in both the private and public sectors to secure financial assistance for parents, the primary educators of their children, so that they can better exercise their right to choose the best schools for their children.

† Catholic schools will be staffed by highly qualified administrators and teachers who would receive just wages and benefits, as we expressed in our pastoral letter *Economic Justice for All*.

Much has changed in our Church and our nation in the ensuing years. Catholic schools continue to be valued and successful; but they still encounter numerous challenges. The bishops have addressed many of the goals that we set in 1990, but much is still left to be done. Therefore, we believe that

221

the time has come to revisit and reaffirm our commitment to Catholic elementary and secondary schools as invaluable instruments in proclaiming the Good News from one generation to the next. This catechesis is a privileged way of "initiating the hearers into the fullness of Christian life" and is "intimately bound up with the whole of the Church's life" (*Catechism of the Catholic Church*, nos. 5, 7). We believe that now is the appropriate time to renew our challenge to the entire Catholic community to join in this critical endeavor. We are convinced that Catholic schools continue to be "the most effective means available to the Church for the education of children and young people" who are the future of the Church (*To Teach as Jesus Did*, no. 118).

Why We Value Our Catholic Elementary and Secondary Schools

Young people of the third millennium must be a source of energy and leadership in our Church and our nation. Therefore, we must provide young people with an academically rigorous and doctrinally sound program of education and faith formation designed to strengthen their union with Christ and his Church. Catholic schools collaborate with parents and guardians in raising and forming their children as families struggle with the changing and challenging cultural and moral contexts in which they find themselves. Catholic schools provide young people with sound Church teaching through a broad-based curriculum, where faith and culture are intertwined in all areas of a school's life. By equipping our young people with a sound education, rooted in the Gospel message, the Person of Jesus Christ, and rich in the cherished traditions and liturgical practices of our faith, we ensure that they have the foundation to live morally and uprightly in our complex modern world. This unique Catholic identity makes our Catholic elementary and secondary schools "schools for the human person" and allows them to fill a critical role in the future life of our Church, our country, and our world (*Catholic Schools on the Threshold*, no. 9).

It is made abundantly clear in an unbroken list of statements, from the documents of the Second Vatican Council to Pope John Paul II's 1999 exhortation *The Church in America* (*Ecclesia in America*), that Catholic schools play a vital role in the evangelizing mission of the Church. They are

> the privileged environment in which Christian education is carried out . . . Catholic schools are at once places of evangelization, of complete formation, of inculturation, of apprenticeship in a lively dialogue between young people of different religions and social backgrounds. (*Catholic Schools on the Threshold of the Third Millennium*, no. 11)

Catholic schools are often the Church's most effective contribution to those families who are poor and disadvantaged, especially in poor inner city neighborhoods and rural areas. Catholic schools cultivate healthy interaction among the increasingly diverse populations of our society. In cities and rural areas, Catholic schools are often the only opportunity for economically disadvantaged young people to receive an education of quality that speaks to the development of the whole person. As we continue to address the many and varied needs of our nation's new immigrant population, the Church and its schools are often among the few institutions providing immigrants and newcomers with a sense of welcome, dignity, community, and connection with their spiritual roots.

As important as a sound Catholic school education is for the new immigrant and the poor, it continues to be of prime importance to those children and grandchildren of the generations who earlier came to our shores.

Our Catholic schools have produced count-less numbers of well-educated and moral citi-zens who are leaders in our civic and ecclesial communities. We must work with all parents so they have the choice of an education that no other school can supply—excellent aca-demics imparted in the context of Catholic teaching and practice.

Catholic Schools Today

Overview Since 1990

The National Catholic Educational Asso-ciation's annual statistical report shows that there are currently 7,799 Catholic elementary and secondary schools in the United States, which enroll over 2.4 million students. These schools currently account for almost 30 per-cent of all private and religious schools in the United States and enroll over 48 percent of the students in these schools. Since 1990, the Church in the United States has opened more than 400 new schools. Regrettably, there has been a net decline of more than 850 Catholic schools in the country during the same pe-riod of time. Almost all of this loss has been in urban, inner-city, and rural areas of our na-tion. In the last decade of the twentieth cen-tury, Catholic schools experienced a period of growth in enrollments. Since the year 2000, however, that trend slowed, then reversed, and now shows a net loss of over 170,000 stu-dents.

Currently, there are more than 2,500 Catholic schools in the country with waiting lists. Almost all of these schools are located in suburban areas. Twenty-six percent of cur-rent students in Catholic schools are members of minority groups—a figure that is steadily growing. The enrollment of students who are not Catholic has grown to 13.6 percent. Staff-ing trends in Catholic elementary and sec-ondary schools show a steady increase in the number of lay people who are administrators and teachers (currently 95 percent). Since 1990, the average tuition in both elementary and secondary Catholic schools has more than doubled; in that same time, the portion of the total cost of educating a student which parents pay in tuition has risen by almost 13 percent.

The Good News

We, the Catholic bishops of the United States, wish to offer our deep gratitude to those individuals who staff our Catholic ele-mentary and secondary schools, the dedicated lay and religious administrators and teachers. We applaud their professionalism, personal sacrifices, daily witness to faith, and efforts to integrate learning and faith in the lives of their students in order to "accomplish the very purpose of evangelization: the incarnation of the Christian message in the lives of men and women" (*Lay Catholics in Schools: Witnesses to Faith*, no. 31). We take this opportunity to encourage all who are devoted to working in Catholic schools to "persevere in their most important mission" (*Ecclesia in America*, no. 71).

Research conducted by the United States Department of Education, the National Catholic Educational Association, and other independent agencies shows that Catholic schools make a major impact in closing the achievement gap for poor and minority stu-dents in inner-city environments. Catholic schools have a lower dropout rate (3.4 per-cent) than both public (14.4 percent) and other private schools (11.9 percent). Ninety-nine percent of Catholic high school students graduate, and 97 percent go on to some form of post-secondary education. Catholic school students continue to score well on standard-ized tests (such as the National Assessment of Educational Progress) in subjects such as reading, mathematics, social studies, and sci-ence, often surpassing standards established by federal and/or state agencies. A Harvard University study issued in 2000 reported that Catholic school students performed better than other students on the three basic objectives of civic education—the capacity for civic engagement (e.g., voluntary community service), political knowledge (e.g.. learning and using civic skills), and political tolerance (e.g., respect for opinions different from their own).[1]

We are encouraged by the laity's increased involvement with school boards, commissions, and councils. We commend the efforts that are being made to develop programs for the spiritual growth of staff, students, and parents; to create safe environment programs for children and young people; to open development and endowment offices in dioceses and schools; to market schools; and to establish parent organizations that advocate for the rights of Catholic school students and teachers to be treated equitably in government-sponsored programs and services.

We are grateful to the individuals who have joined us on the federal and state levels and from the private sector to assist parents in financing their children's education. The passage of programs that provide for government-funded parental choice scholarships, tax credits, deductions, and individual and corporate donations for privately funded scholarships makes it possible for children of the poor and lower middle class to attend Catholic schools.

A 2002 study of Catholic school students with disabilities conducted by an independent agency, the Center for Educational Partnerships, found that 7 percent of children enrolled in Catholic schools had disabilities identified in the *Individuals with Disabilities Education Act*. We applaud the increasing number of our school administrators and teachers who have taken steps to welcome these children and others with special needs into our Catholic schools.

We recognize the positive contributions of those Catholic colleges and universities that are providing specialized programs to train administrators and teachers in the unique mission of the Catholic school, particularly those that work in our inner-city and rural Catholic schools.

The Challenges of the Future

While we look with pride to the many successes and achievements of our Catholic elementary and secondary schools, the entire Catholic community must now focus on the future and the many challenges we face. We, the Catholic bishops of the United States, with the cooperation of diocesan, school, and community leadership, should pursue effective responses to the challenges we face. We must then move forward with faith, courage, and enthusiasm because Catholic schools are so important to our future.

The Face of Our Church

We must face the reality of our Church as it exists today and as it will be in the future. We must be prepared to address the changing diversity of the Church's membership. The Catholic Church in the United States is larger than ever. Many of our people are more financially successful, and they have moved into areas of our nation where, in the past, Catholics were a rarity. Catholic parishes and schools face the challenge of addressing the spiritual, educational, social, and cultural needs of a new wave of immigrants. In responding to the needs of these individuals, we must continue our evangelizing efforts by maintaining our schools' Catholic identity and mission. It is critical that we work with our people to erase any lines of prejudice and bias that may exist and create welcoming communities for these immigrants. People involved in this effort often suffer from meager human and financial resources. We need to seek support from the larger Church and civic communities to assist them in this work.

Our young people are the Church of today and tomorrow. It is imperative that we provide them with schools ready to address their spiritual, moral, and academic needs. Our challenge today is to provide schools close to where our Catholic people live. In areas where there currently are no Catholic schools, we should open schools that have a mission to evangelize. We also need to consider providing new or expanded facilities where we currently have schools with waiting lists. Wherever possible, Catholic schools should remain available and accessible in all areas of a diocese for children who are from poor and middle-class families who face major economic challenges. In addition, Catholic schools should be available to students who are not Catholic and who wish to attend them. This has been a proud part of the history of Catholic schools in the nineteenth and twentieth centuries. We must continue this outreach in the new millennium. We must also serve the increasing Hispanic/Latino population, which makes up 39 percent of our current Catholic community. Hispanics/Latinos make up 41 percent of Catholics under the age of thirty, and 44 percent of Catholics under the age of ten. It is currently estimated that by the second decade of this century, the Hispanic/Latino population will compose 50 percent of all Catholics in the United States.[2] Catholic parishes and schools must reflect this reality and reach out and welcome Hispanics and Latinos into the Catholic faith communities in the United States.

A positive contribution that we enthusiastically support is the opening, by so many of our dioceses and religious communities, of schools that offer reduced or no tuition for at-risk students. These schools utilize comprehensive and innovative educational approaches to improve the academic progress of some of the most disadvantaged young people.

Catholic schools must also continue to look for ways to include and serve better the needs of young people in our Church who have special educational and physical needs. Recognizing that educating students with disabilities often requires more intensive instructional support, we call on government to allow special education monies to follow and support students with disabilities no matter where they attend school.

Personnel

Ninety-five percent of our current school administrators and teachers are members of the laity.[3] The preparation and ongoing formation of new administrators and teachers is vital if our schools are to remain truly Catholic in all aspects of school life. Catholic school personnel should be grounded in a faith-based Catholic culture, have strong bonds to Christ and the Church, and be witnesses to the faith in both their words and actions. The formation of personnel will allow the Gospel message and the living presence of Jesus to permeate the entire life of the school community and thus be faithful to the school's evangelizing mission. We gratefully acknowledge the contributions of school personnel who are not Catholic, but who support and cooperate in accomplishing the mission of the Catholic school.

We must provide a sufficient number of programs of the highest quality to recruit and prepare our future diocesan and local school administrators and teachers so that they are knowledgeable in matters of our faith, are professionally prepared, and are committed to the Church. These programs will require even more active involvement and cooperation by our Catholic colleges and universities in collaboration with the diocesan educational leadership.

Ongoing faith formation and professional development programs must also be available so that administrators and teachers in Catholic schools can continue to grow in their ministry of education. These programs will introduce new and effective initiatives, educational models, and approaches, while always maintaining a sound Catholic identity in our schools. This is especially important when new Catholic school administrators and teachers come from private and state colleges and universities or from careers in the public school system.

Finances

We call on the entire Catholic community—clergy, religious, and laity—to assist in addressing the critical financial questions that continue to face our Catholic schools. This will require the Catholic community to make both personal and financial sacrifices to overcome these financial challenges. The burden of supporting our Catholic schools can no longer be placed exclusively on the individual parishes that have schools and on parents who pay tuition. This will require all Catholics, including those in parishes without schools, to focus on the spirituality of stewardship. The future of Catholic school education depends on the entire Catholic community embracing wholeheartedly the concept of stewardship of time, talent, and treasure, and translating stewardship into concrete action.

While we have made progress in opening offices for development, endowments, marketing, and institutional advancement, we must expand those efforts on both the diocesan and local levels. If we are to respond to the need for more Catholic schools we must seek innovative ways, including the use of tax free bonds, to finance them and to maintain those that currently exist. These programs will allow our Catholic schools to maintain quality programs, hire quality staff, and attract more students. We will need to utilize the collective wisdom of the members of our Church and the society in which we live if we are to be successful in this effort. We need to remind the business and civic communities of the contributions made by the graduates of Catholic schools who help to build the success of these enterprises. Diocesan and school leaders should continue actively to pursue financial support from the business and civic communities.

Our total Catholic community must increase efforts to address the financial needs of our Catholic school administrators, teachers, and staff. Many of our employees make great sacrifices to work in Catholic schools. The Catholic community must not ignore the reality of inadequate salaries, which often require these individuals to seek supplemental employment (*Lay Catholics*, no. 27) to meet living expenses and expenses due to limited or non-existent health care and retirement benefits. These benefits are very often lost if a school employee moves from one diocese to another. The Catholic community needs to study the success of the Michigan Catholic Conference's portable employee benefit program as a possible model for others to replicate. Catholic social teaching on the provision of just wages and benefits is both strong and clear. It is our community's responsibility to take action to address these issues now.

Advocacy

Finally, we need to intensify our efforts in advocating just and equitable treatment of our students and teachers in federal and state-funded educational programs. While we are pleased with the progress made in developing parent advocacy groups since 1990, the Catholic community must work to increase the number and effectiveness of these groups. Advocacy is not just the responsibility of parents and teachers, but of all members of the Catholic community. As the primary educators of their children, parents have the right to choose the school best suited for them. The entire Catholic community should be encouraged to advocate for parental school choice and personal and corporate tax credits, which will help parents to fulfill their responsibility in educating their children.

As we said in our 1995 statement *Principles for Educational Reform in the United States*, we believe that "government at all levels, acting in partnership with parents, has a responsibility to provide adequate professional and material resources to assist all children to attain a quality education" (7).

We also stated in that same document,

> When services that are aimed at improving the educational environment—especially for those most at risk—are available to students and teachers in public schools, these services should also be available to students and teachers in private and religious schools. These individuals should not be penalized for choosing to enroll or work in these schools since they also serve the common good of our nation. (8)

Parents have the constitutional right to direct the upbringing and education of their children (*Pierce v. Society of Sisters*), and we call on the entire Catholic community to join in advocating for the opportunities and resources to implement this right through constitutionally permissible programs and legislation (e.g., *Zobrest v. Catalina Foothills School District*, *Mitchell v. Helms*, and *Zelman v. Simons-Harris*).

In some states, so-called "Blaine" amendments, which ban or severely limit assistance to private and/or religious schools, make the attainment of this goal very difficult, if not impossible. These amendments are part of an anti-religious and, more specifically, anti-Catholic legacy in our nation's history. We need to advocate for the repeal of these relics of unfortunate bigotry.

Future Action

In addition to recommendations we have already made, and to ensure that our Catholic elementary and secondary schools not only continue to exist, but will grow and prosper, we call on bishops and those in educational leadership to

† Convene gatherings of educational, business, and community leaders, in either the fourteen episcopal regions or in each state, to address the critical issues of Catholic identity, cultural diversity, finances, just wages and benefits, academic quality—especially in the area of religious education—alternative governance models, and the marketing of our Catholic schools.

† Develop programs to assist pastors, clergy, seminarians, and laity to understand, appreciate, support, and promote the critical value of our Catholic schools in fulfilling the teaching ministry of the Church.

† Develop strategies to increase the effective advocacy for the equitable treatment of Catholic school students and teachers in government programs. This would include support for existing and creation of new parent advocacy groups in each state and diocese.

† Work with the leaders of Catholic colleges and universities to address the critical staffing needs of our Catholic elementary and secondary schools. This would include steps to ensure that sound and effective programs of teacher education and administration are available and affordable to those interested in working in our Catholic schools.

We call on the Committee on Education of the United States Conference of Catholic Bishops, and its staff, to collaborate with all appropriate groups and individuals in the development of procedures to implement the goals that are outlined in this statement.

We also call on the Committee on Education to collaborate with the National Catholic Educational Association in the development of a strategic plan produced from the proceedings of its Centennial Symposium on the *Vision for the Future of Catholic Education in the United States.*

Finally, we call on the Committee on Education to review the status of Catholic elementary and secondary schools and to report back to the body of bishops and the Catholic community on a regular basis, beginning no later than our annual November General Assembly in the year 2007.

Conclusion

As we, the Catholic bishops of the United States, and the entire Catholic community continue our journey through the twenty-first century, it remains our duty to model the Person of Jesus Christ, to teach the Gospel, and to evangelize our culture. We are convinced that Catholic elementary and secondary schools play a critical role in this endeavor. "Thus it follows that the work of the school is irreplaceable and the investment of human and material resources in the school becomes a prophetic choice…it is still of vital importance even in our time" (*Catholic Schools on the Threshold*, no. 21).

According to *Ecclesia in America,*

> It is essential that every possible effort be made to ensure that Catholic schools despite financial difficulties, continue to provide a Catholic education to the poor and marginalized in society. It will never be possible to free the needy from their poverty unless they are first freed from the impoverishment arising from the lack of adequate education. (no. 71)

The Catholic community is encouraged at every level to support the work of our Catholic elementary and secondary schools, keeping them available and accessible to as many parents as possible. Therefore, we the Catholic bishops of the United States strongly encourage our clergy and laity to market and support Catholic elementary and secondary schools as one of our church's primary missions.

Our vision is clear: our Catholic schools are a vital part of the teaching mission of the Church. The challenges ahead are many, but our spirit and will to succeed are strong. We, the Catholic bishops of the United States, in cooperation with the total Catholic community, are committed to overcoming these challenges. Adversity often brings out the best in men and women. We must respond to challenging times with faith, vision, and the will to succeed because the Catholic school's mission is vital to the future of our young people, our nation, and most especially our Church.

Endnotes

[1] David Campbell, "Making Democratic Education Work: Schools, Social Capital, and Civic Education" (paper presented at the Conference on Charter Schools, Vouchers, and Public Education, March 2000), 25ff.

[2] USCCB Department of Communications, *Catholic Information Project: The Catholic Church in America—Meeting Real Needs in Your Neighborhood* (Washington, DC: USCCB, 2003), 3-4.

[3] See *United States Catholic Elementary and Secondary Schools 2004-2005* (Washington, DC: National Catholic Educational Association, 2005).

Resources

Catechism of the Catholic Church, 2nd ed. (Washington, DC: USCCB-Libreria Editrice Vaticana, 1997).

Congregation for Catholic Education, *The Catholic School on the Threshold of the Third Millennium* (1997), http://www.vatican.va/roman_curia/congregations/ccatheduc/documents/rc_con_ccatheduc_doc_27041998_school2000_en.html (accessed June 13, 2005).

John Paul II, *The Church in America* (*Ecclesia in America*) (Washington, DC: USCCB, 1999).

Sacred Congregation for Catholic Education, *Lay Catholics in Schools: Witnesses to Faith* (1982), http://www.vatican.va/roman_curia/congregations/ccatheduc/documents/rc_con_ccatheduc_doc_19821015_lay-catholics_en.html (accessed June 13, 2005).

United States Conference of Catholic Bishops, *Economic Justice for All: Tenth Anniversary Edition* (Washington, DC: USCCB, 1997).

United States Conference of Catholic Bishops, *In Support of Catholic Elementary and Secondary Schools* (Washington, DC: USCCB, 1990).

United States Conference of Catholic Bishops, *Principles for Educational Reform in the United States* (Washington. DC: USCCB, 1995).

United States Conference of Catholic Bishops, *To Teach as Jesus Did: A Pastoral Message on Catholic Education* (Washington, DC: USCCB, 1973).

The document *Renewing Our Commitment to Catholic Secondary Schools in the Third Millennium* was developed by the Committee on Education of the United States Conference of Catholic Bishops (USCCB). It was approved by the full body of U.S. Catholic bishops at its June 2005 General Meeting and has been authorized for publication by the undersigned.

Msgr. William P. Fay
General Secretary, USCCB

Educating Together in Catholic Schools: A Shared Mission Between Consecrated Persons and the Lay Faithful

CONGREGATION FOR CATHOLIC EDUCATION
September 8, 2007

Introduction

1. The unexpected and often contradictory evolution of our age gives rise to educational challenges that pose questions for the school world. They force us to seek appropriate answers not only as regards contents and didactic methods, but also as regards the *community experience* that is a mark of educational activity. The relevance of these challenges transpires from the context of the social, cultural and religious complexity in which young people are actually growing up, and significantly influences their way of living. They are widespread phenomena such as lack of interest for the fundamental truths of human life, individualism, moral relativism and utilitarianism, that permeate above all rich and developed societies. Add to that rapid structural changes, globalization and the application of new technologies in the field of information that increasingly affect daily life and the process of formation. Moreover, with the process of development, the gap between rich and poor countries grows and the phenomenon of migration increases, so emphasizing the diversity of cultural identities in the same territory with the relative consequences concerning integration. In a society that is at once global and diversified, local and planetary, that hosts various and contrasting ways of interpreting the world and life, young people find themselves faced with different proposals of values, or lack thereof, that are increasingly stimulating but also increasingly less shared. There are also the difficulties that arise from problems of family stability, situations of hardship and poverty, that create a widespread feeling of disorientation at the existential and emotional level in a delicate period of their growth and maturation, exposing them to the danger of being "tossed to and fro and carried about with every wind of doctrine" (Eph 4:14).

2. In this context it becomes especially urgent to offer young people a course of scholastic formation which is not reduced to a simple individualistic and instrumental fruition of service with a view to obtaining a qualification. As well as gaining knowledge, students must also have a strong experience of sharing with their educators. For this experience to be happily accomplished, educators must be welcoming and well-prepared interlocutors, able to awaken and direct the best energies of students towards the search for truth and the meaning of existence, a positive construction of themselves and of life in view of an overall formation. In the end, "real education is not possible without the light of truth."[1]

3. This perspective regards all scholastic institutions, but even more directly the Catholic school, which is constantly concerned with the formational requirements of society, because "the problem of instruction has always been closely linked to the Church's mission."[2] The Catholic school participates in this mission like a true ecclesial subject, with its educational service that is enlivened by the truth of the Gospel. In fact, faithful to its vocation, it appears "as a place of integral education of the human person through a clear educational project of which Christ is the foundation,"[3] directed at creating a synthesis between faith, culture and life.

4. The project of the Catholic school is convincing only if carried out by people who are deeply motivated, because they witness to a living encounter with Christ, in whom alone "the mystery of man truly becomes clear."[4] These persons, therefore, acknowledge a *personal and communal adherence* with the Lord, assumed as the basis and constant reference of the inter-personal relationship and mutual cooperation between educator and student.

5. The implementation of a real *educational community*, built on the foundation of shared projected values, represents a serious task that must be carried out by the Catholic school. In this setting, the presence both of students and of teachers from different cultural and religious backgrounds requires an increased commitment of discernment and accompaniment. The preparation of a shared project acts as a stimulus that should force the Catholic school to be a place of ecclesial experience. Its binding force and potential for relationships derive from a set of values and a *communion of life* that is rooted in our common belonging to Christ. Derived from the recognition of evangelical values are educational norms, motivational drives and also the final goals of the school. Certainly the degree of participation can differ in relation to one's personal history, but this requires that educators be willing to offer a permanent commitment to formation and self-formation regarding a choice of cultural and life values to be made present in the educational community.[5]

6. Having already dealt in two previous separate documents with the themes of the identity and mission of Catholic lay persons and of consecrated persons in schools respectively, this document of the Congregation for Catholic Education considers the pastoral aspects regarding cooperation between lay and consecrated persons[6] within the same educational mission. In it, the choice of the lay faithful to live their educational commitment as "a personal vocation in the Church, and not simply as...the exercise of a profession"[7] meets with the choice of consecrated persons, inasmuch as they are called "to live the evangelical councils and bring the humanism of the beatitudes to the field of education and schools."[8]

7. This document constantly refers to previous texts of the Congregation for Catholic Education regarding education and schools[9] and clearly considers the different situations encountered by Catholic Institutions in various parts of the world. It wishes to call attention to three fundamental aspects of cooperation between lay faithful and consecrated persons in the Catholic school: communion in the educational mission, the necessary course of formation for communion for a shared educational mission and, lastly, openness towards others as the fruit of that communion.

I.
Communion in the Mission of Education

8. Every human being is called to communion because of his nature which is created in the image and likeness of God (cf. Gen 1:26-27). Therefore, within the sphere of biblical anthropology, man is not an isolated individual, but a *person*: a being who is essentially relational. The communion to which man is called always involves a double dimension, that is to say vertical (communion with God) and horizontal (communion with people). It is fundamental that communion be acknowledged as a gift of God, as the fruit of the divine initiative fulfilled in the Easter mystery.[10]

The Church: Mystery of Communion and Mission

9. God's original plan was compromised by the sin that wounded all relations: between man and God, between man and man. However, God did not abandon man in solitude, and, in the fullness of time, sent his Son, Jesus Christ, as Savior,[11] so that man might find, in the Spirit, full communion with the Father. In its turn, communion with the Trinity rendered possible by the encounter with Christ, unites persons with one other.

10. When Christians say *communion*, they refer to the eternal mystery, revealed in Christ, of the communion of love that is the very life of God-Trinity. At the same time we also say that Christians share in this communion in the Body of Christ which is the Church (cf. Phil 1: 7; Rev 1: 9). Communion is, therefore, the "essence" of the Church, the foundation and source of its mission of being in the world "the home and the school of communion,"[12] to lead all men and women to enter ever more profoundly into the mystery of Trinitarian communion and, at the same time, to extend and strengthen internal relations within the human community. In this sense, "the Church is like a human family, but at the same time it is also the great family of God, through which he creates a place of communion and unity through all continents, cultures and nations."[13]

11. As a result, therefore, in the Church, which is the *icon of the love incarnate of God*, "communion and mission are profoundly connected with each other, they interpenetrate and mutually imply each other, to the point that communion represents both the source and the fruit of mission: communion gives rise to mission and mission is accomplished in communion."[14]

Educating in Communion and for Communion

12. Because its aim is to make man more man, education can be carried out authentically only in a relational and community context. It is not by chance that the first and original educational environment is that of the natural community of the family.[15] Schools, in their turn, take their place beside the family as an educational space that is communitarian, organic and intentional and they sustain their educational commitment, according to a logic of assistance.

13. The Catholic school, characterized mainly as an educating community, is a school for the *person and of persons*. In fact, it aims at forming the *person in the integral unity of his being*, using the tools of teaching and learning where "criteria of judgment, determining values, points of interest, lines of thought, sources of inspiration and models of life"[16] are formed. Above all, they are involved in the dynamics of interpersonal relations that form and vivify the school community.

14. On the other hand, because of its identity and its ecclesial roots, this community must aspire to becoming a Christian community, that is, a community of faith, able to create increasingly more profound relations of communion which are themselves educational. It is precisely the presence and life of an educational community, in which all the members participate in a fraternal communion, nourished by a living relationship with Christ and with the Church, that makes the Catholic school the environment for an authentically ecclesial experience.

Consecrated Persons and the Lay Faithful Together in Schools

15. "In recent years, one of the fruits of the teaching on the Church as communion has been the growing awareness that her members can and must unite their efforts, with a view to cooperation and exchange of gifts, in order to participate more effectively in the Church's mission. This helps to give a clearer and more complete picture of the Church herself, while rendering more effective the response to the great challenges of our time, thanks to the combined contributions of the various gifts."[17] In this ecclesial context the mission of the Catholic school, lived as a community formed of consecrated persons and lay faithful, assumes a very special meaning and demonstrates a wealth that should be acknowledged and developed. This mission demands, from all the members of the educational community, the awareness that educators, as persons and as a community, have an unavoidable responsibility to create an original Christian style. They are required to be witnesses of Jesus Christ and to demonstrate Christian life as bearing light and meaning for everyone. Just as a consecrated person is called to testify his or her specific vocation to a life of communion in love[18] so as to be in the scholastic community a sign, a memorial and a prophecy of the values of the Gospel,[19] so too a lay educator is required to exercise "a specific mission within the Church by living, in faith, a secular vocation in the communitarian structure of the school."[20]

16. What makes this testimony really effective is the promotion, especially within the educational community of the Catholic school, of that *spirituality of communion* that has been indicated as the great prospect awaiting the Church of the Third Millennium. Spirituality of communion means "an ability to think of our brothers and sisters in the faith within the profound unity of the Mystical Body, and therefore as 'those who are a part of me,'"[21] and "the Christian community's ability to make room for all the gifts of the Spirit"[22] in a relationship of reciprocity between the various ecclesial vocations. Even in that special

expression of the Church that is the Catholic school, spirituality of communion must become the living breath of the educational community, the criterion for the full ecclesial development of its members and the fundamental point of reference for the implementation of a truly shared mission.

17. This spirituality of communion, therefore, must be transformed into an attitude of clear evangelical fraternity among those persons who profess charisms in Institutes of consecrated life, in movements or new communities, and in other faithful who operate in the Catholic school. This spirituality of communion holds true for the Catholic school, founded by Religious families, by dioceses, by parishes or by the lay faithful, which today takes into itself the presence of ecclesial movements. In this way, the educational community makes room for the gifts of the Spirit and acknowledges these diversities as wealth. A genuine ecclesial maturity, nourished by the encounter with Christ in the sacraments, will make it possible to develop "whether of the more traditional kind or the newer ecclesial movements...a vitality that is God's gift,"[23] for the entire scholastic community and for the educational journey itself.

18. The Catholic professional associations form another situation of "communion," a structured aid for the educational mission. They are a space for dialogue between families, the local institutions and the school. These associations, with their break-down at local, national and international levels, are a wealth that brings an especially fruitful contribution to the world of education as regards both motivations and professional points of view. Many associations have among their members teachers and persons in responsible positions both from the Catholic school and from other educational situations. Thanks to the pluralism of their origins, they can carry out an important function of dialogue and cooperation between institutions that differ but which have in common the same educational goals. These associative realities are required to consider how situations change, so adapting their structure and their way of operating in order to continue to be an effective and incisive presence in the sector of education. They must also intensify their reciprocal cooperation, especially in order to guarantee the achievement of their common goals, fully respecting the value and specificity of each association.

19. It is, moreover, of fundamental importance that the service carried out by the associations is stimulated by full participation in the pastoral activity of the Church. The Episcopal Conferences and their continental versions are entrusted with the role of promoting the development of the specificities of each association, favoring and encouraging more coordinated work in the educational sector.

II.
A Journey of Formation for Educating Together

20. Educating the young generations in communion and for communion in the Catholic school is a serious commitment that must not be taken lightly. It must be duly prepared and sustained through an initial and permanent project of formation that is able to grasp the educational challenges of the present time and to provide the most effective tools for dealing with them within the sphere of a shared mission. This implies that educators must be willing to learn and develop knowledge and be open to the renewal and updating of methodologies, but open also to spiritual and religious formation and sharing. In the context of the present day, this is essential for

responding to the expectations that come from a constantly and rapidly changing world in which it is increasingly difficult to educate.

Professional Formation

21. One of the fundamental requirements for an educator in a Catholic school is his or her possession of a solid professional formation. Poor quality teaching, due to insufficient professional preparation or inadequate pedagogical methods, unavoidably undermines the effectiveness of the overall formation of the student and of the cultural witness that the educator must offer.

22. The professional formation of the educator implies a vast range of cultural, psychological and pedagogical skills, characterized by autonomy, planning and evaluation capacity, creativity, openness to innovation, aptitude for updating, research and experimentation. It also demands the ability to synthesize professional skills with educational motivations, giving particular attention to the relational situation required today by the increasingly collegial exercise of the teaching profession. Moreover, in the eyes and expectations of students and their families, the educator is seen and desired as a welcoming and prepared interlocutor, able to motivate the young to a complete formation, to encourage and direct their greatest energy and skills towards a positive construction of themselves and their lives, and to be a serious and credible witness of the responsibility and hope which the school owes to society.

23. The continuous rapid transformation that affects man and today's society in all fields leads to the precocious aging of acquired knowledge that demands new attitudes and methods. The educator is required to constantly update the contents of the subjects he teaches and the pedagogical methods he uses. The educator's vocation demands a ready and constant ability for renewal and adaptation. It is not, therefore, sufficient to achieve solely an initial good level of preparation; rather what is required is to maintain it and elevate it in a journey of permanent formation. Because of the variety of aspects that it involves, permanent formation demands a constant personal and communal search for its forms of achievement, as well as a formation course that is also shared and developed through exchange and comparison between consecrated and lay educators of the Catholic school.

24. It is not sufficient simply to care about professional updating in the strict sense. The synthesis between faith, culture and life that educators of the Catholic school are called to achieve is, in fact, reached "by integrating all the different aspects of human knowledge through the subjects taught, in the light of the Gospel...[and] in the growth of the virtues characteristic of the Christian."[24] This means that Catholic educators must attain a special sensitivity with regard to the person to be educated in order to grasp not only the request for growth in knowledge and skills, but also the need for growth in humanity. Thus educators must dedicate themselves "to others with heartfelt concern, enabling them to experience the richness of their humanity."[25]

25. For this reason, Catholic educators need "a 'formation of the heart': they need to be led to that encounter with God in Christ which awakens their love and opens their spirits to others," so that their educational commitment becomes "a consequence deriving from their faith, a faith which becomes active through love (cf. Gal 5:6)."[26] In fact, even "care for instruction means loving" (Wis 6:17). It is only in this way that they can make their teaching a school of faith, that is to say, a transmission of the Gospel, as required by the educational project of the Catholic school.

Theological and Spiritual Formation

26. The transmission of the Christian message through teaching implies a mastery of the knowledge of the truths of the faith and of the principles of spiritual life that require constant improvement. This is why both consecrated and lay educators of the Catholic school need to follow an opportune formational theological itinerary.[27] Such an itinerary makes it easier to combine the understanding of faith with professional commitment and Christian action. Apart from their theological formation, educators need also to cultivate their spiritual formation in order to develop their relationship with Jesus Christ and become a Master like Him. In this sense, the formational journey of both lay and consecrated educators must be combined with the molding of the person towards greater conformity with Christ (cf. Rm 8:29) and of the educational community around Christ the Master. Moreover, the Catholic school is well aware that the community that it forms must be constantly nourished and compared with the sources from which the reason for its existence derives: the saving word of God in Sacred Scripture, in Tradition, above all liturgical and sacramental Tradition, enlightened by the Magisterium of the Church.[28]

The Contribution of Consecrated Persons to Shared Formation

27. Consecrated persons who profess the evangelical counsels show that they live for God and of God and become concrete witnesses to the Trinitarian love, so that people can experience the charm of divine beauty. Thus, the first and foremost contribution to the shared mission is the evangelical deep-rootedness of the lives of consecrated persons. Because of their vocational journey, they possess a theological-spiritual preparation that, centered on the mystery of Christ living in the Church, needs to unceasingly progress in step with the Church that progresses in history towards the "complete truth" (Jn 16:13). Again within this exquisitely ecclesial dynamic, consecrated persons also are invited to share the fruits of their formation with the laity, especially with those who feel that they are called "[to share] specific aspects and moments of the spirituality and mission of the Institute."[29] In this way, Institutes of consecrated life and Societies of apostolic life involved in education will manage to assure an essential openness to the Church and keep alive the spirit of the Founders and Foundresses, while also renewing a particularly precious aspect of the tradition of the Catholic school. From the very beginning, in fact, Founders and Foundresses paid special attention to the *formation of the educators* and they often devoted their best energies to this. Such formation, then as now, is not only aimed at strengthening professional skills, but above all, at highlighting the vocational dimension of the teaching profession, promoting the development of a mentality that is inspired by evangelical values, according to the specific characteristics of the Institute's mission. Therefore, "formation programs which include regular courses of study and prayerful reflection on the founder, the charism and the constitutions of the institute are particularly beneficial."[30]

28. In many religious Institutes, sharing the educational mission with the laity has already existed for some time, having been born with the religious community present in the school. The development of "spiritual families," of groups of "associated lay people" or other forms that permit the lay faithful to draw spiritual and apostolic fruitfulness from the original charism, appears as a positive element and one of great hope for the future of the Catholic educational mission.

29. It is almost superfluous to note that, within the perspective of the Church-communion, these programs of formation for sharing in the mission and lives of the laity, in the light of the relative charism, should be designed and implemented even where vocations to the consecrated life are numerous.

The Contribution of Lay Persons to Shared Formation

30. While invited to deepen their vocation as educators in the Catholic school in communion with consecrated persons, the lay faithful also are called in the common formational journey to give the original and irreplaceable contribution of their full ecclesial subjectivity. This involves, first and foremost, that they discover and live in their "life of a lay person...a specific 'wonderful' vocation within the Church"[31]: the vocation to "seek the kingdom of God by engaging in temporal affairs and directing them according to God's will."[32] As educators they are called on to live "in faith a secular vocation in the communitarian structure of the school: with the best possible professional qualifications, with an apostolic intention inspired by faith, for the integral formation of the human person."[33]

31. It should be emphasized that the special contribution that lay educators can bring to the formational journey derives precisely from their secular nature that makes them especially able to grasp "the signs of the times."[34] In fact, by living their faith in the everyday conditions of their families and society, they can help the entire educational community to distinguish more precisely the evangelical values and the opposite values that these signs contain.

32. With the gradual development of their ecclesial vocation, lay people become increasingly more aware of their participation in the educational mission of the Church. At the same time, they are also driven to carry out an active role in the spiritual animation of the community that they build together with the consecrated persons. "Communion and mutuality in the Church are never one way streets."[35] If, in fact, in the past it was mostly priests and religious who spiritually nourished and directed the lay faithful, now it is often "the lay faithful themselves [who] can and should help priests and religious in the course of their spiritual and pastoral journey."[36]

33. In the perspective of formation, by sharing their life of prayer and opportune forms of community life, the lay faithful and consecrated persons will nourish their reflection, their sense of fraternity and generous dedication. In this common catechetical-theological and spiritual formational journey, we can see the face of a Church that presents that of Christ, praying, listening, learning and teaching in fraternal communion.

Formation in the Spirit of Communion for Educating

34. By its very nature, the Catholic school requires the presence and involvement of educators that are not only culturally and spiritually formed, but also intentionally directed at developing their community educational commitment in an authentic spirit of ecclesial communion.

35. It is also through their formational journey that educators are called on to build relationships at professional, personal and spiritual levels, according to the logic of communion. For each one this involves being open, welcoming, disposed to a deep exchange of ideas, convivial and living a fraternal life within the educational community itself. The parable of the talents (Matt. 25:14-30) helps us to understand how each one is called to make his or her gifts bear fruit and

to welcome the riches of others within the shared educational mission.

36. The shared mission, besides, is enriched by the differences that the lay faithful and consecrated persons bring when they come together in different expressions of charism. These charisms are none other than different gifts with which the same Spirit enriches the Church and the world.[37] In the Catholic school, therefore, "by avoiding both confrontation and homologation, the reciprocity of vocations seems to be a particularly fertile prospect for enriching the ecclesial value of educational communities. In them the various vocations…are correlative, different and mutual paths that converge to bring to fulfillment the charism of charisms: love."[38]

37. Organized according to the diversities of persons and vocations, but vivified by the same spirit of communion, the educational community of the Catholic school aims at creating increasingly deeper relationships of communion that are in themselves educational. Precisely in this, it "expresses the variety and beauty of the various vocations and the fruitfulness at educational and pedagogical levels that this contributes to the life of the school."[39]

Witness and Culture of Communion

38. This fruitfulness is expressed, above all, in the witness offered by the educational community. Certainly in schools, education is essentially accomplished through teaching, which is the vehicle through which ideas and beliefs are communicated. In this sense, "words are the main roads in educating the mind."[40] This does not mean, however, that education is not accomplished in other situations of scholastic life. Thus teachers, just like every person who lives and works in a scholastic environment, educate, or they can also dis-educate, with their verbal and non-verbal behavior. "The central figure in the work of educating, and especially in education in the faith, which is the summit of the person's formation and is his or her most appropriate horizon, is specifically the form of witness."[41] "More than ever this demands that witness, nourished by prayer, be the all-encompassing milieu of every Catholic school. Teachers, as witnesses, account for the hope that nourishes their own lives (cf. 1 Pt 3:15) by living the truth they propose to their pupils, always in reference to the one they have encountered and whose dependable goodness they have sampled with joy. And so with Saint Augustine they say: 'We who speak and you who listen acknowledge ourselves as fellow disciples of a single teacher' (Sermons, 23:2)."[42] In educational communities, therefore, the style of life has great influence, especially if the consecrated persons and the lay faithful work together, fully sharing the commitment to develop, in the school, "an atmosphere animated by a spirit of liberty and charity based on the Gospel."[43] This requires that each one contributes the specific gift of his or her vocation to construct a family supported by charity and by the spirit of the beatitudes.

39. By giving witness of communion, the Catholic educational community is able to *educate for communion*, which, as a gift that comes from above, animates the project of formation for living together in harmony and being welcoming. Not only does it cultivate in the students the cultural values that derive from the Christian vision of reality, but it also involves each one of them in the life of the community, where values are mediated by authentic interpersonal relationships among the various members that form it, and by the individual and community acceptance of them. In this way, the life of communion of the educational community assumes the value of an educational principle, of a paradigm that directs its formational action as a service for the achievement of a culture of communion. Education in the Catholic school, therefore, through the tools of teaching and learning, "is not given for the purpose of gaining power but as an aid towards a fuller understanding of, and communion with man, events and things."[44] This principle affects every scholastic activity, the teaching and even all the after-school activities such as sport, theatre and commitment in social work, which promote the creative contribution of the students and their socialization.

Educational Community and Vocational Pastoral Activity

40. The shared mission experienced by an educational community of lay and consecrated persons, with an active vocational conscience, makes the Catholic school a pedagogical place that favors *vocational pastoral activity*. The very composition of such an educational community of a Catholic school highlights the diversity and complementarity of vocations in the Church,[45] of which it, too, is an expression. In this sense, the communitarian dynamics of the formational experience become the horizon where the student can feel what it means to be a member of the biggest community which is the Church. And to experience the Church means to personally meet the living Christ in it: "a young man can truly understand Christ's will and his own vocation only to the extent that he has a personal experience of Christ."[46] In this sense, the Catholic school is committed to guiding its students to knowing themselves, their attitudes and their interior resources, educating them in spending their lives responsibly as a daily response to God's call. Thus, the Catholic school accompanies its students in conscious choices of life: to follow their vocation to the priesthood or to consecrated life or to accomplish their Christian vocation in family, professional and social life.

41. In fact, the daily dialogue and confrontation with lay and consecrated educators, who offer a joyful witness of their calling, will more easily direct a young person in formation to consider his or her life as a vocation, as a journey to be lived together, grasping the signs through which God leads to the fullness of existence. Similarly, it will make him or her understand how necessary it is to know how to listen, to interiorize values, to learn to assume commitments and make life choices.

42. Therefore, the formational experience of the Catholic school constitutes an impressive barrier against the influence of a widespread mentality that leads young people especially "to consider themselves and their lives as a series of sensations to be experienced rather than as a work to be accomplished."[47] At the same time, it contributes to insuring strong character formation...capable both of resisting the debilitating influence of relativism and of living up to the demands made on them by their Baptism."[48]

III.
Communion for Opening Oneself Towards Others

43. The communion lived by the educators of the Catholic school contributes to making the entire educational sphere a place of communion open to external reality and not just closed in on itself. *Educating in communion* and *for communion* means directing students to grow authentically as persons who "gradually learn to open themselves up to life as it is, and to create in themselves a definite attitude to life"[49] that will help them to open their views and their hearts to the world that surrounds them, able to see things critically, with a sense of responsibility and a desire for a constructive commitment. Two orders of motivation, anthropological and theological, form the basis of this opening towards the world.

Anthropological and Theological Foundations

44. The human being, as a person, is a unity of soul and body that is dynamically realized through its opening to a relation with others. A person is formed for *being-with* and *for-others*, which is realized in love. Now, it is precisely love that drives a person to gradually broaden the range of his or her relations beyond the sphere of private life and family affections, to assume the range of universality and to embrace—at least by desire—all mankind. This same drive also contains a strong formational requirement: the requirement to learn to read the interdependence of a world that is increasingly besieged by the same problems of a global nature, as a strong ethical sign for the people of our time; like a call to emerge from that vision of man that tends to see each one as an isolated individual. It is the requirement to form man as a person: a subject that in love builds his historical, cultural, spiritual and religious identity, placing it in dialogue with other persons, in a constant exchange of gifts offered and received. Within the context of globalization, people must be formed in such a way as to respect the identity, culture, history, religion and especially the suffering and needs of others, conscious that "we are all really responsible for all."[50]

45. This requirement assumes even more importance and urgency within the sphere of the Catholic *faith*, experienced in the *love* of ecclesial *communion*. In fact, the Church, the place of communion and image of Trinitarian love, "is alive with the love enkindled by the Spirit of Christ."[51] The Spirit acts as an "interior power" that harmonizes the hearts of believers with Christ's heart and "transforms the heart of the ecclesial community, so that it becomes a witness before the world to the love of the Father."[52] Thus, "beginning with intra-ecclesial communion, charity of its nature opens out into a service that is universal; it inspires in us *a commitment to practical* *and concrete love for every human being.*"[53] In this sense, the Church is not an end in itself, it exists to show God to the world; it exists for others.

46. In the same way, inasmuch as it is an ecclesial subject, the Catholic school acts as the Christian ferment of the world. In it, students learn to overcome individualism and to discover, in the light of faith, that they are called to live responsibly a specific vocation to friendship with Christ and in solidarity with other persons. Basically, the school is called to be a living witness of the love of God among us. It can, moreover, become a means through which it is possible to discern, in the light of the Gospel, what is positive in the world, what needs to be transformed and what injustices must be overcome. A vigilant acceptance of the contributions of the world to the life of the school also nourishes and promotes open communion, especially in some educational environments, such as education to peace, to living together, to justice and to brotherhood.

Builders of Open Communion

47. Sharing the same educational mission with a diversity of persons, vocations and states of life is undoubtedly a strong point of the Catholic school in its participation in the missionary life of the Church, in the opening of ecclesial communion towards the world. In this respect, a first precious contribution comes from communion between lay and consecrated faithful in the school.

Lay persons who, because of their family and social relationships, live immersed in the world, can promote the opening of the educational community to a constructive relationship with cultural, civil and political institutions, with various social groups—from the most informal ones to those most organized—present in the territory. The Catholic school also assures its presence in the locality through its active cooperation with other educational institutions, especially with Catholic centers for higher studies, with which they share a special ecclesial bond, and with local bodies and various social agencies. In this sphere, faithful to its inspiration, it contributes to building a network of relationships that helps students to develop their sense of belonging, and society itself to develop a sense of solidarity.

Consecrated persons also participate, as "true signs of Christ in the world,"[54] in this opening to the outside world by sharing the gifts they bear. They must demonstrate especially that religious consecration has much to say to every culture in that it helps to reveal the truth of the human being. The witness of their evangelical life must reveal that "holiness is the highest humanizing proposal of man and of history; it is a project that *everyone* on earth can make his or her own."[55]

48. Another pillar of *open communion* is formed by the relationship between the Catholic school and the families that choose it for the education of their children. This relationship appears as full participation of the parents in the life of the educational community, not only because of their primary responsibility in the education of their children, but also by virtue of their sharing in the identity and project that characterize the Catholic school and which they must know and share with a readiness that comes from within. It is precisely because of this that the educational community identifies the decisive space for cooperation between school and family in the *educational project*, to be made known and implemented with a spirit of communion, through the contribution of everyone, discerning responsibilities, roles and competences. Parents in particular are required to enrich the communion around this project, making the family climate that must characterize the educating community more alive and explicit. For this reason, in willingly welcoming parents' cooperation, Catholic schools consider essential to their mission the service of *permanent formation offered to families*, to support them in their educating task and to develop an increasingly closer bond between the values proposed by the school and those proposed by the family.

49. The Christian-inspired associations and groups that unite the parents of Catholic schools represent a further bridge between the educational community and the world that surrounds it. These associations and groups can strengthen the bond of reciprocity between school and society, maintaining the educational community open to the wider social community and, at the same time, creating an awareness in society and its institutions of the presence and action carried out by Catholic schools in the territory.

50. At an ecclesial level also, the communion experienced within the Catholic school can and must be open to an enriching exchange in a more extensive communion with the parish, the diocese, ecclesial movements and the universal Church. This means that lay persons (educators and parents) and consecrated persons belonging to the educational community must take a meaningful part, even outside the walls of the Catholic school, in the life of the local Church. The members of the diocesan clergy and the lay persons of the local Christian community, who do not always have an adequate knowledge of the Catholic school, must discover it as a *school of the Christian community*, a living expression of the same Church of Christ to which they belong.

51. If lived authentically and profoundly, the ecclesial dimension of the educational community of the Catholic school cannot be limited to a relationship with the local Christian community. Almost by natural extension, it tends to open onto the horizons of the universal Church. In this sense, the international dimension of many religious families offers consecrated persons the enrichment of communion with those who share the same mission in various parts of the world. At the same time, it offers a witness to the living strength of a charism that unites, over and above all, differences. The richness of this communion in the universal Church can and must be shared, for example, through regional or world level formational occasions and meetings. These should also involve lay persons (educators and parents) who, because of their state of life, share the educational mission of the relative charisms.

52. Structured in this way, the Catholic school appears as an educational community in which ecclesial and missionary communion develops in depth and grows in breadth. A communion can be experienced in it that becomes an effective witness to the presence of Christ alive in the educational community gathered together in His name (cf. Matt 18:20) and that, precisely for this reason, opens to a deeper understanding of reality and a more convinced commitment to renewal of the world. In fact, "if we think and live by virtue of communion with Christ, then our eyes will be opened,"[56] and we will understand that "real revolution, the decisive change in the world, comes from God."[57]

53. The communion experienced in the educational community, animated and sustained by lay and consecrated persons joined together in the same mission, makes the Catholic school a community environment filled with the spirit of the Gospel. Now, this community environment appears as a privileged place for the formation of young people in the construction of a world based on dialogue and the search for communion, rather than in contrast; on the mutual acceptance of differences rather than on their opposition. In this way, with its educational project taking inspiration from *ecclesial communion and the civilization of love*, the Catholic school can contribute considerably to illuminating the minds of many, so that "there will arise a generation of new persons, the molders of a new humanity."[58]

Conclusion

54. "In a world where cultural challenge is the first, the most provocative and the most effect-bearing,"[59] the Catholic school is well aware of the onerous commitments it is called to face and it preserves its utmost importance even in present circumstances.

55. When it is animated by lay and consecrated persons that live the same educational mission in sincere unity, the Catholic school shows the face of a community that tends towards an increasingly deeper communion. This communion knows how to be welcoming with regard to people as they mature, making them feel, through the maternal solicitude of the Church, that God carries the life of each son and daughter of His in His heart. It knows how to involve young people in a global formation experience, to direct and accompany, in the light of the Good News, their search for meaning, even in unusual and often tortuous forms, but with an alarming urgency. A communion, finally, that inasmuch as it is based on Christ, acknowledges Him and announces Him to each and everyone as the only true Master (cf. Matt 23:8).

56. In presenting this document to those who live the educational mission in the Church, we entrust all Catholic schools to the Virgin Mary, Mother and educator of Christ and of persons, so that, like the servants at the wedding of Cana, they may humbly follow her loving invitation: "Do whatever He tells you" (Jn 2:5) and may they, thus, be together with the whole Church, "the home and the school of communion"[60] for the men and women of our time.

The Holy Father, during the Audience granted to the undersigned Prefect, approved this document and authorized its publication.

Rome, 8th September 2007, Feast of the Nativity of the Blessed Virgin Mary

† **Zenon Cardinal Grocholewski**
Prefect

Msgr. Angelo Vincenzo Zani
Undersecretary

---

[1] Benedict XVI, Address to Rome's Ecclesial Diocesan Convention on the Family and Christian Community (6th June 2005): *AAS* 97 (2005), 816.

[2] John Paul II, Speech to UNESCO (2nd June 1980), n. 18: *AAS* 72 (1980), 747.

[3] Congregation for Catholic Education, *The Catholic School on the Threshold of the Third Millennium* (28th December 1997), n. 4.

[4] Vatican Council II, Pastoral Constitution on the Church in the Modern World *Gaudium et spes* (7th December 1965), no. 22: *AAS* 58 (1966), 1042.

[5] Cf. Sacred Congregation for Catholic Education, *The Catholic School* (19th March 1977), no. 32.

[6] In this document reference is made to the priests, men and women religious and persons who, with different forms of consecration, choose the path of following Christ to wholeheartedly devote themselves to him (Cf. John Paul II, Post-synodal Apostolic Exhortation *Vita consecrata* (25th March 1996), nos. 1-12: *AAS* 88 (1996), 377-385.

[7] Sacred Congregation for Catholic Education, *Lay Catholics in Schools: Witnesses to Faith* (15th October 1982), no 37.

[8] Congregation for Catholic Education, *Consecrated Persons and their Mission in Schools*, no. 6; Cf. John Paul II, Post-synodal Apostolic Exhortation *Vita consecrata*, no. 96: *AAS* 88 (1996), 471-472.

[9] *The Catholic School* (19th March 1977); *Lay Catholics in Schools: Witnesses to Faith* (15th October 1982); *Educational Guidance in Human Love. Outlines for Sex Education* (1st November 1983); *The Religious Dimension of Education in a Catholic School* (7th April 1988); *The Catholic School on the Threshold of the Third Millennium* (28th December 1997); *Consecrated Persons and their Mission in Schools. Reflections and Guidelines* (28th October 2002).

[10] Cf. Congregation for the Doctrine of the Faith, Letter to the Bishops of the Catholic Church *Communionis Notio*, (28th May 1992), no. 3b: *AAS* 85 (1993), 836.

[11] Cf. Roman missal, Eucharistic prayer IV.

[12] John Paul II, Apostolic Letter *Novo millennio ineunte* (6th January 2001), no. 43: *AAS* 93 (2001), 297.

[13] Benedict XVI, Homily at the Prayer Vigil in Marienfeld (20th August 2005): *AAS* 97 (2005), 886.

[14] John Paul II, Post-synodal Apostolic Exhortation *Christifideles laici* (30th December 1988), no. 32: *AAS* 81 (1989), 451-452.

[15] Cf. Vatican Council II, Declaration on Christian Education *Gravissimum educationis* (28th October 1965), no. 3: *AAS* 58 (1966), 731; C.I.C., cann. 793 and 1136.

[16] Paul VI, Post-synodal Apostolic Exhortation *Evangelii nuntiandi* (8th December 1975), no. 19: *AAS* 68 (1976), 18.

[17] John Paul II, Post-synodal Apostolic Exhortation *Vita consecrata*, n. 54: *AAS* 88 (1996), 426-427. For cooperation between lay faithful and consecrated persons see also nos. 54-56: *AAS* 88 (1996), 426-429.

[18] Cf. Congregation for the Institutes of Consecrated Life and the Societies of Apostolic Life, *Starting Afresh from Christ* (14th June 2002), no. 28.

[19] Cf. Congregation for Catholic Education, *Consecrated Persons and their Mission in Schools*, no. 20.

[20] Sacred Congregation for Catholic Education, *Lay Catholics in Schools: Witnesses to Faith*, no. 24.

[21] John Paul II, Apostolic Letter *Novo millennio ineunte*, no. 43: *AAS* 93 (2001), 297.

[22] Ibid., no. 46: 299.

[23] Ibid., no. 46: 300.

[24] Sacred Congregation for Catholic Education, *The Catholic School*, no. 37.

[25] Benedict XVI, Encyclical Letter *Deus caritas est* (25th December 2005), no. 31: *AAS* 98 (2006), 244.

[26] Ibid.

[27] Cf. Sacred Congregation for Catholic Education, *Lay Catholics in Schools: Witnesses to Faith*, no. 60.

[28] Cf. Vatican Council II, Dogmatic Constitution on Divine Revelation *Dei Verbum* (18th November 1965), no. 10: *AAS* 58 (1966), 822.

[29] Congregation for Institutes of Consecrated Life and Societies of Apostolic Life, *Starting Afresh from Christ*, no. 31.

[30] Congregation for Institutes of Consecrated Life and Societies of Apostolic Life. *Fraternal Life in Community*, (2nd February 1994), no. 45.

[31] Sacred Congregation for Catholic Education, *Lay Catholics in Schools: Witnesses to Faith*, no. 7.

[32] Vatican Council II, Dogmatic Constitution on the Church *Lumen gentium* (21st November 1964), n. 31: *AAS* 57 (1965), 37.

[33] Sacred Congregation for Catholic Education, *Lay Catholics in Schools: Witnesses to Faith*, no. 24.

[34] Vatican Council II, Pastoral Constitution on the Church in the Modern World *Gaudium et spes*, n. 4: *AAS* 58 (1966), 1027.

[35] Congregation for Institutes of Consecrated Life and Societies of Apostolic Life, *Starting Afresh from Christ*, no. 31

[36] John Paul II, Post-synodal Apostolic Exhortation *Christifideles laici*, no. 61: *AAS* 81 (1989), 514.

[37] Cf. Congregation for Institutes of Consecrated Life and Societies of Apostolic Life. *Fraternal Life in Community* (2nd February 1994), no. 45.

[38] Congregation for Catholic Education, *Consecrated Persons and their Mission in Schools*, no. 21.

[39] Ibid., n. 43.

[40] Benedict XVI, Speech to the Representatives of some Muslim Communities (20th August 2005): *AAS* 97 (2005), 918.

[41] Benedict XVI, Address to Rome's Ecclesial Diocesan Convention on the Family and Christian Community (6th June 2005): *AAS* 97 (2005), 815.

[42] Benedict XVI, Speech to the Bishops of Ontario, Canada, on their ad limina Apostolorum Visit (8th September 2006): *L'Osservatore Romano* (9th September 2006), 9.

[43] Vatican Council II, Declaration on Christian Education *Gravissimum educationis*, no. 8: *AAS* 58 (1966), 734.

[44] Sacred Congregation for Catholic Education, *The Catholic School*, no. 56.

45 Cf. John Paul II, Post-synodal Apostolic Exhortation *Christifideles laici*, no. 20: *AAS* 81 (1989), 425.

46 Benedict XVI, Address to Seminarians (19th August 2005): *AAS* 97 (2005), 880.

47 John Paul II, Encyclical Letter *Centesimus annus* (1st May 1991), n. 39: *AAS* 83 (1991), 842.

48 Sacred Congregation for Catholic Education, *The Catholic School*, no. 12.

49 Ibid., no. 31.

50 John Paul II, Encyclical Letter *Sollicitudo rei socialis* (30th December 1987), no. 38: *AAS* 80 (1988), 566.

51 Benedict XVI, Encyclical Letter *Deus caritas est*, no. 28b: *AAS* 98 (2006), 240.

52 Ibid., no. 19: 233.

53 John Paul II, Apostolic Letter *Novo millennio ineunte*, no. 49: *AAS* 93 (2001), 302.

54 John Paul II, Post-synodal Apostolic Exhortation *Vita consecrata*, no. 25: *AAS* 88 (1996), 398.

55 Congregation for Catholic Education, *Consecrated Persons and their Mission in Schools*, no. 12.

56 Benedict XVI, Homily during the Eucharistic Celebration in Marienfeld (21st August 2005): *AAS* 97 (2005), 892.

57 Benedict XVI, Homily at the Prayer Vigil in Marienfeld (20th August 2005): *AAS* 97 (2005), 885.

58 Vatican Council II, Pastoral Constitution on the Church in the Modern World *Gaudium et spes*, no. 30: *AAS* 58 (1966), 1050.

59 John Paul II, Speech to Parents, Students and Teachers of Catholic Schools (23rd November 1991), n. 6: *AAS* 84 (1992), 1136.

60 John Paul II, Apostolic Letter *Novo millennio ineunte*, n. 43: *AAS* 93 (2001), 296.

About the Editors

RONALD J. NUZZI is a priest of the Diocese of Youngstown, Ohio. He is Senior Director of The Mary Ann Remick Leadership Program in the Alliance for Catholic Education at the University of Notre Dame, where he leads a dedicated graduate program to prepare principals for service in Catholic schools.

A nationally known speaker and scholar, Nuzzi has led dozens of staff development days, in-services, and retreats for Catholic school teachers and administrators in the United States, Canada, Mexico, Australia, and Italy. He has published widely, including several research handbooks and an encyclopedia, all focused on Catholic education. He holds a Ph.D. in Educational Administration from the University of Dayton and Master's degrees in Philosophy, Theology, and Education.

THOMAS C. HUNT received his Ph.D. in 1971 from the University of Wisconsin-Madison. From 1971 to 1996 he served on the faculty of Virginia Tech University where he received a number of awards for teaching, research, and service. In 1996, he joined the faculty of the University of Dayton where in 2002 he received the University's Alumni Scholarship Award. Prior to this book, he authored or edited fourteen books in the last fourteen years, with all but one on religion and education. From 1998 to 2008 he served as co-editor of *Catholic Education: A Journal of Inquiry and Practice*, at the time the only refereed journal on Catholic schools in the nation. A Professor in the School of Education and Allied Professions, Hunt is also a Fellow in the Center for Catholic Education at the University of Dayton.